Beginning Research in Psychology

D0488706

We begin our studies in psychology from the fact that our nature as human beings is a puzzle to us.

John Shotter (1975)

There is a wonderful truth in saying [that] next to being right in this world, the best of all things is to be clearly and definitely wrong, because you will come out somewhere.

Thomas Huxley (1910)

Beginning Research in Psychology

A Practical Guide to Research Methods and Statistics

Colin Dyer

BLACKWELL
Publishers

First published 1995
Reprinted 1996, 1997, 1999, 2001

Blackwell Publishers Ltd
108 Cowley Road
Oxford OX4 1JF, UK

Blackwell Publishers Inc
350 Main Street,
Malden, Massachusetts 02148, USA

British Library Cataloguing in Publication Data
A CIP catalogue record for this book is available from the British Library

Library of Congress Cataloging in Publication Data
Dyer, Colin.
Beginning research in psychology : a practical guide to research methods and statistics / Colin Dyer.
p.   cm.
Includes bibliographical references and index.
ISBN 0–631–18928–9 — ISBN 0–631–18929–7 (pbk)
I. Title
BF76.5.D94   1995   94–33768
150'.72—dc20   CIP

Commissioning editor: Alison Mudditt
Desk editor: Alison Dunnett
Production controller and
Text designer: Lisa Eaton

Typeset in 10.5 on 12pt Sabon
by Graphicraft Typesetters, Hong Kong
Printed and bound in Great Britain
by T. J. International Limited, Padstow, Cornwall

This book is printed on acid-free paper

For Sue,
Rowena
and
Madeleine

Contents

Appendices

Figures

Boxes

Preface

Beginning Research in Psychology is for anyone who wishes to begin to carry out investigative work in psychology, and who is looking for a practical introduction to research methods and statistics. It is particularly, though not exclusively, intended to meet the needs of students of psychology at A level or the International Baccalaureate, or those who are pursuing courses at a similar level, such as Access to Higher Education. In some sections (notably in chapter 8) the discussion extends a little beyond the boundaries of the current A level syllabus. I hope it may therefore also be useful to degree students who are looking for a relatively straightforward introduction to some of the main techniques of behavioural research.

As a glance at the contents page shows, the book reflects the fact that modern psychology is methodologically more diverse than is sometimes recognized. While it is still true that the experimental method is for many researchers the method of first resort, many also do research by other means, including the 'soft' methods such as interviews and participant observational studies. The appearance of these in the book alongside the traditional experimental approach is intended to reflect the main methodological choices available to psychological researchers, and will, I hope, encourage people who are beginning their studies in this area to try such methods for themselves. In addition to the usual description and discussion of the key issues surrounding each approach, each of the method chapters also contains a section on implementing the method in practice, which is intended to support readers during their early encounters with the task of planning an investigation.

In writing the statistical chapters, I have tried to provide a clear exposition of the fundamental ideas while making as few assumptions as possible about what information may already be possessed by a reader. This is perhaps especially evident in the approach taken to descriptive statistics in chapter 6, where it may be felt that I fail to credit the reader with a grasp of even a simple procedure such as placing data values in order. However, throughout these pages, I have tried to bear in mind that the ability to work easily with numbers is by no means as common as it might be, and I have therefore tried to make the approach to all statistical work, and especially to the material in chapters 7, 8 and 9 as clear and straightforward as possible. The simple, structured manner in which data analysis is tackled is designed to bring the researcher close to the data, to enable him/her to spot patterns and regularities. From the simple structures used the student can proceed to analyse data with calculators and computer packages.

Any book of this kind contains several different categories of information and clearly it is possible to take more than one path through that information depending on one's specific needs and interests. For most readers, guidance will be available from a syllabus or teaching staff but, for absolute newcomers to psychology who lack advice and who want to get started, it may be helpful to begin by looking at the material in chapter 1, then go on to review the descriptive statistics in chapter 6, working through the data collection projects at the end of that chapter in order to gain experience of working with quantitative data before approaching either the methods or inferential statistics for the first time.

Acknowledgements

This book is the work of more minds than mine alone and I would like to thank everyone who has contributed in any way to its writing.

I am indebted to the anonymous reviewers who read the first draft, and were both generous and unsparing with their comments, thereby saving me from making many errors, both of omission and commission. My students at North Warwickshire College, on whom I tried out various sections of the book, were likewise generous with their time and interest. I have tried to incorporate the suggestions I received from all sources into the book, and these have helped make it much more useful to its readers than it would otherwise have been. Any errors and imperfections which remain are of course solely my responsibility.

In addition to the many friends and family members who looked over my shoulders as I wrote, Alison Mudditt of Blackwell's has been consistently supportive throughout the long gestation period, and has cheerfully put up with my ignorance of the publishing business. Ken Browne took an interest in the project from its inception, and was responsible for my continuing with it on several occasions when I was tempted to throw in the towel. Malcolm Tillotson bore me patiently through a sea of statistical difficulties.

Last, but of course not least, I thank the members of my immediate family, Sue, Rowena and Madeleine, for making me a gift of the time and space needed to work on the project over a long two years. I hope they feel their unquestioning support is vindicated by the result.

I would also like to record my gratitude to the following: The Longman Group UK Ltd on behalf of the Literary Executor of the late Sir Ronald A. Fisher, FRS and Doctor Frank Yates, FRS, for permission to reproduce tables III, IV, VII and XXXIII from *Statistical Tables for Biological, Agricultural and Medical Research,* 6th Edition, (1974). The Biometrika Trustees for permission to reproduce table 23 from *Biometrika Tables for Statisticians* by E. S. Pearson and H. O. Hartley, 1966, Cambridge University Press. The American Statistical

Association for permission to reproduce Table 1 from Zar, J.H. 'Significance Testing of the Spearman Rank Correlation Coefficient', *Journal of the American Statistical Association*, 67, 578–80. The Addison-Wesley Publishing Company, Inc. for permission to reproduce tables 11.4 and 12.1 from Donald B. Owen, *Handbook of Statistical Tables* 1962.

1 Science and Psychology

This chapter provides an introduction to ideas from the philosophy of science which make up the background to practical investigative work in psychology.

- It describes the connection between psychology and science and discusses the goals of scientific research from the perspective of psychology.

- It introduces the important philosophical doctrines of empiricism and positivism and considers their significance for scientific research in general, and for psychology.

- It considers the critique of positivism offered from the humanistic wing of psychology, and briefly introduces the hermeneutic approach as a way of reconciling these opposing perspectives on scientific research.

- It describes each of the main stages in the process of doing research in science.

- It outlines and explains the process by which scientific theories are developed and scientific hypotheses can be tested and evaluated.

- It introduces key scientific terms and concepts such as variables, hypothesis, and theory.

Introduction

Our human nature is, as John Shotter has observed, largely a puzzle to us, (Shotter, 1975), and I'd like to begin our approach to looking at research methods in psychology by giving you a description of a short series of events which happened to me quite recently which, to me at least, illustrates this rather clearly. It happened that I had decided to phone Bob, a friend who, for as long as I have known him, has always had the same phone number which I thought I had memorized perfectly. Unusually, on this occasion it took me four tries before I actually got through and was able to speak to Bob, because something went wrong with each attempt.

The first time I found myself talking to a complete stranger. A wrong number. Probably, I wasn't thinking what I was doing when I dialled. With more concentration, and using what I was still sure was the correct number, I dialled again. This time there was a different voice on the other end of the line but the same net result. Another wrong number. I began to wonder whether I was suffering from a selective amnesia of middle age, and so I went and looked my friend's number up in the phone book, which in our house is kept in a different room from the telephone. I checked the number noticing, as I did so, that on the previous attempt the digits I had dialled had been the right ones, but that the last two had been in the wrong order. I checked the number again, and, leaving the book behind, went back to the phone. When I got there, finger poised to press the buttons, I found that my mind was almost blank. One or two random digits floated past on the stream of consciousness, but there was nothing there which resembled the six digit number which I had verified only fifteen seconds earlier. Failure again. Those members of my family who had been taking notice of this short pantomime nearly fell off their chairs with laughter at this point, and I felt very irritated, by my inability to complete such a simple task, as much as by the humour it was generating among those around me. Trying not to let it show, but naturally failing, I fetched the phone book and dialled again. This time, I read off each digit from the book as I did so, and, of course, I got through to Bob without any further difficulty.

During the conversation which followed, I found that I was able, by concentrating hard, both to carry on the phone conversation and also to listen in to parts of the talk in the room around me. For short periods of time – perhaps ten or fifteen seconds in duration – I had the feeling that I was simultaneously taking part in two quite different conversations. This was interesting in itself, and useful, since I was able to monitor my family's reasonably affectionate, but profoundly disrespectful speculations about the probable effects of alcohol on a middle-aged memory.

When the call was over, and I had dealt with the jokes, I found myself reflecting on what it could be that holds a friendship together. Bob and I have been phoning each other up and meeting reasonably regularly, for over twenty years. We have some interests in common, such as a deep devotion to the memory of the Great Western Railway, but in many respects we are quite different. He is on the right politically, and a bit of an idealist, while I am a fairly cynical left-leaner. He pursues sports of all kinds with intimidating amounts of enthusiasm, and competence, but hardly ever goes to the theatre. I, on the other hand, limit my exertions to walking and an occasional swim, and I go the theatre as frequently as I can. He thinks psychology is mostly a lot of mumbo-jumbo, while I, a bit predictably, think it is one of the most interesting and rewarding of all possible ways to spend one's time. When I consider all the ways in which we differ it seems to me to be a rather improbable friendship. Why, I wonder, do we continue to meet and phone each other when we seem to have so few attitudes and interests in common? What can it be that keeps our friendship alive?

The point of retailing these fragments of behaviour and experience from my recent past is that despite the fact that they strike us as so very unsurprising, even banal, they nevertheless have a puzzling side to them. They do, clearly, represent some of the more taken-for-granted aspects of life which virtually everyone reading this is likely to have experienced at some time, and in that sense they are each profoundly ordinary. For example, everyone has problems with phone numbers from time to time. We all find we are able to monitor more than one conversation at once, and we all have friends who are both similar to and different from ourselves. However, despite, or possibly because of, the fact that they represent generally experienced features of our existence, each of these phenomena – remembering and forgetting, divided attention and friendship are nevertheless full of questions and puzzles for both psychologists and non-psychologists alike. To list a few of the most obvious:

- Am I perceiving my friend as he really is, or do I somehow mis-perceive his qualities and interests? If so, why can I not see him as he 'really' is?
- Why did I dial the wrong number in the first place instead of the number I intended?
- Why couldn't I remember the number after I checked it in the phone book?
- What is it about the way the brain processes information which allows me to take in information from two different sources?
- What is it that keeps my friendship with Bob alive? Why do people have friends anyway?

There is an uncomfortable edge to questions like these because they demonstrate, yet again, the truth of John Shotter's observation. Almost always, when we ask them, the unsatisfactory answer which comes back to us in response is that we are unable (so far) to offer any full or final explanation. We simply don't know the full reason why phenomena like these occur in the way they do, and although parts and fragments of some likely answers have been uncovered by psychological research, the complete picture still eludes us. The uncomfortable fact is that we are still much less informed than we would like about the why and wherefore of our own functioning as human persons. There is a gap between the large, difficult, but extremely interesting questions which we pose to ourselves about human nature, (such as why I continue to be friends with Bob), and the rather narrow and limited amount which is actually known about things like friendship, (or indeed about relationships in general).

The task of reducing this gap is one which engages psychological researchers of all kinds, but is has to be said that there is more to the conduct of psychological inquiry than simply 'doing psychology'. Historical experience and human reason both suggest that the only approach to research which offers any prospect of success is to pursue it in a particular way, by means of the concepts and techniques of science. To do psychology, therefore, is always to find oneself engaged also in 'doing science', and this is something which is occasionally a source of surprise to people who have come to study psychology for the first time, and who may have expected to find themselves engaged in something rather less hard-nosed than it turns out to be. In a sense, though, their surprise is itself surprising. 'Science' is no more than the name for a set of concepts and procedures which have been proved by experience to be the best yet devised for dissecting all kinds of natural phenomena, of which human nature is only the most complicated and least tractable example. But, it is well known that science can appear a complex, and to an outsider somewhat mysterious process, almost a form of esoteric rite directed towards uncertain ends. In fact, as you will find as you work through the contents of this book, it is much more interesting and useful. Science, as distinct from the various disciplines which use it as a method of attack on specific problems, is at bottom really no more than a set of ideas and procedures. These often appear complex, particularly to a beginner, but they are always learnable. And, since they offer the only productive way of tackling the extremely tough and complex questions about human nature which psychologists seek to answer, their learning assumes considerable importance.

The fact that the ideas of science occupy such a central place in psychological research means, perhaps rather obviously, that in order to understand something of what is really involved in pursuing a problem of research in psychology it is essential to have a picture of what it means to 'do science'. It is true that you can (possibly) manage to carry out an experiment in a purely mechanical way without needing to understand very much about how science works although I wouldn't be totally certain on that point. However, if you did this, you would almost certainly be working in a kind of mental fog – going through the motions of doing research without comprehending any of the reasons for your actions. It follows that the greater your understanding of what science is, and how it works, then the better will be your understanding of how research in psychology operates, and hence, the more competent and satisfying your own investigations are likely to be. So, I hope I have succeeded in convincing you that you need to know at least something about science in order to become a competent researcher in psychology. Because it is unlikely that everyone reading this will share exactly the same ideas about science, the natural point to begin is with the bedrock question of why science in general exists and what its goals are.

What is Science?

One of the important features of science is that it possesses a set of general goals, principles and procedures which are shared to some degree by all the rather disparate disciplines which call themselves sciences and which serve to direct their activities. What unites the very different disciplines of psychology with physics, palaeontology, astronomy and all the other scientific disciplines is the fact that beneath their surface differences they have the same basic approach to the construction of explanations: a way of going about their business which is common to all and which is distinctive to the activity of 'doing' science.

The goals of science

The primary goal of science, as we have already said, is to generate explanations for various puzzling natural phenomena, which will enable us to understand something of why things are the way they are and what events and processes are hidden beneath the surface of perceived reality.

In psychology, the goal of research is to answer our curiosity about human beings, to offer explanations about why people are the way they are, both in mind and behaviour. To take a random set of concerns as illustrations, psychology seeks an understanding of such varied natural phenomena as learning and forgetfulness, thinking and reasoning, the perception of people and objects, altruistic behaviour, the formation of friendships, and the different forms of mental disorder: the examples could be multiplied indefinitely.

The first goal of all scientific research, then, is to obtain new knowledge, which we might call 'the truth', about the natural world. However, truth by itself is not sufficient. Science searches for a particular type of truth which can take us beyond simple observation towards explanation. To illustrate this by means of an obvious example from physics, it is a truth, which we verify for ourselves every time we drop something, that objects always fall towards the earth. However, on reflection it should also be clear that the observation by itself tells us no more than the fact that objects fall down instead of up. It does not, in itself offer any kind of explanation about why falling should take the direction which it does. Of course, it is always possible to suggest possible explanations, such as that objects have a natural tendency to seek the lowest point available , or that some form of attraction exists between the earth and nearby objects, but such 'explanations' can be multiplied indefinitely, since there is nothing in the observation itself to suggest which of all the possible explanations might be the correct one.

This is not, of course, to suggest that observation alone is of no value. The simple process of looking, and noticing the character of the phenomena around us is an essential part of science, since it is this which identifies the existence of a problem in the first place. However, while it is the only way to get a process of scientific inquiry started, observation by itself is not capable of delivering the explanation we seek for why dropped objects always end up on the floor. We need to know the truth about why such effects occur, and that only becomes accessible if we apply the procedures of science to the problem. As the famous philosopher of science, Sir Karl Popper has put it:

'Truth is not the only aim of science. We want more than mere truth: what we look for is interesting truth – truth which is hard to come by ... what we look for is truth which has a high degree of explanatory power ...' (Popper, 1963, p. 229)

Science, then, is the way we get at the truth of things, the way in which we are able – eventually – to achieve the explanations we seek for the way the natural world functions. And clearly, in many fields of inquiry, including psychology, there have been some important successes. For example, we now possess a considerable amount of information, and some understanding, about the phenomena of human memory thanks to the work of a long line of researchers running from Hermann Ebbinghaus in the nineteenth century onwards into our own day.

Prediction ...

The goal of filling the gaps in our knowledge of why things are the way they are is clearly important in its own right, and one which needs no further justification. At the same time, however, there is a further benefit to be had, beyond simply accounting for what has been observed. Explanations of natural phenomena which are accurate and complete also make it possible for predictions to be made about what would happen if certain conditions are met: in effect, knowledge also makes possible true descriptions of phenomena which have not yet been encountered in reality. Some of the clearest examples of this predictive capability of scientific knowledge can be found in subjects such as physics and chemistry, where knowledge is so precise and detailed that very exact predictions can be produced. A chemist, for example, is able to predict exactly what result can be expected when certain compounds are allowed to react under particular conditions, even though that combination may never before have been observed to occur.

In psychology also, knowledge in some areas is sufficient to enable predictions to be made, although at a lower level of precision than would be possible in chemistry and physics. For example, social psychological research into prosocial (helping) behaviour has developed the idea of the 'diffusion of responsibility' (Latane and Darley, 1968) which suggests that in an emergency, or similar situation in which helping behaviour is called for, the probability that aid will actually be given is related to the number of people in the vicinity. That is, a prediction can be made about the likely behaviour which will be observed when certain specified conditions are met. Note though, that the prediction consists of a statement about the *likelihood* of help being given, and not a firm statement about whether or not help will actually be given in that situation. What psychology cannot yet do, and may never achieve, is to predict *exactly* what will happen in any particular situation where helping is needed, and this is the position in most, if not all of the rest of psychology. People's behaviour is too variable, and our theories are as yet too weak to allow that kind of predictive power and precision.

The making of predictions and then testing them against what actually happens when the necessary conditions are met is a crucial part of the scientific process since it provides valuable feedback on the accuracy of the knowledge on which the prediction was based. Clearly, if a prediction proves to be false, then the information on which it was based will need to be reconsidered. It may be that it was the result of an erroneous reading of correct information, or it might be that the information itself was wrong. Either way, the process of making and evaluating predictions provides an important source of feedback which permits existing knowledge to be refined. We shall see much more on this later in this chapter and when we consider the foundations of the experimental method in chapter 5.

... and control

In some disciplines of the natural sciences the acquisition of knowledge and the development of understanding has permitted scientists to pass beyond making predictions about what would happen under certain conditions to reach a still further stage in which control of a particular phenomenon can be achieved.

Nuclear physics, for example, has developed such a detailed understanding of the physical processes involved in a nuclear reaction that not only can predictions be made about when, under what conditions, a nuclear reaction can be expected to occur and its consequent results, but it also enables a nuclear reaction to be initiated and controlled inside a nuclear power installation in order to produce electricity.

In psychology, the idea that the development of detailed knowledge and understanding might one day permit the control of human behaviour or experience in the same way as a nuclear scientist is able to control a nuclear reaction raises important ethical questions. On the one hand, it is clearly unacceptable simply to treat people as if they are passive objects to be manipulated at will, if the purpose is then to exploit them in some way. On the other hand, if some good for the individual is involved, then the issues become much less clear cut. In fact we already accept the control of human experience when a doctor gives a patient a drug to relieve pain. In this case there is no ethical objection because the interests of the patient are being served, and because the doctor is acting within the framework of a relationship which is clearly understood by both parties. The ethical hurdle is thus not insurmountable.

More problematic are the practicalities. At present psychology possesses embarrassingly few theories which are precise and detailed enough to provide a basis for the control of behaviour or experience. We simply do not know enough about what makes people behave and experience as they do to be able to make precise predictions about them with much confidence and, lacking accurate predictions, control, at least in the sense in which it has so far been discussed, is still impossible.

There is, however, more than one definition of what it means to take control. To concentrate on the assumption of power by one person over another is certainly one way in which control can be defined, but there is also a second way of looking at it. This is the possibility that the knowledge generated by psychological research may offer control in the sense that it enables individuals to exert control over their own behaviour and experience, rather than to experience a lack of control, or control by others. In this interpretation control is clearly both a worthwhile and ethically acceptable goal for psychology since it involves the good of empowerment rather than its reverse. An example of this might be a person who suffers from a crippling fear, the fear of open spaces, perhaps, who seeks psychological help. If that person, by the application of the specialist knowledge of the clinical psychologist, can be helped to cope with the fear, so that normal life becomes possible, then clearly that is an example of control, of the unwanted behaviour and experience, being attained in the positive sense. In such a case the person is empowered to regain control of his life through the application of knowledge obtained from psychological research.

We have begun by focusing on the goals of science. We now need to move on to explore some of the principles and ideas which scientists – including psychologists – use to guide their work towards these goals. To use an architectural analogy, we have established something of why the edifice of science exists in terms of what its purposes are. We now have to enter the building, and go down into the basement in order to examine the foundations.

The Foundations of Science

This part of the chapter introduces the fundamental questions raised by the theory of knowledge, and shows how and why the philosophical doctrine of empiricism is able to provide effective answers to those questions.

The ideas of positivism are explained, and their significance for psychology is identified.

The aims of psychological research, and the problems posed by the desire to study mental activity by the methods of science are reviewed.

The humanistic critique of positivism is reviewed, and the hermeneutic method which brings together the humanistic and positivist strands of thought is briefly described.

Epistemology and empiricism

Science, in Karl Popper's memorable phrase, is involved in the pursuit of that 'interesting truth' which is capable of explaining why things in nature are the way they are, and which results in the generation of new knowledge. For this process to have any hope of success, however, it has to know what it is looking for, and this means, in turn, that there must be answers available when researchers ask themselves the following questions:

- What, among all the different kinds of information available, is to count as real knowledge; or, put differently, how is truth is to be recognized when, if, it is encountered?
- How can knowledge of the truth be reliably achieved, so that we can be sure that whatever we identify as true today will also be true tomorrow?

The first of these questions arises because scientists are confronted by information of many kinds and from many sources all of which may make claims to be factual and to therefore contain truth. This does not mean, however, that all such claims can automatically be taken at their face value. Information does not emerge into the light of day complete with a certificate attesting to its validity, and practitioners of science are therefore in need of a way of assessing whether or not an assertion which claims to be factual is likely to be true.

The second question represents the recognition that science is potentially handicapped by the very human and understandable tendency to seek an easy path to knowledge. Unless research procedures are sufficiently rigorous to provide some guarantee that the results obtained are indeed as close to the truth as it is possible to get, then it is unlikely that they will be able to generate the kind of explanatory truth which is looked for.

Fundamental questions of this nature, which deal with this very basic issue of what it means to 'do science', are the concern of the philosophical discipline of epistemology. The task of epistemology is to describe and evaluate the various claims which have been made about what knowledge is and how it can reliably be obtained. Particular versions of such claims, and there are several, are also known as epistemologies, and, when used in this sense, 'an epistemology' defines a particular view of what constitutes scientific knowledge, and how it can be acquired. From about the seventeenth century onwards, philosophers working in this field have tried to define the logical foundations of science, in order to explain how it is that science, by applying some relatively simple procedures, is able to generate new knowledge. Thanks to their work it is now relatively clear to us how and, more importantly, why science is required to operate as it does if knowledge is to be produced. The key to the answer, in which is contained much of the explanation for the spectacular successes of scientific research over the past three hundred or so years, lies with the philosophical doctrine of empiricism.

The ideas of empiricism are important because they offer a convincing answer to one of the most fundamental problems of all. All researchers, in whatever discipline, will wish to be satisfied before they embark on an investigation that the information they are going to acquire can be relied on to give an accurate picture of the facts. Without such prior confidence in the basic procedure the whole business of research becomes, in effect, an empty charade which is unable to separate the truth from mere speculation. From its development in the seventeenth century, onwards into our own time, the doctrine of empiricism has provided a solution to this problem by specifying clearly how a researcher should set about the process of acquiring knowledge. By working in the way which empiricism dictates, researchers in all scientific disciplines have been able to develop powerful explanations for a wide range of natural phenomena. These, because they have been found to be both accurate and reliable have in turn provided starting points for yet further researches and discoveries. In effect, by following the empiricist approach scientific knowledge develops by a process of bootstrapping itself onwards, using what is already known in order to gain knowledge of the unknown.

Empiricism

To begin to understand why empiricism was able to provide such a powerful understanding of how science should proceed, and also why it continues to be the cornerstone of science still today, we need to look more closely at what it has to say. It consists, in essence, of the following three closely linked propositions, which though they may appear to be saying much the same thing, are in fact making quite distinct statements about the nature of scientific knowledge.

The first principle of empiricism is that an understanding of natural phenomena can only be constructed from information which has been obtained directly through the senses, (or by means of apparatus such as a microscope which acts as an extension of the senses). Empiricism thus sets as the minimum standard in the pursuit of scientific knowledge that research should proceed by careful observation of the object of inquiry in order to find out what may be the case.

Secondly, empiricism argues that the only valid criterion of truth for science, that is, the only standard against which the truth of an idea is able to be measured, is whether an idea describes a situation which is able to be observed by any competent person. This means that all sources of information other than direct observation, such as beliefs, prejudices, wishful thinking, or old wives' tales, are excluded as potential sources of scientific knowledge.

Finally, empiricism defines the content of scientific knowledge solely in terms of what is publicly observable, although, as in the case of sub-atomic particles, the observation process may require vast quantities of expensive apparatus. This point says two things. Firstly, it says that science is only competent to pronounce on those phenomena which are capable of being objectively verified (i.e. can be observed by more than one person); and secondly, that there are no hidden sources of scientific knowledge which are accessible only to those with special powers. On the contrary, scientific knowledge is in principle available to anyone who is able to apply the required observational techniques to a problem.

It is possible that this last point may have a familiar ring. It was, in fact, the crux of the behaviourist argument against the introspectionist psychology prevailing in the early part of the twentieth century (Watson, 1913). And, of course it still causes a certain amount of difficulty for psychologists interested in researching such non-objective phenomena as dreams, and other mental states.

One of the difficulties with discussing empiricism, is that you sometimes find yourself wondering what all the fuss is about. The principles of empiricism are now so much part of our understanding of science that it is easy to feel that they are no more than self-evident truths, and, for that reason, if for no other, it may be quite difficult to appreciate their full significance. However, it is possible to see why they are, in fact, so central to a full understanding of how science operates, if you consider the nature of the alternative.

Before the rise of empiricism the dominant epistemology had been idealism. This had argued that knowledge of the truth could be attained directly, without recourse to anything other than the unsupported activity of the mind – i.e. simply by thinking. Knowledge, considered from this point of view, consisted only of ideas which were not required to be anchored to objective reality in any way. The process of research, of searching for explanations of natural phenomena could be pursued simply by constructing explanations for various problem phenomena from the ideas available, with the main criterion for the acceptance of such explanations being how well they fitted in with ideas and assumptions which already existed. If the fit was good, then an explanation was likely to be accepted. If, however, the fit between explanation and assumptions was poor then they would be regarded as incorrect, and consequently rejected.

Idealism, which perhaps seems to us to be little more than an eccentric blip on the screen of history was, in its time the most powerful epistemology in the West. So powerful was it as a view of the nature of reality that examples of the rejection of empirical data in favour of explanations constructed out of prior assumptions can be found cluttering the pages of history from the fifteenth century onwards. Possibly the most the famous was the refusal of the authorities in fifteenth-century Italy to accept Galileo's heliocentric theory because it clashed with the ideas about the cosmos which were derived from the doctrines of the church. But even as late as the middle of the nineteenth century, the debates between the evolutionists and creationists over Charles Darwin's theory of evolution showed that that the general approach offered by idealism still possessed considerable attractions for some thinkers.

The weakness of idealism as an approach to doing science is simply that ideas which are just assumed to be true because they appear plausible, or because they fit in with other ideas, can never provide any kind of basis for understanding the objective world. From the seventeenth century onwards, the work of empiricist philosophers such as John Locke showed that idealism was wholly inadequate as a basis for scientific research, since it was incapable of leading to reliable knowledge. Eventually, though, and not without a struggle that lasted well into the nineteenth century, idealism became discredited, and in its place empiricism emerged as the dominant epistemology for science.

The importance of empiricism for science is two-fold. First, it directs a researcher's attention outwards into the world of natural objects. It says that knowledge of the truth about things is only to be obtained through a process of active inquiry, so that if you want to know the reason why some phenomenon occurs then you have to go out and actually collect information about it. The reasons for things lie outside in the world, rather than in the interior of the human mind. Research can't be done by simply sitting and thinking. Moreover, the doctrine of empiricism means that research which is pursued according to its principles will generate knowledge which genuinely corresponds with reality, and with the way things actually are. These are outcomes which could never be achieved by any alternative means.

The second reason for the importance of empiricism to the development of science is that it provides a route by which the correspondence between observation and reality, once discovered, can be verified objectively. The fact that knowledge is defined in terms of what can be directly known through the senses means that it is possible for the findings of one researcher to be checked by others. This is crucial to the development of knowledge, because it provides an in-built guarantee against error, as long as procedures are honestly applied, though not of course if there is a deliberate intention to deceive. The knowledge gained from scientific work thus becomes *objective* knowledge, in the sense that it can be shown to have an existence which is independent of any particular observer. It is also the case, of course, that each independent verification of a given result increases confidence that this is a genuine effect which requires an explanation to be found.

Positivism

Empiricism provides the philosophical foundation for the building work of science – and this is as true for the more recently developed social sciences, as it is for the old-established 'natural' sciences, such as physics and chemistry. In the former group, which includes psychology and sociology, the general epistemological position of empiricism, has, since the nineteenth century, been expressed in the shape of the extremely powerful and influential doctrine known as positivism. First formulated by the pioneer French social scientist Auguste Comte in the 1850s, the fundamental tenets of positivism consist of the following five points:

- Science is a unitary activity, representing a seamless whole. There is no essential difference between the natural and the social sciences so that research in these fields can share the same basic assumptions and follow the same fundamental processes and procedures.
- Reality consists of what is available to the senses. Ideas can count as knowledge (facts) only if they have been tested against actual experience and been found to correspond to it. (This, of course, is a statement of the empiricist position.)
- The world of nature, which includes the social world, operates according to strict laws of cause and effect, such that every effect has one or more discoverable causes.
- Scientific research consists of identifying the casual links which explain the existence of various natural phenomena.
- There is a fundamental distinction to be drawn between facts and values. Science should concerns itself only with matters of fact (i.e. with what can be objectively known) and should be entirely neutral (value-free) on matters

concerning values (i.e. opinions about what *ought* to be the case in any particular situation).

(Like the tenets of empiricism which were discussed earlier, the positivist position may also be thought to do little more than state obvious truths. If this is the case, however, it is again only because the principles and assumptions of positivism have become generally accepted as the correct – indeed at times the only – approach to research in the social sciences.)

As you can probably see, these doctrines perform two main functions. They define, first of all, what it means to do research in the social sciences by placing all social science research, including psychology, in a clear relationship to the other sciences, while at the same time specifying the nature of the phenomena with which the social sciences must be concerned, (points 1, 4 and 5 above). Secondly, they sketch the general outline of a programme of research for all social science disciplines to follow, and specify the method by which such research should be pursued (points 2 and 3).

These ideas go a long way to explaining why research in psychology presents the appearance it does, and we will consider some of its effects in more detail below. Before we do, we can get a clearer appreciation of the effect of these ideas on the social and human sciences in general, and psychology in particular, by looking more closely at what it means to pursue research in those subjects which positivism adopted as models of 'science'.

In the 'natural' sciences, such as physics and chemistry, researchers are seeking to identify 'laws of nature', which can be observed as regularities in the relationship between variables. One such is 'Boyle's Law' in physics, which describes the relationship between the pressure and the volume of a given mass of gas. The relationship between these variables which the law defines, turns out to be such that if the pressure on a given mass of gas which is held at a constant temperature is increased by a given amount, then it becomes possible to predict the corresponding change in its volume.

The process of identifying such 'laws of nature' by empirical means has, in the natural sciences, generally involved doing experiments, in which precisely defined variables, (such as pressure, volume and temperature), are manipulated and their changes carefully observed and measured. The power of this specific method lies in the fact that it permits causal relationships between the variables to be identified, and measured. (A causal relationship is one in which any change to one variable causes a concomitant change to occur to another.) By this means, then, it then becomes possible to identify which variables cause which others to change, and hence to build up a picture of how the different forces in nature interact with each other. In the natural sciences, these causal relationships provide the basic building blocks of knowledge, and as they accumulate, patterns and consistencies emerge which eventually may permit large-scale principles – laws of nature – to be identified.

If we look back over the past three hundred years or so, we can see that the method of experimentation has been applied with considerable success to a wide range of problems in the natural and biological sciences. In fact, so great has been the success of experimentation in delivering the triple goals of under-standing, prediction and control, that to modern minds, 'doing science' is to a large extent synonymous with 'doing experiments'.

The very striking successes which followed from the application of the ex-perimental method to the problems of the natural and biological sciences can largely be explained by two facts. First, many of the phenomena which interest the natural sciences have (so far) proved themselves to be extremely stable; they exist in relationships with each other which appear to be largely fixed and unchanging. (Indeed, it seems probable that some features of the natural world, such as the basic physical constituents of matter, could probably only be changed if the fundamental nature of the universe were to be altered also.) Relation-ships between variables which are fixed in this way are called *deterministic*, because any given set of conditions can always be relied on to produce exactly the same results, or put another way, the antecedent conditions wholly deter-mine the nature of the consequences. For example, one would expect two chemical elements brought together under the same conditions always to react, if they react at all, in precisely the same fashion, and with precisely the same results. The antecedents, that is, the elements and the conditions of heat or pressure under which they are brought together, in this case also determine the nature of the consequences in the form of the kind of reaction (or non-reaction) which is obtained. The relationship is a deterministic one.

Clearly the deterministic nature of many natural phenomena is very helpful to a researcher in the natural sciences since there can be confidence that an observation, once made, can be repeated, as long as the necessary pre-conditions can be reconstructed. The important effect of this is to make it possible for different investigators to confirm the validity of others' data, since if one researcher is unable to repeat the results of another by reconstituting the original conditions, it suggests that the original research was flawed in some way. In this respect the existence of deterministic relations in nature can be said to provide ideal conditions for the detection of various kinds of error in experimentation.

The second reason for the success of the method of experiment is because the variables studied by natural scientists have been capable of precise meas-urement using the language of mathematics. Experimental research in, say, physics, works with descriptions of the relationships between variables (heat, light, electricity and so on) which are expressed in quantitative (numerical) form, and which are often referred to as 'hard' data in order to emphasize the close correspondence which exists between the actual phenomenon and the measures which have been made. The use of mathematics to provide the lan-guage in which these sciences describe phenomena carries significant advan-tages. One is that phenomena can be described with precision and objectivity, and this is obviously important, since it facilitates the replication of research results which was mentioned above. More than this, though, mathematics provides a way of expressing theories which are, above all, perfectly clear and unambiguous in what they say. Unlike theories expressed in verbal form, there can be no argument about what is really said by a theory which is expressed in mathematical form: arguments are possible only about whether what it says is justified in terms of the available data.

Despite the considerable success which has followed from applying the experimental method to the problems of the natural sciences, it would be wrong to see doing experiments as the *only* way to do science. The experiment is, in fact, only one of the several research methods which scientists in general have at their disposal. Even in the natural sciences, the experiment is far from being the only way in which knowledge is pursued. In astronomy, and palaeontology (the study of extinct life-forms), for example, it is clearly impossible to conduct experiments. One cannot manipulate galaxies in order to test theories, nor is it yet possible to bring back extinct species in order to study their biology more closely. Researchers in both these disciplines can only do their work by making observations and then trying to interpret what the results might mean for the theories which they hold. It is, therefore, quite possible to conduct research which is perfectly 'scientific' without ever doing an experiment.

So it is not the question of which research method is used which determines whether or not a particular discipline is a 'science' or not, and experiments, in particular, are not, in any way, a necessary part of what it means to 'do science'. What ultimately matters is the nature of the supporting framework of ideas – including the concepts of empiricism and positivism, but also, as we shall see later, extending more widely. These ideas, because they determine the approach which is taken to research at a very fundamental level, are much more critical to whether a discipline is scientific or not than the bare details of the method. This can be seen quite clearly in the contrast between astronomy and astrology. The former is a scientific discipline, which uses observational methods in order to test theories about the natural history of various cosmological phenomena, such as stars, planets, galaxies, and so on. Astrology on the other hand, also uses cosmological phenomena, and makes observations (of a very limited kind), but is interested only in using these to support a particular theory of human nature. The crucial difference between these two activities lies in the fact that while in astronomy the validity of its theories are decided by the observational data, in astrology the fundamental theory (in so far as it has one) is not available to be challenged by data.

This example raises the very important issue of exactly what kind of criterion can be used to distinguish between the 'genuine' sciences, such as physics, astronomy and psychology and other subjects, like astrology or psychoanalysis, which may pretend to the status of science, but which are in fact fundamentally unscientific. However, we will postpone a more detailed examination of this issue until a little later in this chapter.

To return to the basic point, made earlier: the experimental method, though extremely important as a method of doing research, is not the whole of what it means to do science. Whether or not a discipline can be regarded as a science is much more to do with how its practitioners set about the task of research, and much less about which specific method is used. This is a particularly important point for psychologists because, although many of them do conduct their investigations by means of experiments, this is by no means true of all.

As you may already be aware, many interesting and important questions in psychology simply are not accessible to experimental investigation, and have therefore, of necessity, to be pursued by other means. All however, are of equal standing scientifically, as long as they work within the same set of principles which are recognized by the scientific community at large.

Positivism, psychology and research methods

We can now begin to draw together some of the strands of the discussion so far, by considering how psychology has responded to the positivist agenda. What are the implications of these ideas for the way in which psychology sets about the investigation of human behaviour and its accompanying mental events?

A widely quoted definition of psychology calls it 'the science of mind and behaviour' (Gross, 1992). As a discipline, it aims to study and, if possible account for, a wide and varied range of human phenomena running from observable behaviour on the one hand, through to the hidden processes of the mind, such as dreaming, thinking or remembering on the other. It has often been noted that psychology is unique among the sciences in that it is the only discipline which includes the contents of consciousness among its objects of study. Whereas the other sciences study processes and phenomena which are clearly physical in nature, for example, astronomy studies the physical phenomena of the universe, and medicine studies the physical phenomena of disease, psychology includes within its scope all the non-physical phenomena of the mind, the precise status of which is much more problematic. Clearly mental processes are somehow related to the physical structures of the brain, but it is not at all clear how they are related to each other.

Modern psychology rests on the foundation provided by positivism, and this, as we have seen, involves accepting the general view that the investigation of human behaviour and experience can be pursued in precisely the same way as the natural sciences approach other natural phenomena. What this means in practice, for many psychologists is a process of research which is pursued by undertaking the careful observation of objectively defined phenomena, by making quantitative measurements of specified variables, and, often by doing so under the controlled conditions of an experiment.

However, this approach to research in psychology is not without its difficulties, and these can be traced back to the fact that human beings are sources of both mental and behavioural events, which are related to each other in highly complex, and little-understood ways.

One problem is the sheer variability of human behaviour, which makes the ordinary behaviour of human beings less predictable than the behaviour of almost any other species. This may seem unlikely, because often we are more conscious of the large-scale regularities of our lives: we know we get up at much the same time in the morning, eat meals at regular and predictable times, or go on holiday at roughly the same time of year. However, if you drop down into the minute details of behaviour, then the predictability visible in the large-scale view largely vanishes. Shall I watch TV tonight? Or read a book, or go for a walk, or just go to the pub? Anyone trying to predict my decision from outside, would almost certainly have great difficulty. And even if an observer were brave enough to make a prediction, I could easily spoil things by doing none of these, but going to the cinema instead.

The source of this variability, as a moment's reflection on our own lives will indicate, lies in our mental life which contains a whole range of different-seeming entities such as thoughts, feelings, ideas and the like, all of which are capable of influencing behaviour. The result is that anyone who is rash enough to try to predict my (or your) actions in any detail without first acquiring quite a lot of information about our thinking is almost certainly doomed to fail. It just isn't possible to make predictions of this kind without access to at least some of the contents of consciousness, which may include among other things, a person's plans for the day, their interests and recreational preferences, and their emotional state.

What all this means for psychology is that it has not been possible for its practitioners to seek the kind of deterministic explanations which have been found for the phenomena studied by the natural sciences. The variability of human behaviour and the difficulty which this poses for the attempt to identify the links between one piece of behaviour and another, or between different mental states and behaviour, has meant that psychology has had to develop as a *probabilistic* rather than a deterministic science . That is to say, psychological research proceeds by trying to identify statistical regularities in data, and by expressing the relationships between variables in terms of their probability of occurrence, rather than in terms of fixed and deterministic relationships. This, ultimately, is the reason why inferential statistics play such a key role in much psychological research.

There is also a further difficulty. Whereas behaviour is public, overt, and relatively easily lends itself to quantification, the private phenomena of the mind present a much harder challenge to a psychology which aims to be scientific. How is psychology to set about the study of mental events and processes given that they are neither directly observable nor measurable, and can only be manipulated, if at all, by indirect means? The answer to this problem, which was hit on quite early in the history of psychology is to employ *operational definitions*.

These require whichever (inaccessible) variable is to be researched to be defined in terms of another, related variable which *can* be observed and measured directly. The second variable is then said to represent an operational definition of the underlying psychological variable, and it consists of a precise description of the variable itself, together with the conditions under which the observation are to take place. The example in box 1.1 below illustrates this point.

The connection between a psychological variable and its operational definition can be made in one of two ways: by logic or by means of psychological theory. In the example in box 1.1 the connection is made by logic, since the

---

Box 1.1   *Operational definitions*

Operational definitions clearly always have to be used to study memory, because memory processes are not directly observable, and the most obvious approach is to use the amount of information recalled as an operationalization of the amount of information stored in memory. However, as noted above, the operational definition is highly specific – that is, it represents a particular and highly specific decision by the researcher on the way in which an underlying psychological variable is to be observed in a particular situation.

For example, in one investigation into memory, the operational definition of stored information might consist of the number of common nouns recalled from a list of thirty items after a two minute memorization session and a five minute interval between memorization and recall. In another investigation, the operational definition it might be the number of words correctly recognized from a list, while in a third it might be the number of errors made in placing words in their correct order. The point is that a single psychological variable can be operationalized in a number of different ways, with the choice of one operationalization rather than another dependent on the nature of the inquiry, and the precise hypothesis being tested.

---

ability to recall is necessarily dependent on prior memorization having taken place. In other areas of psychological research the connection is made by theory. For example, an intelligence test is generally used to provide an operational definition of the inaccessible variable of intelligence, and this relationship is encapsulated in the well-known, but erroneous saying that 'intelligence is what intelligence tests measure'. Actually the connection between the two is provided by whichever theory about the nature of intelligence the test was based on.

As you may have realized, the fit between a psychological variable and its operational definition can never be perfect. There will always be some degree of error in the measure of the psychological variable which is provided by its operationalization. This is true for all operational definitions of all variables (that I can think of). This means, for example, that simply because a given item of information cannot be recalled on a particular occasion does not mean that it isn't in memory: only that it is not retrievable at that moment. The indication of how much is remembered provided by recall thus includes a degree of error, since it may underestimate how much is remembered. The problem is that we can never know how large the error may be.

The hidden nature of mental events combined with the variability inherent in behaviour has also meant that psychologists have found it extremely difficult to follow the example of the natural sciences and express their theories in the language and concepts provided by mathematics. One attempt to achieve descriptions of behaviour (of rats) using mathematics was made by the American behaviourist, Clark Hull in the 1940s (Hull, 1943). However, this now seems to be generally regarded as a courageous effort rather than an outright success, and it appears to have had no imitators. It seems that the descriptions of processes, theories and ideas which make up the subject matter of psychology, as well as some of the raw research data itself, are really only capable of being expressed in verbal language, which though rich in descriptive power, also lacks the clarity and precision of mathematics.

Despite all the difficulties, though, psychologists have proved themselves to be ingenious and tenacious researchers, and seemingly insurmountable problems have been, if not overcome, at least tackled sufficiently for progress to be made towards experimental investigation even of such impossibly difficult phenomena as mental images. See box 1.2 below.

The experiment represents the dominant method in psychology, reflecting the profound influence which the doctrine of positivism has exerted on the development of the discipline. For many psychologists, the experiment offers the only truly rigorous and scientific way of pursuing a research question. At the same time, however, many psychologists can also be found who employ one of the non-experimental methods in their researches. The reason is simple: there are many topics of great interest which cannot be explored experimentally, either for ethical or practical reasons. For example, a question about the

---

Box 1.2   *Studying mental images by experimental means*

Mental images – the fleeting pictures in the mind which we enjoy when daydreaming – had generally resisted study by any method other than introspection, i.e. having a subject look inside their own mind and try to report what was there. However, R. N. Shepard and his co-workers succeeded in developing a technique for studying these images experimentally, in a way that gave precision and objectivity to the process (see Cooper and Shepard, 1984).

Shepard's approach exploited the fact that we typically use mental imagery in situations when we are required to make difficult decisions about three-dimensional objects. The experimental task in one example involved presenting subjects with pairs of pictures of three-dimensional block figures, in which each figure was in a different orientation to the other. The subjects were then asked whether the figures were the same or different. In order to answer the question, subjects had to form a mental image of one block and then mentally rotate it in two or three dimensions until they could check whether the two figures were the same. The subjects were able to do this quite easily, but the time they took to reach a decision was shown by Shepard to be closely related to the amount of rotation required to get the figures into the same orientation.

The more rotation the longer it took to decide, and rotation in two dimensions took less time than rotation in three. In fact Shepard was able to show that the relationship between the rotation of mental objects in the mind bore the same relation to time as did the rotation of physical objects in the hands. The research aptly demonstrates the way in which the ingenuity of individual researchers has enabled seemingly inaccessible mental events to be reached and studied experimentally.

role of play in the social and emotional development of the child should probably only be approached by a non-experimental method, since it is clearly a breach of research ethics to prevent a child from playing for a period of time in order to observe any consequent effects on its development.

Partly because of difficulties like this, psychologists have, in association with other social scientists, helped to develop a varied range of other methods of data collection, such as the questionnaire and the interview. These offer ways of collecting data which can be used on those research questions, like the example above, for which an experiment is inappropriate. More interestingly, they can also be used to obtain a very different kind of information about a problem from that produced by an experiment. Whereas experiments are, almost exclusively, geared to the generation of 'hard data' in the form of quantitative measures of a variable, the alternative methods are able to provide the researcher with 'soft' qualitative information consisting of verbal descriptions of psychological events and processes.

This distinction proves to be useful and important for two reasons. The first is that the latter, qualitative type of information is of particular value when the focus of an inquiry lies with private mental events and processes, such as dreams, which can be reported verbally, but which do not easily lend themselves to meaningful quantification. It therefore offers a way of tackling the problems of researching into the phenomena of the mind.

The second reason is that the distinction between 'hard' and 'soft' data represents an important part of a debate between humanistic psychology and positivism about how psychological research should proceed, and what its real aims should be. We now turn to look briefly at some of the issues which this debate raises.

Humanistic psychology's critique of positivism

Positivism represents, as we have seen, the dominant framework of ideas within which most psychological research is currently carried out. Nevertheless, it would be a misconception to suppose that it represents the only available approach to doing research in psychology. There is a competing perspective, which though so far less influential, offers a significant alternative to the positivist line. This is the approach offered by the humanistic wing of psychology which argues that positivism can never provide an appropriate perspective from which to explore human behaviour and experience.

Humanistic psychology, the so-called 'third force' in psychology (after behaviourism and psychoanalysis), represents an approach to psychology which consciously presents itself as an alternative to the fragmented and partial view of humanity which it regards as the positivist tradition's only offering. Rather than seeing people as (say) information-processing systems, or sets of conditioned responses, the humanistic psychologists take the view that people are rational organisms of great complexity, each of whom possesses a range of unique qualities, and is continually striving to achieve psychological completeness and self-fulfilment. They therefore argue that the real business of psychology should be to try to understand people as wholes by studying the phenomenal world of individual experience rather than by concentrating on narrowly defined and objectively observable features of behaviour.

Given this generous view of what psychology should be, it is scarcely surprising to find that humanistic psychology has, in general, been extremely critical of the research conducted from within the positivist approach. In particular, the experimental method has been singled out for special criticism on the grounds that while it may be able to deliver explanations of limited and artificial fragments of behaviour, when viewed from the perspective of humanistic psychology, it is seen as incapable of providing anything like an adequate understanding of human beings.

Humanistic psychology argues that traditional, positivist, experimental research represents a distortion of what psychology should be because it involves the translation, without reflection or examination, of the approach of the natural sciences into psychology. This has resulted in a psychology which is mechanistic, impersonal, obsessed with quantification and precise measurement, in which research is directed towards the examination of a limited number of 'variables' which are represented as isolated units of behaviour or experience. This when it should really be pursuing questions about how people experience, and deal with the different elements which make up their lives.

The distinction between humanistic and 'scientific' psychology can be summed up in Child's (1973), distinction between 'hard' and 'soft' psychologies. In this distinction, the traditional, positivist scientific approach is 'hard', – i.e. is quantitative, claims to be objective and value-free, and is oriented towards analysing parts of complex phenomena rather than to examining their wholes. It is therefore unable to deliver any understanding of the human person as a whole. The humanistic approach, on the other hand, is 'soft' in that it is concerned with existential and phenomenological questions, and takes a holistic approach to its subject matter, preferring to collect qualitative over quantitative data, and regarding the values of the researcher as an integral and necessary part of the research situation.

It has to be admitted that the humanistic critique of the 'traditional' positivist approach to doing research has not so far been particularly influential. There are few signs, for example, of the wholesale abandonment of experimentation in favour of alternatives, although on the other hand, there are indications that more and more psychologists are learning to appreciate the contribution which non-experimental methods can make to a research project. Although the progress of change is difficult to assess accurately, it seems that gradually, the inferior status suffered by non-experimental methods is being worn away, and researchers are now rather less likely to see experimentation as the research method of first resort.

A way of doing research which has been much influenced by the ideas of humanistic psychology – which in fact brings together both the humanistic and positivist strands – is known as the hermeneutic approach (Reason and Rowan, 1981). This takes its name from the literary technique of hermeneutics, which is the process of establishing the meaning and interpretation of religious texts. The key idea of this approach to research is that people are not to be seen as passive subjects, to be mined for information by an omniscient researcher, but rather as active co-participants and partners in the research process. Doing research from this perspective involves both parties – the researcher and the informants–in the creation of a constructive *dialogue* about the research topic, to which each contributes their own unique insights and ideas.

What this means in terms of actual research practice probably varies from practitioner to practitioner, since in some ways hermeneutic research is more of an attitude than a clear set of procedures to be followed. If you wish to try the hermeneutic approach to doing research then the following recipe will take you some way towards the humanistic position, without necessitating the complete abandonment of the principles of positivism:

- First, one should always include as data in an investigation some of the research participants' own accounts of their experience alongside more objective measures. The research participants are always to be regarded as active partners in the research process rather than as 'subjects' or passive sources of data.
- Secondly, one should use qualitative methods alongside the quantitative ones (rather than simply as alternatives) whenever it is possible to do so.
- Finally, one should try to conduct research into how people function in natural situations and compare the results with those obtained from the laboratory.

With this rather compressed introduction to the hermeneutic approach to research we end this review of a small part of the philosophical background to psychological research. We began by considering the fundamental principles which inform all research in science. In the remaining part of this chapter we look in more detail at the procedures which scientists follow in the pursuit of knowledge.

Testing Theories: A View of the Process of Doing Research

In this part of the chapter the process of doing research in science is examined both in overview and in detail.

Key scientific terms and concepts such as 'variable', 'hypothesis' and 'theory' are defined.

The four main stages in the process of doing research are described and explained, and related to the development of practical applications.

The importance of the process of theory development is reviewed, and the logic of the process is explained by reference to Popper's principle of falsification.

The use of the principle to distinguish science from 'non-science' is briefly touched on in relation to the theories of psychoanalysis.

Box 1.3   *Some terms and concepts of science*

As you may already be aware, from studies in other science disciplines, 'doing science' always involves acquiring a set of new words and concepts, and psychology is no exception. The following is a short list of some of the basic terms and ideas which you will need from this point onwards as you work through this book. More detailed explanations of each concept are provided later in the chapter.

Data
'Data' (the plural form: the singular is 'datum') is the name given to the information collected in the course of an investigation.

Quantitative data
Quantitative data are those in which information is represented by numbers. IQ scores, reaction times, and the tally of the different responses to a questionnaire, are all examples of quantitative data. Quantitative data can be analysed by means of descriptive or inferential statistics (see chapters 6 to 9).

Qualitative data
In qualitative data the information is represented in the form of verbal descriptions. For example, a description of the interaction between two people which conveyed what was said, in what tone of voice, and with what gestures, would be qualitative data.

Variables
A variable is any entity, or 'thing', which can take more than one value. Intelligence, handedness, or liking for another person are all variables. Quantitative data consists of measurements made of the behaviour of variables, while qualitative data provides descriptions of the same behaviour.

Continuous variables
A variable whose value forms a perfect continuum is called a continuous variable. This means that within the range of values which it is possible for it to take, it is able to hold absolutely any value at all.

Discrete (discontinuous) variables
A discrete variable is one whose values within the possible range are discontinuous from each other. This means that there is a gap between each of the values in the range and only those values can be observed. A five-point rating scale generating possible scores of 0, 1, 2, 3 and 4 is a discrete scale since only these values (and not, values of 3.7 or 2.4) are possible as data.

Theories
A theory is an explanation, often partial or incomplete, and always temporary, which is proposed for some puzzling aspect of nature. Research in science is

directed towards the testing of a theory in order to assess the adequacy of the explanation which is offered, and to enable a better theory to be developed.

Hypothesis
A hypothesis is a prediction, made on the basis of a theory, about the kinds of result which may be expected from an investigation.

Scientific hypotheses
Scientific hypotheses are those which make a general prediction about how the value of one or more variables might be expected to change if the conditions required by the theory are met and, of course, if the theory itself is correct.

Statistical hypotheses
Statistical hypotheses are highly specific versions of general scientific hypotheses, which lead to predictions of how a particular variable is expected to change its value under precisely defined conditions in an investigation. These hypotheses come in pairs consisting of a null and an alternate (or experimental) form. See chapter 7 for more information.

Introduction

In what follows we first of all look at the major elements which constitute 'doing research' in psychology. Then, having established the picture in large scale, we will move in to look at the some of the key details of what is involved.

We begin, then, by considering the process of doing research from the high-level perspective offered by figure 1.1. At this very general level of description, scientific research can be described in terms of four linked stages or processes. They are:

1   **The stage of problem identification,** at which the research problem is isolated and defined.
2   **The stage of data gathering and evaluation,** at which empirical data relevant to the problem are collected and evaluated.
3   **The stage of theory development,** when data are used to generate explanations which form the actual content of what is known.
4   **The stage of the development of applications,** when the insights contained in theory are used to solve practical problems.

The main value of taking such a high-level perspective enables us to focus closely on two key areas: those of problem identification and theory development, and also to say something about the development of applications. Not much will be said at this stage about data gathering and evaluation, as this will be dealt with in more detail later.

One of the most important features of this diagram is the existence of the feedback loop between the theory stage and the stage of problem identification

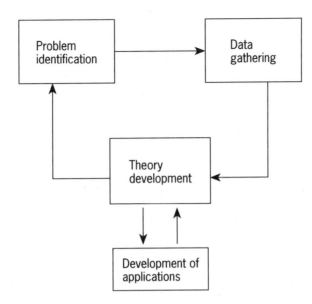

Figure 1.1 An overview of the research process

which means that the result of what happens at the stage of theory development can influence what happens at that first stage of problem identification.

When it is viewed at this level, then, the research process appears as a cycle which can be repeated infinitely many times, and not simply as a 'straight-through', once-for-all process. In simple terms (and this will become more apparent to you as you do more research of your own) it means that whatever is identified as a problem is itself partly determined by the nature and content of the theories which are being proposed as explanations. Theories, it turns out have a dual function. They not only provide explanations, for observed phenomena , but also help to identify further problems for the research process to work on.

However, although the stages can be laid out neatly in a diagram in a way which suggests that each is completed before the next is begun, it is also important to remember that this represents a very simplified and idealized picture. Like life itself, the reality of doing science is much less straightforward, messy even, but also rather more interesting, than the diagram suggests.

The stage of problem identification

The necessary first step in doing research is obviously to identify the problem which is to be pursued. But research problems do not necessarily present themselves to the investigator in a clearly defined form. They don't, as it were, spring fully formed from nature demanding to be solved. How, then, do they emerge? Where do the problems which engage researchers come from?

At a very deep level, this is probably asking a question about human nature for which there is no real answer available. Perhaps the nearest one can get to an answer is to say that problems present themselves for solution because curiosity is a fundamental human urge which we are all driven to satisfy. The scientist's curiosity is not different from that of the non-scientist: it is simply directed towards a different set of problems from those which preoccupy non-scientists.

Psychologists, and philosophers have tried to analyse the process of problem identification in science in more detail. One suggestion is that what happens is that scientists see and respond to something with a sense of puzzlement. They finds themselves, to use Karl Popper's phrase, in a 'problem-situation', as the idea develops that there is something which requires investigation.

The 'something' itself might come from any one of a number of different sources. It could come, for example, from the discovery of what have been called 'surprising facts' – i.e. facts which, when discovered, demand an explanation. It could come from a theory which has been shown not to match the facts of a situation, or from another scientist's research report. Or, it may come from a much less clear source. The autobiographical accounts of many scientists suggest that important research can often spring from a sudden hunch, or an awareness of a gap in knowledge, even from an experience in everyday life. On different occasions these have all provided starting points for successful research.

These are, though, what might be called the 'official' answers to the question of where problems come from because they match closely a simplified and rather idealized version of how science operates. From this point of view scientists are depicted as being driven by wholly disinterested motives, with the process of discovery, and scientific progress in general, taking place in something of a social and cultural vacuum. There is some truth in this picture, but it is far from being the complete truth. In fact there are a whole range of other motives for pursuing research including those which may be regarded as somewhat less than worthy, and these must also be acknowledged if the picture is to be complete.

One is the desire to develop exploitable applications of knowledge – the area of so-called 'applied research' in which scientific knowledge is applied to the solution of practical problems. The selection of the research problem in these cases is driven not so much by the desire to develop theoretical understanding, although this may be one outcome, but by the desire to develop products or processes which have a direct application in the world outside the research environment.

In psychology, applied research has always played a part in the development of the discipline. In the late nineteenth century, for example, in the wake of the establishment of universal education for all French children, the psychologist Alfred Binet was asked by the French government to construct a psychometric test to be used to distinguish those children who had learning difficulties, and who would therefore be unable to benefit from the normal curriculum, from those who did not. The results of Binet's efforts, which included the concept of mental age as the basis for measuring intellectual development, provided many of the foundations for the later development of the whole field of mental testing. Since World War Two, psychological research directed towards applied ends has grown into a significant (though unaccounted) part of the total of research activity, as government agencies have tried to recruit psychologists to find solutions to their various problems. One particularly intriguing example is described in box 1.4 below.

The example of the military sponsorship of research in box 1.4 provides an important reminder that all scientific research is likely to be driven by a mixture of motives on the part of the researcher. Curiosity, and the disinterested pursuit of knowledge are certainly important factors, but there are likely to be other, less straightforward motives mixed in with the simple desire to add to the sum of human wisdom. These will also play a role, both in the choice of a research topic, and in the selection of a particular research method. Obviously, it is difficult to say much about these, since they will certainly vary from person to person, and from one occasion to another, but it is plausible to suppose that considerations such as the desire to advance a career or to obtain the recognition of professional peers, and the inevitable need to obtain funding to allow the research to be undertaken at all, will help push a researcher towards one particular problem rather than another. And as the beginning of this chapter has already suggested, psychological research may often be stimulated by the wish to find an explanation for a puzzling piece of personal experience.

All of this emphasizes one further point that has so far been rather glossed over. It is that science as a human activity, and therefore all science including, of course, psychology, is carried on in an environment which is formed by a particular social, political and economic context, and affected by influences and pressures from that context in complex ways. And of course, even our understanding of what science is, and what its purposes and functions might be are formed by the notions available to us within the society in which we live. The example of John Bowlby's 'maternal deprivation' hypothesis in box 1.5, shows how psychological theorizing can arise from, and be supported by, a particular social context.

Once an idea has emerged as a problem to be investigated, the processes involved in getting research underway become a little clearer. The philosopher Karl Popper has suggested that the initial stage in finding a way to a solution involves the formation of what he calls 'conjectures'. These are 'jumps to conclusions': tentative, ill-formed, hunch-like explanations which constitute the scientist's first response to the emergent problem. Conjectures are important because they provide a platform of initial ideas from which a research enterprise can be launched. They may be rapidly discarded once the research gets under way, but this is of no consequence. They will have served their purpose because they will have provided the vital starting point without which there could have been no further progress. Though disposable, they nevertheless make a vital contribution to the overall research process.

There is also one more reason why conjectures should be seen as an important part of the research process. They represent the intuitive, creative, almost playful side of science, which contrasts sharply with the formal, rigorous application of method which characterizes the later stage of research activity.

Box 1.4   An example of the military sponsorship of psychological research

An example of a military-sponsored investigation which has generated consider-able debate and controversy, is the research on the simulated prison which was directed by Philip Zimbardo during the late 1960s. With funding from the US Office of Naval Research, Zimbardo and his associates constructed a simulated prison in the basement of the University of California, and placed in it a group of guards and a group of 'prisoners', both of which were formed from volunteers from the student body of the university. Zimbardo's avowed intention was to test the 'dispositional hypothesis' – the theory that the poor state of relations between prisoners and guards is due to the 'nature' of the people in each group which determines how each is likely to behave towards the other. The idea was that prison guards (particularly in the USA) will behave in a dominating and vindic-tive way towards prisoners and, equally, prisoners will behave in a hostile and negative way towards guards, because of the kind of people who naturally gravi-tate into each group.

The results of this research were extremely striking. Beginning with groups of prisoners and guards who had been selected at random from a pool of partici-pants, and who were therefore initially indistinguishable from each other, Zimbardo found that the behaviour of the two groups rapidly diverged. The 'guards' became ever more aggressive, cruel and vindictive in their treatment of prisoners, while the 'prisoners' became mostly submissive, passive and depressed. The effects on the 'prisoner' group were, in fact so severe that the experiment was terminated after only six days, although the investigation had been planned to run for fourteen days.

This is a particularly interesting piece of research, not least because once the details were released opinion became divided about the real reasons why it had been carried out. Zimbardo and his co-workers give their own explanations in their publications (see, for example, Haney, Banks and Zimbardo, 1988) and the Office of Naval Research, as one would expect, has to date released no official comment on the matter. However, it has been pointed out (e.g. Watson, 1978), that it is implausible to suppose that the US Navy could really be interested in the interpersonal dynamics of a civilian prison. Had that been the case, it was already responsible for a number of penal establishments in which research could have been done, without the need to simulate a prison environment. On the other hand, as Watson also says, the Navy, along with other arms of the military, is very likely to be interested in the behaviour of prisoners of war, and this is rather harder to research in either a civil or military prison where routines are already firmly established, and where there are limits on how the prisoners may be treated.

By constructing a simulation of a prison both these obstacles could be circum-vented. Watson suggests that a more plausible reason for doing the research would be in order to investigate how newly captured servicemen would respond to confinement under harsh conditions. If this was the case, it would have been intended to lead to the development of strategies to help them to cope with the experiences of capture, imprisonment and interrogation by an enemy which could have been taught to all US military personnel. Whether this is really the expla-nation is, of course, still not known.

Box 1.5   Social context and psychology – John Bowlby and the maternal deprivation hypothesis

Bowlby's thesis, which he developed in a number of reports and books published through the 1950s and 1960s (e.g. Bowlby, 1969) was that biological mothers, as distinct from others who might perform the mothering role, provide a quality of care for their children which is, in some sense unique. He appeared to believe that it is, literally, better for a child to be cared for by a bad or incompetent biological mother than by a competent caretaker who is unrelated to it.

Bowlby's research appeared to show that children who experience any disruption of the normal maternal care-taking during infancy or early childhood (such as might be caused by the mother going out to work, or by a period of hospitalization) suffer serious social and emotional disadvantage, which could lead, Bowlby believed, to personality disorders and delinquent behaviour in later life.

Bowlby's theory was extremely influential in the period between the late 1940s to the 1960s, and this may be linked to the fact that government policy of the time aimed to squeeze as many women as possible out of the labour market in order to create space for the men who, with the post-war shrinkage of the armed forces, needed to find jobs.

Clearly, Bowlby's ideas were very timely since they were able to provide politicians and economic planners with independent 'scientific' support for the idea that 'a woman's place is in the home'. They therefore played a role in creating a climate of opinion which made it harder for a woman to continue to work after having a child.

This is not, of course, to suggest that Bowlby was simply a stooge of the government who produced the 'evidence' needed to support a government policy which had already been decided. Nevertheless, as later researchers on this topic have argued (e.g. Rutter, 1976), Bowlby did take a highly simplistic, not to say idealistic, view of the process of parenting and the formation of affectional bonds, and there can be no doubt that his views found ready acceptance in Whitehall. The only conclusion which one can draw from the theory of maternal deprivation is that it demonstrates how very closely it is possible for scientific research, public opinion, and government policy to become entwined, so that it is extremely difficult to tell where one ends and the others begin.

The stage of data gathering and evaluation

Once a problem has been adequately identified, the research can move on to the data gathering stage. This is a rather complex process, involving several distinct operations which we will return to in detail a little later. For now, though, it is enough simply to identify each of the operations contained in this stage. They are:

- The selection of an appropriate research method
- The formation of hypotheses for testing, (if appropriate)

- The acquisition of data by means of observation and, in the case of quantitative data, measurement, of one or several variables
- Data analysis and evaluation.

From figure 1.1, you can see that the outcomes of these processes go on to contribute to the crucial activity of theory building. As the nature of theory, and its precise role in the development of knowledge is often misunderstood, we now need to examine these matters in some detail.

The stage of theory development

The reason why research is undertaken is not primarily to collect information about some problem, but to help with the process of developing theories. In fact, theory development represents a major part of what it means to 'do science', and in doing research you need to have the idea of what a theory is and what its role is in science at the front of your mind.

What is a theory? The most straightforward definition is to say that it is an explanation for some puzzling aspect of nature. However, this needs to be qualified by two further pieces of information. First that a theory may only offer a partial or incomplete explanation of the phenomenon in question, and secondly that any explanation which it offers can never be regarded as the final word on the subject. All theories, no matter how venerable and apparently unassailable, are essentially temporary structures. They exist only until a better theory comes along, and then they are discarded.

Theories play a central role in science because as well as providing explanations for puzzling phenomena they also guide the thinking and investigative activities of researchers. Contrary to the view that they are essentially impractical and divorced from reality, a good theory is an intensely useful thing because it provides a source of research problems and basis for the development of understanding, prediction and possibly also control. As the social psychologist Kurt Lewin once said, 'There's nothing so practical as a good theory.'

Obviously, though, not all theories are the same. They will inevitably vary from discipline to discipline and from problem to problem: they may be elaborate or simple; they may be founded on little more than a guess or hunch, or on quantities of data; they may be expressed mathematically in formulae or described in words, and so on. Whatever their outward appearance, however, all good theories, will be found to share certain important characteristics in common. To be 'good' a theory should be:

Testable and refutable
Parsimonious (economical)
A good generator of predictions
A fertile source of new ideas.

We'll take a closer look at each of these characteristics in turn.

Testability

All scientific theories propose an explanation for some phenomenon. That is, all theories try to explain something in nature which is a source of puzzlement, either because there is no explanation available, or because it fails in some way to fit in with existing assumptions or expectations. The purpose of any theory is to remove that puzzlement by offering an explanation, but science, in line with the doctrine of empiricism, still needs some way of confirming independently that what is offered is a valid explanation which does in fact account for the observed phenomena. This is where theory testing – comparing predictions from the theory to the observed facts – becomes vitally important, since this is the way in which the validity of the explanation offered by a theory can be assessed.

Clearly, for this to take place, the theory concerned has got to be testable. And if it is to be testable, this means, in turn, that it must be explicit. That is, it must be couched in a way that allows propositions to be derived from it which are so clear and precise that it is possible to say, without equivocation, whether or not the observed data match the prediction. Any vagueness or ambiguity of formulation in the theory are extremely undesirable because they make it very difficult to pin down its exact meaning. They also undermine the very task which the theory should be supporting, i.e. to advance knowledge. As we shall see a little later, theories can be regarded as the suicide pilots of science in that they are launched only in order for attempts to be made to shoot them down. If, as happens, a theory is untestable for some reason, that places it beyond the reach of criticisms which are based on empirical data. It is also difficult in such cases to show that the testing process has been exhaustive, and there will always remain doubt about whether the theory has been fully examined. Theories have to be explicit and clear in order to be testable: unclear or otherwise defective theories cannot be tested adequately.

The process of testing a theory is absolutely central to the development of knowledge. It is only by subjecting a theory to testing and thereby showing that it is either incorrect or *not* incorrect (and note that this is not the same thing as showing a theory to be *correct*), that it can count as a contribution to knowledge. For this to be possible, as we said, a theory also has to be expressed in a form which allows us to say how it could be shown to be incorrect. This is the further principle of refutability: the idea that it is possible to identify exactly what kind of data one would have to collect in order to demonstrate with certainty that a theory is incorrect. This latter point may seem a perverse one, since the idea of showing a theory to be incorrect is the exact opposite from the generally held view that it is the business of scientists to show that theories are correct. However, as you will see shortly, there is a very sound reason for putting it this way. (If you can't wait to find out what it is, turn to the section headed 'A more detailed view of theory development and the principle of falsification', on p. 34.)

For the moment, we simply have to note that, in principle, the testing process can lead to one of only three possible outcomes. Either the theory is shown to be incorrect and it is discarded; or it is shown to be incorrect and undergoes modification to bring it closer to the explanation suggested by the results of the empirical data. Such a modified theory then has to undergo a process of re-test in order to check that the modifications have actually improved the theory. The final possibility is that the theory is shown to be not incorrect, and it then becomes a candidate for general acceptance as an explanation of what has taken place.

Research in all the sciences, and not just in psychology, is directed towards such testing of theories in order to ascertain whether they can be shown to be inadequate in some respect. This is why it is so necessary for different research-ers to go over the same ground again and again so that they can become increasingly sure (but never finally certain) that a theory offers the best avail-able (but not the final) explanation of the phenomenon in question.

Parsimony

A good theory should also be parsimonious or economical in seeking to ex-plain the known facts in a way which is as simple, and involves as few special assumptions, as possible. There are two reasons for this. The first is that a theory which is simple is likely to be more easily testable, and, as we have just seen testability is one of the criteria against which a theory has to be measured. Important though this is, it is probably true to say that it comes slightly behind the second reason. This is that the simpler the theory, the better the quality of the thinking which it is likely to express. So simple theories which can easily be scrutinized for logical flaws or cases of special pleading, are better than those which are complicated, and contain buried within them ill-defined con-cepts, inadequately worked arguments or assumptions which can only be jus-tified by reference to special cases.

You may be interested to know that we owe this criterion of a good theory to a medieval logician called William of Ockham, who was apparently the first to enunciate the principle of parsimony (called 'Ockham's Razor', because, when wielded in appropriate circumstances it permits weak arguments to be cut to ribbons). Ockham naturally wrote in Latin, but a loose translation of his idea would be that the simplest possible explanation is always to be pre-ferred to more complicated alternatives.

A good generator of predictions

As we have already seen, one of the goals of science is to be able to make predictions about what will happen when certain preconditions are met. These predictions which must be based, however loosely, on a theory of some kind, can only be as good as that theory. If the theory is good (i.e. provides an accurate explanation of why things occur the way they do) then it will allow clear predictions to be made about what will happen if the conditions are fulfilled. And, of course, the better the understanding given by the theory, the more accurate these predictions are likely to be. Eventually, if a theory is so clear and precise that very precise and successful predictions can be based on it, then it may make it possible to go beyond simple prediction to allow control of the phenomena covered by the theory.

Fertility

As its name suggests, this criterion is concerned with the generative powers of a theory, that is with its ability to stimulate new thinking, new ideas, and eventually the production of new knowledge. One popular misperception of theories is that they try to provide final and complete answers to research questions, but this is not the case. Good theories provide open rather than closed systems of explanation, which means that while they provide explanations for the phenomena which need to be explained they are also capable of suggesting new ideas for further investigation, new interpretations of existing data, or new ways of attacking previously intractable problems, so that far from closing off a line of inquiry with a final explanation, they actually open up new avenues to be explored.

To summarize we have seen, perhaps somewhat to our surprise, that theories are multifaceted entities, possessing a number of important characteristics which are responsible for their fundamental role in the process of developing new knowledge.

First, because they are able to provide explanations of the way things are, which can be tested, they make the world a less ambiguous and more predictable place, and the more general these explanations are, the better is our grasp of what it is that makes the world as it is. Moreover, as the development of science means that knowledge comes to consist of a range of ever more powerful theories, we thereby extend our ability to explain, predict, and sometimes control, new and hitherto unexplained phenomena.

The stage of the development of applications

Lastly, we come to the development of applications. This process, by which the results of the work to develop scientific theories is applied to answering practical needs, has already been mentioned in connection with the motives which drive scientists to do research. However, it would be wrong to regard the process of applying theoretical knowledge for practical ends as a one-way traffic which simply solves practical problems but does nothing for scientific advance. In fact, as figure 1.1 suggests, the relationship is more like a two-way street. Not only does a good theory make it possible to try to deal with practical problems, but the theory itself may be refined and improved by the attempt to produce applications. In psychology, one example of this process has been the way in which endeavours to apply learning theory to the control of certain mental disorders has resulted in a clearer understanding of the limitations of the theory.

This completes an overview of what is involved in doing research, which has described each of the different stages of the process, and explained something of the part played by each one in the generation of new knowledge. As we indicated earlier, we will shortly need to examine one of those elements – data gathering – in much more detail. But we will first take a closer look at the process by which theories, which were discussed earlier in connection with the third of the four stages – theory development – are tested.

A more detailed view of theory development and the principle of falsification

Having examined the research process in overview, we now need to return to a question, touched on earlier, which lies at the very heart of understanding exactly how science works. This is the question of how theories can be tested. What exactly does it mean to 'test' a theory, and how can we be certain that an adequate test has been carried out?

In reading what follows you need to bear in mind that the process of theory testing requires description and explanation on two levels. On the more abstract level it is possible to explain the principles or the logic of the process – that is, to say how it is that theories can be satisfactorily tested in a way which leads to a growth of knowledge. This is the level, if you like, of the theory of theory testing. Secondly, and more concretely, there is the level of actual real-world activity by which theories are tested and evaluated through research. At this level we are dealing with what happens when scientists actually try to apply the abstract principles of the first level. In what follows, although we will touch lightly on the practicalities of theory testing, we will be concentrating mostly on providing the first level of description, leaving the matters on the second level to be explained in detail in chapter 7.

First, then, the principles. The problem posed by the question of how theories are tested was tackled with some success by Karl Popper in the 1930s, when he was able to provide a convincing account, not of the process itself, but of the logic which underlies it (see, for example, Popper, 1963).

His explanation centres on a concept called the principle of falsification. Popper argued that falsification – the process of showing an argument to be false – was absolutely central to understanding how science works, because it explained exactly how the testing of theories was able to generate knowledge. His argument ran as follows.

Firstly, he argued that from the point of view of strict logic, it does not matter how much information is amassed which confirms or supports a particular theory, because one can never *prove* that a theory is finally and completely correct. No matter how many mountains of supporting evidence are collected, there always remains the possibility, which may be extremely small but which, because it exists, has nonetheless to be taken into account, that there exists somewhere a piece of information which shows that the theory is false. Because of this, Popper argued, we can never be completely *certain* that any theory is correct, no matter how powerful and convincing the evidence which supports it. Always we have to take into account the possibility that the theory is wrong. Therefore, Popper argued, science can only arrive at certain conclusion about the theory by taking a different approach. It cannot arrive at certainty by trying to prove a theory to be correct, for the reason given; but if it takes the opposite tack, and tries to prove a theory to be incorrect, then a certain conclusion can be achieved. While the theory can never be finally confirmed, it is quite definitely possible to falsify it.

Popper illustrates this argument by the famous 'black swans' example. Imagine a man, representing a scientist, who has lived all his life on a desert island and who spends his time watching birds fly overhead (corresponding to the data-gathering process in science). Now suppose he only ever sees black swans, and never a white one. The question is whether he would have good grounds for supposing that all the swans everywhere else were black (the theory). Popper says not. He points out that no matter how many black swans the man may see, there is always the possibility that somewhere in the world there is a white swan which has never flown anywhere near the island, and hence has never been observed by the scientist. On the other hand, the scientist has only to see the one white swan to know immediately that the theory that all swans are black is false.

The importance of falsification is, therefore, that it provides science with a way of obtaining certain knowledge. Although it is impossible to confirm a theory because of the possibility of a piece of negative evidence, and therefore confirmation cannot provide any kind of certainty, it is on the other hand possible, to *dis*confirm a theory (i.e. prove it false) on the basis of a single piece of negative evidence, and thereby to achieve certainty that the theory is incorrect. The process of attempting to falsify a theory involves gathering data from the kinds of situation covered by the theory, and then determining whether the data match the predictions of the theory, i.e. whether or not they look the way the theory says they should.

Earlier, the distinction was made between the logic of theory testing and its practice. How, then, does the falsification principle work in practice? As we have seen, the logic of the process demands that if the data which are gathered do not match the theory (assuming that the data have been collected in ways which the theory requires), then that theory has been shown to be false, and should be abandoned or modified. However, in practice it is rare for a single disconfirming result to force the abandonment of a theory, and almost invariably in the few such cases which can be found, the theory has been doubted all along, so that research simply confirms suspicions held on other grounds. Scientists are rightly cautious about abandoning previous work which has appeared to be correct, and so rather than abandoning a theory after the first instance of disconfirmation, they will almost invariably continue to test it in a variety of ways. If the repeated tests continue to throw up a range of discrepant results, then that theory becomes progressively weakened and will eventually be modified or replaced.

On the other hand, it is possible that a theory may survive repeated and ever more ingenious attempts at falsification. If it does, then confidence grows that the theory is essentially correct; and the more times this happens, the stronger the confidence. After many such unsuccessful attempts a theory may come to be regarded as unassailable – virtually correct. However, as Popper has shown it is *still* possible (though increasingly unlikely) that even such a very strong theory could ultimately be shown to be incorrect.

There is a further important point to be made here. Scientific knowledge consists essentially of *theories* – the explanations which have been constructed in order to account for natural phenomena. *Data*, the results of a scientist's investigations, are not knowledge in the same sense, since they lack explanatory power. The importance of data lie purely in their ability to provide a test of a theory.

This view of the relationship of data to theory accounts for our experience of science itself. If it is the case that the knowledge generated by scientific activity is contained in theories rather than in data, then it means also that as existing theories are superseded by new and more powerful explanations so scientific knowledge is also continuously changing and developing. And this in fact is what happens. Through the activities of scientists we feel that we understand more and more of how the world works, but this is not in any sense due to the fact that we are accumulating more and more data. On the contrary, it is due to the increasing power and sophistication of the theories which are produced from the data.

Popper's principle of falsification also provides a useful way of distinguishing between genuine science and those subjects, such as astrology and psychoanalysis, which call themselves scientific, but are in fact not so. In Popper's view, to be genuinely scientific a discipline is required to generate theories which are genuinely testable–falsifiable, and any failure to do this is to abandon the strict criterion of what makes a science. Psychoanalysis provides a classical example of what, for Popper, is a 'non-science'. Critics of psychoanalysis argue that it is impossible decisively to falsify any psychoanalytic theory, because any instance of failure to confirm the theory can always be explained away by reference to some other part of the psychoanalytic canon. Such systems of ideas are said to be 'self-sealing' because any attempt to show that the theory is false can always be repaired by the ad hoc application of ideas from another part of the theory. For example, Freud's theory of the Oedipus complex (see Freud, 1986), proposes as a universal feature of psychosexual development that all males will at some stage experience incestuous feelings towards their mothers and aggressive wishes towards their fathers. But any male who cannot produce memories of such feelings for his mother does not, for a convinced Freudian, demonstrate the failure of the theory. The inability to remember such feelings and wishes is instead seen as evidence for powerful and conflicting motives which have been denied or repressed as an ego-defensive strategy which is aimed at keeping the psychological conflict and anxiety which they generate out of consciousness.

This means that statements in psychoanalysis are extraordinarily difficult to test in any final sense, although various efforts have been made over the years (see, for example, Kline 1989). It seems probable that the nature of psychoanalysis is such that its propositions cannot rigorously be tested in the sense that one can say clearly and with certainty what observations would definitely result in the theory being shown to be incorrect. For this reason, psychoanalysis is generally regarded by many as lying outside the boundary which separates science from non-science, and its statements, although interesting, and possibly useful, as not really to be counted as a part of scientific knowledge.

This completes our review of the Popperian view of theory development, which, it is probably fair to say, currently represents the most widely held view of how science operates. As you may be aware, there is more that could have been said, but to do so would have taken us well beyond what is necessary to appreciate the logic of how theories are tested, into deeper philosophical waters lying beyond the scope of this book. Instead, we will continue by honouring the earlier promise to examine the data gathering and evaluation part of the process of scientific research more closely.

Hypothesis Testing: A More Detailed View of the Process of Data Gathering and Evaluation

This section of the chapter reviews in more detail the activities of the hypothesis testing stage of the research cycle, and distinguishes between hypothesis testing and exploratory research.

Introduction

The process of pursuing research in science was earlier described as consisting of four distinct stages, beginning with the identification of a problem to be investigated, continuing with data gathering and the generation of a theory or explanation, and ending with the development of applications. It was also said that the key to this process was the *principle of falsification*, by which possible theories are tested against data which has been gathered specifically for that purpose. We now have to look in more detail at that part of the process which lies between problem identification and theory development, and which is concerned with data gathering and evaluation.

However, before go on to look at it more closely, we need to clarify exactly what the term 'hypothesis' refers to and how it fits in to the overall scheme of things in a psychological inquiry.

Hypotheses

In science, a hypothesis is simply a prediction concerning the kind of results which are expected from an investigation. However, they are more than just free-standing guesses, plucked from the air, about what might possibly be the case. To be of any value at all they must be based on a theory of some kind, and the prediction they make must be justifiable in terms of the theory. Otherwise they have no status other than as more or less informed guesses about what might possibly (or possibly not) be the case. Hypotheses are predictions about what the data from an investigation can be *expected* to look like *if the theory is correct.*

It is obviously also important to get the relationship between theory and hypothesis as close as possible, and this means that any test of the hypothesis which results in a failure to confirm its prediction will weaken the theory. The continual failure to confirm the predictions of hypotheses eventually result in the abandonment or modification of the theory.

From this angle, you could say that the whole purpose of doing research is to collect data which will enable, via one or more hypotheses, a theory to be tested – i.e. to find out whether the predictions drawn from a theory are supported by actual data.

Note that it is *always* essential that hypotheses be formulated before any data are collected, rather than after. Otherwise, logically speaking, the hypothesis cannot constitute a prediction about what is expected, but is a description of what has been already found.

For example, someone who is investigating human reasoning and problem solving might, on the basis of the relevant theory, decide to pursue the question of whether people's expectations about a problem (such as whether or not they believe that it is hard to solve) is capable of determining how quickly or easily the solution can be arrived at, irrespective of the problem's actual difficulty.

Before going any further in pursuit of this question, the researcher will typically formulate an hypothesis, such as the following, which expresses this idea in the form of a prediction:

> **Hypothesis: People who believe that a problem is difficult will in general take longer to solve it than those who believe that it is easy, even if there is no difference between the problems in terms of difficulty.**

The next step, is then to pursue this question by collecting some data from people who have been asked to solve some problems under controlled conditions. The precise way in which that might be done is described in chapter 5.

Hypotheses are required to have two related qualities. They have to be highly explicit in that they must state as precisely as possible what the data are predicted to look like, and they must be testable. That is, it must be possible to actually to find some data against which the hypothesis can be tested. These requirements are crucial: hypotheses which are vague, or which require data which cannot actually be collected are of no value since, in the first case, they cannot be tested with certainty, and in the second, cannot be tested at all.

Statistical hypotheses

When quantitative data are to be collected in an investigation and subsequently evaluated using the techniques of inferential statistics, it becomes necessary that the hypotheses which frame the investigation have to be re-written in statistical form. These re-written hypotheses differ from the sort described above only in that as well as leading to a prediction about a given configuration of data arising from the investigation, they also provide the logical framework for making a decision about whether or not the data support the theoretical prediction. Such statistical hypotheses play a key role in the evaluation of data and they come in two forms, called the null and the alternate hypotheses. We don't need to pursue this distinction at present, although if you are curious to see what the difference between a null and alternate hypothesis might be, you can look ahead to chapter 7. The worked examples of the statistics in chapter 9 also contain examples of these hypotheses being used to make decisions about data.

This is all you need to know for now about the nature of hypotheses. We now turn to examine the individual processes which make up hypothesis testing in more detail.

Consider figure 1.2, which offers a detailed picture of the processes involved in data gathering and evaluation. It shows that the stages of 'problem identification' and 'theory development' are connected by a series of procedures which make up a hypothesis testing cycle. It is this cycle which requires closer inspection, since it is absolutely central to much research in psychology.

The hypothesis testing cycle

Once a hypothesis has been formed, the process of testing can follow. Testing a hypothesis involves gathering data, using an appropriate method such as an experiment, and then subsequently evaluating the data to determine whether the hypothesis is correct or not. From one point of view, the sole function of the whole process of gathering data within an investigation could be said to be to enable a particular hypothesis to be put to the test.

The actual testing of hypotheses involves the following stages, which are shown as the lower row of boxes in figure 1.2.

1   Selection of research method

The selection of a research method involves making a decision about how the data are actually to be collected in an investigation. A number of factors contribute to this decision. One is the question of what kinds of data are actually needed in order to meet the requirements of the hypothesis you wish to test. Statistical hypotheses, for example, can only be tested if the data are in quantitative form, and this requirement almost certainly rules out the use of participant observation as a method of research.

Another consideration may be the need to generate exploratory data in order to examine whether a theory fully explains all aspects of a problem. Exploratory research need not be as closely focused as that directed towards testing explicit hypotheses, and this in turn may suggest the use of one of the non-experimental methods and the collection of qualitative rather than quantitative data.

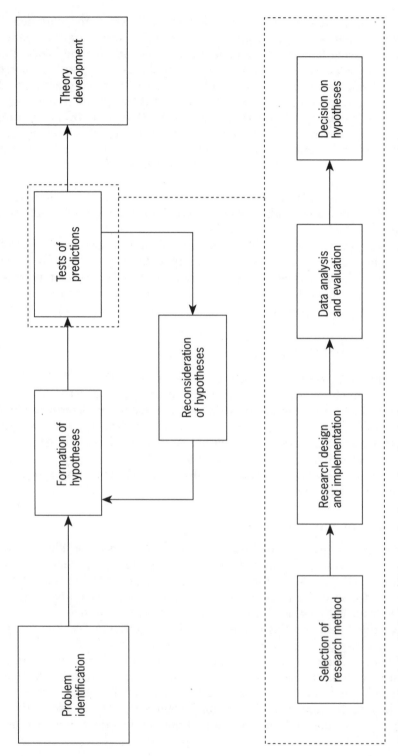

Figure 1.2 A detailed view of data gathering and evaluation

Yet a third consideration could be the nature of the researcher's own skills and preferences which may direct the choice of method. Not all researchers who are good at conducting experiments, for example, are equally adept at conducting interviews, and you will therefore also need to consider which method of research is likely to provide the best match to your own inclinations.

There is no need to go further into these issues at this point. You will find that the information you need to help you select a research method for a particular project is contained in the four chapters following this one.

2   Research design and implementation

Once the specific research method has been selected, the investigation has then to be designed in detail and implemented. This means essentially that the exact procedures which are to be followed have to be put together, materials, such as questionnaires, have to be constructed, informants have to be obtained and the data gathered. Again the information you need in order to undertake the design and implementation of your own investigations can be found in the method chapters which follow this one.

3   Data analysis and evaluation

The immediate outcome of an investigation is data. This is information which comes from your informants and which should provide an answer to the question you are pursuing. However, it usually needs to be processed in some way before it becomes capable of providing answers to the question which is being researched. Numerical data have to be subjected to statistical analysis (see chapters 6 to 9), while qualitative data, which consists of descriptions in words rather than numbers, needs to be simplified and summarized to render it more manageable. This can be done by constructing a set of categories into which the raw data can be fitted, either by means of a tally chart which converts qualitative data into numerical frequencies, or in some other way which preserves the qualitative form. See the section in chapter 3 on question-naire analysis for some suggestions on the analysis of qualitative data.

4   Decision on hypotheses

Finally, the hypotheses of the investigation have to be submitted to a decision process, involving comparison against the data in order to determine whether they should be accepted or rejected. (The exact details of how this should be done when data are in quantitative form can be found in chapter 7, with examples in chapter 9.)

Only two possible decisions exist. If the data are as predicted in the hypoth-esis then the hypothesis is formally accepted. This means that the investigation adds further support to the underlying theory on which the hypothesis was based. If on the other hand, the data are not as predicted in the hypothesis, then the hypothesis is rejected, and *no support* can be offered to the theory by the data. Note that this does not mean that the theory is necessarily incorrect: it just means that *in this case* data have not been found which support the theory.

If the hypothesis is rejected, and if the line of research is not to be completely abandoned, then two actions need to be taken. First, the original theory should be reconsidered and, if possible, the hypothesis should be reformulated, so as to provide a prediction of data which is closer to the theory. It may be that the theory has been misunderstood, or it might be that it is simply inadequate as an explanation for the problem. Alongside this, the conduct of the investigation itself should be reviewed to check whether the data were gathered as competently as possible. It is always possible that failure to accept a hypothesis is due to poor procedure at the stage of data gathering. It is no exaggeration to say that the effectiveness of the whole hypothesis testing process depends crucially on the quality of the data gathered. If the data are of poor quality, then a misleading decision may be taken about the correctness of the hypothesis. (See also the description of type 1 and type 2 errors in chapter 7.)

Over a longer period, a theory which is repeatedly not confirmed when it is tested by different investigators is inevitably weakened and is likely eventually to be modified or abandoned. This in turn is will generate many new hypotheses for testing, and so the cycle continues.

As you can see, then, hypotheses function to enable the correctness of theories to be tested in an actual situation, and under highly specific circumstances. They are essentially disposable parts of the scientific process since they exist only to be tested and once the outcome of the test is known, they have no further function and are discarded.

The account of the research process which is given here represents what might be called the 'official view' of what goes on in science. That is, it represents attempts by scientists and philosophers to explain the research process, and account for its obvious success in providing explanations for natural phenomena. However, it should be pointed out that although this is the 'official' view, it is also, in some ways, an unrealistic one. The reality of doing science is not necessarily as clear or as straightforward as the description suggests. The reason for this is that the image of science given above is largely an image of an activity with the humanity removed. It virtually ignores the fact that scientists are people and that science itself is an intensely human process. But the fact that science does have 'a human face' as someone once put it, means that the everyday reality of 'doing science' is unlikely to match the clear, and somewhat idealized description which you have just been given.

The main reason for this is that this description divides into discrete stages what is, in terms of the cognitive processes of the individual scientist, a seamless whole. Although it is possible for descriptive and analytical purposes to generate a view of science such as that in figure 1.1, in which it consists of a clearly labelled sequence of different activities, in fact, these activities when they occur in the mind of an individual scientist are far from separate. It is unlikely, for example, that any scientist compartmentalizes the task of theory generation neatly away from the data gathering tasks in the way suggested by the diagrams. Much more likely is that the two tasks will interact closely and continuously with each other, and with others, throughout the whole process of investigation.

With this thought, we have completed all that needs to be said immediately about the nature of science. You should now have enough information, at least about the 'official' version of what is involved, to enable you to understand some of the background issues which lurk behind your own research projects.

Before we move on, there is one further point to be made about the useful distinction often drawn between two different forms of research: research directed towards the testing of hypotheses, as described above, and the much looser form which has been dubbed 'exploratory research'. (If this distinction seems familiar, it may be because I mentioned exploratory research recently on p. 39, when talking about research method selection.) While there is no need to say any more here about research which aims to test hypotheses, you do need to know something about the distinction between that kind of research and the other kind – exploratory research.

Exploratory research

Exploratory research is research which simply aims to find out more about a particular problem or phenomenon rather than to test specific predictions. It is therefore more likely to be used when psychologists are venturing into new or ill-defined research territory, or where there is no theory which could provide guidance on formulating hypotheses.

As an example of a situation in which the exploratory mode might be employed, take a researcher who is interested in the coping strategies employed by the newly bereaved. Finding that the topic has been left virtually untouched by others, she would probably not want to test any specific hypotheses about the question until the dimensions of the problem have been fully explored. This would involve collecting information in an open-ended way about as many different aspects of the problem as possible in order to get some idea about how the different variables or features of the situation might be related to each other. Once this has been done, it may be possible to identify regularities in the data which may, in turn, suggest precise hypotheses which can later be tested.

When does a researcher make the decision that a particular piece of research should be exploratory rather than directed towards the testing of some hypothesis? As you may already have seen for yourself, there are two points to consider.

First, there is the question of the degree of precision with which the original research question can be formulated. Sometimes a problem can be expressed only in a rather vague form which does little more than identify that an interesting question exists which needs to be answered. For example, a developmental psychologist might feel that an examination of male–female sibling relations might throw some light on the way in which gender roles are acquired and reinforced within the family, though without necessarily being able to do much more than simply pose the question. In such a case, there is a need to carry out purely exploratory research in order to clarify the dimensions of the problem.

Secondly, there is the question of whether or not a relevant theory exists. There may be no theory on which precise predictions can be based, and if this is the case then, again, an exploratory approach is indicated. However, theory is unlikely to be completely absent even from the most speculative of exploratory researches. Even if there is no formal theory to guide the research, it is virtually certain that the researcher will be entertaining ideas of some kind – which may, in effect, amount to an informal theory – about whatever phenomenon is being pursued. Once the data are in, these ideas may subsequently harden into a more explicit and formal explanation.

This is all we need to say for now about the theory and philosophy of doing research in a science such as psychology. I hope that enough has been said to give you a reasonably clear idea of the more prominent features of the background to 'doing science' – enough, at least, to enable you to feel comfortable with what follows in the remaining chapters of the book.

The next four chapters contain descriptions of the four main methods of research used in psychology, and as these represent different ways of implementing the ideas we have just been discussing, I hope you will detect a number of connections and recurrent themes as you work through them. Following those four chapters, we turn to the theme of data analysis, and pick up, in much more detail, the topic of hypothesis testing in the light of the powerful ideas provided by inferential statistics.

Summary of chapter 1

The general goal of science is to develop explanations, in the form of theories, for the various phenomena of nature, including the various forms which may be taken by human behaviour and experience. These may, in turn, lead to an ability to make predictions and, sometimes also, to take control of the phenomena in question.

Psychology as a scientific discipline is clearly committed to the first of these goals, but the extent to which it is able to predict behaviour is limited by the variability and unpredictability of much of human behaviour, and by the inaccessibility of mental processes to direct inspection. The possibility that psychological knowledge might be used to control behaviour is highly contentious and raises important ethical questions.

The philosophical foundations for the modern science of psychology are to be found in the related doctrines of empiricism and positivism. In the former the fundamental principle is that only a process of active collection of information, in the form of sensory data, can lead to knowledge. Positivism likewise argues that the study of human behaviour and experience can only be truly scientific if it is pursued by methods and procedures derived from the natural sciences, and this view has led research in modern psychology to concentrate on the observation and measurement of objectively defined 'variables' in experimental settings.

The positivist position is contested by humanistic psychology which instead takes the view that the business of psychological research is to seek an understanding of the subjective world of each individual rather than the construction of general explanations of behaviour. It has therefore strongly criticized mainstream psychology for what it sees as an over-reliance on the experimental method, and for its generally positivist stance.

The hermeneutic approach offers a way of doing research in psychology which is a compromise between the extremes of postivism and humanism. In essence, this means using a combination of different research methods to investigate a problem, while at the same time seeking the active co-operation and partnership of the participants in the research.

The process of doing research in science can be divided into the four stages of problem identification, data collection, theory development and development of applications. Of these, data collection and theory development represent the central core of the scientific enterprise.

The role of a theory in science, often misunderstood, is to provide an essentially temporary explanation for some phenomenon which can be tested by empirical research. Good theories, in the sense that they contribute to the development of knowledge, are those which are productive – they should be testable, enable precise predictions to be generated, and should be successful in stimulating new research.

The stage of data collecton and evaluation, represents the 'active' part of the research process, since it centres on the collection of empirical data by means of one of the various research methods for the purpose of testing hypotheses. These latter consist of precise predictions, derived from a theory and made in advance of data collection, about what data could be expected to be obtained under certain specified conditions. Data are then collected, and compared to the prediction, and a decision made about the hypotheses, and the outcome is fed into the research cycle, resulting in either a strengthening or a weakening of the original theory.

Theory development in science rests ultimately on Karl Popper's principle of falsification, which states that certain knowledge can only be achieved by showing theories to be false rather than correct, and the business of science is thus the falsification of theories rather than showing them to be true.

Not all research in psychology is directed towards the testing of explicit hypotheses. There is also an important role for purely exploratory research. This is descriptive research aimed at establishing the nature or scope of a phenomenon about which little is known, the results of which may lead later to the development of a theory and the testing of precise hypotheses.

Scientific research in general, and psychological research in particular, reflect a range of motives on the part of the researchers. The wish to contribute to the sum of human knowledge is certainly one important factor, but there are others, including the desire to develop applications which can be exploited, and personal advancement. Like all scientific activity, psychology is heavily influenced by its social and political context, with government agencies of various kinds acting as major sponsors of research activity.

2 Case Studies and Interviews

This chapter provides information and guidance on the construction of a case study, and on using interviews as a way of collecting detailed qualitative data from informants for that purpose. It contains:

- A description of the main features which distinguish the case study from other approaches to research.

- A description of the main features of a research interview, including a comparison of its structured and unstructured forms, the importance of rapport, and the ethical issues raised by this method of research.

- Help with planning and carrying out an interview for a case study, including information on how to devise schedules of questions, how to approach the task of obtaining information, and how to conduct the actual interview.

- Guidance on how to write up the results of an interview into a case study.

- Two suggestions for interview-based research projects.

The Case Study

Introduction

The writing of case studies as a research method originates in clinical medicine. There, the 'case history', consisting of a patient's personal history, a description of the symptoms, diagnosis, record of the treatment and the eventual outcome may be written up – particularly as a way of recording any unusual cases which appear. This record then becomes part of the collection of medical data which may later be used to help with investigations of the suspected cause(s) of a disorder, its symptoms, and to establish the most effective approach to treatment. Comparison between different case histories of patients suffering from the same disorder establishes such vital information as the range of different symptoms which have been found to be associated with a particular disease, or the results typically observed after a particular form of treatment.

In psychology, the aim in putting together a case study is to explore, in some depth, some aspect of the behaviour and subjective experience of a single individual. This is typically done by collecting detailed qualitative (i.e. descriptive) data from the person concerned by means of an interview, rather less commonly by observation, or by some combination of the two.

This approach can be applied to either of two general types of research question, although there is no restriction as to the specific topics which can be studied. Closest to the medical usage are those occasions when it is used to provide a detailed description and analysis of an example of a rare or unusual facet of behaviour or experience. Luria's (1968), study of the mnemonist, and the case of 'SB', the blind man who recovered his sight, studied by Gregory and Wallace (1963), are both examples of this type. In these, when the interest lies in the differences between the subject of the case history and people in general, the case study approach permits the unique features of the case to be studied in depth.

The other main application of the case study method is to provide descriptions of individuals who, far from being extraordinary in any particular respect, can be regarded as representative of people in general. The power of the case study approach here is that it allows features of behaviour or experience which are shared by many people to be studied in detail and depth. For example, the study of the development of language in small children has often employed a case approach in which diaries and audio recordings of children's utterances provide the basis for a detailed description of linguistic ability at different stages of development. (See, for example, Berko & Brown, 1960.)

What makes the case study different?

The list below sets out the main characteristics of a case study which distinguish it from other approaches to research in psychology. As you will probably notice, there is a close fit between these characteristics and the kind of research problems for which it might be used. A case study is:

1 **A descriptive method** The data collected in a case study constitute descriptions of psychological processes and events, and of the contexts in which they occurred. Quantitative data may be collected, but the main emphasis is always on the construction of verbal descriptions of behaviour or experience.

2 **Narrowly focused** Typically a case study offers a description of only a single individual, although it is also possible (but rarely done) to write case studies of groups. In general a case study concerns itself with only one limited aspect of the person, such as their psychopathological symptoms, or, as in the case of 'SB' (Gregory & Wallace, 1963), visual perceptual abilities.

3 **Highly detailed** The focusing of inquiry on a single person, and on particular aspects of that person's behaviour or experience, means that the descriptions which are achieved can be extremely detailed.

4 **Combines objective and subjective data** The information collected in a case study can represent almost any combination of objective and subjective data. Alongside the objective description of behaviour and its context, the case study can equally include details of the subjective aspect, such as feelings, beliefs, impressions or interpretations. All are regarded as valid data for analysis, and as a basis for inferences within the case study. In fact, a case study is uniquely able to offer a means of achieving an in-depth understanding of the behaviour and experience of a single individual.

5 **Process-oriented** The case study method also enables the researcher to explore and describe the nature of processes which occur over time. In contrast to, say, the experimental method, which basically provides a stilled 'snapshot' of processes which may be continuing over time, the writing of a case study enables on-going processes, which continue over time, to be investigated and described in some detail. The use of case studies in the field of developmental linguistics, mentioned above, is an example of this.

Case studies contain two kinds of information

Bromley (1977) has pointed out that a case study represents more than a simple reconstruction of a set of facts which have been first collected by an investigator and then assembled into the case study. It is, in fact, a rather more complex form of record than it at first might appear.

Firstly, as we have already said, it will contain a description of the features of the 'case' which are regarded by the researcher as being of interest. These might include such things as descriptions of pieces of behaviour, which the researcher has directly observed, and the context in which they occured, or they could be reports of behaviour by the informant or, more subjective and uncheckable, accounts of the feelings or attitudes of the informant on a given occasion.

Secondly, it will hold a set of interpretations of the meanings which can be attached to the various pieces of information which have been collected into the study. In particular, the implications of the data for any relevant theory which may exist, will need to be explored. Obviously, this aspect of the case study can only be contributed by the researcher who is writing it up.

There are two further important points which need to be made here. One of these is that the decision about what is, and what is not important information, and thus the decision about what to include and what to leave out of the case study, is in almost every case, made by the researcher alone. It is, I suspect, extremely rare for the opinions of the informant to be taken into account, although, as is clear from the above, much of the information in the case study comes from an informant's own privileged knowledge of their own mental processes.

This means that a case study has always to be read with an awareness that a process of selecting information has taken place to which only the author(s), but not the source of the information has been party. This is not, in itself a major difficulty, although is seems odd to me that informants are generally excluded from the process of selecting information. The real problem arises however, when, as often happens, the criteria on which information has been selected are not made sufficiently clear or, worse, are not made clear at all. Yet without this information in a case study it is impossible to form a reliable judgement about the information which *has* been included. You need to be able to see the whole picture, and not just the part the researcher has selected.

One further point. It is extremely important to maintain as clearly as possible the distinction between the two categories of information in a case study, i.e. that between knowledge and inferences. The readers of a case study should always be able to decide whether they are reading a description of relevant details, whether at first or second hand makes no difference, or an inference about what those details might mean in relation to a theory. Freud's work is instructive in this respect. Although he was in other respects a gifted and perceptive writer of case studies, his work provides several examples of the tendency for the boundaries between fact and supposition to become blurred in a case study. You might like to test this for yourself by reading any of the cases so vividly depicted in *Studies on Hysteria* (Freud & Breuer, [1894] 1974), while asking yourself what is fact and what is inference, and whether Freud is careful to make the distinction between the two entirely clear at all times.

The role of theory in a case study

The great value of the case study approach is that it enables a more detailed, qualitative and exploratory approach to be taken to research. However, writing a case study is not simply a matter of doing a bit of creative writing on a psychologically interesting theme. If it is to have any scientific value, a case study must be firmly grounded in empirical facts – that is, in the discoverable features of the case – and should also be linked to a clear theoretical background.

It should always represent a disciplined and systematic exploration of a specific research question. Although the case study approach to research has an important role as an exploratory method, the exploration still needs to possess a clear direction if it is to generate information of psychological interest. And, as always, the best source of guidance is theory.

This is not of course to say that it is necessary for every single case study to be tightly grounded in a theory. However, the aim should always be, as far as possible, to answer a research question which has been derived from a theory of some description. This means that, in the writing of the case-study, the theoretical origins of the research, however far in the background they may be, must always be made explicit. Otherwise there is the risk that the research will provide answers to questions which no one wanted answering.

In science, as we have already seen, data collection serves the goal of theory development. However, the single individual who is typically the subject of a case study represents an extremely narrow data base, and this makes it difficult for anything like a full test of the correctness of a theory to be undertaken. It is, to put it simply, unlikely that case study evidence will be sufficiently clear or straightforward to cast serious doubt upon a theory. Nevertheless, a case study can offer much valuable information. As well as providing evidence which supports or confirms a theory, the case study may also contribute to theory development in a number of other ways. It may, for example, suggest ways in which the theory is inadequate, by enabling missed dimensions to the problem to be identified. A well executed case study can also suggest ways in which a theory needs to be extended, or can provide new insights into a problem. Finally, of course, the case study method is always capable of providing a starting point for attacks on the problem which use one of the alternative methods. For example, possible causal variables can be identified from case study data which can subsequently provide the rationale for an experimental investigation.

Ways of using the case study approach

There are two general ways in which the case study can be used to provide a test of a theory, and it will obviously helpful to have these alternatives in mind when you are considering undertaking a case study of your own. They are rather different, and since they require different approaches to questioning a respondent, they need to be planned rather differently. Note that both require the research effort to be grounded in a clearly articulated theoretical background.

The first approach is to use the case study to focus closely and in some detail on one clearly defined range of behaviour or experience within a single individual. An illustration of this approach might be for a researcher to try to obtain evidence which supports or refutes the Freudian theory of the Oedipus complex.

In psychoanalytic theory, the Oedipus complex is a developmental crisis which occurs at around the age of six or seven years, and centres on the child's emotional attachment to the parent of the opposite sex. As you can appreciate, in pursuing this research, the questioning will need to focus closely on the individual's memories of that point in development and on the possible sexual content of remembered thoughts and feelings. This approach can clearly be most successfully taken when the research question is clearly defined and the underlying theory has enabled fairly precise predictions to be made.

The second and alternative approach is to follow a much more exploratory line, where the broad limits of the inquiry may be set by a theory, if one exists, but where the researcher is free to range within those limits depending on the nature of the data which are uncovered. It is possible that such theory as exists is too vaguely expressed to be very much help to the investigation, in which case one of the aims of the case study should be to collect information which will enable the theory to be improved.

In this, the case study is still to some extent *guided* by theory, but the guidance is very much looser and less restrictive than it is in the more focused approaches. An example of this approach is the study by Luria (1968) of an individual with an extraordinary memory, in which theory provided little help in directing the inquiry. Clearly this strategy is most appropriate where, as in Luria's study, precise predictions cannot be made on the basis of theory, or where the theory itself is inadequate.

You can probably see from what is said above that the decision to use the case study method does not so much limit the problems which can be tackled as *determine the kind of questions which can be asked* about a problem. You can, in fact, use the case study method to investigate almost any topic in psychology, as the range of examples illustrates.

The main thing to remember is that the case study requires the construction of clear, precise and relevant descriptions of those aspects of the informant's behaviour and experience which are of interest. In essence, it allows you to conduct a detailed exploration for one individual, of the relationships between behaviour, its physical and social context, and your informant's own ideas and feelings.

A brief evaluation of the case study approach

The main criticisms to be levelled against case studies have in fact already been made in connection with the nature of the information which case studies typically contain, and in connection with the ability of case study data to contribute to the testing of theories.

On the first point, the main issue concerned the way in which information may be selected for inclusion in a case study against unknown criteria, and the tendency, apparent in some work, to blur the distinction between information and inference. It was suggested that neither of these arguments succeeded in weakening the value of a case study, since they could be removed if researchers adopted a more careful approach to the construction of their case studies. On the second point, the question concerned whether data from individual cases could provide an adequate basis for theory testing, and here it was earlier suggested that while a case study cannot provide a full test of a theory it can nevertheless contribute to the process by providing information about relevant processes.

There is also a variation of this argument, which asks whether the insights into individual behaviour or experience which can be obtained from a case study can be generalized to apply to other individuals. In other words whether one can reason inductively, from the evidence of a particular case in order to say something about people in general. Those psychologists who see their task as the pursuit of general truths which are applicable to everyone would say not, arguing that a case study represents an exploration into the private experience of a single unique individual. No matter how typical of the experience of others such a record may seem, they would argue that it is essentially unique and unrepeatable since it is informed by the person's own life history, which by definition can never be the same as anyone else's. Case studies, from this perspective, can provide a way of researching aspects of human uniqueness, but have no general truths to teach.

I feel this is unnecessarily pessimistic. While a case study is essentially a one-off piece of research, which may be unique and unrepeatable, (though not necessarily), it may still shed more general light on some psychological questions. The case of 'SB' (Gregory & Wallace, 1963) is an example of this. While SB himself was a unique individual, his experience of undergoing a cataract operation, and having his sight return after spending almost his whole life as a blind person, offers a number of interesting clues to the development of visual perception in normally sighted people. It is, therefore, on the evidence of the case of 'SB', possible for psychologists to draw general conclusions on the basis of unique cases.

Although these criticisms have raised important issues, the case study should not be written off as of little value to psychological research. It also has important strengths which it only partly shares with alternative methods.

First, because it involves the collection of mainly qualitative data, it is capable of providing a much richer and more detailed description of human behaviour and experience than can be obtained from the collection of quantitative information. For some psychologists, only qualitative data has the power to provide a faithful description of what goes on inside a person's head. Numbers, from this perspective, may be useful for providing summaries of data, but they fail to capture the intricate detail of human experience.

Secondly, case studies are good ways of capturing and describing changes which occur over time to psychological processes. It was earlier said that data obtained from an experiment represent a 'snapshot' – one frozen moment of time extracted from a continuous process of change – and this is also true of other methods of research. In a case study, on the other hand, it is possible to track the changes and to develop an understanding of the happenings in a person's life over a period of time.

Finally, almost uniquely among the research methods of modern psychology, the case study focuses on the experience of a person. It represents an affirmation of the uniqueness of each individual and tries to work with that uniqueness instead of, as often happens, ignoring it or denying that it exists.

By now, I hope that you will be sufficiently interested in the case method to be thinking about putting together one of your own. If you are, you need to know more about the best way to collect the data, so we now move on to look at what is involved in conducting a research interview.

Some examples of the case study method

The following are a selection of well known, and therefore reasonably accessible, examples of research using the case study method. You may like to use these to explore the wide range of research topics to which the case approach can be applied.

1   **Freud and Breuer ([1894] 1974)** provide accounts of some early cases, such as the famous case of 'Anna O'. These are specimens of the case history from within the clinical research tradition of psychoanalysis, and are emphatically not intended to be models for imitation: they are long and detailed, and, as we have already noted, they blur the distinction between theorizing and data. Nevertheless, they do offer extremely interesting examples of this approach to research.

2   **Gregory and Wallace (1963)** applied the case study method to the study of perceptual processes in the case of 'SB'. They provide an account, which is unfortunately difficult to obtain in its original form, of the process of recovery from an operation to restore the sight of an individual – identified as 'SB' – who had been blind almost from birth. The study throws some light on the 'nature–nurture' question in relation to visual perception.

3   **Gardner and Gardner (1969)** used an approach which was substantially based on the case study method in order to explore the question of whether animals could acquire and use language. Their account of their research into the linguistic capabilities of the chimpanzee 'Washoe' is an example of how a case study can be written on the basis of a combination of observational and experimental data.

4   **A. R. Luria (1968)** wrote a famous case study, entitled 'The Mind of a Mnemonist', in which he discusses the amazing feats of memory performed by a Russian 'memory man'. By taking the case study approach, Luria is able to present a view of what it feels like to be the possessor of an extraordinary memory in considerable detail, and using many of the individual's own words.

REFERENCES

Freud, S., & Breuer, J. (1974). *Studies on hysteria.* Harmondsworth: Penguin Books. (Original published 1894).
Gardner, R. A., & Gardner, B. T. (1969). Teaching sign language to a chimpanzee. *Science, 165.* 664–72.
Gregory, R. L., & Wallace, J. G. (1963). Recovery from early blindness: A case study. *Experimental Psychology Society Monographs. No. 2.* Cambridge. (Also in: Gregory, R. L. (1974). *Concepts and mechanisms of perception.* London: Duckworth; and Gregory, R. L. (1972, 2nd edn) *Eye and brain.* London: Weidenfeld & Nicolson. World University Library Series).
Luria, A. R. (1968). *The mind of a mnemonist.* New York: Basic Books Inc.

The Interview

In this part of the chapter we take a fairly detailed look at what a research interview is like.

We compare the interview with ordinary conversation, in order to see more clearly exactly what it is that makes an interview distinctive.

Two different forms of the interview – structured and unstructured – are examined and compared.

The importance for successsful interviewing of motivation and rapport is discussed.

The two key ethical issues of confidentiality and right of withdrawal are briefly looked at.

Introduction

Strictly speaking the term 'case study' refers to the *results* of research, rather than to any specific method of data gathering. However, the focus on the individual, and the aim of including experience as well as behaviour within the scope of the inquiry leads naturally to the interview as the main method of gathering data. This is not to say that an interview is the only method available for collecting information for a case study. Interview data may also be supplemented by information, obtained from other methods of doing research, such as by experiments which employ the (same) respondent as a single subject. (See also the section on N = 1 experiments in chapter 5.) Also as the work of the Gardners on sign language learning by apes has shown (Gardner & Gardner, 1969), it is not necessary to interview at all, since a fascinating case study can be constructed on the basis of observations alone.

It is a good idea, therefore, to be alert to the possibility of including data obtained from other methods in your research, either as alternatives to the interview, or as additional sources of information, which will enable you to explore a question from a different angle than the interview allows. More information on such alternatives can be found elsewhere in this book. However, as we said earlier, it is probably true that most people who intend to write a case study will make the interview their method of choice, and therefore the following discussion will be based on that assumption.

What is an interview?

On the surface, an interview simply consists of two people talking together about some topic which is of interest to them both. However, when closer attention is paid to what is actually happening in an interview, it becomes apparent that this is more than just another ordinary conversation. There are, in fact, a number of important differences between interviewing someone and having a normal conversation with them as the following set of comparisons make clear:

Key differences between normal conversation and an interview

A Conversation

1 **A conversation generally lacks an explicitly mentioned purpose.**
It is rather rare (or at least unnecessary) in general conversation for either party to have a clear purpose in mind before beginning to talk, and still rarer for a purpose to be mentioned by either party. More usually, the purpose of a conversation is left unspoken, becoming apparent, if at all, only through the topics covered and the nature of what is said.

2 **There are unspoken rules about avoiding repetition.**
An important rule in ordinary conversation is that you should avoid repeating yourself. You don't normally say the same thing more than once in the course of the same conversation, (or it is likely to be pointed out to you if you do).

3 **Both participants can ask questions.**
It is normal for both participants in a conversation to ask questions of each other. For example an inquiry about the

An Interview

1 **An interview always has an explicitly mentioned purpose.**
Both participants in an interview know that the talk has a purpose and that the purpose of the interview is to enable information on a specified topic to pass from the respondent to the interviewer. The topic which is to be the subject of discussion is also explicitly agreed in advance.

2 **Repetition of questions is required in the interview.**
Repetition of questions and answers is an important tool for an interviewer for two reasons. Not only does it enable the interviewer to check that the informant is reliable, (i.e. gives a similar answer to similar questions asked at different times), but asking the same question in slightly different ways can reveal new information which might otherwise have remained hidden.

3 **Questioning is largely restricted to the interviewer.**
In an interview most of the question are asked by the interviewer. If the respondent asks any questions, it may be at

health of the children of one participant will normally be reciprocated, often in the utterance immediately following.

4 **Both participants are likely to express interest in what the other is saying and/or ignorance of topics which are raised in conversation.**
One of the basic rules of conversation is that the listener must provide the speaker with evidence that what is said is of interest, (possibly by actually saying things like 'Oh, that's interesting', but more commonly by nodding the head, saying words like 'yes' and 'right', and so on). Such expressions of interest are produced approximately equally by both participants while a conversation is in progress, and if they are not, the conversation may come to a fairly rapid halt. Likewise, expressions of ignorance, ('Well, I never knew that!'), are important since they reassure the speaker of the hearer's continued interest.

5 **Conversation depends to a high degree on shared common knowledge.**
All conversation draws on shared knowledge, since without it the interaction becomes a lecture or monologue. The better people know each other, the more their conversation is likely to make use of such shared background knowledge. In such conversations the meaning of what is said is often implicitly present or conveyed indirectly rather than being clearly stated.

the express invitation of the interviewer.

4 **Both interest and ignorance are likely to be expressed only by the interviewer.**
In an interview the aim of the interviewer is to encourage the flow of information, and expressions of interest and ignorance are important ways in which an interviewer is able to stimulate the flow of information, since they reassure the respondent that what is being said is valuable and interesting, i.e. the information is what the interviewer wants. Such expressions are therefore more likely to be produced by the interviewer than the informant.

5 **Interviewing requires that all information in a respondent's answers is explicit.**
The aim of an interview is to draw from a respondent a range of information which includes implicit knowledge, (the informant's assumptions about what the researcher already knows). One of the aims of an interview may be to bring as much as possible of this implicit knowledge out into the open, and to make it explicit.

6   Answers should, in general be as brief as politeness allows: high levels of detail are to be avoided unless specifically requested.

This point can best be illustrated by asking you to imagine how you would respond to the question 'How was your holiday?' You are likely to answer with, probably, a sentence or two. Imagine the reaction if you were to respond with a minutely detailed description of your first day at the beach.

6   Answers should always be as detailed as possible.

The aim of an interview is to collect information on a particular topic. To be useful the information has to be expressed at the right level of detail. An interviewer is likely to pay special attention to eliciting the details from a respondent, by the use of appropriate forms of question, such as 'Could you say a bit more about. ... ?' or 'Can you explain about. ... ?'

Types of interviews

The comparison between conversation and interviewing above suggests that there are a number of important features found in most interviews. However, interviews also differ from one another, and in particular in the extent to which they are structured – organized in advance – by the interviewer. One way to think of this is to regard all the different forms which an interview might take as lying along a continuum. At one end of the continuum is the most structured form of interview, in which the questioning process is tightly organized in advance by the interviewer: at the other is the wholly unstructured form, in which virtually nothing is decided by the interviewer before meeting an informant. We now need to look at these in more detail.

1   Structured interviews

A structured interview is one in which the interviewer determines the precise form and direction of the questioning in advance of actually meeting the interviewee. In its most extreme form, it would consist simply of an interviewer reading through a prepared list of questions, and writing down the respondent's answers. Although it is clearly rather an inflexible approach, it does have some virtues. If the questions are decided in advance, it is much harder for the interview to be deflected from the topic in hand. It provides a relatively quick and easy way of obtaining data, and is economical with the interviewer's time. Also, the interviewer may find it easier to relax in the interview if there is no need to try to think of the next question to ask. You could consider using this approach if you are very new to interviewing and need to gain some experience of interacting with live informants, or perhaps if the direction of your inquiry is perfectly clear from the outset, and if you only need obtain answers to a set of questions which you can formulate in advance.

At the same time, the limitations of the structured approach are considerable. Because the questions are decided in advance, the interviewer is prevented from following any new directions for the inquiry as they emerge from the respondent's answers, and it will not be possible for a researcher to pursue a line of inquiry which has not been anticipated in advance. In other words, the support offered by the precise preparation of questions can rapidly become a straightjacket.

It is also possible that an interview which is highly structured into a question and answer format, may feel more like an interrogation than an interview from the informant's perspective. If this is so, there may well be a tendency for the informant to produce stereotyped and self-protective replies, with a consequent loss of validity to the interview.

2   Unstructured interviews

At the other end of the continuum lies the unstructured interview, in which there is no prepared list of questions, but where the interviewer decides what questions to ask from moment to moment depending on the information volunteered by the informant. It might begin with the interviewer explaining to the respondent what matters or topics are to be explored in the interview, and with the posing of an initial question. When the flow of ideas in answer to that first question comes to an end the researcher may ask further questions to obtain clarification of some points, or may raise a new topic, and the questioning repeats itself in a chain-like process in which one answer suggests the next question. One of the strengths of unstructured interviewing lies in the fact that the interviewer is not narrowly pursuing a predetermined set of questions, but is allowing the respondent's answers to influence the questioning process.

It is, therefore a much more flexible approach to interviewing, which to an observer, can look something like an ordinary conversation, except that one of the parties does most of the talking. However, when transcripts are examined, it should become clear that in fact the discussion was firmly anchored to a specific question or set of topics.

It requires skill to carry out an unstructured interview successfully. Considerable attention needs to be given to the content of the informant's replies, and you have to have a good grasp of all the issues which are likely to emerge from the questioning process. Extensive preparation before the interview is implied by this last requirement, and it is unlikely that a good interview can be obtained simply from asking questions in an unprepared manner.

Probably, the most successful approach to interviewing is one which uses a combination of these two forms. Although respondents differ greatly from one another in the extent to which they require their thought processes to be steered by questioning, all need to have their thoughts gently guided by questions of some kind. A semi-structured format, in which the interviewer works from a number of prepared questions, while allowing the respondent plenty of opportunity to expand answers, and pursue individual lines of thought seems to offer the best approach. Some suggestions about how this process can be organized within an interview are made below.

Interviewing: the importance of motivation and rapport

Motivation

The single most important factor in determining whether an interview is successful is not the level of skill possessed by the interviewer, but the motivation
of the informant. Motivation – the desire to help you in your research – is, to
put it fairly crudely, what determines how hard an informant will be prepared
to work for you in the interview. It should be remembered that talking, thinking, remembering, and similar cognitive activities require effort, and can be
tiring, especially when they have to be done to order, and you need to try to
ensure that informants are as well-motivated as possible in order to maximize
the work which they are prepared to put in to the process. This is particularly
true of interviews where you are asking for very detailed accounts or explora-
tions of behaviour or experience.

Motivation can also be adversely affected if the person to be interviewed is
uncertain about any aspect of the process of being interviewed, and particularly if there is any doubt about the eventual use which is to be made of the
information. If this should be the case, some degree of censorship of the information is likely to occur.

How can you maximize an informant's motivation?

The ideal is for an informant to be just as interested in and committed to your
research goals as you are yourself, but clearly this is asking a great deal! You
should be aware before you begin that you are unlikely to obtain such a high
level of co-operation from the average informant. Nevertheless, what you will
find is that people can still be extraordinarily helpful and tolerant of the odd
demands which researchers sometimes make of them, and you need only to
observe a few simple guidelines to make sure that even if your informants'
interest in your research is not screwed up to fever pitch, they are nevertheless
ready to do their best to help you.

- Don't take any help for granted. Take care to tell all informants, from the
  very first contact, how grateful you are, and how useful and valuable their
  information will be – even if you fear that it may be nothing of the kind.
- Do take the time to explain the aims and background of your research
  project in terms which your listener is likely to understand. Be particularly
  careful to say just why you want that particular person to help you, (otherwise they may be left wondering 'why me?').
- Explain what will happen to the information (both as rough notes and in
  the final report) once it is in your care, and make it clear that all information is protected by a confidentiality rule (see below). In addition you
  should always give, and respect, any further assurances about confidentiality which are demanded.

Rapport

As well as endeavouring to ensure that an informant is as well motivated as possible, an interviewer should also aim to build a good sense of rapport with the person they are interviewing. Essentially, this means trying to develop a relationship with the other person in which both of you feel you are 'on the same wavelength', and are therefore able to communicate clearly and honestly with each other on the topic in hand. In some ways, having a sense of rapport is like having a friendship, though without the strong emotional commitment that friends also make to each other. Like a friendship, though, a sense of rapport does not emerge instantaneously at the beginning of an interview, but develops over a period of time. So, if you are planning to collect information in a single interview session, you should be prepared for the strong possibility that a sense of rapport may not develop at all.

It is helpful to think of the development of rapport as occurring in three phases:

1   Initially rapport will be low, and an informant may be wary, even mistrustful of the interviewer and his/her motives. Personal and/or sensitive information is likely to be held back, or at least heavily censored in this phase.
2   Later, as the interview progresses and rapport starts to build up, there is a greater willingness to reveal personal details, and to make self-disclosing statements. The way in which such information is received by the interviewer is important for the continuing development of the sense of rapport. Only if the interviewee feels reassured by the response of the researcher to such information will the development of rapport continue.
3   In the third phase, the continued self-disclosure of personal information by the interviewee, and appropriate responses from the researcher enable a good sense of rapport to emerge, with a high degree of trust between the participants. In cases where there is a very high degree of rapport, the informant may adopt the role of a collaborator in the research, using privileged knowledge to direct the interviewer's attention to particular items of information, rather than simply taking a passive role. In this, both now share the goal of developing as complete a picture of the topic as possible.

How can you build rapport with an informant?

The development of a sense of rapport between interviewer and interviewee comes largely as a result of the efforts from the researcher's side of the relationship. The aim should be to provide the kind of conditions in which rapport has the best possible chance of emerging. What can you do?

- The first rule is to try always to communicate as fully and honestly as you can to your informant about the research. Nothing hinders the development of a rapport between researcher and informant as much as suspicions about the researcher's motives or integrity. Any hint of evasiveness is likely to be viewed particularly seriously, since it will only confirm to an informant that his initial wariness was fully justified. The aim must be to endeavour to demonstrate on all occasions that you will conduct your research with integrity and respect for other people.

- Try as far as possible to maintain an awareness of what the process of being interviewed is probably like from the informant's point of view. Interspersing comments like 'I understand that you probably find all these questions tedious . . .', or 'This must seem an odd question to ask, but . . .' reassure the other person that you do not just view him or her as a source of information, to be milked as quickly and efficiently as possible, but as someone who has their own perspective on what is going on. Encourage your informant to express those views, and show that you understand them, even if they are not directly relevant to your inquiry. It may indicate a significant advance in rapport, depending, of course on how this is done, if your respondent feels able to express negative views on your research.

- Take your research, but not yourself, seriously. A few self-deprecating remarks scattered here and there among the more serious stuff will help your informant to relate to you as a person, and make them more disposed to help. (Remember research shows that people who appear flawlessly competent in all areas are liked less than people who appear to have a few flaws.)

- Finally, don't confuse rapport with liking the other person. Liking is not necessary to rapport, though it may come as a bonus. And beware the negative effects of rapport – there is always the danger that the work of developing and maintaining rapport can become almost an end in itself. If it does, it may be hard for a researcher to ask the hard, probing questions which can generate real insights into the research topic, but which it may be difficult for an informant to answer, or even consider.

Ethical issues in interviewing

Because of its similarity to everyday conversation an interview needs to be planned and executed with ethical issues very much in mind. Two aspects in particular need to considered carefully.

Confidentiality

Qualitative data is, by its nature, highly accessible – it consists of verbal descriptions which can easily be read by anyone. It is therefore essential to take great care to maintain the confidentiality of the written record. This is particularly necessary since informants may be led to reveal more than they either intend or desire, particularly when a good rapport has been established between interviewer and informant.

This requires that all records – interview notes, as well as subsequent rewritings – should be such that there is no possibility that the source of the information can ever be identified. The minimum necessary to achieve this is to remove the name of the informant from all documents (or, better never to

---

Box 2.1 *Interviewing skills*

Although successful interviewing is a complex skill which can only be learned over time through practice and attention to the feedback obtained from interviewees, the following lists of do's and don'ts should help you to avoid those things which can kill an interview stone dead, while pointing you towards those features of interviewer behaviour which are essential to good interviewing practice.

When interviewing, try to avoid
- Asking questions to satisfy your own curiosity.
- Showing impatience, criticism or indifference.
- Staring or looking preoccupied.
- Wanting to fill any short silences with a question.
- Looking away from the speaker.
- Interrupting what is being said.
- Planning what you intend to say next while listening.
- Making judgements about the other person, or what they have to say.
- Feeling you want to control what is going on.

Try to make sure you
- Attend fully to your informant all the time.
- Give good eye contact, without staring down.
- Read your informant's body language for clues to attitudes and feelings.
- Use your posture and facial expression to show interest and a sympathetic attitude.
- Leave plenty of spaces in the flow of question and answer in which your informant can think about what to say.
- Spend less time talking than your informant.
- Adopt a neutral attitude to everything that is said, even if your opinion is asked for.
- Try to remember as much as possible, not only what was said, but how it was expressed.

---

put it on in the first place), and to substitute either letters or a fictitious name chosen at random. If it should be necessary to have a record of an informant's personal details, these should be kept entirely separate from the interview data, and there should be no way in which a casual reader could connect the two. This rule should be regarded as absolute even when informants give permission for real names to be used.

Beyond this minimum, every researcher should satisfy himself that all personal information, such as place of residence, occupation, and the like, which could lead to an identification, and which is not absolutely essential to the topic of inquiry, has either been removed or effectively disguised.

The right to withdraw from the interview

You must also ensure that the right of every informant to withdraw from an interview at any time is clearly stated, repeated, if necessary at intervals, and acted on promptly.

The nature of the interview is such that the possibility always exists that an informant will wish to withdraw, especially if it approaches matters which are of deep personal significance such as bereavement, or divorce. Since the feelings caused by these events are hard to predict, the only counter-measure is to try to make sure that an informant is quite clear that the interview can be ended at any moment, and for any reason. You should remember that a change in an informant's willingness to continue with an interview can be signalled in a number of ways – by sudden restlessness, changes to tone of voice, or by a shift from a self-disclosing to a self-defensive reply, as well as by simply asking for the session to end. As interviewer you need to remain conscious of all these possibilities, and offer to end the interview any time you sense that the inform-ant's willingness to continue has undergone a change, although sometimes simply changing to a new topic will be enough to make the interviewee more comfortable. However, it is always better to have an interview unexpectedly cut short than to subject an informant to questioning on a subject which is painful to them.

If you feel at the planning stage that your proposed interview may lead you to touch on topics which may evoke painful feelings or ideas in your inter-viewee, then you should first seek the advice of a more experienced researcher, and secondly consider carefully whether you need some more training to help you to conduct an interview on such sensitive topics.

A brief critique of the interview method

The main criticism of the interview as a method of research comes from those who argue that, like any account of a conversation, the information obtained from an interview will consist almost exclusively of interpretations or para-phrases of the respondent's words. In evaluating the results of an interview, it is argued, one is faced with the problem of (1) whether this is what the informant actually said, and (2) whether this is what she actually meant. Unless detailed transcripts of an interview are provided, say the critics, the first point can never be decided, but even with that information, the second point will always be open to debate and disagreement. From this perspective, interview data are thus to be regarded as inherently unreliable as a source of information about human behaviour or experience.

However, this criticism can largely be answered by adopting the process of 'triangulation'. This involves checking the information or insights obtained by using one method against the information obtained from one or more different approaches. For example, data that had been obtained from an interview could be partially 'triangulated' against data relevant to the same research question, obtained from an experiment, or from running a procedure such as the Semantic

Differential (Osgood et al., 1957) or Repertory Grid (Kelly, 1955). If it then turns out that there is a convergence between the different sets of data, then some confidence can be reposed in the reliability of the data obtained from the interview.

This completes the review of much of what you will need to know for now about the background to research interviews. The next thing we look at is how these ideas can be applied when you want to do interview based research yourself. How do you set about planning and implementing research of your own which uses this method? The next section of this chapter supplies some answers.

Planning and Implementing an Interview

In this section of the chapter we go through the various tasks involved in planing and implementing an interview, and point out some of the more dangerous pitfalls which can trap the newcomer to this method of data collection.

We look, in some detail, at how questions can be generated and organized into an interview schedule.

The process of planning the face-to-face part of the interview is discussed.

A number of the important issues and problems in interviewing, such as the self-presentation of the interviewer, are examined.

Introduction

It has to be said from the outset that using the interview method to collect the data for a case study is almost certainly one of the more difficult approaches to research described in this book. It *can* be a relatively (note the qualification) straightforward and simple process to interview someone and turn the results into a case study, but the experience of many researchers has been that it also has the potential to turn into a time-consuming, personally demanding and frustrating experience. While careful planning can remove some of the problems before they appear, you certainly need to be aware that research using this approach *can* be hard and time-consuming work.

If you have only limited time available for carrying out an interview and writing up the case study, perhaps because you are aiming to produce a piece of course work against a tight deadline, you will certainly need to plan extremely carefully, and try to build in as much insurance as you can against mistakes or omissions. If you should be extremely time-limited, for example, then take a highly structured approach to the interview, and plan for a single interview session, during which you will aim to collect all the information you

---

Box 2.2   *A checklist for interview planning*

1   The preliminaries to the interview

Have you

- Clearly described the research problem?
- Stated the aim of the interview?
- Linked the problem to an appropriate theory?
- Identified the general categories of data which you will need to collect?
- Developed an explanation of why the case study approach can enable the problem to be tackled?

2   The questions

Have you

- Generated an appropriate set of questions?
- Planned the order in which the questions will be presented?
- Planned the interview to obtain the required balance between structured and unstructured interviewing?

3   The interview procedure:

Have you

- Considered the issues of self-presentation?
- Identified and approached potential respondents?
- Planned the pre-interview meeting?
- Planned the post-interview debriefing?
- Decided how the information is to be recorded in the interview?
- Considered the ethical issues raised by the proposed research and sought advice if necessary?

---

need (as far as you can foresee). If you adopt this strategy, it is obviously vital to make sure that you plan the interview as closely as you can, and try, as far as possible, to anticipate everything you will want to ask. Except on very rare occasions you probably won't be able to achieve the goal of the perfect interview, but you can certainly minimize the chances of things going seriously wrong. In particular, careful planning reduces the probability of finding later that you have some key information missing and need to use some of your precious time to re-interview the informant (who may be much less co-operative on the second occasion).

Because there is a quite a lot to say about planning an interview, and the information is quite dense and detailed, you may find it helpful to have an overview of the process to enable you to orientate yourself in what follows.

A checklist to help with planning interview-based research can be found above in box 2.2. This sets out the main tasks which you will certainly need to consider on the way to successfully completing your research.

Interview planning

The planning process, which ought to precede any interview carried out for research purposes, should include each of the following operations. After listing them, we'll look at each in turn.

The key operations in planning an interview

- Find a starting point for the investigation in a theory
- Develop a set of questions
- Find a respondent to interview
- Plan the interview itself.

Finding a starting point

Once you have found a research problem which you wish to approach by means of the interview method, the first tasks before planning proper begins, are to identify the theoretical basis for the research and to define the purpose of the interview in terms of the theory. You may also at this point begin to form an idea of which precise approach to data gathering may be most appropriate for your purposes, such as the structured or semi-structured interview, or a combination of interview and observation, or possibly even interview and experiment.

When you have decided to go ahead the next step is to develop a set of questions around which the interview can be organized.

Developing questions for the interview

It is an obvious point, but the questions you ask in an interview are extremely important since they play a major role in determining the kind of data you collect, and hence in how successfully an interview achieves its aims. If you don't ask the right questions, you are unlikely to get the information you seek, since you can't expect your informant to be able to read your mind. So, clearly, it is worthwhile to spend as much time as you can in mulling over the list of questions you propose to ask your informant.

One way of ensuring that your questions are directed towards the issues that really concern your research is to adopt a structured approach to generating interview questions. This involves making several passes over the problem with each pass providing a new set of questions at a deeper and more specific level.

Why do it this way? Simply because it provides a clear and logical path from the initial posing of the problem down to the questions which are actually asked in the interview. This enables you to check the process by which you arrived at the questions – you can see where they came from – and it makes the business of evaluating the research much easier. This approach can be divided into three phases:

1   Identify the general problem.
2   Generate from this a set of subsidiary questions which direct attention to particular aspects of the problem.
3   Generate a set of specific questions of different types which can be put directly to your informant.

We'll now look at each of these in more detail. To show you how the whole process might look in one particular case, the following description will use as an example a piece of research which might be carried out to investigate gender stereotyping.

1   Identify the general problem

State as clearly as you can the general problem which is to be tackled. Don't be put off by the fact that at this stage you may only be able to make a general statement, (which may be *very* general indeed), about the problem area.

As an example, consider the issue of 'gender stereotyping' – the idea that there exist in society stereotyped ideas about what constitutes maleness and femaleness which, effectively, define what 'proper' men and women are like, and which we frequently use to guide our notions of 'proper' behaviour.

Virtually everyone is likely to have some experience of the gender stereotyping process from one side or the other, and it would be interesting to try to explore part of the topic in the depth and detail which the interview/case method provides. Suppose, then, that we wish to use this approach to take a closer look at some of the ways in which childhood experience might influence the development of such stereotypes.

2   Generate from this a set of subsidiary questions which direct attention to particular aspects of the problem

The next step is to put together (perhaps by means of a 'brainstorming' or similar technique) as many subsidiary questions as you can. These are questions, possibly suggested by a particular theory, which deal with a limited part of the basic problem and they are therefore much more precise, pinpointing specific issues which could be explored further in an interview.

Given that we intend to look at the acquisition of gender stereotypes, then among the subsidiary questions which might be identified at this stage could be:

- To what extent do people possess clear and stereotyped views on different genders?
- How clear are people's ideas on different genders?
- What kind of picture of the different genders do their views describe?
- How do they think they acquired them?
- If they hold stereotyped views on gender, are they aware that they are stereotypes?
- Do gender stereotypes change over the lifetime of an individual?
- In what ways and for what kinds of reason do they change?

- In what kinds of situation have such stereotypes been applied to them by others?
- With what effects in the short or long term?
- Have particular individuals been more influential than others in defining gender stereotypes for them?
- How did this come about? What kinds of feeling are associated with stereotypes, and with unstereotypical behaviour?
- How can these feelings be explained?

This is far from being a complete list of the possible areas which could be explored, and they come from simply turning the problem of gender over in the mind, without any prior assumptions about what aspects in particular it might be worthwhile to pursue.

If some theory is also injected into the process a whole new set of ideas emerges. For example, the question of the development of gender identity, and gender stereotypes could fruitfully be looked at from the perspective of psychoanalytic theory, and this generates a new set of questions centred on the idea that identification with the same sex parent during the Oedipal phase might be connected to the formation of stereotyped ideas about gender. (See, for example, Gross, 1992, for an account of the psychoanalytic theory of psycho-sexual development, and the significance of the Oedipus complex.)

From the standpoint provided by Freud's theory, then, a further set of questions, suggest themselves:

- How does the process of identifying with the same sex parent during childhood seem to influence the development of ideas about gender?
- Do people who make a relatively weak identification with the parent of the same sex during childhood possess strong or weak gender stereotypes as adults?
- How does rewarding or punishing behaviour by the same sex parent affect the child's ideas and feelings about his own gender?
- How, if at all, does the child's relationship with the opposite sex parent appear to influence ideas about people of the opposite sex in general?
- Again, does rewarding or punishing behaviour appear to affect the kinds of ideas about gender which are formed?

When this process of generating ideas, whether by brainstorming or by some other method, has gone on for some time, it will be necessary to pause to take a careful look at what you have. Probably, you will be able to identify a number of clusters of ideas, each of which offers a slightly different angle on the basic issue you are hoping to address. If any such clusters are present, any one of them can provide the main focus for your interview.

For example, in the set of sample questions listed above, you will note that they can be organized into three overlapping groups. One is concerned with mapping the extent to which gender stereotyping exists, the second looks at the experience of stereotyping others and with being stereotyped in return, and the third considers some of the possible ways in which identification with a same sex parent could interact with the development of ideas about gender roles.

Of course, you aren't limited to pursuing the ideas in any single cluster or group. If you want to, or your inquiry seems to require it, you can attempt to answer questions from any number of clusters. However, by organizing your preliminary ideas into groups in this way, you can help your inquiry to become more focused and more structured, and increase the probability that your questions will really enable you to dig down beneath the surface of your chosen topic.

3   Generate a set of specific questions of different types which can be put directly to your informant

The final stage of the process is to turn some of the subsidiary questions, from one or more of your question groups, into specific questions which can be used, either as part of an interview schedule or questionnaire, or as 'memory joggers' to help with the framing of questions in an unstructured interview.

A useful guiding principle should be that whatever questions you decide to ask they should be framed in such a way that they are questions which only that person will be able to answer. That is, they should take as their point of reference the concrete situation and particular life experiences of the individual respondent. Gregory and Wallace's (1963) study of the cataract patient who was given back his sight did not simply ask general questions about how people in that situation would or might behave: instead they asked very specific questions which only that person could answer.

Suppose we assume that you have decided to pursue the cluster of questions which are concerned with the experience of gender stereotyping. Among the specific questions which might be asked in connection with an inquiry into this aspect of gender are:

- Can you remember behaving in a way which people around you regarded a being contrary to what was proper for a person of your gender?
- Can you explain what kind of behaviour that was? Can you remember the feelings and thoughts you had when you were doing that? What were they?
- What happened subsequently? How did the people around you react? What did your mother or father say?
- How would you respond if one of your own children did that? Why do you think that is so?
- What do you think would have happened if your behaviour on that occasion had been different?

And so on . . .

It is important when you are generating questions to be aware that different types of question are required in order to obtain a full picture. Different kinds of question allow different aspects of the problem to be explored and you should aim to have a full range available for the final interview schedule (that is, the list of questions which are to be asked). Note that it is also possible to combine different categories within single questions.

Descriptive questions are those which ask for straightforward descriptions of events or processes, e.g. What did your mother say when she found you helping your father saw logs?

Structural questions are questions about relationships between different parts (structures) of a person's experience, e.g. How did your behaviour differ at school from what it was like at home?

Hypothetical questions are questions which pose a possible situation and invite a response. e.g. What would your mother have said if . . .

General questions are questions which invite the informant to generalize from their experience. e.g. Do you think that boys today identify with their fathers as strongly as they did thirty years ago?

Specific questions are those which (obviously) ask something specific for which only a small range of answers is possible. e.g. Do you feel your identification with your father was very strong?

So, at this point you will, if you are still with me, have generated a set of questions which you are reasonably confident will address your chosen issues. You now have to organize them into a sequence which, you hope, will lead the respondent painlessly through the problem area. It is very helpful at this point to have an overall plan for the interview which will enable you to see from the beginning how all the different parts (questions) will fit together. The aim is to place the questions in an order which facilitates the detailed exploration of the topic, while if possible also enabling your respondent to understand the reasoning process which lies behind them. This sequence should be written out to form the schedule of questions for the interview. The question schedule for the issue of gender identity is given in box 2.3.

Finding a respondent

In most cases, the characteristics of the respondent you need for your case study will be defined quite clearly by the research question you wish to explore. If the research question concerns (say) the psychological functions of friendship in older people, then of course you need to find a person of the right age, however you choose to define 'older'. She must also, of course, be willing and able to participate in the interview.

You may be able to find suitable informants from among your family or friends, or you may have to cast your net somewhat further afield. In all cases, the respondent must be fully informed in advance about both the purpose and the form of the interview.

There should be an initial meeting held a few days before the main interview between yourself and your respondent in order to establish the general range of questions which you are interested in exploring, and to answer any questions which the respondent may have about the process in general. For example, some respondents may be anxious about the eventual fate of the information they are preparing to give you, and wish to be reassured that their anonymity

Box 2.3   An example of an interview schedule

The following is an example of how a schedule of questions on the subject of the contribution of early school experience to the development of gender identity might look. The extreme right-hand column is used to place a tick against each question as it is asked, to prevent the embarrassing possibility of asking the same question twice. Note the heading to the schedule which ensures that you have a record of the basic details of the research stored with the questions, and the range of question types covered.

Title of project   A case study of the development of gender identity
Topic   Contribution of early school experiences
Date of interview

---

1   Can you begin by giving me a general description of the school you attended at the age of five, so I can begin to understand what kind of a place it was?
2   Looking back, how did your school deal with the issue of gender in general? For example, were boys and girls treated in very different ways? Could you give me some examples of that?
3   How did this compare with what you experienced at home?
4   How was children's behaviour dealt with? For example, was a clear distinction made between what was considered appropriate behaviour for boys compared to girls?
5   Did the school generally reinforce or challenge stereotyped gender definitions? Examples?
6   How do you now think this affected you during your early school life? Can you give some examples?
7   Can you give me some examples of the kind of thing that would have happened if a boy behaved in a way the teachers thought was more appropriate to a girl?
8   Can you give me any examples of the ways in which the rules about appropriate behaviour were enforced? How do you feel about them now?
9   What would have happened if you had been found breaking a rule like that?

---

will be preserved. At this meeting you can tell the respondent what form the interview will take, and can begin to build a good working relationship.

As a matter of good practice, some time before you intend to do the interview you should prepare a written statement of the aims and scope of your research project, and a note of the specific topics which you would like the interview to cover. Your informant can then consider these at leisure and decide whether to be interviewed.

It is very important to establish in the preliminary meeting how long the interview is expected to last and whether your respondent is prepared to spend that length of time in talking to you – make sure that you don't overstay the time. Complex topics may be better broken down into sub-topics and spread over a number of interview sessions, if you have time and the respondent agrees, rather than being rushed through in a single session.

Planning the interview

The simplest approach to planning an interview is to think of it as having three phases – a beginning, middle and end, with each phase containing certain tasks which have to be done to complete the work of collecting information.

1   The beginning phase

The beginning phase of an interview besides the initial greeting, and any small talk, both of which are important to the development of rapport, should be directed towards two other tasks. First, the purpose and scope of the interview should be re-stated, in case the informant has forgotten, or misunderstood, and you should again obtain your informant's consent to be interviewed. Secondly, if you need to collect any items of information about your informant, such as name, age or marital status, then this is the best time to do it. From your point of view, it gets the routine information safely gathered, while from the interviewee's perspective, it helps to become accustomed to your style of asking questions, as well as to the (generally new) feeling of being interviewed.

Among the questions you will need to consider about this phase of the interview will include how you intend to manage the preliminaries. What information do you need to provide for your respondent? How (in what terms) are you going to present the research project? What will you do if your respondent doesn't want to proceed, or is uncooperative?

2   The middle section

The middle section of the interview is when the main information gathering takes place, and it is important to approach the planning of this with some care. You will already have generated a set of questions dealing with the one or more topics which you have identified as relevant to your basic research question, and you now need to organize these into a framework for the interview. In doing this, the following principles will be found helpful:

- If you intend to cover more than one topic in the interview place them in an order, with those which are likely to be easiest for the respondent to answer, and which depend least on the development of rapport, before the harder and more emotionally demanding ones.
- If you are planning to take an unstructured approach, you still need to plan the order in which broad topics are to be broached. But because, in this case, the direction of the interview is much more in the hands of your

respondent, you won't be able to plan on a question-by-question basis. However, you should nevertheless have a clear view of which questions would be appropriate if a particular topic is opened up by a respondent's answers.

- Make sure that all related questions (i.e. those which bear on the same topic) are grouped together.
- Decide which questions you are going to use in the structured part of the interview, and which you are going to hold back for when the conversation takes an appropriate turn, or in case your respondent 'dries up'.
- Ensure that any changes of topic are clearly signalled to the informant by saying something like, 'Leaving that topic on one side for now, I would like to ask you about . . .'.

Within each specific topic you should try to organize the questioning process in the following ways:

- Ask general questions before specific ones.
- Move from questions about behaviour to those about feelings and emotions as rapport develops.
- Use hypothetical questions in order to test ideas about what might have happened in a situation under other circumstances.
- Ask questions about the informant's mental state as often as questions about behaviour – try to find out how the informant responded to, or made sense of, particular events and experiences.
- Periodically use questions which re-state an earlier answer in different terms to enable you to check that you have understood what has been meant, as well as what was said.

The key to success is to treat the interviewee exactly as you would wish to be treated yourself if your roles were to be reversed. If possible, try to establish a sense that the research is a joint activity to which you both contribute, even if you are using a highly structured questionnaire which requires straightforward answers.

Try to plan for all the things which you think *could* happen in the main interview. For example: how will you respond if there is an unplanned interruption to the interview, or if the respondent doesn't wish to focus on the topic area you have in mind, or has changed her mind about helping you? This may never happen, and probably won't, but knowing that you have a contingency plan ready in case it does will do wonders for your confidence – and a relaxed interviewer is more likely to conduct a successful interview than one who is tense.

3 The closing section

Once you are satisfied that the information gathering is as complete as you can make it on this occasion, you should begin to close down the interview. The key elements in this will be:

1 Some element of debriefing to check that your informant is not going to leave the interview with negative feelings about the experience. It is particularly important to do this conscientiously if you have any reason to suppose that the interview has touched on painful events or feelings. You should already have some idea of whether this is likely, but you must also check after the interview, and allow your informant time to express any feelings which may be necessary. If for any reason you feel that you have been unable to help your informant fully you should always seek the advice of a more experienced researcher.

2 Secondly, give your interviewee some information about how you feel the interview has gone. You could, for example, comment on any aspects which you found particularly interesting or which you think will be especially helpful to your project. The aim should always be to leave the interviewee feeling good about participating in your research, irrespective of whether the interview has been wholly or only partly successful (or even not successful at all). It should always be possible to make positive remarks of some kind without compromising your integrity.

3 Finally, you have to manage the return from interview mode to a more normal style of interaction with your informant. Comments such as how tiring it must be to have to answer so many questions, or how you now see that you had been anticipating doing the interview with unnecessary anxiety, are good for helping the transition from interview to normal conversation, and will merge quite naturally into general leave-taking remarks and the departure of the interviewer.

The Conduct of the Interview

Having generated your questions and done all the careful planning, you now arrive at the moment when you have actually to conduct the interview itself.

Being an interviewer means that you have to attend to several tasks simultaneously. You have to ask questions, and attend to the answers, take notes and plan the next question, all while you are endeavouring to build up a rapport with the person you are interviewing. Not easy.

When you are about to set out on an interview for the first time it is tempting to suppose that the many models available from the mass media will be of help in forming your interviewing style. This is a mistake. There are plenty of models of interviewing available on the mass media, but these are more likely to be a hindrance to you in forming an interviewing style for research purposes. If you try to emulate the rather confrontational style adopted by some TV and radio journalists you will almost certainly make your respondent shut up like a clam, and you will find it very difficult to obtain any information. The most effective approach is likely to be an altogether softer and more conversational style which never makes an informant feel that he or she is undergoing a grilling on TV.

In the sections which follow we look at a number of specific issues to do with the conduct of an interview.

Self-presentation

The way in which you present yourself to your informant will play a part in deciding how successful you are as an interviewer. You have to remember that your informant will be constantly looking for clues about you.

Facial expression

Smiling is interpreted by others as indicating a generally relaxed state and a liking for the person one is talking to. However, it doesn't do to smile too much as this can also be interpreted as indicating a lack of confidence, nervousness, or an eagerness to please which may unsettle the informant, and cause them to wonder whether they should have confidence in you. Punctuated smiling is best – that is, smile frequently, but not all the time, and try to provide your informant with a reason for smiling also, such as a mild joke or a bit of wordplay.

Dress

You should aim to minimize, as far as possible, any gross indications of status differences between yourself and your informant, since the greater the difference in status perceived by your informants, the less likely it will be that they will relax and speak easily. The way you dress is one very important indicator of social status, which is easily, even unconsciously 'read' by almost everyone, and therefore you need to pay some attention to choosing what you are to wear to conduct an interview. Specifically, you need to consider how the clothes you intend to wear are likely to be 'read' by your informant. For example, if you were to wear an extremely smart suit to interview someone, you would almost certainly trigger a whole range of speculations about what the kind of person who wears a suit like that could be doing running interviews about whatever kind of subject you happen to be pursuing. Such speculations, or at least the conclusions which may be drawn from them, can easily ruin your chances of obtaining a frank interview.

The aim, as we have already noted, is to dress so as to minimize status differences as far as possible. Thus, you need to take care not to dress up too much, especially if you intend to interview people, who, for one reason or another (such as homelessness, substance abuse or economic disadvantage) may not give a high priority to purely sartorial concerns.

Equally, you need to beware of over-enthusiastic dressing down. If you turn up to conduct the interview in torn and oil-stained jeans, for example, this may well be read as an indication that you are not to be taken seriously as a researcher in psychology.

The best strategy, as usual, is to try to strike mid point between excessive formality of dress and complete scruffiness. Jeans, a jacket and a shirt, usually worn with a tie would probably meet this requirement for males, and handily it also fits the stereotyped view of what an academic looks like.

The environment of the interview

You won't necessarily have much, or any, control over the environment in which the interview takes place. If it happens to be the informant's living room, for example, you will just have to accept the situation as you find it.

A meeting on neutral territory has both pros and cons. On the one hand you may have more control over the conditions under which the interview is conducted, but on the other hand, your informant may feel less relaxed than if you agree to hold the interview on his or her home territory.

The basic requirement is for a space where you can both relax and be free of possible distractions or interruptions by others, while you concentrate on the interview itself. It also needs to be possible to take notes for an extended period, and as this is tiring when done from a standing position, you will need to be able to sit down.

The seating arrangements can make a difference to the success of an interview, and you need to try to get the seating arranged for maximum effectiveness. Essentially you want to try to make sure that you get as close as possible to the following conditions:

1 You are both sitting on the same level, or if this is not possible, that you, the interviewer are sitting at a lower level than your informant. The reason for this is that height is another powerful indicator of status, and if you are seated so that your informant is at a lower level than yourself, it sends an inhibiting message.
2 You are sitting at an angle of about 90 degrees to your informant. This will make it easy to maintain eye contact with the other person, without seeming to dominate or appear adversarial. The alternatives – side-by-side, and face-to-face – are both less good and should be avoided if possible, the first because it makes it difficult to maintain eye-contact and write notes, and the second, because it may call up associations with official interviews of one sort or another – employment interviews, for example, it may help generate a feeling of formality which will seriously hinder the development of a rapport between you.

Note-taking

The purpose of every interview is the collection of information which, naturally, needs to be recorded in some way so that it can be examined and analysed later. This, unless you are one of those rare people with perfect recall, raises the perennial problem of how you manage the recording process.

Perhaps the most likely course of action is to try to take written notes throughout the interview. This means that the whole interview will become a slower process, as you will have to ask the informant to speak slowly enough for you to write down the gist of what is said. This isn't a major problem, however, as you will probably find that with a little practice you will be able to get most of what is said down in writing fairly fast. It won't be necessary to write down every single word uttered by your interviewee, simply the sense and meaning of what is said.

It is probably as well to try to avoid taking very brief notes in the hope of reconstituting what was said into a full record at some later point. First, for this to have any chance of success the reconstitution process needs to take place almost immediately after the interview itself and, for practical reasons, this is not always possible. Secondly, as memory research has shown, human memory does not so much reproduce stored information as reconstruct it around a set of expectations or assumptions about what was originally given. A similar reconstructive process is likely to apply to the recalled information from the interview, and it will almost certainly contain a number of errors generated by the interviewer's assumptions and expectations. The best strategy is always to rely on memory as little as possible, and if possible not at all.

One solution to the difficulties of taking written notes is to use a tape-recorder to record the respondent's words, and transcribe them on to paper at your own convenience. This has the great advantage of allowing you to concentrate your whole attention on listening to what your informant is saying, and in considering your next question. On the other hand, it is possible that some people may be inhibited by the thought of being continuously recorded, and you should certainly check with your informants beforehand to make sure that it is acceptable to them. If possible run a preliminary test to make sure that you can obtain a clear recording from the place where the interview is to take place – it may be acoustically poor, with lots of echo or intrusive noise. It also goes without saying that you also need to be totally sure of the reliability of the equipment that you will be using.

Some problems and pitfalls of the interview

In addition to the rather varied range of difficulties which have already been mentioned, there are others which arise out of the nature of the interview itself. You will need to be constantly aware of these and should try, by planning the interview carefully, to minimize their effects as far as possible.

1   Social desirability effect

This is also known as 'evaluation apprehension' or, more plainly, as 'faking good', and it arises because an interview is a situation in which the respondent can easily feel herself to be 'on trial', or at least under rather intense scrutiny.

In such a situation, the normal, socially learned response is to answer questions in a way which is most likely to ensure the approval of the questioner. Respondents who adopt this strategy tend to provide answers which are socially acceptable, and/or which place them in the most favourable light rather than to tell the truth. If your questioning covers matters about which a social desirability effect seems at all likely, (for example, if it is concerned with money, about which people can be notoriously evasive and misleading), then you should interpret the results with some caution. The possibility of social desirability affecting your data can be minimized to some degree by the development of trust and rapport between the interviewer and respondent.

2 Response bias

It has been found that even where the social desirability effect seems unlikely to operate, respondents can still show unconscious bias in their answers to questions. For example, some respondents have been found to have an 'acquiescent response set', that is, a tendency to agree to questions which offer them a choice of a 'yes' or 'no' answer. The root cause of this form of bias is probably similar to the social desirability effect mentioned above. Respondents may unconsciously regard negative answers as unhelpful, and therefore tend to produce positive answers when they have the choice. Their need to feel that they have assisted the researcher outweighs their need to tell the strict truth.

3 The impact of the interviewer

Finally, you need to be aware of, and plan for, the probable effect of yourself as interviewer on your respondent. All interviews are social situations, and an interviewee's answers will invariably be affected by complex factors such as the age, sex, social class and race of the interviewer, especially when these are different from her own. This means that you should consider carefully the possibility that you will be unable to get the information you are looking for, simply because your interviewee will be unwilling to give it to you because of the way basic demographic characteristics can influence perceptions. For example, it has been shown that working-class interviewees provide much fuller information in response to questioning if the interviewer is perceived to be working class also, than if she is perceived to be middle class.

Writing up a Case Study

This section of the chapter makes some suggestions about how the data obtained from an interview can be written up into a case study.

It also contains outlines of two research projects which can be pursued using the interview method.

Introduction

Interview data can be written up into a case study using the framework provided by the standard format for psychological reports. You will obviously
have to omit those sections for which you will have no information (such as
'apparatus'), but apart from such points, the standard format can be used quite
satisfactorily. The main weakness of using the standard approach is that it
separates your data – an informant's replies to your questions, which go into
the results section – from your analysis of what they mean from the point of
view of theory, which belongs in the discussion. There doesn't seem to be any
way around this problem other than by merging the results and discussion
sections which, of course, destroys the point of using the standard format in
the first place.

   Don't worry that published case histories, such as those of Freud, do not use
the standard headings – he wasn't producing coursework for examination
purposes. You, on the other hand, probably are, and you need to make sure
that your work is organized in a way which the marking scheme recognizes.
You should therefore always use the standard format, unless you are explicitly
advised otherwise.

   Similarly a case study written for assessment purposes should be no longer
than the official guidelines – you should always check on the exact length
which is required, but for many assessment purposes around 1500 words will
probably be acceptable. Again, don't be influenced by the fact that a full-scale
case study (and Freud again springs to mind) can stretch to around 10,000
words. In writing work for assessment, the quality of the reasoning and the
depth of understanding of the issues which you display are always more important than the sheer number of words you are able to generate.

   The following represents the main ways in which the content of a report
written in case study style will need to differ from a report of an experiment
(which is what the standard format was designed for). However, I must point
out again that when you are producing work to meet a course requirement you
always seek information on the content and layout which are required by the
assessing authority. Guidance on writing up a psychological report for both
qualitative and quantitative data can be found in appendix 2.

The Introduction

You should present a statement of the theoretical background relevant to the
case study as succinctly and as clearly as possible. A statement of hypotheses
is not appropriate, but you should show how and why the aims and objectives
of the study follow from the theory.

Subjects

Present a 'thumbnail sketch' of your informant. In this, the details of physical
appearance may be less important than your assessment of intangibles such as

mood, manner and personality. How easy did you feel it was to establish a co-operative relationship? How open or truthful did you feel the respondent was being? Did your initial assessment of your informant change at all during the interview? If so, what caused the change?

Procedure

State the date(s), time(s), duration(s) and place(s) of the interview(s). Say whether any other persons were present, why they were there, and for how long. Record the sex, age and any other characteristics of the respondent, such as the presence of a disability, if they are relevant to your inquiry.

Results

The results, either of a structured or an unstructured interview, will be a mass of data which, depending on how well you have mastered the art of note-taking, may make more or less sense when you sit down to sift through it later. The problem of analysing interview data is to find a way to organize what you have collected, so as to be able to discuss the information you have acquired and to draw some valid inferences. Without some form of organization, the case study is likely to consist of little more that a collection of your informant's remarks, loosely strung together into some kind of order. This can produce interesting results, but is not likely to be an approach which permits research questions to be answered, or the correctness of a theory to be assessed.

One strategy, which *is* able to permit such questions to be answered, is to organize the information by means of a set of categories which have been identified as possibly relevant from the background theory. Pieces of information from an informant can then be sorted into the categories, and the task of writing up then becomes a question of working through the information placed in each of the categories, and evaluating its significance in terms of the theory.

As an example of how the categorization process could operate, suppose that a case study is to be written on the development of gender identity from within the theoretical viewpoint provided by social learning theory. You will be about to conduct an interview covering someone's childhood experiences in which you will be focusing on gender relevant matters. Before doing the interview, however, you identify some of the key categories of information which you will need in order to analyse the answers you will obtain, and these might well include some of the following:

Category 1 Instances of reinforced (rewarded) imitation of the same and/or opposite sex parent.
Category 2 Instances of punished imitation of the same and/or opposite sex parent.
Category 3 Instances of imitation of the same and/or opposite sex parent which were ignored by parents.
Category 4 Examples of gender specific behaviour in that family.

Category 5   Evidence relevant to the strength of gender identification, such as remembered feelings of pleasure following imitation of the same and/or opposite sex parent.

Two points need to be observed in order to ensure the validity of the categorization process. Firstly, it is important that a set of categories should be identified *before* the interview is carried out, otherwise, if they are established afterwards, they may simply be chosen to match the categories which are already perceived to be in the data.

Once the interview has been conducted and data have been collected, you then go through your notes identifying different elements – sentences or longer sections – which represent examples of those categories of behaviour or experience which you have already set up. Each example in the interview record is then marked in some way (different coloured felt-tip pens are useful) to indicate which category it fits. If you have conducted a highly structured interview, based on a prepared list of questions, then you will probably find the analysis into categories a reasonably straightforward process.

The less structured the interview, however, the more likely you are to have obtained information that cannot easily be fitted into the category framework, with the result that you will end up with a less than perfect match between data and categories. This doesn't matter. It is simply an indication that you have been scrupulous about establishing your categories before the interview (and in avoiding leading questions designed to produce answers which fit the categories). From the point of view of completing the case study, all that matters is that you have identified some key categories which appear to have some significance from the point of view of the theory you wish to explore. Any unclassifiable material can be treated as a source of examples, speculations, or ideas for further research.

Discussion

The discussion section of a case study should contain three main types of information:

1   It should contain a discussion and evaluation of the data you have obtained from the point of view of the aim(s) of the case study.

This can be structured around such questions as:

- Did you achieve the aims and objectives of the research? Explain how.
- To what extent are your questions answered by the data you have obtained? What have you found out? Give examples, referring to the data you have obtained.
- Did it prove to be difficult to obtain information on any particular aspect of the problem? Why do you think this was?
- To what extent do the data force you to reconsider the questions you were asking?

- Did you realize at any point that you were thinking about the problem in an inappropriate way?
- If you used data obtained from more than one method, do they all point in the same direction, or do data obtained in different ways suggest different answers to the same problem?

In writing this part of the discussion section you must always take care to distinguish clearly between those words actually spoken by your informant, and those which are your own paraphrase or interpretation of what was said. The simplest method is to underline everything which is a direct quotation. It is also a good idea to place a sample transcript of the interview in an appendix to the report so that the reader can obtain an idea of the 'flavour' of the interview.

2 **It should include an evaluation and discussion of the case study material in terms of the background theory.**

Although you cannot undertake a formal test of a theory by this means, you should still be able to outline the connections between the data you have uncovered and any underlying theory. The main questions to be considered here are:

- In what instances do the data support, or fail to support the theory?
- Where, and why do they suggest that the theory needs to be extended, and in what ways?

3 **Finally it should contain an evaluation of the data gathering process itself.**

- If you used the interview method alone, how successful do you feel you were in obtaining data relevant to the question(s) you were asking?
- If you used more than one method, to what extent were you successful at exposing different aspects of the problem using the different methods?
- How did your informant respond to the different methods?

Appendix

The appendix to the main case study should contain a copy of the interview schedule, or interview plan, in the case of a wholly unstructured interview, together with any data which you think have value, but which you have been unable to fit into any of the categories of analysis.

After the write-up

Once you have completed a draft of the case study, it is a courtesy to offer the respondent the opportunity to read and comment on your write-up of the interview. This establishes that you value the respondent's contribution to your research, and enables you to correct any unintentional error arising from misunderstanding or misinterpretation.

Suggested Topics for a Case Study

The following are two suggestions, either of which could provide the basis for case study research, although they are not intended to prevent you from thinking up topics of your own. In fact, the best way to use them is as a guide to how to frame interesting research questions in order to make them accessible to research by the case study method.

Topic 1:   Forgetfulness and the experience of forgetting

The aim of this investigation is to use the case study approach to explore one individual's experience of forgetting. If you are able to enlist the help of an elderly person, you are likely to find this a particularly rich field of inquiry, but don't worry if you have to make do with a younger person. Everyone is prone to forgetting, even if they don't think they are. In fact, it's an interesting research question in itself to try to uncover the extent of forgetting in healthy young adults.

Among the specific aspects of this problem that you could explore are:

The effects of situation   Does more forgetting seem to occur in one kind of situation than another? Does it depend on what the person is doing at the time or on the nature of the material which is forgotten, such as faces, names, ideas, or images?

The experience of forgetting   How does it feel to be forgetful? What effect does this seem to have on other aspects of the individual's life, such as her relationships, her self-image, and so on?

Coping techniques   What techniques or strategies has the person worked out for dealing with forgetting? How effective do these seem to be?

What do the data suggest about theories of forgetting? Do they confirm the classical view of different sources of forgetting – interference, unlearning, transfer effect and so on? Do your data confirm the picture we get from experimental studies of memory?

REFERENCE

Baddeley, A. (1983). *Your memory: A user's guide*. Harmondsworth: Penguin Books.

Topic 2:   Friendship

Investigate the experience of friendship by one person. How do friendships come to be formed and ended? What influences were there on the formation and end of friendships? Why are some maintained and others not? What factors are responsible? Does the idea of a friendship 'career' seem to have any validity? How do relationships change over time, and in response to what kinds of event? What are the positive and negative aspects of friendships; what costs and benefits? How do these vary with circumstance and situation? What did the experience of the friendship offer to the respondent?

You could also explore your respondent's attitudes and values concerning friendship. How do these compare to attitudes and values concerning significant others such as family and other relatives? What was the effect of friendships on relations within the family, especially relations with any siblings?

How far are the respondent's answers predicted by the various theories of friendship such as the contiguity effect, or social exchange theory?

REFERENCES

Baddeley, A. (1983). *Your memory: A user's guide.* Harmondsworth: Penguin Books.
Duck, S. (1988). *Relating to others.* Milton Keynes: Open University Press.

Summary of chapter 2

The case study approach to research involves the construction of a detailed qualitative description of the behaviour and/or experience of a single individual 'case'. In general, data for a case study are collected by means of an interview with an informant, though other methods of data collection such as observation or experiment may additionally be employed to provide information on specific points of detail. The main value to psychologists of the case method lies in the fact that it permits the exploration of those hidden aspects of human behaviour such as thoughts, feelings, and subjective perceptions, which it is difficult, if not impossible, to approach in any other way, and which are therefore relatively neglected as topics of study. At the same time, its very ability to provide access to the other's subjective world is seen as a major weakness, since it is impossible directly to verify the data obtained.

The most usual way of collecting data for a case study is by conducting an interview with an informant, an approach which bears some superficial similarities to an ordinary conversation, but which, on closer inspection, proves to be different in a number of important ways. The most obvious, perhaps, is the fact that the asking of questions in an interview is almost wholly one-sided, whereas in an ordinary conversation either party is likely to ask questions of the other.

In structured interviewing, the questioning process is based on a schedule of questions which have been worked out in advance, and the informant therefore plays no part in determining the direction or content of the interview. In unstructured interviewing, on the other hand, the questioning is likely to be directed by some general ideas or interests in the mind of the researcher, but little advance planning of questions takes place. Rather, the content of questions is prompted by the information progressively communicated by the informant during the interview. In terms of the control of the interview, and the power of each participant to influence the outcome, the two approaches are clearly very different. In structured interviewing control lies almost wholly with the researcher while in unstructured interviewing the informant is in a much more equal position.

Clearly, both types of interview have their own spheres of application, with structured interviewing being best in situations where the area to be covered by the research can be precisely identified in advance, or when relatively simple research questions are being pursued to no great depth. Unstructured interviewing requires a much greater level of skill on the part of the interviewer, but allows questions to be pursued in an exploratory fashion, and to greater depth. For general research purposes (if such exist), the best approach is probably to devise some mixture of the two types, since this allows the high level of control offered by the structured approach to be modified by the flexibility and responsiveness of the unstructured approach.

Whichever form of interview is adopted, the critical variable in an interview will almost certainly be whether a sense of rapport develops between the interviewer and the informant, which in turn plays a large part in determining the informant's motivation. Without these crucial ingredients, the interview may founder entirely, and will almost certainly be less than fully effective as a means of collecting information. An interview represents a particularly delicate and intense social situation and it is, therefore essential for interviewers to be aware of the different ways in which their behaviour may affect the outcome.

The planning of an interview does not only require careful attention to the organization of the questioning process itself. It is also – obviously – necessary to make sure that the questions are pertinent to the research aims, and as the interview proceeds, that they reflect earlier answers which have been given. If a partly structured approach to interviewing is contemplated, the places at which the unstructured questioning is to take place must also be determined. Less obviously, perhaps, an interviewer should also give thought to making sure the environment in which the interview is to take place is arranged in a way which facilitates the questioning process. Sitting face to face with an interviewee, rather than side by side will, for example, almost certainly make it harder for them to communicate information which is of deep personal significance.

The interview contains a number of potential pitfalls and difficulties arising out of the particularly exposed nature of the informant's position. The issue of rapport has already been mentioned, but in addition, informants may offer distorted or incorrect information, sometimes deliberately to mislead, but more probably in order to try to present the best possible image of themselves to the interviewer. Either way, some degree of error may be introduced into the data and this can be extremely difficult to detect with certainty. Ethically, too, the interview holds potentially sensitive aspects. Because the whole purpose of an interview is to encourage the communication of personal information there is always the possibility that informants will be led to reveal more about themselves than they either intend or want. It is therefore extremely important that the interviewer promises, and does everything possible to assure, the absolute confidentiality of all information obtained in an interview.

The process of writing up the information obtained from an interview, and turning it into a case study may require the organization and analysis of a considerable mass of raw qualitative data. One strategy for dealing with this problem is to impose order on the chaos by analysing the raw data into a set of categories which can then be used to structure the content of the case study itself. The standard psychological report structure is likely to be the preferred format for many assessment purposes, and can easily be used to organize the writing of a case study if the sections which are not required (such as 'apparatus'), are omitted.

3 The Survey Method

This chapter provides information about the survey method, covering issues of survey design, sampling, the construction of questionnaires and attitude scales, and the analysis of results.

- It describes some of the more widely used survey designs, and points out the differences between them.

- It describes the main methods of obtaining a sample from a population.

- It discusses the process of questionnaire construction, showing the range of question types which can be used.

- It describes the Likert procedure for attitude scale construction.

- It explains key concepts in sampling such as 'population', 'sample', 'sampling frame' and 'sampling error'.

- It provides two suggestions for research projects using the survey method.

Doing Research by Survey

Survey research is a way of collecting information from a large and dispersed group of people rather than from the very small number which can be accommodated in a case study. If you wish to do this, and you are aiming to collect the sort of information which can be obtained by pencil and paper methods – for example, by means of a questionnaire – then you are likely to choose the survey method.

The two foundation concepts of this method of research are the concepts of the *population* and the *sample*, and you will need to have a clear understanding of how these fit together before you can really understand how the survey approach works, and why it is able to deliver useful information to a researcher.

The notion of population has two distinct, though overlapping meanings. In the demographic sense it refers to the group of people who simply occupy a given area of space – the 'population' of Huddersfield, for example. In this sense, a population could conceivably be of interest to psychologists, for example, if a bizarre mental disorder were to suddenly strike all the inhabitants of Huddersfield, but it is somewhat unlikely.

On the other hand, in the statistical sense in which psychologists tend to use the term, a 'population' is simply a set of individuals (of which there may be a large number) who share a given set of identifiable characteristics. It is simply a set of individuals who happen to be alike in some way. Thus, there exists a population of left-handed people and another population of right-handed people, and both of these overlap with yet a third population of red-haired people, and with the populations of men and women and so on, and so on. It is no exaggeration to say that, viewed from the standpoint of statistics, the universe consists only of an infinity of overlapping populations. The aim of all survey research is to obtain information about some specified population, generally referred to as 'the population of interest', and in order to do this it is necessary to take a sample.

A sample is the group of individuals, who are selected from within a larger population by means of a sampling procedure, and who actually generate the data for the research. Sampling is a necessary procedure whenever a researcher wishes to draw some conclusions about a group of individuals, but when it is not possible to gather information from each individual member of the group, usually because the group is simply too large for every member to be contacted. The purpose of a sample is to 'stand in' for the population from which it was taken, and therefore a researcher is not so much interested in the sample data itself, but in what it can tell *in general* about the population from which the sample was taken. The critical factor in determining the validity of these generalizations is the extent to which the sample can be regarded as truly representative of the population in question. Providing an answer to this question requires the concept of 'sampling error' which is discussed a little later in this chapter.

Before we look, in some detail, at what is involved in the design of a survey, you may wish to look at the examples of survey research at the end of this chapter in order to get an idea of the kinds of question and the results which are possible.

Designing a Survey

The process of designing a survey can be divided into the following three activities; we shall look at each in turn:

- The selection of a survey design
- The selection of a sampling method in order to obtain the necessary number of subsets from the population(s) of interest
- The design of a standardized set of questions as an instrument for collecting data.

The selection of a survey design

When we consider some of the different types of survey research below, it is helpful to bear in mind that it can be undertaken with either of two rather different intentions in mind. Either it can be done in order to establish a description of some phenomenon of interest, or it can be done in order to try to explain why a particular phenomenon has occurred, and these types are called, logically enough, descriptive and explanatory surveys.

> **Descriptive surveys** are those common forms of survey in which the aim is simply to establish the features of a particular group – to provide a description of the group in relation to some specific characteristics which it possesses.

For example, an educational researcher might decide to survey a representative group of school-leavers in order to try to find out to what extent they are motivated to succeed in their chosen fields of work. The aim in this will be to provide a clear and complete description of the motive to achieve of those individuals studied, with the assumption that such information will also apply to the wider group of school-leavers to some degree.

> **Explanatory surveys** on the other hand, are those which aim to push beyond straightforward description to try to provide explanations for phenomena, by permitting a researcher to ask questions about possible cause and effect relationships between different variables. These surveys are naturally rather more complex than the descriptive type, and are therefore more difficult to carry out successfully.

An example of this kind of survey would be one which looks at how far parents' behaviour contributes to children's motivation to achieve highly at school. To carry out such a study, the researcher will need to design the research so that it not only allows conclusions to be drawn about the population on the basis of the sample data, but also, as far as possible, permits parental example (if any) to be isolated from all the other possible influences on the motive to achieve.

As you will appreciate, explanatory research can be difficult to design and carry out successfully by means of the survey method, not least because it is almost always impossible to exclude all possible alternative explanations for a given result. The researcher is almost always in the position of trying to figure out what the probability might be of correctly identifying an explanation for the data.

The distinction between descriptive and explanatory research, although clear enough in theory, becomes considerably blurred in practice, since the two concepts are best thought of as representing the opposite ends of a continuum, rather than a simple dichotomy. When it comes to the actual conduct of research, a survey is much more likely to occupy a position somewhere along the continuum, rather than sitting neatly at one of the ends. This is for two reasons. Towards the descriptive end of the scale, researchers are still likely to be equally interested in forming explanations for their data, as in producing straightforward descriptions of it, even though any such explanations must always remain highly speculative.

Secondly, towards the explanatory end of the continuum, the fact that the survey method is unlikely to identify any single explanation for a set of data means that the explanatory power of even the more highly controlled kind of survey is necessarily partial and incomplete. The four types of survey, described below should be seen as occupying different positions on this continuum rather than as members of two distinct categories.

Survey Designs

This part of the chapter describes the four main survey designs, and discusses some of reasons for choosing among them in research.

The four basic types of survey design are:

- **The one-shot survey**
- **The before–after design**
- **The two-groups controlled comparison design**
- **The two-groups before–after design.**

You will need to know something of the differences between each of these designs, their strengths and weaknesses, and the criteria for choosing among them for your research. Incidentally, when you come to chapter 5 you will notice that these same designs appear again, although they are described in slightly different terms. This is because they represent basic ways of organizing an investigation which are essentially the same whether data are to be collected by survey, observation or experiment.

The one-shot survey

The simplest form of survey is the 'one-shot' type (see figure 3.1), in which the data are collected from a single sample drawn from the population of interest.

This design permits only descriptive research to be carried out, since it makes no provision for the collection of data with which a comparison could be made, and without which there is no possibility of drawing any inferences

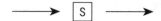

Figure 3.1   The one-shot survey design. Note that in this and the following figures, the 'S' in the square box represents the process of sampling from a population, while the arrows indicate the passage of time.

about the possible causes of the data. This must be emphasized, even though often there may appear to be an implied comparison with another group of people.

In the research conducted by Rees (1971), described at the end of this chapter, there is just this kind of an implied comparison between the experiences of bereaved people and those of the non-bereaved. However, although Rees found that his sample of bereaved people did suffer from post-bereavement hallucinations, we can't simply draw the conclusion that bereavement was the cause because the design made no provision for collecting data about the incidence of hallucinations among the non-bereaved. Most of the sample were rather elderly, and some were unwell, and it is always possible that the hallucinations could be attributable to the effects of age or medication, as much as to bereavement.

The before–after design

The before–after survey design provides one way of repairing the worst weakness of the one-shot design, namely its lack of provision for the collection of control or comparison data. In this design (see figure 3.2), data are collected from the members of a single sample on two distinct occasions, which are separated from each other by some kind of treatment or event, and where the presumption is that the second set of results will be influenced by the intervening process. It follows, then, that by comparing the second set of data with the first, it can be seen whether the second set of results has changed in response to the intervening event.

Figure 3.2   The before–after design

To use the example of Rees's research again, the design used on that occasion could have been adjusted in order to provide additional explanatory power, by arranging to survey members of the sample at some point before their partners died. Then, following their bereavement, to sample again. A comparison of the results of the two questionnaires would then have indicated whether the frequency and content of any hallucinations had changed as a result of the experience of bereavement.

However, the validity of this line of reasoning clearly depends crucially on being able to show that only the intervening event, and no other, could have influenced the second set of results, and this may be extremely difficult to arrange in a survey.

As an example, consider a researcher who is interested in the (quite likely possibility) that the experience of getting married might influence attitudes towards those who choose to remain unmarried. That is, that people who marry might undergo a shift in attitudes towards the unmarried, caused by the change in their own marital status. This question could be addressed simply by taking a sample of to-be-married couples and administering an appropriate attitude questionnaire to them, say, six months before they are due to get married.

Once the wedding is over, and the new couple have started married life together, say six months after the wedding, the same questionnaire (or its equivalent form) could again be administered to the same people. The two sets of results, (the 'before marriage' set and the 'after marriage' set), could then be compared. If they differed significantly, the argument could be advanced that the difference was due to the fact that the couples were married in the interval between the first and second data collection points.

Essentially, this argument, that an intervening event can be used to explain any differences between two sets of data collected on different occasions, stands on two legs. The first is that the event occurred in time before the second set of data were collected. Since, in logic, causes must always precede effects, the argument is made that the intervening event is qualified in logic to be considered as a possible cause of any difference between the two sets of data. Secondly, it must also be possible to argue from theory for an intervening event to exert an influence on the variables or qualities which are being measured. That is, there has to be some reason for supposing that there is a connection between the variables being measured and the intervening event so that the intervening event could provide an explanation of the results.

In the case of the newly-weds, Festinger's (1957) theory of cognitive dissonance would predict some change in attitudes as a result of the decision to marry, and it is reasonable to suppose that this is likely to be accentuated by the occasion of the wedding ceremony itself.

However, this reasoning still needs to be treated with some caution, since, as we noted above, it is difficult to ensure survey data are collected under anything like controlled conditions. While it may be true that the experience of marriage changes attitudes towards the unmarried, there are other possible explanations which should also be considered. Among the alternatives are:

Change due to the passage of time

Is it certain that the observed difference between the two sets of data would not have been observed anyway, even if the couples had not married in the interval between them? It could be argued that the difference is simply due to developing a more mature outlook on life in general over the year covered by the survey.

Uncontrolled variables

Even if the effect of the passage of time is excluded, there is still the possibility that the observed difference is due not to marriage as such but to a variable related to it. It could be that all the marriages have turned out after six months to be particularly happy ones, and that the second set of survey results owe more to the happiness of the marriages than to the fact of marriage as such. And, of course, having good relations with in-laws, the lack of financial problems, and owning one's own home may, in their turn all play some part in generating marital happiness.

The repeated measures effect

A yet further source of difficulty lies in the fact that the research design involves administering the same group of individuals with the same test instrument on two different occasions. In such a situation there is a possibility that, unless the researcher takes steps to prevent it, respondents may try to replicate their first answers on the second occasion.

The problem is made worse by the fact that any attempt to avoid the repeated measures effect by using a different measure to collect information on the second occasion brings the problem of weakening the extent to which the two sets of results can be validly compared.

As you will probably appreciate, any conclusions which might be drawn about the sources of attitude change in newly-weds on the basis of a before–after design will need also to be subjected to a very careful reasoning process which takes fully into account a whole range of possible alternative explanations. And even when this is done, there will still remain the possibility that something crucial has been overlooked.

The two-groups controlled comparison design

Another alternative to the one-shot approach is provided by the two-groups comparison design. In the simplest version of this, data are collected from two separate samples, when each of the samples has received a different form of treatment before the data are collected. In the most powerful case, one sample should be treated while the other remains untreated (see figure 3.3). In such a situation, it can be argued that any difference between the different sets of data can be attributed to the fact that they have come from two samples of which one has been treated in particular way, and one has not. The fact that one of the groups is an untreated 'control' is crucial to this reasoning.

Taking again the earlier example of the (fictitious) research into the attitudes of newly-weds, you can probably see that it would also be possible to pursue the same research question (i.e. whether attitudes change as a result of marriage), by obtaining data from an attitude questionnaire administered simultaneously to two different samples. One sample would consist of individuals

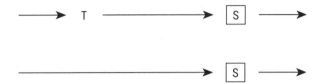

Figure 3.3   The two-groups controlled comparison design. The 'T' in the figure indicates the treatment or the intervening event applied to one of the samples.

who are unmarried, and the other of those who have recently been married. After the data have been collected, a comparison between the two sets of data might be used to try to throw some light on the research question, since if a difference between them can be shown, it could plausibly be argued that it was because members of one group has all been recently married, while members of the other had not. In this case the argument is that if a comparison is made between two otherwise apparently similar groups who differ in one important respect, then any other differences which are later discovered (such as a difference in attitude scale scores) can be held to be caused by the earlier difference.

However, as you will probably have worked out for yourself, this line of reasoning is, again, somewhat problematic. It is clearly not acceptable to simply conclude that there is a causal link between a treatment and a dependent variable – in this case between getting married on the one hand, and having a different attitude to marriage compared to unmarried people on the other. One problem is that in many cases the samples are constituted from naturally occurring groups – that is, from people who have naturally developed the characteristics which place them in one group or the other. The same would be true if the two groups consisted of males or females, or single and joint parents: their membership of one group or the other would be the result of nature, or their life-history, rather than the decision of the researcher, and they therefore may possess any number of additional characteristics or life experiences which could cause the observed result as well as, or instead of, the one in which the researcher is interested.

A rather less powerful version of the same design that looks at the possibility of a relationship of co-variation between variables would be one in which there is no untreated control, but in which the two samples could actually consist of people who can be regarded as naturally having been treated in different ways. For example, an investigation into the relationship between gender and risk-taking would necessarily require two samples each composed of the members of a different sex.

In this case, the possibility of identifying a causal relationship between gender and risk-taking does not arise. The lack of an untreated control, and the fact that neither gender can be regarded as a control for the other, means that this version of the design is only capable of revealing the extent to which risk-taking varies with gender, and not at all whether any observed variation is caused by gender differences.

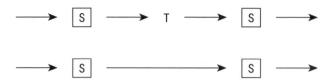

Figure 3.4   The two-groups before–after design

The two-groups before–after design

The before–after design with controls which combines features of both the preceding ones, is the most powerful of the survey designs dealt with here. In essence, it involves taking two (or more) samples which are each pre-tested before being given different treatments, and then subsequently tested again, using a comparable test to the first (see figure 3.4).

So far, much like the before–after design. Where the more complicated version really comes into its own is that it allows further comparison between the different sets of data which considerably strengthens any inferences of a causal nature which you might wish to make. The comparison of one set of pre-test data with the other will reveal the extent to which the two samples are equivalent at the beginning of the research. This is important, since if the two groups are demonstrably equal in the crucial respect, and yet respond differently to different treatments, and if one group moreover is an untreated control, then the case for arguing that the difference is caused by the difference in treatments becomes all the stronger.

One example of a possible situation in which this design could be used might be a project researching the effectiveness of a TV commercial intended to promote increased awareness of the need for economic aid to countries in the Third World. The research would require two samples to be formed by allocating the members of a large sample pool at random to one or other of the two groups. Both groups would be administered a test designed to measure their attitudes to a range of Third World development issues. One group would then be required to watch TV for an evening, during which the commercial would be shown a number of times, while the other group, would watch a different TV channel which did not show the commercial. Subsequently both groups would be tested again to determine whether attitudes to Third World issues had changed. If a difference should be found at this point then, providing the two groups were virtually indistinguishable at the start of the research, the conclusion might be drawn that viewing the commercial had indeed caused a shift in attitudes. However, as with all survey research it would be necessary to exercise considerable caution in drawing any firm conclusion about the possible cause of the results.

This design can also be used to explore the effects of the same treatment applied to two (or more) groups who differ from each other in some way before the treatment is applied. The post-treatment measures then enable an

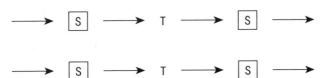

Figure 3.5   A version of the before-after design, in which identical treatment is applied to two initially different groups

assessment to be made of whether the initial difference between the groups has reduced or increased. Figure 3.5 illustrates this second version of the design.

An application of this version of the design might be in a project to investigate the effectiveness of pre-examination relaxation training (to help control the symptoms of anxiety) on performance in an examination, where it was thought that the effectiveness of the training might depend on whether a person was generally highly anxious or not. Following the completion of a test to measure levels of anxiety, the initial sample could be divided into high and low anxiety groups and both groups given training in relaxation techniques. They would subsequently take an examination, the results of which could be used to decide whether the level of pre-training anxiety influenced the later effectiveness of the relaxation training.

The Sampling Process

In this section of the chapter we review the main methods of putting together a sample from a population.

The key distinction between probabilistic and non-probabilistic (purposive) sampling is used as a basis for discussion of the different methods.

The concept of 'sampling error' is introduced and two important sources of this form of error are discussed.

As we have already seen, the function of a sample is to 'stand in' for a much larger but generally inaccessible population of individuals, which forms the real focus of interest of research. Clearly, the extent to which a researcher is able to draw inferences about a population on the basis of a sample is limited by the extent to which it can be claimed that the sample is the same as the population in all significant respects – is representative of the population. No matter how large the sample, or how carefully the data are collected, at the end of the process, if the sampling has produced a sample which is wildly different from the population, most of the effort will have been wasted.

The main aim in obtaining a sample, then, is to try to ensure as far as possible that the sample is an accurate reflection of the population, so that inferences made about the sample can be validly generalized to the population. This involves two issues, one of lesser moment, and one of absolutely vital significance to effective sampling. The lesser matter concerns getting the right sized sample; the vital issue concerns getting the right individuals in the sample.

Sample size

As far as sample size is concerned, bigger is generally better. All other things being equal, the larger the size of the sample that is taken from a population, the greater the likelihood that the sample will accurately reflect the population as a whole. The reason for this is straightforward. Every population will almost certainly contain a number of people who, if sampled, will contribute extreme values to the data. In a large sample, the effect of any extreme values is buried within the mass of more moderate data values. If, on the other hand, a very small sample is taken the presence of extreme values will exert considerably more influence on the overall picture presented by the sample data.

You should also know that quite precise calculations can be made of the sample size which is needed for any particular piece of research providing the sample concerned is to be a random one, and this may be necessary, for example, when every individual sampled is a cost to a slim research budget. In such a situation, the aim is usually to try to make sure that the sample is only as large as it needs to be to achieve the research goals.

The decision on sample size in these cases can be made by consulting specially prepared tables. These give the size of sample needed to achieve any given level of sampling error for a range of confidence levels, and though they are outside the scope of this book can be found in more specialist texts on statistics and sampling theory. As a general rule of thumb when trying to estimate a proportion, say the proportion of left-handed adults in Huddersfield, a random sample of 100 will yield a sampling error of 10% at the 95% 'confidence interval'. In plain English this means that if you take a sample of 100 people you can be 95% certain (or more precisely, the probability is $p = 0.95$) that the proportion obtained will be within ±10% of the proportion which *would* have been obtained had you been able to collect data from the entire population. Thereafter, each halving of the sampling error requires a quadrupling of the sample size, so to be 95% certain that your data came within ±5% of the population values you would need a sample of 400, while to ensure a sampling error of no more than 2.5%, would need a sample of 1600 people. (Note: the concept of 'confidence interval' is mentioned in more detail in the section below on sampling error. Details of how sampling error can be estimated in the case of random samples can be found in chapter 8.)

Sampling methods

As a glance through any specialist text on the survey method will show, there are approximately thirty different ways of putting together a sample. Some of them are rarely used except in particularly problematic sampling situations. For more routine sampling tasks you only need to know about a much smaller set of sampling techniques.

There are two basic types of sample: the probability sample and the purposive sample:

A probability sample is a sample in which every individual has a known probability (between $p = 0$ and $p = 1$) of being included in the sample. Clearly, it is only possible to achieve this if the total number of individuals in a population is known, and all are accessible to the researcher. In practice, this means that it is necessary to be in possession of an exhaustive sampling 'frame' (about which more is said below) which lists all the individual members of the population.

A purposive sample is a sample in which the probability of any individual in the population being included is either $p = 1$, or (the more likely case) unknown. This method can be used whenever the size of the population is very large, or when there would be difficulties in accessing all the members of the population.

The sampling frame

Before we look at some of the specific methods of obtaining a sample, we need to clarify the idea of the sampling 'frame', since it is fundamental to the process of probability sampling, and hence to the problem of obtaining a representative sample. A sampling frame can be defined as a list of all the units of the population from which a sample will actually be drawn. Its function, therefore, is to identify all the individuals who potentially may be included in an eventual sample.

At its simplest a sampling frame will consist of the list of the individuals in a population from whom the sample will be taken. If the population is small or clearly defined, such a list may actually exist to be used by the researcher. For example, the membership list of a particular club, or a class register, might be used as the sampling frame for constructing samples from those particular populations. Sampling frames like these are called 'exhaustive sampling frames' since they contain an exhaustive enumeration of the members of the population.

The basic requirement for probability sampling is that there should exist a sampling frame for the population, and this is relatively easy if the population is defined by membership of some organization. Often though, a researcher finds that it is not possible to identify all the members of a population so easily. For example, if one wished to construct a sample from the population of people who had recently divorced (say within the last year), then the sampling frame would consist of a list of all the names of all such people. However, no such list exists, and though one could in theory be constructed from the scattered records of the divorce courts, in practice the exercise would be prohibitively expensive. And this is also true of many of the populations which a researcher may wish to sample.

In such cases, some method has to be used which will enable the researcher to get round the lack of a detailed sampling frame, and some of the possible approaches are described below.

Probability sampling methods

Four methods of obtaining a probability sample are described below. They are:

- **The simple random sample**
- **The systematic sample**
- **The stratified random sample**
- **Multistage cluster sampling.**

Random sampling: the simple random sample

Random sampling provides the 'gold standard' of sampling procedures against which all other procedures can be compared, since it is essential to use this procedure if you want to obtain a sample which bears a precisely known relationship to the population from which it came. It is also, as will become clear in chapter 5, essential to the ability to draw causal inferences about the relationship of variables in an experiment.

A random sample is a sample taken from a defined population in such a way that:

1   Every individual in the population has an known chance of being included in the sample. This means, of course, that there must be an exhaustive sampling frame listing every individual in the population, since if the size of the population is not known, the probability of any individual being included in the sample cannot be known either.
2   The inclusion of each member of the sample is a wholly independent event – placing any individual in the sample must not influence the placing of any other individual in the sample. Some form of standardized procedure must therefore be used to construct the sample, such as drawing names from a hat, or better, by using tables of random numbers. (See appendix 5 for a table of random numbers and a description of their method of use.)
3   In addition, the variable which is to be sampled must be known, or at least be assumed, to be evenly distributed throughout the population.

Taking a simple random sample

To take a simple random sample, you firstly need a complete sampling frame for the population of interest. If this is not available, it will not be possible to take a true random sample, although an alternative method may provide a sample which approaches randomness. Secondly, you also need to know how large a sample you wish to take from the population, since without this information you will not know when to stop sampling.

As an example suppose you wish to take a simple random sample of 20 from a class of psychology students, which happens to number exactly 50 individuals. The sampling frame for the population will thus contain a list of all the 50 names of the people in the class:

Class list containing 50 individuals

Name			Number	Name			Number
Freud	#		1	Gregory	#		26
Hilgard			2	Bem			27
Festinger	#	$	3	Woodworth		$	28
Binet			4	Thorndike	#		29
Skinner	#		5	Pavlov	#		30
Adler	#		6	Kelly			31
Walster			7	Duck			32
Jung	#	$	8	Maslow	#	$	33
Watson	#		9	Craik			34
Piaget			10	Eysenck	#		35
Aronson			11	Zimbardo			36
Asch			12	Shiffrin	#		37
Newell		$	13	Hubel	#	$	38
Rumbaugh			14	Gardner	#		39
Sperry	#		15	Premack			40
Treisman			16	Hess			41
Hull			17	Klein			42
Laing		$	18	Luria		$	43
Miller	#		19	Spitz			44
Terman			20	Wickelgren	#		45
Wechsler			21	Kluver	#		46
Popper			22	Oswald			47
Fantz		$	23	Gibson	#	$	48
Neisser			24	Wittgenstein	#		49
Postman			25	Dicara			50

= 40% simple random sample
$ = 20% systematic sample

You then proceed as follows:

Step 1   Give each individual in the sampling frame an identifying number as in our class list. Logic suggests that you start with '1' and continue, integer by integer in order, but there is no other reason for doing so. As long as every individual has a different number and you know the range of numbers which is used you can number as you like.

Step 2   Next, consult the table of random numbers of p. 460 in the appendix 5, and starting at any point, and reading in any direction, read off the first 20 pairs of digits which are within the required range, ignoring any which occur more than once, and those outside the range. In this case you need numbers within the range 1–50. So, starting, for example, from the bottom right-hand corner of the table and reading backwards from right to left the first 20 such numbers are:

39, 05, 26, 29, 09, 46, 35, 38, 33, 48, 01, 30, 37, 06, 15, 03, 49, 08, 45, 19

Step 3   Finally, select those individuals identified by the numbers taken from the random number tables, (those with a # beside them in the list of names). These individuals constitute a 40% random sample of the original population of 50.

The advantage of using simple random sampling is that if the procedure is followed conscientiously, it is guaranteed to produce a sample which is likely to be more representative of the population than any other method, and especially likely to be more representative than any sample produced by a non-probabilistic approach. Of course, this isn't the same as saying that a random sample is necessarily perfectly representative. Some degree of sampling error is inevitable in all cases, but if the sample is a random one there is a procedure for estimating how far it is likely to differ from the population. (See chapter 8.)

On the debit side, the obstacle most likely to prevent more widespread use of both random sampling, and its cousin, the systematic sample – see below, lies in the fact that it requires an exhaustive enumeration of all the individuals in the population for the sampling frame. And this, as we have already noted, is not always available.

The systematic sample

Systematic sampling is a simple and straightforward alternative to random sampling which gives results indistinguishable from a random sample as long as the variable of interest is homogeneously distributed throughout the population. Like the random sample it also requires a complete listing of the individuals in the form of an exhaustive sampling frame, but instead of using a table of random numbers the sampling procedure involves drawing individuals at a regular, predetermined interval from the sampling frame.

Taking a systematic sample

Step 1   Determine what proportion of the population is to be included in the sample (also called the sampling fraction). You might, for example, wish to take a 20% sample, using the sampling frame – i.e. the class list – on p. 101 above.

Step 2   Determine the starting place for the sampling. This will be n places from the head of the list where n is a whole number below the larger term in the sampling ratio. In this case, as the sampling ratio is 1:5 (20%), then n must be less than 5, and can be determined by reading the first value in the appropriate range from the table of random numbers in appendix 5. On this occasion, reading from the bottom right of the table gives $n = 3$.

Step 3   Beginning with the third name on the list, then take every fifth name in the list to form a systematic sample of 10 individuals (indicated on p. 101 by a $ against each of the names in the sample).

In many cases systematic sampling is likely to be the method of choice, as it provides a result which is virtually indistinguishable from that obtained from random sampling by a slightly less fiddly procedure. However, if you should elect to use systematic sampling you will need to be alert to the possibility of there being recurring patterns in the sampling frame which will result in a biased sample being produced. It all depends on how the sampling frame has been organized. For example, if a population consists of married couples, and the listing of individuals in a sampling frame is organized by households, then you may find that males alternate with females throughout. If you take a systematic sample of every eighth individual (or any even number) then you will end up with a sample which is completely composed of members of the same sex.

The answer? If you suspect that a sampling frame may contain a recurrent pattern which could bias the sample, you could first randomize the contents of the sampling frame before taking a systematic sample in the usual way, but if you are going to randomize you might as well take a random sample in the first place. An alternative is to choose a sampling interval which does not match the recurrence pattern.

The stratified random sample

As we have seen, the random and systematic sampling methods are really only of use when the population to be sampled is a relatively homogeneous one, at least as far as the variables which are likely to influence the results of the survey are concerned. Often, though, a researcher is faced with the task of sampling from a decidedly non-homogeneous population, in which the individuals making up the population may differ from each other in various ways – by age, by sex, by political attitudes, any of which may influence the data which are to be collected. For example, if a survey is planned on spending habits which doesn't take into account the fact that single, married and divorced people are likely to have different patterns of spending, and different amounts of disposable income, and also that spending patterns vary with age, then the results of the survey may not be at all representative of the population at large. The problem, then, is to find a procedure which can generate a sample which is as closely representative of such a heterogeneous group as possible. This is provided by the technique of stratified sampling.

Use the stratified sampling method when:

- The population to be sampled is heterogeneous with respect to one or more variables which may affect the outcome of the survey.
- There exists an exhaustive sampling frame for the population in question.

The procedure for taking a stratified random sample

Step 1   Decide the variable(s) on which you wish the sample to be stratified. Only those which may be capable of influencing the outcome of the survey need be considered.

Step 2   Identify the sampling frame for the population, and organize it into groups, one for each level of the variables to be stratified. For example, to stratify by age and marital status, you need first to divide the population into married and unmarried people, and then further subdivide each of them into

Box 3.1   A hypothetical population stratified by age

Strata	No. in population	No. placed in sample
15–29 years	3000	300
30–49 years	6000	600
50–69 years	4000	400
70+ years	2000	200
Totals	15000	1500

The third column gives the number of individuals from each stratum who would be placed in the sample if a one in ten sampling fraction had been applied using the random sampling method. Note that the proportion of the population falling into each population stratum is the same as the relationship between each stratum of the sample and the whole sample. For example, people in the 15–29 age group constitute both one fifth of the population, and one fifth of the sample.

a number of different age groups (the same for each). Each of the subdivisions of the population obtained in this way is referred to as a stratum (the plural is 'strata') of the population. Box 3.1 gives an example of such a sampling frame for a hypothetical population.

Step 3   Finally, using the procedure described earlier, take a random sample from each of the strata, applying the same sampling fraction to each. This will have the result of preserving the relative proportions of the different groups in the population into the sample. Note that if any population strata are particularly small relative to the others then a larger sample should be taken than strict proportionality requires in order to deal with the effects such as non-response on the data. If you think this is likely to be a problem for you, consult a specialized sampling text for detailed guidance.

Multistage cluster sampling

If, as is quite likely, a sampling frame is not available, then the technique of multistage cluster sampling can be used. This enables a representative sample to be generated without the need for an exhaustive listing of the population, and it is a useful method to use when, for example, the population is dispersed across a geographical area, but when it is possible to subdivide the population according to some principle or other. These subdivisions constitute the 'clusters' which give the method its name. The basis of the technique is to subdivide the population into a number of relatively large units, then sample from these to obtain a further group of smaller units, and so on, until the level of individual respondents who will make up the final sample is reached.

One way in which clustering can occur is if the population to be sampled consists of members of some kind of formal group which is structured into several different layers of organization. All that is necessary for cluster sampling is that the different layers of organization form a hierarchy, so that each higher level includes all those at the lower levels. This enables cluster sampling to dispense with the need for an exhaustive sampling frame containing the entire population. Instead, all that is necessary is for the researcher to be able to construct an exhaustive sampling frame for each level or cluster. Because each higher level cluster contains all those at a lower level, all that is necessary is to move down through the clusters, sampling as you go. For example, many groups, such as trade unions, and many clubs and societies possess different levels of organization which run from the national level through regional, county, city or town levels to the individual branches and the grass-roots members. Cluster sampling is able to exploit this hierarchical organization to get around the fact that an exhaustive sampling frame of members may not exist.

The procedure for taking a multistage cluster sample

Step 1   Identify the progressively smaller set of subgroups into which the population can be divided, and compile an exhaustive sampling frame for the top level (largest) groups.

Step 2   Using the simple random sampling technique, obtain from the largest groups a sample of clusters at the next level down: compile an exhaustive sampling frame for the clusters at the next level down, and sample again: repeat this process until the level of individual respondents is reached.

Step 3   Use random sampling from the groups on the lowest level to compose the final sample of respondents.

For example, the multistage cluster technique could be used in order to develop a sample of 11- to 16-year-old school students. In this case, to reach the individuals in the population to be sampled it is necessary to take into account the layers of organization in the education system, and sample from each of a series of clusters which include the Local Education Authorities, schools, and classes before arriving at individual schoolchildren. (See box 3.2 below.)

This example also illustrates the important point that, in practice, the sampling frame probably defines the nature of the population which is to be sampled just as much as the other way round. This is because the sampling frame lists only those members of the population actually known to qualify for the sample. There may also be many other individuals who would qualify for inclusion in the sample, but whose existence is not known, and who therefore lie outside the scope of the research. In the example above, the sampling can include only those individuals who are registered at schools in the state system. Chronic non-attenders, those unknown to their LEA, and those attending fee-paying schools are therefore excluded, and this consequently limits the conclusions which may be drawn from the research.

As you have probably also realized, an important decision in cluster sampling concerns the question of how many elements to sample at each stage of the process. How many Local Education Authorities, for example, should one

---

Box 3.2   *Constructing a multistage cluster sample*

Population   British schoolchildren aged 11–16 (state system only)
Sampling frame   List of Local Education Authorities, lists of schools within selected Authorities, lists of forms (classes) within selected schools, and lists of children within selected forms.

Sampling procedure

Step 1   Take a random sample of LEAs
Step 2   Take a random sample of schools from each LEA in the sample
Step 3   Take a random sample of forms from within each school sampled
Step 4   Take a random sample of pupils aged 11–16 from each of the forms.

---

sample in order to ensure that the final result is a sample of individuals which is representative of the population? If it is too large, the final sample may be unmanageably enormous, while if it is too small, the claim to representativeness of the final sample may be in doubt. It turns out that the answer is straightforward. The best chance of obtaining a representative sample which is also of the desired size by the end of the cluster sampling process is to make the early samples (those from the most inclusive groups in the population) as large as possible, and then to allow them to become smaller as the sampling approaches the actual individuals who are to be the members of the final sample.

Non-probabilistic sampling methods

Non-probabilistic sampling is a way of getting around the difficulty posed by not being able to specify exactly how many individuals there are in a population. These are, with the exception of quota sampling, much weaker sampling methods than those discussed above, since they are unlikely to produce a representative sample, neither is it possible to estimate the extent to which the sample is not representative. However, despite these drawbacks, in many cases they may offer the researcher's only possibility of obtaining a sample of any kind. The four basic types of non-probabilistic sampling are:

- **Quota sampling**
- **Judgemental sampling**
- **Opportunity sampling**
- **Volunteer sampling.**

Quota sampling

Quota sampling is a technique which can be used when the aim is to sample from a heterogeneous population for which no exhaustive sampling frame exists. The basic idea is that a representative sample can be obtained without recourse to an exhaustive sampling frame if the population can be subdivided on one or more variables, and if the subdivisions constitute known proportions of the population, and if these relationships are preserved within the sample taken from each subdivision. Thus, to take a simple example, if a population is known to be made up of 55% females and 45% males, then the proportion of males and females in the final samples are also required to be 55% and 45% respectively. Note, though, that like the stratified sample, the quota sample is representative of the population only in relation to the variable on which the population is initially divided.

Where quota sampling differs from stratified sampling is in the nature of the sampling process itself. Whereas stratified sampling is probabilistic and requires an exhaustive sampling frame and objective sampling method of selecting individuals for inclusion in the sample, quota sampling is non-probabilistic. This is because the researcher is aiming to obtain data from fixed numbers of individuals (the 'quotas') who possess certain characteristics, and will make decisions about which individuals to include in the sample on the basis of whether they possess those characteristics, rather than by applying a fixed procedure, as in probabilistic sampling. The probability of any particular individual being included in a sample obtained by the quota method therefore cannot be known.

The procedure for taking a quota sample

Step 1   Decide the variable or variables on which the sample is required to be representative of the population, and determine what proportions of the population fall into each of the different categories which are to be used.

For example, if a population is to be quota'ed on the basis of income, then the population would need to be divided into several income levels and the proportion of the population falling into each level found. This might give the result in the table in box 3.3 below.

Step 2   Decide the desired final sample size, and determine the quota for each category in the sampling frame. Thus, in the example in box 3.3, 33% of the population have an income of between £15,000 and £19,999. If the total sample required is to consist of 200 individuals, then the quota for the £15,000–19,999 income group will be 33% of 200 – or 66 individuals. Similarly the quota for the £5000–9999 income group will be 20 individuals.

Step 3   Finally, sample from the population using one of following non-probabilistic procedures until each quota is filled.

Judgemental sampling

Judgemental sampling simply involves the application of the researcher's judgement or expert knowledge to decide which members of a population should be taken into the sample.

As an example, to form a sample of 11- to 16-year-olds, by the judgemental

---

Box 3.3   *Proportions of a hypothetical population falling into five income groups*

	Income group	Percentage of the population in each group
1	£0– 4,999	5
2	£5,000– 9,999	10
3	£10,000–14,999	12
4	£15,000–19,999	33
5	£20,000+	43

---

sampling method would mean a researcher using judgement (guessing or esti-mating) about whether any particular individual in the population was aged between 11 and 16, rather than by checking birth certificates or similar official records. This means that only the researcher's subjective judgement about who is aged under 11 or over 16 determines who is included in the sample rather than the objective facts, and the chances of obtaining a sample which is at all representative therefore depend on how that judgement is exercised. The prob-lem of the unrepresentative nature of the samples obtained by this method is often exacerbated by combining the judgemental approach with opportunity sampling.

Opportunity sampling

An opportunity sample simply consists of those individuals who are willing to take part in the research at the time that the sample is being put together, and thus consists only of people who are able to take the opportunity to be in the sample when it is offered. The usual method of putting together an opportunity sample is simply to ask members of the population whether they would like to participate in the research.

Volunteer sampling

Volunteer sampling is the form of sampling which occurs when a researcher accepts into the sample those individuals who have volunteered to take part in the research in response to an advertisement or a similar invitation.

The important point about volunteer samples is that they are self-selected. They reverse the usual roles compared to other forms of sampling since, in-stead of the researcher approaching each individual in order to ask them to be in the sample, the volunteer instead approaches the researcher and asks to be included. For this reason, it is generally accepted that the members of self-selected samples are likely to be significantly different in personality and atti-tudes from the general population. Clearly, you need to be extremely cautious about generalizing from a self-selected sample to the general population since its members may not be representative of any population other than the (ill-defined) population of volunteers.

Sampling decisions

Clearly, in the process of planning a survey you are required to make a decision about which sampling method should be used. But which to choose? The first consideration is that some methods require specific conditions to be present before they can be used – the requirement of an exhaustive sampling frame for random sampling is an example: these requirements have all been mentioned already, and do not need to be gone through again.

Beyond this, you may find the following checklist helpful in arriving at a decision. Remember that the aim is always to arrive at a sample which is as representative as circumstances allow – and that this very often may be less representative (or at least less demonstrably representative) than you would like.

1 Do you have an exhaustive sampling frame? If not, you will have to forget about random or systematic sampling, but quota sampling may be an alternative option. If you can, you subdivide the population into known proportions on some variable.
2 Consider what resources of time/money/assistance are available to support you in the sampling process. In general the probabilistic methods require more resources, and this also needs to be taken into account when research is being planned.
3 Be clear about how important it is to your research that you should be able to show that your sample is representative of the population of interest. If you don't need to be able to show this beyond reasonable doubt, then you may not need to use a probabilistic sampling technique. For some purposes, even non-probabilistic samples can be plausibly be argued to be representative of a population (see, for example, Milgram, 1963).

This last point is particularly important for psychologists to consider, since their research often requires sampling from a population which is both of unknown size, but extremely large, and widely dispersed, for example, the population consisting of people in general. In such cases, there may be little alternative to using one of the non-probabilistic methods such as opportunity sampling.

The important point to bear in mind is not that the use of non-probabilistic sampling methods should be avoided, but that one should always be conscious of the limitations which such techniques place on the inferences which can be drawn from the data. A sample which bears an unknown relation to its parent population cannot provide a secure basis for confident generalizations about the population at large. It may be possible to make some generalizations, but these should always be cautiously drawn, and hedged about with qualifications about the (possibly) unrepresentative nature of the sample.

Sampling error

It is inevitable that any sampling process, no matter how carefully carried out will always result in a sample which is less than perfectly representative of the population. To put it another way, one can say that no matter what sampling method is used, sample data, will always differ to some degree from the values which would have been obtained had it been possible to sample the entire population. The value of the mean of a sample, for example, will always differ to some degree from the mean of the population from which it came. This difference, which is due to **sampling error**, comes from two main sources; the sampling process itself, and from the problem of non-response.

Error due to sampling

Error due to sampling arises simply from the fact that any sampling method (except in one special case) is always unable to generate a sample which reflects exactly the characteristics of the population from which it came. There will always be some degree of difference, and one of the main tasks of the researcher who undertakes a survey is to try to figure out as exactly as possible just what magnitude of error is likely to be present in the data. (The special case is, of course the case of the 100% sample, where the entire population is sampled, and thus the representative character of the sample is guaranteed.) Apart from this, even random sampling will result in a sample which is unrepresentative of its population to some degree, though not to anything like as great an extent as that obtained by any of the non-probabilistic methods.

Where non-probabilistic methods are used the extent of error can never be more than the subject of guesswork, but in those cases where sampling has been random it is possible for a researcher to use the sample data, to identify the range of values – called the **confidence interval** – within which a population parameter, such as the mean would be likely to lie. This means that the difference between sample and population can be characterized quite precisely, and therefore that it is possible for a researcher to know how representative of its parent population any data might be. More information on how to determine the confidence interval from a random sample can be found in the section on parameter estimation in chapter 8.

Systematic error due to non-response

The design and interpretation of survey data has also to take into account the fact that not all those people who are originally selected for a sample will eventually contribute data. Refusal to participate in the survey, or simple difficulties in contacting every member of the sample, may make it unlikely that information will be collected from a full sample in any but quite rare cases. Even if all possible measures are taken to include all intended members of a sample, a non-response rate of around 25 per cent can be expected, and the response rate can slide even lower in particularly difficult environments.

To some extent, this can be corrected by taking a larger sample which allows for the possibility of a given level of non-response. If the aim is to collect data from a sample of 100, then selecting an initial sample of 125 individuals will be likely to result in around 100 sets of data, given a non-response rate of 25 per cent. However, such a strategy, although it keeps the numbers straight, does little to address the fundamental problem of non-response, namely the bias which it may introduce into the data. Basically, the problem is that even if a sample of the desired size is obtained by the compensating procedure mentioned above, the data obtained will still not be the same as they would have been if the non-responders had been included. And, to make matters worse, it is not possible to say with any precision how they differ or by how much. All that can be said is that non-responders are probably rather different from people who do respond. It is known, for example, that they tend to be working class rather than middle class, but there may be a whole range of other important, but barely recognized, differences between the two groups.

The existence of non-responders carries important implications for the integrity of the sample, since the greater the extent of non-response, the less likely it will be that the sample is actually representative of the population. And over-sampling (that is taking a larger sample than is needed in the expectation of non-response) really only compounds the problem, since it just ensures that you have a larger group of responding individuals, and not a smaller group of non-responders.

The best solution is to try to find ways of reducing the proportion of non-responders in a sample to as close to zero as is practicable. Persuasion and simple persistence can often be effective, but it is as well to recognize from the outset that this will not be successful in every case, as some proportion of non-responding is always inevitable.

An additional strategy, which can be run alongside the previous approach is to try to find out the nature of the bias introduced by non-responding. If this can be determined, then there are statistical techniques, (for which you will need to consult a specialist text on sampling), which allow sample data to be corrected to allow for the non-responders. For example, if social class is thought to be a variable relevant to the survey, then it would clearly be important to know what the social class of non-responders might be in order to gauge what their effect on the sample data would have been if they had been included. In Britain, at least, social class can be estimated with a fair degree of accuracy from residential address so it might be possible to determine the social class of non-responders from their addresses and the sample data could then be corrected to allow for those individuals who had not actually contributed data.

Data Collection by Questionnaire and Attitude Scale

In this section we review the tasks involved in putting together a questionnaire. A process for generating questions is described in detail.

The main types of question are identified and explained, and examples are provided.

Some important aspects of question design are explained, including the avoidance of bias, and the need to use clear language. Types of question which should be particularly avoided are also identified.

The task of putting a set of questions together to form a questionnaire is addressed, and an outline structure is given.

The concepts of reliability and validity of survey instruments are explained, and the main types of reliability and validity are described.

Two of the most commonly encountered forms of data gathering instrument in psychology surveys are the questionnaire and the attitude scale.

The **questionnaire** is the basic research tool in the social sciences which is capable of being tailored to the demands of almost any research topic. In psychology, it can be used to elicit information on almost any aspect of a participant's attitudes, behaviour, beliefs or experience. It may be helpful to see questionnaires as belonging to two different types. One type is the exploratory questionnaire which is wide-ranging, but relatively shallow. This might be used when the researcher is trawling for information during the early stages of a project when the precise shape of a problem has still to be discovered. The other is used for more in-depth data gathering, and takes a deep, but relatively narrow approach. This type can be used when a researcher's intention is to gather data in detail about some specific question.

At its simplest a questionnaire is no more than a list of questions to which answers are being sought. However, to ensure that misunderstandings or ambiguities in the questioning are reduced to a minimum, and to enable data to be compared across the members of a sample, a number of different ways of presenting questions have been developed, and these are described below.

An **attitude scale** is a rather specialized version of the questionnaire which is used where the intention is to measure the strength with which one or more attitudes are held. This type of instrument is thus intended for a quite different purpose from the general questionnaire, and this means that a somewhat different approach also needs to be taken to putting one together.

We'll begin by considering first the process involved in putting together a questionnaire. More information on the 'Likert method' of attitude scale construction will be given later.

Questionnaire Construction

Survey research possesses an uncomfortable feature which should be borne in mind by every questionnaire designer from the very start of the process. It is that when you administer a finished questionnaire to an informant, it may (and probably will) be your one and only opportunity to collect data from that person. Unlike in an experiment, where a researcher can relatively easily detain a subject until certain that the data are as good as the experimental procedure can make them, in a survey, where perhaps the questionnaires are taken away and completed by respondents in private, this is not an option.

The guiding principle, therefore, is that you have to be as sure as possible at that point that the questionnaire is complete – in the sense that it answers all the questions which you would like answered – and also clear and concise, so that the possibility of your respondent failing to understand what a question requires is as close to zero as possible.

The process of questionnaire construction can be divided into the following sequence of steps, which we'll look at in turn:

- **Generating a preliminary set of questions**
- **Refining the raw ideas into questionnaire items**
- **Organizing the items into an appropriate sequence to form the questionnaire**
- **Testing the questionnaire by means of a pilot study, and evaluating the result.**

Generating a preliminary set of questions

This part of the process of questionnaire design involves generating a preliminary body of questions or, more tenuously, ideas about what questions it might be worthwhile or interesting to ask. These preliminary thoughts about what directions the research may take need not be very precise or very carefully worked out – they are worked into finished questions only at the next stage of the process.

The main aim at this point is to try to get lots of ideas – the more the better. The technique of brainstorming can be helpful if you feel you suffer from an ideas block at this point. The important thing is to develop as many angles on the research question as you can. It doesn't matter if, when you have a closer look at them, some are discarded. This is inevitable. It is equally certain that you will have many usable ideas as well.

As an example of the way this initial process might go, suppose a psychologist is researching the factors affecting the relationship between married couples during the first year of their marriage, and has decided to use a questionnaire in order to explore the factors which affect the stability of marriages during that first year.

The first task is to identify questions or topics or ideas which appear to be related to the question of the stability of the marriage, and which could be turned into questionnaire items. What kinds of issue might be relevant to this question and could be used in order to assess the relationship?

Obviously, there are a great number of possibilities here, but the range of ideas which might be generated at this stage of the process might include questions about such matters as:

- The way in which disagreements are managed in the relationship
- The partners' subjective perceptions of the stability of their relationship (i.e. how they feel about it)

- How critical issues such as money and friendships with people outside the marriage are managed within the relationship
- The amount of time which each partner spends away from the other, and the reasons for this
- The partners' attitudes to divorce
- Whether either partner is violent towards the other.

and so on.

Having generated an initial list go through the cycle again: take each idea on the first list and try to break it down into a set of smaller, more precise questions, which look more like the kind of question you might find in an actual questionnaire. The purpose in this is partly to do some work towards the final questionnaire, but mainly it is to ensure that each idea or issue has been looked at in as much detail as possible before you get to the questionnaire design stage.

As an example, you can probably see that each of the ideas listed above suggests a range of further, more specific questions which could be asked. For example, the first item on the list above deals with disagreements in a relationship, and it might well be useful to the research to inquire further on some of the specific features of marital disagreements, such as:

- How frequent are disagreements?
- What are the disagreements usually about?
- How are disagreements normally settled?
- How long do disagreements generally last?
- How much bad feeling do disagreements cause?
- Does the acrimony linger after the disagreement has been settled?

Note that at this stage, these are simply ideas for questionnaire items, not the items themselves. These will emerge during the next stage of the process.

Refining raw ideas into questionnaire items

Having generated a pool of ideas which seem, on the surface at least, to be relevant to the research question, the next step is to begin to construct the questionnaire by discarding the topics or ideas which are not to be used as a basis for questions.

The key criterion here is the intended range and size of the questionnaire. Questionnaire research is most effective when it is used to obtain relatively precisely defined information about a fairly restricted range of topics or issues. It is better to ask carefully designed and quite detailed questions about a few precisely defined issues than the same number on a wide range, or, worst of all, a very large number of questions on a very wide range of topics.

You therefore need to sift through the list of possible issues in order to identify those which are central to your research concerns, and those which are more peripheral. And it may not always be apparent which these are until you begin to do it. The process of designing the research instrument is also part of the wider process of defining the precise focus of the research: you may find that your ideas about your research project change quite significantly at this point as you begin to look closely at the ideas you have generated. Don't forget, also, that you can always follow up with another questionnaire to cover any untouched topics on another, later, occasion. You could also follow up the questionnaire with some interviews designed to fill in the details already obtained.

For example, from the first list above, you might decide that on this occasion, the question of marital disagreements was the area of primary interest to your research. You would therefore aim to design the questionnaire in order to collect data on this specific question (with possibly a few questions included in order to explore one or two side issues, such as, perhaps friendships outside the marriage). The remaining ideas, which are not to be used, now go back 'on hold' in the ideas file for later consideration.

Having identified the specific issues and ideas which are to be the subject of the questionnaire, the task is now to turn them into a set of finished questions. The involves two parallel processes which take place together: the formulation of precise questions from the raw ideas already identified at the previous stage and simultaneously identifying an appropriate format for each. We now turn to consider the range of formats which are available to the questionnaire designer.

Question formats

It is important to choose the right format for each question. This depends partly on the nature of the question and on the kind of information which is sought, and partly on the characteristics of the sample on which it is to be used. The main distinction to bear in mind in question design is between open and closed questions.

Closed questions   Closed questions, which provide the backbone of most questionnaires, are questions in which the range of possible responses to a question is completely determined by the researcher: respondents are simply required to select one from a range of the possible answers. For example:

Q1   *Which sex are you?*   *Male   Female*
      (tick to indicate)
Q2   *How old are you? (tick to indicate)*   *20–29 years*
                                                 30–39 years
                                                 40–49 years
                                                 50–59 years
                                                 60 years or older

Asking people to underline or tick the item which applies to them is generally more reliable than asking them to indicate those answers which do not apply. Note that the identical form of response, (ticking an item from a list) is required in both cases. It is good design practice to use, as far as possible, a single standard form of responding throughout the questionnaire. This minimises any possibility of inaccurate answering due to the respondent having been confused by the different requirements of by different questions.

Closed questions are best used for collecting straightforward factual information such as details of the age, sex, or the marital status of a respondent, or for establishing baseline data on behaviour which can later be explored using more open ended questions (see below). For example, a closed question directed towards establishing some baseline information about marital disagreement might be,

Q3   Do you remember the first occasion when you had a serious disagreement with your partner?   *(tick one)*

Yes/No

If so, what was it about?   *Sharing of household tasks*
(tick one only)   *My personal habits*
                              Partner's personal habits
                              Partner's attitude to my family
                              Partner's attitude to my friends
                              My attitude to partner's family
                              My attitude to partner's friends
                              Money
                              None of these

Closed questions possess a number of useful features. They are straightforward and quick to answer, lie within the intellectual reach of the majority of the population, the answers are easy to code and analyse, and can readily be compared with each other across different respondents. For these reasons closed questions are likely to form the majority on a questionnaire when the need is to get a limited amount of information from a large number of people in a short time. Market research interviewing, or opinion polling at general election time are two such situations which rely largely on closed questioning as the main ingredient in their research. A number of specific forms which closed questions can take are described below. However, the amount of information which such questions can elicit is rather limited, and in most situations they will need to be supplemented by a range of open-ended questions which enable more varied and more individual answers to be collected.

Open-ended questions Open-ended questions are those which do not limit the nature of the response in any way. A question is asked and the respondent is simply provided with a space in which she can answer in her own words. Thus as a follow-up to Q3 above, a questionnaire might offer the following open-ended question:

Q4   Describe in the space below the specific event which precipitated that disagreement. If you can't remember, or if there was no such specific event, please say so.

_____

_____

_____

Open-ended questions like this enable a respondent to answer a question wholly in her own words rather than having them provided for her. This brings both rewards and costs. On the one hand, it may mean that a more precise and personal response can be obtained than if the closed form of question had been used. On the other hand, the answers provided to open-ended questions may be difficult to analyse in any neat and tidy fashion. Because people are free to answer in their own words, the range of possible responses is infinitely wide, and this needs to be taken into account when planning the data analysis.

This type of question also assumes that respondents all possess the ability to express themselves reasonably fluently in writing, and this may or may not be the case. Those who are not able to do so may not be able to complete the open-ended questions, and this will cause uneven sampling. In any case there will almost certainly be wide differences between individual responses, with some respondents writing extremely terse or single-world responses, and others writing several sentences, or more. Again, these matters need to be taken into account when planning the data analysis.

More designs for closed questions

In addition to the closed question forms already mentioned, the following can also be used:

Checklists   A checklist is a variation on the basic form of closed question in that it presents of a range of possible answers, but instead of requiring the selection of a single possible answer the respondent is invited to choose as many of the options as may apply. For example:

Q5   The following is a list of common leisure-time pursuits. Place a tick against any that you have carried out with your partner during the past week.
Gardening or DIY   Watching TV   Reading
Visiting friends   Going for a drive   Entertaining at home
Participating in sport or fitness activity   Shopping
Going to pub or restaurant

Rankings   Ranking-style questions enable more information to be obtained from a checklist, since rather than simply select from a list of possibilities, the informant is also required to place them in a rank order. This means that information on the relationships among the different options, in terms of preference, frequency or some other variable, can be collected. Thus:

Q6   Here is a list of some possible causes of disagreements in marriage. Place a 1 against whichever seems to you to be the most frequent cause of your disagreements, a 2 against the next most frequent, and so on. If you feel that two (or more) of the items are equally frequent, give them the same number.
  Please make sure that you number all the possibilities in the list.
☐ *Sex*   ☐ *Money*   ☐ *In-laws*   ☐ *Holidays*
☐ *Housework*   ☐ *Food*   ☐ *Friends*
☐ *Work outside the home*   ☐ *Political or religious beliefs*
☐ *Possessions*   ☐ *Personal habits*

Graded response questions   Often a questionnaire designer needs to be able to provide a way to enable those people who will be completing the questionnaire to express degrees of magnitude in their answers. For example, it may be desirable to measure degrees of agreement or disagreement, or frequency. There are three types of graded response question which enable this kind of information to be collected:

1   **Attitude statement questions**
2   **Likert-type questions**
3   **Semantic differential type questions.**

Attitude statement questions are those in which the informant is provided with a statement which reflects an attitude to a particular issue or topic and is then invited to select an answer from a continuum which most closely matches to their response to that statement. (This is a further example of the scaled response type of question which is dealt with below.)

Q7   Here is a statement which describes a belief which some people hold about marriage. When you have read it, choose the answer which most closely matches your response to the statement.
'In a marriage, both partners should work equally hard to avoid serious disagreements occurring.'
Do you: Strongly agree   (tick one only)
*   Agree*
*   Neither agree nor disagree*
*   Disagree*
*   Strongly disagree*

Likert-type questions (so named after a mildly famous social psychologist of the inter-war period), are virtually the same as attitude statement questions in structure, except that they include a numerical scale which enables the informant's response to be expressed directly as a numerical value. (More information on the Likert scale is provided later in this chapter.) An example of a Likert-type item would be:

Q8   How close emotionally would you say you are to your partner? Indicate how close you feel you are now by placing an x on the scale below. 1 indicates 'hardly close at all' and 5 indicates 'extremely close'
$$|\_|\_|\_|\_|\_|$$
$$1\ \ 2\ \ 3\ \ 4\ \ 5$$

Scale items such as this can have either an odd (typically 3, 5, 7 or 9), or an even number of points or divisions. Scales with an odd number of points possess a central neutral zone, and depending on the nature of the question, it may be better to use a scale with an even number of divisions so as to provide a 'forced choice' between the two halves of the scale.

Among the advantages of Likert scale questions are the fact that they generate numerical data which can easily be summarized across a sample. However, the presence of numbers can lend a spurious aura of precision to the data. It has to be remembered that the numbers represent subjective assessments of the strength of variables which are essentially unquantifiable, and should be treated as representing measures only on the ordinal scale of measurement.

Semantic Differential type questions use a technique invented by Osgood and his co-workers (Osgood et al., 1957) for providing a way of quantifying feelings, emotions, perceptions and similarly subjective variables which are otherwise difficult to express numerically. All that is required is that a number of dimensions of the target variable are able to be represented by one or more pairs of bi-polar adjectives (that is adjectives which can be regarded as representing the extreme ends of a continuum – see example below). Informants are then asked to identify the position on each of the continuums which best describes their feelings. Each of these can subsequently be represented numerically when the data are analysed.

Q9   Place an X on the scale to indicate how you would describe your relationship with your partner as it is at this moment.

Satisfying	I.......I.......I.......I.......I.......I.......I.......I	*Unsatisfying*
Undemanding	I.......I.......I.......I.......I.......I.......I.......I	*Demanding*
Unstable	I.......I.......I.......I.......I.......I.......I.......I	*Stable*

Language and the questionnaire

It is an obvious point to make, but it is important to ensure that questions are formulated in such a way that, as far as possible, there is no possibility of misunderstanding. The main defect to be found in questionnaires lies in the imprecise wording of the questions which can leave the respondent wondering what you mean, or worse, taking an entirely different meaning from the one intended. You want, ideally, each respondent to extract from each question exactly the same meaning or intention as was in your mind when you formulated the question in the first place. This is far from being the automatic process it can appear to be. Human language offers at best only rather a blunt instrument for conducting research and it is rarely possible to check that the meaning received by the reader of a questionnaire is the same as that intended by its designer.

In everyday life we trade off precision of meaning against a host of other pressures such as the sheer need to keep information moving. And of course we rely on the imprecision and vagueness of language in general to cover our uncertainties and lack of knowledge. However, when it comes to writing the items for a questionnaire you can't allow yourself the luxury of assuming that your meaning will automatically be clear to all respondents. You have to try to ensure that it is, and that means manoeuvring words around until you feel that the meaning you require is absolutely crystal clear on the page. You may feel that this results in questions which sound somewhat stilted and awkward when you read them out, but it is the only way to ensure that any possibility of misinterpretation is reduced to an absolute minimum. It is perhaps stating the obvious to point out that there are special problems of language where a questionnaire is intended for children, non-native speakers of the language, or similar groups. In these cases special attention will need to be paid to the comprehensibility of the language, which should be checked if possible by means of a careful pilot study.

An example of the kinds of problem which our imprecise language can create is people's differing use of words to do with time. Often in doing research one would like to obtain the respondent's estimates of the frequency with which some event occurs, and on occasions this can result in a question which looks like the following:

Q13a   How often do you think that you have disagreements with your partner? (tick one)

> *Never*
> *Seldom*
> *Sometimes*
> *Frequently*
> *Always*

The problem for the questionnaire designer is that one person's 'Seldom' is another person's 'Frequently', and while research has shown that 'Always' is generally interpreted to mean 99–100% of the time and 'Never' 0–1% of the time, between these limits, 'Sometimes' can mean anything between 20% and 46% of the time, and 'Seldom' from 9% to 22% of the time. This makes it very difficult to interpret the results of the questionnaire with any precision: did the respondent who answered 'sometimes' mean 20% of the time, 30% of the time or even more? There is obviously no way of knowing.

The solution in this specific instance is to avoid all such subjectively defined terms and to try to write questions which specify exactly what kinds of time intervals you mean, and avoid vague words as far as possible. The example above is better as:

Q13b   How often do you think that you have disagreements with your partner? (tick one)

> *Once a week or less*
> *Between once a week and once a month*
> *More than once a month*

However, the more general solution, which applies to a whole set of further linguistic problems in questionnaire design is for the researcher to try to develop a more heightened sense of the many pitfalls of meaning that language can contain, and which can result in additional error in the data.

An example is the use of emotionally charged language which, if not removed, may effectively cause a respondent to select one particular response rather than another. Thus:

Q14   How do you think the police should deal with the young thugs and hooligans who currently terrorize the streets?

To obtain a sense of how powerfully such language can affect a person's perception of the meaning of a question, try substituting an innocuous alternative phrase such as 'young people who break the law' in the question above. Notice how the emotional 'tone' of the question changes quite significantly when the emotionally laden words are replaced, so that a moderate and considered response becomes more likely.

Careful attention to the language in which questions are couched can also help with the problem of trying to collect information on topics which may be highly sensitive to some people. Not everyone, for example, is prepared – for perfectly good reasons – to answer questions concerning their sexual relationships or their income or polities, and if a questionnaire contains a direct question on these, or similarly sensitive subjects, it may be ignored by those who prefer not to answer. Worse, such respondents may simply abandon the questionnaire completely, thereby adding to the problem of non-response in the survey.

Clearly, the designer of the questionnaire has to make an important judgement about whether questions which deal with matters so sensitive are really essential to the research. If they can be removed from the questionnaire without making it impossible to achieve the aim of the research, then this should be done, but sometimes this is not an option. In such cases, a way has to be found of presenting the same question in a way which minimizes any possible offence. One way of doing this is to change the 'voice' of the questions from the personal to the impersonal. So, for example the blunt question 'What is your income?', which some people might find a little too direct on a sensitive matter, could be altered to the less stark impersonal form, 'What are average earnings for people who do your job?'.

The problem of positive response bias – the fact that people tend to reply to certain sorts of questions (such as those concerning income) by 'faking good', that is by answering in ways which are calculated to reveal them in the best possible light can also be reduced by using the same strategy.

Questions to avoid

When you are in the process of putting together a questionnaire it is all too easy to concentrate on the intention behind the questionnaire, and to forget how each question may appear to the respondents, and how, in turn, this may affect the answer given. It is all too easy to generate questions which, though they appear unproblematic at first glance, are clearly defective when given a closer inspection. If allowed to remain as they are, such questions will almost certainly causes serious difficulties when the data come to be analysed. The following are three of the more common kinds of defective question which, if found, should always be removed from a questionnaire before it is used.

1 Double-barrelled questions A double-barrelled question is one in which two entirely different issues are merged to form a single item in the questionnaire. This causes confusion, since an informant cannot separate them in order to provide an answer to each. The question may therefore remain unanswered. For example the question:

Q15   Do you think that families are more democratic in their decision making these days, or do you feel that young people need to be given more say in what is decided?

combines into one question the issues of whether families are more democratic than they were with the entirely different question of whether young people should have more say in decision making. The two matters are clearly related, but they each need to be dealt with in separate questions of their own.

2   **Negative questions**   Negative questions are those (perhaps obviously) in which a question is posed in a negative rather than in a positive form. For example:

Q16a   Do you agree that young people today do not have as many pressures to contend with as the young of previous generations?

The positive form of the question is clearer:

Q16b   Do you agree that young people today have fewer pressures to contend with than the young of previous generations?

The difference may appear insignificant, but research has shown that some respondents tend to 'read over' the negative and treat the question as a positive one.

   The best way to deal with this possibility is to try to avoid writing negative questions and since, in general, every negative has positive this should not be too difficult. However, should you feel that you absolutely must write a question in the negative form, you can reduce the probability that the negative part will be ignored by underlining or otherwise trying to make it stand out in some way.

3   **Biased, or leading questions**   These are questions of the 'Have you stopped beating your wife?' variety which require that the assumptions of a question are accepted if an answer is to be given. For example:

Q17   Given that the police always do their best to catch criminals, what do you think is the best way to tackle that increasing level of crime in society?

Sometimes leading statements such as this are inadvertently included in a questionnaire because the question writer wishes to include some important background information for informants, and this somehow becomes mixed up with the question itself. If you feel you absolutely must provide background information before your questionnaire can be answered, this should always be clearly separated from the questions – preferably on a separate sheet of paper. In this way the important distinction between the information you are giving, and that which you are seeking from your informant can be maintained. If you do need to do this, though, you should consider whether you are sampling from quite the right population, and asking the right questions.

   Leading questions can also produce quite unintended effects. In the example above, if an informant felt that the police were not doing a particularly good job, the statement might only cause irritation, and the result might be no answer to that question. The risk of inadvertently including a leading statement can be reduced if all questions are reduced to their essentials.

Some principles of questionnaire design: a summary

To help you avoid some of the more frequently encountered difficulties, linguistic and otherwise, in the design of a questionnaire, the following summarizes the key points which you need to bear in mind when you are putting your questionnaire together. However, it can be difficult to identify all the flaws in one's own work, so if possible have one or two other people read through your questionnaire as well.

1 Keep the language as simple as possible. Check especially for emotional language, ambiguity and technical terms. Remove the first two, and put technicalities into ordinary language unless your questionnaire is intended for respondents who you are certain will have the necessary technical knowledge.
2 Short questions are always better than long ones. Always ask yourself whether a question is likely to be immediately comprehensible to everyone.
3 Check each question for double-barrelled structure, negatives and leading questions.
4 Make sure you have both positive (inviting a 'yes' response) and negative, (inviting a 'no' response) questions in your questionnaire in approximately equal numbers.
5 Consider whether any question asks something the informant may not know. If this is a possibility, embed it in a contingent question so that only those respondents with the necessary knowledge will need to answer.
6 Does the questionnaire deal with sensitive topics, such as income or sexuality, on which is there the possibility of response bias? If so consider whether you have designed the question in a way which maximizes your chance of obtaining an accurate answer.
7 Is the content of all questions likely to be acceptable to all informants? If you think there is any possibility that any question could give offence then it should be examined carefully, removed if possible, and if not, then rewritten.
8 Is the frame of reference of all questions quite clear and explicit? Check that you are not relying on any assumptions about how a particular question will be interpreted – as far as possible make absolutely everything explicit, even when it seems superfluous to do so. This means, for example, that all units of measurement should be clearly stated, as well as the degree of precision expected in an answer.

Putting the questionnaire together

By now you will have developed a set of precise questions which you intend to use in order to carry out your research. The final stage of the process of designing a questionnaire is to put these together to form the questionnaire itself. As you have may already realized, this needs to be done with some particular considerations in mind, and it is helpful, at this stage, to divide a questionnaire into three sections – an introduction, a middle section and a conclusion.

The introduction   The first page of the questionnaire should consist of an introduction which contains the following basic information about the research project in general and the questionnaire. The title of the questionnaire should be given, such as 'Marital stability questionnaire', and this should be followed by a brief paragraph, addressed to the respondent, which explains the general purpose of the research and the nature of the sample, and which requests the respondent's help in completing the research. It is also a good idea to say in broad terms what kind of ground the questionnaire will cover, and roughly how long it will take to complete. This last point is a necessary courtesy because some respondents may not wish to spend very long in answering a questionnaire.

   Finally, since the ethics of psychological research require that all data should be held in confidence, you should provide clear and unequivocal reassurance on the first page that this will be the case.

The middle section   The central section of the questionnaire contains the questions which are to be asked on the substantive research problem. The following simple principles will help you to organize the contents of a questionnaire to maximum advantage:

1   Make the early questions as factual and as non-threatening as possible. Try also to ensure that they have clear relevance to the research topic as you described it in the introductory section.
2   Organize the questions to run from easy ones at the beginning to the more demanding ones. One criterion of this is how much careful consideration you think they will require. Put open-ended questions towards the end of the questionnaire.
3   Try to ensure that there is a sense of connectedness between the different questions – that one question leads smoothly and reasonably logically into another. Above all, avoid jumping backwards and forwards between topics. If you do need to introduce questions on different topics signal that this is about to happen, either by sectionalizing the questionnaire (Section A, Section B, and so on), with a heading which clearly identifies the topic with which each section is concerned, or alternatively by inserting a verbal 'signpost' into the questionnaire which tells the reader clearly that questioning on a new topic is about to be opened. For example, you might say something like, 'Turning now to your relationships with your partner's relatives will you please answer the following questions?'.
4   Save questions on demographic matters, such as age, sex, martial status, and the like to the very end of the questionnaire.

5   Use contingent questions to steer respondents away from questions which they need not answer. They allow specific questions to be targeted on different categories of respondents (such as, for example, on people of particular ages or sexes), without he need for obtaining a separate sample, and designing a new questionnaire, as in the following example:

Q18   How do you believe that your relationship has changed over the past year? (tick one)

> *Has it   Grown more satisfying*
> *Grown less satisfying*
> *Stayed about the same*

If you answered 'Grown more satisfying' to Q18 go on to answer Q19 below. Otherwise skip Q19 and continue with Q20.

Q19   You said in response to Q18 that you feel your relationship has grown more satisfying over the past year. Can you describe any particular ways in which this has occurred?

_____

_____

_____

6   Use as wide a variety of question formats as is appropriate to the research topic, but don't include too many open-ended questions, as informants may find these fatiguing and difficult.
7   Check the length. This will depend of the topic and the nature of the target population, but medium length questionnaires of 30 to 50 items are generally found to be adequate. If you think you need a longer questionnaire consider whether all your questions are really necessary.

The conclusion   The last page of the questionnaire should contain a request that respondents check that hey have answered all the questions. You should also express your thanks to respondents for their help in completing the questionnaire and say how useful the information will be to you. Offer to answer any questions which respondents may have, and say how they can obtain information on the final results of the survey if they wish to do so.

It may seem an obvious point, but it is well worth spending time adjusting the layout of the questionnaire on the page. You will obviously want to avoid cramming the questions together so that it is difficult to tell where one begins and the next ends. Also, your respondent is likely to complain that it is difficult to tell where the answers are supposed to be written, and may lose motivation as a result, with unfortunate effects on the data you collect.

Less obviously, perhaps, it is also a good idea not to space questions out too generously. Too much white space between the questions can be intimidating (informants may believe they are expected to fill it all), and if there are a lot of pages, it may suggest that providing answers will be an unpleasantly lengthy business. Either way, you may find your respondents melting away into the distance when they catch a clear view of your research instrument. Your problem as a questionnaire designer is to find the middle road between the two extremes which will prevent either of the unwanted outcomes from occurring.

In addition, the following ideas may help you to turn out a more effective questionnaire:

1   Print the questionnaire on only one side of the paper – if you use both sides it makes it easier for an informant inadvertently to miss out some questions.
2   Make sure you have left sufficient space for the answers to all the open-ended questions – up to a half a page may be necessary if you anticipate, or want to encourage, relatively lengthy responses.
3   Always list alternatives to an answer down rather than across the page. Listing across makes it harder for informants to pick them out as alternatives.

Testing the questionnaire

Once the first version of a questionnaire has been produced it is essential that it should be subjected to some form of evaluation before it is used to collect data. It is unsafe to assume that because it looks right to you, the questionnaire designer, it will also necessarily be a valid and reliable instrument for use in your research. Of course, it may well be the case that it is both valid and reliable, but you need to try to collect some evidence before you use it on real respondents from whom you wish to collect data.

There are two ways of going about this. The first is to conduct a pilot study to evaluate the questionnaire. This involves taking a very small sample (per-haps amounting to only at most a couple of dozen individuals) from the population on which it is eventually intended to be used, and administering the questionnaire exactly as you would for the main sample. The results of this should provide clear evidence of the extent to which the questions have been fully understood, and responded to appropriately by the members of the pilot sample.

The completed questionnaires are naturally of considerable interest and should be scrutinized carefully to determine whether any signs of misunderstanding or response bias can be identified in the answers. For example, the presence of questions which have not been answered may indicate that the questioning has been insensitive, or if the same individual gives different answers to similar questions it may suggest either that one of the questions was not properly understood, or that an inconsistent answer was given intentionally. If it is possible to arrange debriefing interviews with some of the members of the pilot group then this should also be done. The issues which should be explored in such interviews have already been covered in some detail when we were con-sidering the design and construction of the questionnaire. These include such questions as whether the 'feel' of the questionnaire is acceptable. That is, does it ask questions which are at best on the borderline of acceptability? Are there any particularly sensitive questions which have caused people to not answer, and which therefore need to be removed or revised? Another set of questions might concern the layout of the questionnaire and the order in which the questions have been posed. Is it easy to find a way through the contingent questions? Are the different sections of the questionnaire sufficiently clearly signposted? And of course, are there any questions which are difficult to comprehend?

A pilot study along the lines indicated above is the ideal to be aimed for, and should really be regarded as an essential preliminary to any serious survey work. However, one has to recognize that the full-scale piloting of a questionnaire may not always be possible, and so it may be necessary, for one reason or another, to carry out a rather less exacting programme of evaluation. At its simplest this would mean reducing the sample size down to a single individual. Nevertheless useful information can be obtained from even one person, always providing they are asked the right questions.

You may also wish to set about assessing the reliability and validity of your questionnaire in a more formal way than that discussed above. Information on how this can be done is provided below.

The reliability and validity of survey instruments

Reliability and validity are key concepts in survey research in that they provide the assurance that a questionnaire, or similar instrument, is really capable of providing an accurate and meaningful answer to whichever research question is being pursued.

Validity

The validity of a questionnaire or similar survey instrument concerns the extent to which it is actually capable of providing the information which it claims to provide. A valid questionnaire designed to assess (say) marital stability, would be one which actually does provide true information about marital stability and not about some other aspects of the relationship. In the same way, an invalid questionnaire would be one which claims to measure (say) attitudes to marriage among men, but which actually measures their attitudes to women, which is not the same thing at all.

The important point is that general questions about the validity of a scale or questionnaire are not really meaningful when they are considered in isolation. As well as knowing the subject of the questionnaire, you also need to know which of the different types of validity is being applied as a criterion, and what purpose the data obtained from the questionnaire are intended to serve. Only then is it possible to make a final judgement about whether or not it is a valid instrument.

The types of validity with which the researcher needs to be concerned are:

Criterion-related validity In this form, the validity of a questionnaire or attitude scale is established by comparing the prediction made on the basis of the test instrument with some external criterion. For example, a questionnaire intended to assess the stability of marital relationships during the first year of marriage could be administered to a sample of married couples soon after their wedding, and the results compared to the number of marriages in the sample which broke up before their first wedding anniversary. A valid questionnaire in terms of criterion-related validity would be one which successfully predicted which relationships would end, and which would continue.

Another approach to establishing criterion-related validity is to compare the results of a questionnaire with results obtained from some other established psychometric test or procedure which can be given at the same time as the questionnaire. This form of validity is known as concurrent validity.

Content validity Content validity assesses the content of the questionnaire against its intended purpose or aim. A questionnaire which is intended to assess the stability of friendships will not have validity as an indicator of (say) educational experience, simply because the kinds of questions which need to be asked are quite different from each other. They reflect the entirely different purposes behind their design.

The content validity of a questionnaire or scale is established by checking that the questionnaire items reflect the issues or topics which theory has identified as related in some way to the behaviour which is being investigated.

Construct validity A more precise and refined approach to content validity is construct validity. Essentially, a construct is a concept or an idea. A scale or questionnaire which possess construct validity is one which has been explicitly based on one or more particular theoretical concepts (such as anxiety), so that the individual test items provide measures of the construct in question.

Face validity Face validity is concerned with the extent to which a scale or questionnaire appears to be appropriate for its purpose when viewed by non-psychologists. Ensuring that a research instruments has face validity is a matter of ensuring that in terms of its surface features, it is capable of meeting the sample members' expectations of what a psychological research instrument should look like. This is not at all the trivial issue that it might appear. A research instrument which has face validity may be much more effective in practical terms than one which doesn't simply because respondents perceive it to be appropriate for its task. Such perceptions can markedly affect the willingness of respondents to take part in research.

Reliability

As well as validity, a researcher also needs to be concerned about the reliability of the research instrument which is being used. This is concerned with the extent to which the procedure is capable of returning an accurate result despite the presence of factors which might influence the outcome in one direction or another. So, for example, a reliable questionnaire would be one which is capable of producing the same result when given to the same individuals on different occasions. Its reliability therefore consists of its ability to resist any influences related to the passage of time, such as learning, fatigue, or changes to motivation. There are two main methods of assessing the reliability of a survey instrument:

Test-retest reliability   Test-retest reliability is concerned with the question of whether the scale or questionnaire possesses consistency over time, and is assessed by having the instrument completed by the members of the same sample on two different occasions with a long enough interval between them to prevent remembering from influencing the results. A reliable questionnaire on this measure, will be one in which the same answers are produced on the second occasion as on the first, and this can be expressed numerically by means of a correlation coefficient (see chapter 6).

Internal consistency   The internal consistency of a scale is the extent to which the different items in it can be said to be measuring the same variable, and it can be assessed by means of either the *split-half* or the *alternate form* procedures.

In the split-half procedure, the measuring instrument is divided into two equivalent halves, each is administered separately to the same sample, and the two sets of scores are then correlated with each other. A high correlation between the two halves of the scale indicates that the instrument is internally consistent, since it indicates that a high score on one half of the test predicts a similarly high score on the other half.

The alternate form procedure requires the preparation of two equivalent questionnaires. These are then administered separately to the same sample on different occasions, and the two sets of scores correlated. Again, a high positive correlation between the two sets of scores indicates that the two scales are probably measuring the same variable.

Some of the ethical issues in questionnaire-based research

It might be assumed that apart from the need to ensure basic ethical standards such as the confidentiality of information, doing survey research using a questionnaire or similar pencil and paper instrument is, in terms of research ethics a largely unproblematic activity. It seems reasonably certain, for example, that respondents are not likely to be subjected to the kinds of situational pressures which can occur when some of the alternative research methods are employed.

Though largely true, the survey is not quite as ethically straightforward as it might appear. In particular the possible effect on respondents of asking questions of certain kinds needs to be considered quite carefully when the survey is being designed. Research has shown, for example, that even answering an apparently innocuous questionnaire on personal relationships can generate effects which carry over into those relationships.

Rubin and Mitchell (1976), conducted a survey on the development of relationships between dating couples, and as part of the research respondents were also asked whether they felt that answering the questionnaire had any effect on their relationship. Half the couples said that it had. It appears that one unintended effect of completing the questionnaire (which most couples had discussed together), was to highlight areas of difference and potential conflict, and thus, in some cases, to accelerate the process of breaking up.

The moral to be drawn from this is that it cannot be assumed that completing a questionnaire is a simple on–off activity which has no consequences beyond the completion of the instrument. People are open to all kinds of influences on their behaviour, including the items in a questionnaire, and the researcher has an obligation to take this fact into account in the design of any research instrument.

Constructing an Attitude Scale by the Likert Procedure

The collection of information on attitudes requires the use of an attitude scale rather than the general form of questionnaire which has been discussed so far.

This section explains how to construct an attitude scale using the Likert procedure.

The Likert procedure (Likert, 1932), named after a prominent social psychologist of the 1930s and 40s, is commonly used for the construction of attitude scales – paper and pencil instruments for measuring the strength of attitudes and beliefs.

Attitude scales

The basis of an attitude scale is an attitude statement. This is a statement which is relevant to the attitude which is to be measured and with which a person who holds that attitude can be expected to agree (or disagree). For example, a (hardhearted) statement which is relevant to the attitude to people suffering from AIDS might be:

AIDS sufferers have only themselves to blame for their condition.

People who are knowledgeable about the causes of AIDS, and who consequently have a favourable (unprejudiced) attitude to the sufferers from the condition are likely to disagree with that statement, while people who exhibit prejudice towards the sufferers from AIDS would be likely to agree with it. The statement thus discriminates between those people who possess a negative attitude to AIDS and those who possess a positive one. An attitude scale consists of a set of such statements, together with a scale on which the strength

---

Box 3.4   Internal consistency of attitude scales

The internal consistency of an attitude scale is the extent to which the different
scale items (or questions) appear to be measuring the same underlying attitude.
Internal consistency is measured in the Likert procedure by determining the extent to which scores on each test item correlate positively with the overall score.
The higher the correlation the more it can be said that the item measures what
the other items are measuring while, conversely, a low correlation suggests that
an item is measuring a quality or variable unrelated to that measured by the other
items.

---

of response to each statement can be registered. This enables enable the presence and strength of a particular attitude to be assessed.

An extremely desirable characteristic of an attitude scale is that it should
possess internal consistency (see box 3.4). This means that the different statements can be said to be measuring the same underlying attitude. The particular
value of the Likert procedure lies in the fact that it produces an attitude scale
which has a known degree of internal consistency, so that having developed a
scale by means of the Likert procedure the researcher can have confidence that
the items of a scale do provide a reasonably consistent measure of the same
attitudes or group of attitudes.

The Likert procedure

The Likert procedure for constructing an attitude scale consists of six steps
which are listed in box 3.5. Note that to use the procedure you need to be
familiar with Spearman's rank order correlation coefficient: a description of the
procedure for computing this statistic, and guidance on interpreting the result,
can be found in chapters 6 and 9.

**Step 1   Generate as many candidate statements relevant to the attitude as
possible.**

The first step is to collect a large pool of attitude statements which are relevant
to the attitude in question. As a rule of thumb you need to generate at least
twice as many statements as you expect to use in the finished scale. If you want
the scale to be about twenty items long, then you will need to make up about
forty statements at this stage. Brainstorming, and similar techniques or loosen-
ing up one's thinking processes can be a great help at this point.

Attitude scale items do not need to be factually accurate – they simply need
to reflect one possible perception of the truth. When the scale is actually put
into use, the members of the sample will not be assessing the factual accuracy
of each item, but will rather be responding to the feelings which the statement
triggers in them. As you develop your initial pool of statements you need to

---

Box 3.5 *Summary of the Likert procedure for constructing an internally consistent attitude scale*

Step 1 Generate as many candidate statements relevant to the attitude as possible
Step 2 Administer the candidate statements to a sample asking respondents to rate their agreement on a five-point scale
Step 3 Convert the scoring of negative statements so that agreement to a favourable statement scores the same as disagreement to an unfavourable statement
Step 4 Using Spearman's rank order correlation coefficient, correlate scores for each item with the total scores
Step 5 Discard all negative and low positive correlating items
Step 6 Review the result. If too few statements have been retained, keep the highly correlating items already generated, and return to step 1 to repeat the process with a new sample until enough statements have been obtained.

(See chapter 9 p. 431 for information and computational instructions for the Spearman rank order correlation coefficient.)

---

try to make sure that you are maintaining an approximately even balance between positive (favourable) statements with which a person holding the attitude would be likely to agree, and negative (unfavourable) statements, with which such a person would be likely to disagree. For reasons which will shortly become apparent, you also need to keep track of which statements fall into each of these categories.

When you have devised an initial set of forty or so statements you now provide each statement with a scale on which the strength of response can be registered. It is usual to employ a five-point scale for this, although seven- or nine-point scales may be used as an alternative:

Strongly disagree:___:___:___:___:___:Strongly agree
                1   2   3   4   5

Step 2 Administer the candidate statements to a sample asking respondents to rate their agreement on a five-point scale.

The next step is to administer the whole set of initial statements to as large a sample from your target population as possible, asking the members of the sample to indicate the extent to which they agree with each statement on the scales provided.

Step 3 Convert the scoring of negative statements so that agreement to a favourable statement scores the same as disagreement to an unfavourable statement.

When all members of the sample have indicated the extent of their agreement to every item in the pool, the next step is to remove the internal contradiction in the scaling process which prevents us from simply taking the raw scores at face value.

The contradiction is caused by the fact that the body of statements contains both positive and negative statements. So, at the moment, agreement to a positive (favourable) statement is given the same score (5) as agreement to a negative (unfavourable) statement. Clearly this represents a logical nonsense in terms of the underlying attitude, and so it is necessary to do something about it. What we need to do is to arrange things so that agreement with a positive (favourable) statement generates the same core as disagreement with a negative statement (since they are logically equivalent) and vice versa.

To do this, you take the existing raw score for each of the negative items only, and change each one as follows. (This is why you needed to keep track of which scale items are positive and which are negative).

Negative items only

Raw score	Converted score
1	5
2	4
3	3 (no change)
4	2
5	1

You can see that once raw scores have been converted in this way, strong agreement to a positive (favourable) item, and its logical equivalent – strong disagreement to a negative (unfavourable) item – both attract a score of 5, and so on down the scale.

Once this rather laborious process is done, we can measure the strength of each person's attitude simply by adding the rating which they have given to each item. The maximum score achievable on a 40 item scale, indicating strong agreement with all favourable items and strong disagreement with all unfavourable items would be $40 \times 5 = 200$. Similarly the minimum raw score would be 40 (i.e. 40 times 1).

Step 4   Correlate the scores for each item with the total scores.

Now the item analysis, which determines the internal constancy of the finished scale, is conducted. This is done by determining the extent to which scores for each scale item correlate positively with the overall score. The higher the correlation for any individual item, the more it can be said that the item measures what the other items are measuring, and conversely, a low correlation suggests that an item is measuring a quality or variable unrelated to that measured by the other items. The aim is to reduce the final set of statements to those which correlate highly with the overall score.

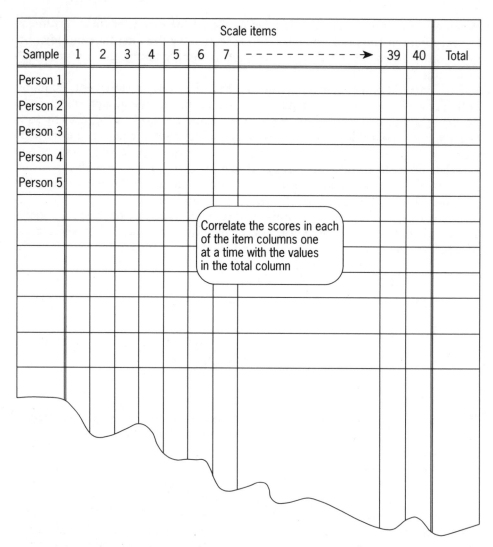

Sample	Scale items										Total
	1	2	3	4	5	6	7	— — — — — — — — — — →	39	40	Total
Person 1											
Person 2											
Person 3											
Person 4											
Person 5											

Correlate the scores in each of the item columns one at a time with the values in the total column

Figure 3.6   Grid for item analysis in the Likert procedure. Enter the raw data obtained at Step 3 in the squares in the body of the table.

To do this, you first need to lay the raw data out into a table such as the one in figure 3.6.

Into each cell in the main body of the table enter the rating on that scale item as made by each member of the sample. Total the ratings horizontally for each individual, and enter the value in the appropriate cell in the column labelled 'Total'.

Now, using Spearman's rank order correlation coefficient in chapter 9, compute the correlation for the set of scale item scores in each of the columns (numbered in the example from 1 to 40), with the set of values in the column labelled 'Total'. List each correlation coefficient against its item number as you go. You should, obviously, finish up with as many coefficients as there are items in the attitude scale.

Step 5   Discard all negative and low positive correlating items.

The highly correlating scale items are the ones needed for the final scale, since these will be the items which are internally consistent with each other. Therefore you have to discard from your set of items those which have produced only a negative or a low positive correlation.

Obviously the level at which the criterion for exclusion is set will be a matter for your judgement. Items with a correlation below +0.5 are unlikely to contribute much in the way of internal consistency, and I suggest that you aim to keep only those items which generate a correlation of at least +0.75.

Step 6   Review the result. If too few statements have been retained, keep the highly correlating items already generated, and return to step 1 to repeat the process with a new sample until enough statements have been obtained.

But what do you do if, as it sometimes does, this means you finish up with a smaller set of items than you actually require for your attitude scale? There are two possibilities. One is to compromise the internal consistency of the scale by including in it some of the low correlating items from the original pool. However, the methodologically correct decision is go back to the beginning of the process, and to brainstorm some new items, add them to those items from the original pool which were found to correlate highly with the total score, and repeat the whole procedure from step 2.

You can, to some extent, insure yourself against having to repeat the process by starting out with a sufficiently large sample of candidate statements. The more statements relevant to the attitude in question you generate to start with, the greater the probability of having a sufficient number of highly correlating items in the group. With luck, you may even find yourself in the position of being able to set the cut-off correlation as high as +0.90!

You now have a final set of attitude statements of known internal consistency, which you can use for your research. Note that, as always, before you employ it for any serious purpose, it is a very good idea to run some pilot trials to ensure that the items are readily comprehensible, and to assess the reliability and validity of the scale.

Analysing the data obtained from a Likert scale

To determine the strength with which the attitude of interest is held by each individual in the sample, do the following:

1 For each completed questionnaire, score each item, and remove the logical inconsistency in the scale using the procedure described above in step 3.
2 Sum the revised scores on each scale to obtain a total score for each individual in the sample.

3   The set of scores thus obtained form a sampling distribution, and can be examined and described using the techniques of descriptive statistics mentioned in chapter 6.

To perform an item analysis of completed questionnaires, i.e. to find out whether particular scale items attract consistently positive or negative responses across the sample, follow the procedure described in step 4 above.

REFERENCE

Likert, R. (1932). A technique for the measurement of attitudes. *Archives of Psychology*, No. 140.

Planning and Carrying out a Survey

This section of the chapter deals with the tasks involved in actually doing the survey, and with analysing the results once the data have been collected.

Having designed the questionnaire or attitude scale, the next problem is to get it into the hands of the members of your sample, and have it completed so that data can be analysed. The aim is to get as many fully completed questionnaires returned as possible.

As far as distribution is concerned, three main options exist. These are:

* The mailshot
* Personal distribution
* Collection by respondents from a central point.

The method chosen will depend on a number of factors, such as the nature of the population, the sampling strategy which is to be adopted, and also the extent to which a researcher is prepared to accept response rates which may be considerably below 100%.

The mailshot

In a mailshot, the post office takes responsibility for delivering your questionnaire to the members of the sample. However, the cost of postage these days make it increasingly unlikely that a true mailshot will be contemplated, except by researchers with a research budget. But a simpler version may still be possible. For example, if a true random sample is to be taken from within an organization such as a school or college, for which an exhaustive sampling frame exists, then a version of the postal survey, using the internal mail system could be carried out. This is convenient, and relatively easy, but carries the penalty that the response rate (i.e. the proportion of fully completed question-naires received back), may be low, and will almost certainly never achieve 100%, especially if the completed questionnaires are to be returned by the same method.

Personal distribution

An alternative approach, which is more likely to be used when one of the purposive sampling methods is employed is for the researcher (or assistants) to personally distribute the questionnaire to the members of the sample. The advantage of this technique is that the researcher or her representative is able to make direct contact with the members of the sample, and can give more detailed information about the research than it is possible to provide in writing. Personal contact such as this may well be an important factor in motivating respondents to complete and return the questionnaire. However, this is pro-bably only a feasible strategy when the sample members are easily contacted.

Collection from a central point

The third approach, which can be used if a volunteer sample is required, is to allow respondents to collect a questionnaire from a central point, and return them when completed. This is the least arduous option from the researcher's point of view, since it only requires a supply of questionnaires to be placed at the collection point, and a subsequent trip made back to collect the completed questionnaires. The weakness of this approach is that without adequate pre-survey, and point-of-collection publicity, the questionnaires may simply be overlooked, and very few collected. So although on the surface this strategy conserves the researcher's time and energy, in practice, considerable effort may be expended on making sure that people know about the survey and where they can obtain a questionnaire.

   The process of getting questionnaires into the hands of the sample, and back again without mishap, raises the problem of the low response rates which are typically obtained in survey research. One solution to this problem is to ensure that assistance in the form of someone connected with the research, is present while the questionnaire is being completed.

   One approach to assisted completion, which brings the survey closer to the interview method of research, is for the researcher to read each question out, and to record the answers for the respondent. Alternatively, the researcher may leave the completion of the questionnaire to the respondent, simply remaining present in case any questions arise.

   There are clearly advantages to using these strategies, since they enable the researcher to deal at once with any queries which may arise from any lack of clarity in the questions, and also provide an opportunity to spot any misunder-standings at the time they occur. On the other hand, the method of reading the questions may result in the researcher unwittingly influencing the respondent's answers by stressing certain words in the question. Both approaches make the

Box 3.6   *A checklist of survey design tasks*

The issues involved in planning a piece of research by the survey method have already been discussed throughout this chapter, and this checklist provides a summary of the key tasks. It can be used either to guide the planning and design of a survey, or to enable you to check that nothing important has been omitted once planning has been done.

1   The preliminaries to the survey

Have you
- Clearly described the research problem?
- Stated the precise aim of the survey?
- Developed an explanation which either links the proposed survey to a theory, or says why the survey should be carried out?
- Decided whether a descriptive or explanatory survey is required?
- If appropriate, stated the hypothesis to be tested?
- Identified the target population?

2   The survey design

Have you
- Determined whether an exhaustive sampling frame is available?
- Decided which survey design to use?

3   The sample

Have you
- Defined the sampling frame?
- Decided whether probabilistic or non-probabilistic sampling is required?
- Select the sampling method to be used and justified your choice?
- Decided the size of the sample to be taken, and justified the decision?

4   The questionnaire

Have you
- Generated an appropriate set of questions for the questionnaire?
- Checked that a range of question types have been used?
- Checked that demographic questions are at the end of the questionnaire?
- Reviewed the language of the questions for clarity, simplicity and emotional content?
- Had the questionnaire read over by another person?
- Assessed the questionnaire for reliability and validity?
- Carried out a pilot study, evaluated the results and made any necessary changes to the questionnaire?
- Checked that the research conforms to ethical guidelines?
- Decided how the questionnaire is to be distributed, and collected?
- Considered how the data are to be analysed?
- Calculated the extent of non-response and its effects on any conclusions which can be drawn from the results?

anonymous completion of the questionnaire impossible, and this may in turn influence the extent to which respondents feel free to answer questions as frankly as they can.

Analysing questionnaire data

The data obtained from a survey consist of the set of answers provided by the respondents to the items in the questionnaire or other research instrument. Having collected the data from a sample, the next task is to try to draw some conclusions and provide an answer to the research question. The basic approach, which can be applied to all types of question, is to draw up a tally of all the different categories of response. This provides the material for the basic descriptive analysis of the survey.

The first step is to reduced the data so it can be handled more easily and the information which it contains more clearly seen. The procedure is as follows:

1 Check that all questionnaires have been fully completed, and discard any which are incomplete so as to maintain the integrity of the sample. Do not destroy those which are incomplete, as the information they contain can be used to supplement the main analysis (providing it is clearly labelled as such).
2 Calculate the response rate. The number of fully completed questionnaires divided by the total number of questionnaires originally distributed multiplied by 100 gives you the percentage response.
3 For the analysis of Likert-type and closed questions, draw up a tally chart, such as the one in figure 3.7. For each question which is to be analysed by this method, go through the questionnaire counting the number of answers of each type which have been obtained. Enter the results in the appropriate

Item No.	Response 1	Response 2	Response 3	Response 4	Response 5

Figure 3.7   Tally chart for the analysis of closed questions

cells of the chart. The following table could be used to analyse responses when the maximum number of possible answers to any question is no greater than five, but more could be accommodated simply by expanding it sideways.

When the tally chart is complete compute, item by item, the percentage of the sample placed in each of the categories.

(Note that questionnaires which consist entirely of Likert items require a somewhat different approach: the analysis of these scales has been described earlier in the section on the Likert scale.)

4 Open-ended questions invite a completely free response and each respondent can write as much or as little as they wish, whether relevant to the question or not, so they are more laborious to analyse, and involve the exercise of the subjective judgement of the researcher.

The first step in this process is to devise a coding scheme, consisting of a set of categories, which can be applied to the answers. Sometimes it will be desirable to construct a separate set of categories for each open-ended question in the sample, and sometimes it will be possible to use the same set of categories across all open-ended questions.

As an example of how the coding process could be approached in the case of open-ended questions, consider:

Q20 Could you try to describe in your own words what you think your marriage will be like in about a year's time?

Clearly, this is a question which could elicit a considerable variety of responses, ranging from those who expect positive change in their relationship to those which take entirely the opposite view. To deal with the range of responses which might be obtained, the simplest form of coding would need to involve just four categories, although more complex versions could also be used. The four categories are:

- **Positive responses:**   those which envisage an improvement in the quality of the relationship.
- **Negative responses:**   those which envisage a decline in the quality of the relationship.
- **No change:**   No real difference between the relationship today and a year hence.
- **Irrelevant:**   the response bears no discernible connection to the question.

The next step is the construction of a tally chart (see figure 3.8), containing these categories. Each individual respondent's answer to the question should be carefully scrutinized in order to determine into which category it should be placed, and a mark is then placed in the appropriate cell of the chart. The comments section on the right enables the researcher to make notes on the qualitative aspects of the answers. For example, it might be that there are many uncertain, highly qualified answers among those who take a broadly positive view, while those who take an opposite view tend to be much more dogmatic. This is important qualitative information which

Item No.	Positive answer	Negative answer	No change	Irrelevant answer	Comments

Figure 3.8   Tally chart for the analysis of open-ended questions

should be recorded as it will be needed when the research report comes to be written.

This basic process can in principle be applied to the analysis of all open-ended questions. The main problem, as you have probably noticed for yourself, is to identify the appropriate categories into which the responses are to be divided, but once that has been done, the process is no more difficult than the analysis of closed questions.

Hypothesis testing using the survey method

As well as providing data for descriptive analysis, the survey method can be used to test precise hypotheses using inferential statistics. The following are some suggestions about how this can be approached, but note that if you have not yet done so, you will first need to acquaint yourself with the following information from elsewhere in the book (you'll see why as you read on):

- the general concept of hypothesis testing, the use of null and alternate hypotheses and the role of test statistics in making a decision about hypotheses (chapter 7)
- the characteristics of non-parametric statistics in general, and the chi-squared statistic in particular (chapter 9).

1   Closed questions can be analysed by first determining the number of answers obtained to each of the categories, and then using the chi-squared test for goodness of fit to test the null hypothesis that the observed frequency distribution does not differ significantly from that predicted by random choices.

2   The answers to open-ended questions can be coded using the procedure outlined above, and the results analysed in the same way by means of the chi-squared goodness of fit test.

3   The strength of association between answers to different questions (that is whether a particular answer to one question is associated with a particular

answer to another), can also be assessed using the chi-squared test in its test of association form. To do this, all the possible answers to the two questions to be analysed are arranged along two sides of a data matrix, and the frequency of each of the possible combinations determined from the sample. The chi-squared test of association can then be applied to determine whether the association between the different answers is statistically significant.

Writing up the results of a survey

For most purposes, the best approach to writing up the results of a piece of survey research is to employ the standard headings (discussed in appendix 2), without significant modification. The main differences from an experimental report (see chapter 5) are likely to be:

1   The **Subjects** section should detail the characteristics of the sample and the procedure used for identifying and locating sample members.
2   The information in the **Procedure** section should be clearly divided between the procedure followed in devising and testing the questionnaire, and that required to administer the questionnaire and collect the data.
3   If specific hypotheses are to be tested, the **Treatment of Results** section should report the results of each analysis – this may make for a rather more lengthy section than in the case of other types of research.

Two Examples of Surveys

Example 1   The hallucinations of widowhood

It has long been known that people whose husband or wife has died may subsequently experience vivid visual, auditory or tactile illusions of the presence of the dead person, but the extent to which these might be a common feature of bereavement is generally unclear. In this research, Rees wished to establish whether, and to what extent, the experience of post-bereavement hallucinations might be general among those who had lost a close relative.

The method chosen involved carrying out a survey of the people known to have been bereaved who were living in a particular geographical area in mid-Wales. A total of 363 people were initially identified as potential members of the sample, but after those who had themselves died, or who were incapacitated by age or illness, or who were unwilling to be interviewed, were taken out of the sample Rees was left with a total of 293 respondents (227 female and 66 males).

The data collection process involved a semi-structured interview based on a standard questionnaire, which aimed to establish the frequency of the phenomenon of post-bereavement hallucinations, and to collect information on the extent to which the occurrence of any hallucinations co-varied with a range of variables such as age, duration of marriage, duration of widowhood, age at widowhood, and so on.

Rees found that post-bereavement hallucinations were both common and long-lasting among the people in his sample. About half the sample reported experiencing hallucinations of some kind, often for many years after the death had occurred. They were more common in those who had been widowed after the age of 40, those who had enjoyed a happy marriage, and among middle-class people compared to working-class people.

It was concluded from the research that hallucinations should be regarded as a normal and helpful part of the experience of widowhood which provide psychological support, at a time of a major life stress, and which eventually cease of their own accord. There was no evidence that they were associated in any way with mental illness or abnormality. Rather, most of those interviewed felt that they were helped by their hallucinations, but nevertheless most did not discuss them with the members of their families for fear of being thought odd.

Example 2   Depression: Crisis without alternatives

This research, reported in an article in *New Scientist* is an example of a prospective survey design, in which a prediction is made about some future situation. The research concerned the relationship which was thought to exist between certain critical life events, such as bereavement and redundancy, the availability (or otherwise) of a good social support network, and the probability of developing clinical depression. Earlier research had strongly suggested that social support was the critical factor: if it was weak or absent the possibility that a critical life event would provoke a clinical depression appeared to be significantly higher.

However, up to the time of the research reported by Oatley, the studies which had been carried out on the relationship between thee three variables had only been identified by means of retroactive research, in which people who had suffered a critical life event and then a depression were studied some time later, and it was possible that the passage of time had introduced distortions into their recollections. This prospective study represented an attempt to circumvent the criticisms which had been applied to the earlier research.

In this study, a sample of 49 newly redundant men, who had no previous experience of being out of work were interviewed and measures of depression (using a standard questionnaire) and the extent of their social support networks were taken. The same data were also collected from a control group of 49 who had not suffered redundancy, and who remained employed throughout the period of the research. No significant difference was found between the samples on either of the two measures taken.

The researchers predicted that the men who had suffered redundancy, and who possessed weak support networks would be more likely to become clinically depressed than either those who had similarly lost their jobs, but who also had numerous sources of emotional support available to them, or those who had remained in work.

Both samples were followed up six to eight months later, during which period the measures of social interaction within each sample remained the same. It was found that the prediction of clinical depression among those unemployed who also possessed weak social networks (and had not found work), was confirmed, amounting to 25% of the unemployed sample. By comparison, none of the employed group, nor the unemployed with strong networks, showed any increase in measured depression over the period studied.

REFERENCES

Oatley, K. (1984). Depression: Crisis without alternatives. *New Scientist*, *103*, 29–31.
Rees, W. D. (1971). The hallucinations of widowhood. *British Medical Journal*, *4*, 37–41.

Suggestions for Research Using the Survey Method

Unless you have some experience of doing survey research it will probably be best to attempt these projects in the order in which they appear. To help you get started with the first, a little background explanation and a few hints are provided, while the second, as you can see, represents a bit more of a challenge since it only gives you the barest outline of the problem to be researched.

Is it true that men become emotionally attached to their cars?

Some people have suggested that the evident attachment that men show to-wards their cars (which is sometimes greater than that they show towards their wives) may have less to do with its practical use as a means of transport, than with some deeper motives. A car, it is argued, is much more than a way of getting from one place to another in reasonable comfort and privacy: it is rather a piece of technology which is capable of exerting a powerful grasp on the male psyche. One theory has suggested that a car can be seen as a piece of moveable territory, to which people exhibit attachment, and defend in the same way as their fixed home territory. In a sense, the car could be seen as a mobile part of the home, evoking the same intense emotional responses as the home does. This perhaps goes some way to explaining why some people adorn the interiors of their cars with ornaments of various kinds – pairs of furry dice, for example.

It would be interesting to try to establish whether any empirical support can be found for these ideas. For this project, devise a questionnaire and conduct a survey to investigate the possibility that men do really feel emotionally attached to their motors – and, if possible, compare the answers with those from a parallel sample of women. What are the psychological and social implications of your findings (if any)?

Here are a few ideas to start you off.

Can you think of questions you could ask about how your informants feel about their cars when they are driving it, thinking of selling it, contemplating the damage after an accident, lending it to a friend, or when someone touches it? Do they dream about their cars? What kinds of things or ideas do they associate with their cars? What else do they do in their cars aside from driving? And so on.

It will probably be important not to make these questions too direct. You could try using oblique techniques, such as asking people which adjectives they associate with these different scenarios, from a list of mixed emotional and non-emotional ones, or getting them to free-associate on paper to a list of car-related words as a way of avoiding direct questions.

Are holidays really good for you?

Package holiday advertising would like us to think that we will return from our ten days on the beach relaxed, refreshed and taking a more positive view of life. In short they would like us to believe that there are major psychological benefits to be gained from taking a holiday.

But do holidays really confer any such advantages, or are we likely to return from a vacation more stressed, depressed and uptight than when we left?

For this project, design a questionnaire to allow you to examine this question, and administer it to a sample in an appropriate survey design.

Summary of chapter 3

The survey method tackles one of the basic problems of social science research: how to collect data when the people from whom it must be obtained are either too numerous, or too dispersed across a wide geographical area to be accessible? Such a group (called in statistical terminology a 'population'), can only be studied by a process of sampling, that is, by identifying within the larger group a (relatively) small number of individuals from whom data are to be collected. The extent to which the data obtained from a sample are likely to be representative of the whole population is the central issue in sampling. Understanding the various ways in which samples can be constructed, and knowing how far each type is capable of generating a representative sample are therefore vital elements in successful survey design.

To obtain data from a population by taking a sample which is as representative as constraints allow, means choosing among a number of different sampling options from two main categories. On the one hand there are the probabilistic sampling methods, such as simple random sampling, so called because it is possible to state the probability that any given individual in the population will be included in the sample. On the other hand, there is non-probabilistic sampling, such as opportunity sampling, in which it is impossible to say what the probability of any individual being included in the sample might be. As you would expect, probabilistic sampling is more powerful, but requires more work by the researcher, while non-probabilistic sampling is easier, but yields a sample which bears an unknown relationship to its parent population.

The key to probabilistic sampling is the sampling frame. This is a complete list of all the individuals who make up the population. However, the fact that this is rarely available means that most psychological research relies on non-probabilistic sampling, especially the opportunity and volunteer forms.

All sampling, by whatever method is subject to some degree of sampling error. This can be explained as the difference between the data which is actually collected from a sample, and the data one *would* have obtained had the entire population been sampled. Although the incidence of sampling error can be reduced by careful attention to the detail of the sampling procedure, some proportion of error will always remain in the data. The aim should be to reduce this to the minimum possible.

The data collection part of a survey is carried out by means of a questionnaire or similar instrument, such as the Likert scale, and in general these also have to be designed from scratch as part of the survey planning process. To be an effective collector of information for research purposes, a questionnaire needs to be designed around a clear set of research questions which are subsequently turned into questionnaire items. A range of different types of questionnaire item may be used in the construction of a questionnaire from the 'closed' types which place narrow limits on the kind of answer which can be offered, (such as checklists or rating scales, for example), to the 'open' type in which the respondents are completely free to answer in their own words. The key skill of questionnaire design lies in making sure that the form and the content of each item exactly represent the researcher's intentions and that they will be interpreted by the respondents in the way intended.

A questionnaire is more than just a simple list of questions. The overall logic of the questionnaire should be apparent to all informants, and the ordering of the questions should be done in such a way that respondents experience a gentle increase in the depth and detail of the information demanded, rather than being faced with difficult questions at the beginning of the questionnaire. Open-ended questions are best placed around the middle of a question schedule, while demographic information, such as details of the respondent's age and sex, is best collected by means of questions placed at the end. The placing of contingent questions permits different subgroups within the sample to be steered to answer some questions and to avoid others.

Some types of question, such as those which are posed in the negative form, or leading questions which are based on hidden (or not so hidden) assumptions, should always be removed from a questionnaire at the editing stage since they can act as a potent source of measurement error. The language used in each item should also be carefully checked and any vagueness or ambiguities removed.

Once the sampling procedure, and the method of collecting the data are decided, the implementation of the research follows. The main concern of the research at this point is to place the questionnaire or other document in the hands of the members of the sample, and here again a number of possibilities exist. One way is for the questionnaires to be distributed through personal contact with the researcher, another is to leave them to be picked up by respondents from a convenient point. A third alternative, distribution by mail-shot, is expensive and has a poor response rate, but may be the only way of the reaching the members of a widely dispersed population.

Finally, when the data are collected, the task of analysis begins. The analysis of quantitative data is relatively straightforward, and can be accomplished through a combination of descriptive and inferential statistics. Qualitative data, obtained from open-ended questions is rather more problematic, but even these can be subjected to statistical treatment if first divided among an appropriate system of categories.

4 Observational Research

This chapter provides information about the participant and non-participant methods of making observations, and gives guidance on how to set about doing research using these techniques.

- It reviews key concepts in observational research, such as naturalism, reactivity and the structured/unstructured distinction.

- It describes the important features of participant observation research and reviews the major tasks involved in doing research by this method.

- It introduces the non-participant method of research, and provides an approach to the planning of this type of project.

- It provides suggestions for a number of research projects using both participant and non-participant techniques.

Introduction

Reduced to its bare essentials, observation is simply watching. A basic description of what is involved would be to say that it requires a researcher to enter a situation where some behaviour of interest is likely to take place, to watch the nature and frequency with which particular forms of behaviour occur, and to make a record of what is observed. Subsequently, of course, the record of observations is used to help answer a particular research question.

Stripped to its fundamentals in this way, observational research might appear a delightfully uncomplicated process, especially when compared to the complexities of a really tightly designed experiment. There are, in fact several different ways in which this basic approach can be implemented, representing different elaborations – ways of doing observation – on this basic scheme. As we shall see shortly, observational research is less of a single unitary approach to research than a whole collection of methods, loosely tied together by some general similarities. We shall defer discussion of these issues for a few moments while we focus on two important ideas which lie behind the use of the observational approach within psychology, and which to some extent explain its importance to psychologists as a method of research. These are, first, the idea that the observational method offers a route to doing **naturalistic** investigations, and secondly, that it offers a way around the thorny problem of **reactivity** in research with human subjects.

1   Naturalistic research

Naturalistic research is research which examines situations and behaviour which occur naturally, in contrast to those which are in some sense artificial because they have been engineered by a researcher to serve the purposes of an investigation. In naturalistic research the aim is to carry out research on behaviour (or experience) as it occurs in its *natural*, everyday environment, that is, in the houses, schools, streets and shopping malls of the 'real world' rather than in the artificial situation of a laboratory.

Clearly this approach is of considerable interest, not only because psychologists are (of course) committed to developing a better understanding of the nature of human behaviour and experience wherever it may occur, but also because it provides a way of tackling one of the more difficult problems in research methodology.

The problem is that much, and almost certainly most, psychological research has, so far, been laboratory research. The criticism most often voiced about this type of research is that it possesses only weak ecological validity. That is because one of the functions of a laboratory situation is to provide a very structured (and simplified) environment compared to any 'real-life' situation, and therefore the behaviour which can be observed there may be quite different from what would be obtained in any comparable situation outside. In other words, a laboratory is not an 'ecologically valid' version of the 'real-life' situation outside.

Asch's famous piece of research into conformity (Asch, 1956), illustrates this point. (If Asch's research is unfamiliar to you see almost any general textbook of psychology, such as Gross, 1992, for a fuller account.) The basic experiment placed a single 'naive' experimental subject in a group of six confederates. The members of the group were then asked one by one to look at a set of lines, and then to say out loud which lines were the same length. On some trials, the confederates reported accurately, as indeed did the 'naive' subject, but on others they reported that lines were the same length when they were clearly not. On those trials, the subjects apparently experienced strong pressure to deny the evidence of their own eyes, and conform to the majority decision. Some, in fact did so, and it is generally accepted that these results confirm the existence of strong pressure to go along with the majority view, even when, as in the experiment, this runs counter to the objective evidence.

However, the experiment can be criticized for its poor ecological validity. The fact that (among other issues) it used specially created groups of subjects, and an extremely simple perceptual task, means that it is actually quite unlike any naturally occurring situation in which conforming behaviour might be expected. It can be argued that in fact the experiment tells us much less about conformity in general than about how people will behave when they are placed in the kind of highly structured and artificial situation created by Asch for his research.

The general point is that in many areas of psychological research laboratory based investigations pose problems of interpretation, since it can be argued that they can offer only an understanding of what people are likely to say and do under certain highly specific situations, rather than in the more complex and interesting situations of everyday life. Much of the power and attractiveness of naturalistic research lies in its ability to get around this problem. By opening up many areas of everyday life to closer scrutiny, it holds out the prospect of developing theories which explain behaviour in general, and not just behaviour in the laboratory.

One might well ask at this point what exactly does 'natural' mean in relation to an environment and the behaviour which takes place there? Is it a meaningful concept to use? This is not an idle question, since there is at least one sense in which all human behaviour, including the behaviour of people in experiments, could be said to be 'natural', so that the concept of 'naturalistic research' could turn out, ultimately, to be meaningless, or at least largely empty. Fortunately, however, the notion of what 'natural' might mean in relation to research has been analysed and, it turns out, there are three different criteria of naturalism in research. These are: naturalism of a setting or environment; naturalism of events; and naturalism of behaviour.

A natural setting is any situation or part of the environment which has not been specially set up for the purposes of the research. Streets, parks, or the interiors of public and private buildings of all kinds are therefore examples of natural settings for research.

Natural events are any events which occur in the research setting, which are natural to it, and have not been engineered to occur as part of the research design. For example a car accident (as long as it hasn't deliberately been made to happen) is a natural event.

Natural behaviour is behaviour which is the usual or expected behaviour for a given environment or situation, in the sense that it would have occurred anyway, even if the researcher had not been present. In a shop, looking at the goods on display, asking for information from an assistant, and queuing at the checkout are all natural behaviours in this sense.

As you will see a little later, observational research in general finds it relatively easy to meet all three of these criteria, and it therefore represents the main route by which psychologists are able to study 'natural' behaviour under 'natural' conditions. At the same time, it is also important to know that to qualify as a piece of naturalistic research in the fullest sense, a project needs to meet all three of the criteria. If a researcher deliberately intervenes to modify a situation, or events, or the behaviour of individuals to any degree, then the research can no longer claim to be wholly naturalistic: and, of course, the greater the extent of the intervention, the greater the likelihood that the study will lack ecological validity.

2 The reactivity issue: overt and covert observation

A second criticism of experimental research argues that laboratory-based research is flawed because it too often fails to take into account the reactivity of the research participants. The problem of reactivity is that knowing that one is taking part in research, and that one's behaviour is being studied, can influence behaviour. This means that a researcher can never be wholly sure how much of observed behaviour is due to the effect of being a participant in the research, and how much is the genuine result of the situation. 'Evaluation apprehension', mentioned earlier in chapter 2 is only one example of this phenomenon. The problem which this poses for the researcher is that although such reactive effects are not inevitable, and do not necessarily appear in every piece of research, they are extremely difficult to predict because they are not well understood. Consequently, laboratory studies tend to ignore, or at least gloss over the problem.

A further reason for doing observational research then, is that it is able, again in principle, to offer a way around this problem of reactivity. Observational research can be extremely unobtrusive, since the basic activity consists simply of watching what goes on, and it therefore follows that the researcher's influence on the data can be reduced to a minimum. One obvious way of doing this is to make observations covertly, so that those being observed are wholly unaware of their participation in the research, although, as we discuss below, this approach runs into serious ethical difficulties if it means observing people without first obtaining their consent. In some situations, such as observational research involving non-human species, it may be possible to undertake ethically acceptable covert observation. However, where human subjects are involved, the ethical issues should always be weighed very carefully. Some further discussion of the issues involved appears below.

The alternative to carrying out fully covert observation is to make the observing process overt, so that the people who are being observed are able to see what you are doing and to know that their behaviour is being observed. If the research is then designed so as to allow them to become accustomed to the presence of an observer before data are collected, effectively they no longer notice the researcher, and thus become less likely to change their behaviour. Reactivity effects on the data thus become much less of a problem.

However, even though the data gained from observations may be relatively uncontaminated by the process by which it was obtained, reactivity can never be discounted completely as an influence on the data. Unless anything other than fully covert observation is employed, the planning for an observational research project always needs to take into account the possibility that the observations will be affected by the observation process itself.

Types of Observational Research

As we have already said, to speak of 'the observational method' implies, to some extent, a single method which can be applied equally to all research questions and situations. However, this is not so. As we pointed out earlier, rather than a single observational method, there are in fact several ways of approaching the task of making reliable and informative observations.

The key difference among these different forms of observational research is the extent to which the researcher, as well as observing, also becomes involved as an actor in the events which are being studied. This variable constitutes a continuum, along which it is possible to range all the different forms of observational research. At each extreme are the two possibilities: participant observation at one end, and non-participant observation at the other. We'll take a brief overview first, and then, in the remainder of this chapter look at these two types of observational research in more detail.

1   Participant observation research

As its name implies, in participant observation the researcher plays a dual role, as both a participant and an observer, in the events and processes which are being researched. The process of observation continues (sometimes with considerable difficulty) while the observer is also fully engaged as an active participant in what is taking place, becoming, in effect, a part of the picture which the research describes.

2   Non-participant, or 'observation only' research

'Observation only' research occupies the opposite end of the continuum to participant observation. In this, the researcher simply observes the on-going flow of events as an uninvolved outsider, and plays no direct part in what is being observed. Obviously, in the light of what was said earlier about reactivity effects, this is only certain to be true if observation is carried out completely covertly.

Along the continuum

As we said earlier, observational research can be represented as a continuum with the participant and non-participant forms located at the extreme ends. Along the intervening length of the continuum, therefore, lie all the various possible combinations of these two idea types. Two of these can be mentioned briefly to give you a better picture of the kinds of approach to observation which result when the earlier types are combined in different ways.

The **participant as observer** occupies a position closer to the 'pure partici-pant' end of the continuum than to the other end, and represents an approach to research in which the observer is rather less concerned with participating, and more with collecting data, although the balance is still tipped in favour of the former end of the scale.

The **observer as participant** reverses that balance, and gives the researcher a role in which the primary concern is the collection of data, although she may still be significantly involved as a participant in on-going events.

The precise mix of participation and observation which is used in any par-ticular project will depend on a number of factors such as the nature of the research question, the constraints or demands of the immediate environment in which the research is to be carried out, as well as on the personality, prefer-ences, or theoretical preferences of the observer. In this respect, observational research is quite unlike (say) the method of experimentation in which the scope for individual decision making by the researcher is much narrower.

The last point that needs to be made before we move on to consider another important distinction in observational research is that none of these different approaches to observation is necessarily better than the others. They simply represent different strategies or techniques, each of which allows different kinds of research question to be asked, and different sorts of data to be gathered. It is the researcher's task to decide which approach is best suited to the needs of a particular research question.

The structured/unstructured distinction in observational research

In addition to the participant–observer continuum there is one further basis for distinguishing between participant and non-participant observation which fo-cuses on the extent to which the observing process is structured, or organized.

Unstructured observation in its most extreme form is research where the aim is simply to ensure that everything which appears to be of relevance to the research at a given moment is recorded. The researcher, unconstrained by any prior assumptions about this, simply endeavours to collect all the information which is available in the situation.

However, it is extremely difficult to find an example of unstructured research which is actually this extreme. Most unstructured research turns out to be organized, albeit loosely, by some kind of theory, or at least by a set of ideas which define in general terms the behaviour which is to be studied. The impor-tant point is that any such definitions do not exclude any other pieces of behaviour, or information from the consideration of the researcher if these seem to be of relevance to the research question.

Although this approach may appear to be unfocused, random and at the mercy of changing events, if used effectively, it is also capable of providing a very flexible and open approach to research, which enables an investigator to modify or change the direction of an inquiry with relative ease when the picture presented by the incoming data is examined. At the same time, though, it relies on an observer's own knowledge and understanding of what is going on to direct the observing process.

It should be reasonably clear that, of the two extreme versions of the observational method, it is participant observation which is the more likely to take the unstructured approach. In participant observation, because the researcher is also an active part of the on-going flow of events the flexibility offered by the unstructured approach is a valuable asset, enabling examples of unanticipated behaviour to be captured, when otherwise they would have been lost to the research.

Structured observation on the other hand, is research in which the inquiry is guided by theory, or by ideas which the researcher may have about what is likely to be important or relevant to the research. This means that the researcher has to make a decision about what is to be observed well before any observations are actually made. Moreover, the early commitment to collecting only certain categories of data means that all other categories are excluded from consideration. The key point is that structured observation, because it involves making prior decisions about what to observe, renders the research process relatively inflexible and incapable of responding to unpredictable situations.

The structured approach to research typically means using an observational system of some kind in order to provide a framework for the observing process. However, it is also true that although structured observation is likely to involve an observational system, it can also be rather informally organized around an intention to observe only certain types of behaviour, without the necessity of resorting to the construction of a full-blown observational system. Box 4.1 provides a summary of the main differences between the structured and unstructured approaches to observational research. More information, on the processes involved in undertaking structured observation and an example of an observational system can be found below in the discussion of non-participant observation.

Participant Observation

In this section we look at the method of participant observation in more detail.

The different phases of a participant project are described, and we examine the different tasks which are required in each phase.

Examples of participant research, and suggestions for investigative projects using this method are provided.

Introduction

As its name suggests, in participant observation the investigator is required to occupy simultaneously two quite different roles. On the one hand, to be a

---

Box 4.1   *The main differences between structured and unstructured observation*

Structured observation	**Unstructured observation**
Concerned with recording specific features of behaviour	Concerned with recording all relevant behaviour
The behaviour to be recorded is determined before observation begins	The behaviour to be recorded is decided at the time the observations are made
Permits the testing of precise hypotheses	Provides a description of behaviour in a given situation
Provides a partial record of behaviour on a given occasion	Provides a more complete record of behaviour on a given occasion
Uses a checklist or other written protocol which has been developed prior to observation	No checklist is used
Permits estimates of observer reliability to be made	Observer reliability is difficult or impossible to estimate
Behaviour to be observed can be relatively easily predicted	Behaviour to be studied is largely unpredictable

---

participant, a researcher has to try to become accepted as a full member of whichever social group is being studied. This means taking an active part in the lives of the people who are the sources of information, building relationships with them, interacting with them in all kinds of situations, doing the things they customarily do at the times, and in the ways that they do.

At the same time, the observer part of the role requires the researcher to exercise the skills of the detached observer in the collection of information – by watching what happens, listening to what is said, asking questions and analysing situations and actions as they occur.

Research which uses this approach typically aims to try to understand the nature of life in a particular social group. For example, Patrick in an often quoted piece of research (Patrick, 1973), became a member of a street gang in Glasgow for several months while he pieced together an inside account of their activities, both law-abiding and less so, and their relationships with each other, and also with those outside the gang. Despite some intensely difficult moments, caused by the gang's fairly frequent brushes with the law, he was able to collect data of sufficient richness to throw considerable light on the lives and social relationships of the gang members.

The general goal of participant observation research, then, is to arrive at a detailed appreciation of a particular social situation from the perspective of

---

Box 4.2   Some of the distinctive characteristics of participant observation research

1   In participant research **the researcher plays a dual role – both as participant and observer.**
2   Participant observation research is **unstructured.** The researcher is prepared to collect any and all data which may seem to be relevant. No decision is made about what data to collect before entering the field.
3   Participant observation **focuses on social processes and the interaction between people.** The research is concerned with on-going events, and the meanings which these happenings may have for those involved.
4   Participant observation research is **primarily descriptive.** The results of the research consist of descriptions of events rather than quantitative data.

---

those for whom that situation is their daily reality, to develop an understanding of what it may be like to be a member of that social group, and to acquire what Lofland calls 'an intimate familiarity' with that particular situation (Lofland 1971). Box 4.2 lists the distinctive characteristics of this form of research.

Participant observation: philosophical and practical implications

Participant research is uniquely able to provide an insider's perspective on the behaviour and experience of people in natural situations. In particular, it offers a way for psychologists to gain insight into the daily experiences of 'marginal' groups such as substance abusers, or the members of doomsday cults, who would normally be unreachable by other methods of research. Despite these advantages, and the stimulating examples provided by a range of interesting pieces of research (see the examples below), use of this method is still far from common. There seem to be two reasons for this: the philosophical and the practical.

From the philosophical angle, participant observation, with its emphasis on trying to understand people's experience as against proposing explanations for their behaviour has clearly fitted uneasily with the notions of positivism about how psychological research should be conducted. In particular, positivism argues for a clear separation between a researcher and her data, whereas in undertaking participant observation the researcher's experience becomes a part of the data which is reported. Equally problematic from the positivist point of view are the actual data. Participant observation generates a rich mix of descriptive information rather than the kind of quantitative data which can be easily used to test specific hypotheses. Rather than statistics, participant observation is better suited to providing a source of ideas for hypotheses which can later be tested elsewhere by other means.

On the practical side, doing participant observation research can be very time consuming, with the duration of a full-scale project typically measured in months and years. This is because it can take several weeks just to enter the field, and gain the confidence and acceptance of the people there. In general, it is only when this has been done that worthwhile data can begin to be collected, and such a heavy commitment of time represents a major disincentive to use this method to most researchers.

Because of this, if you are attracted to this method, and feel you would like to begin a participant project of your own, you must consider very carefully the amount of time which it is likely to take to put together a project of even a quite modest nature. It can't be emphasized too strongly that participant research is extremely time consuming, and is certain to take at least three times as long as your most generous estimate. The unpredictable nature of social interaction, and the fact that you are always at the mercy of your informants for the data you collect means that there will probably be long stretches of time when, from your point of view, your research is stalled, because no data can be collected. For these reasons, it is almost certainly best not to begin a participant project if there is a deadline by which you are required to have your research completed.

Two Examples of Participant Observation Research

Example 1   When prophecy fails

In the 1950s the social psychologist Leon Festinger read a newspaper report about a Mrs Marion Keech, who had claimed to be receiving messages from outer space, and who was predicting that the end of the world in the form of a great flood would engulf the local area on the following 21 December.

She had also attracted a little band of followers who had come to share her beliefs, and Festinger became interested in the question of how the cult members would cope when, as he confidently expected, the predicted catastrophe failed to materialize. The cult members had actively publicized the prophecies, and in some cases had sold their houses and resigned from their jobs in preparation for the coming disaster, believing that as the waters rose, they would be rescued by a flying saucer. To find out, Festinger and a number of co-workers joined the group, posing as converts to the cause, and they participated in the group's activities, while making observations and recording the behaviour of the group members. As Festinger had expected, the prophecies from outer space proved to be false. The flood failed to materialize as promised, and no flying saucer landed to whisk the cult members away. After a short, but intense period of adjustment, the cult members eventually went their separate ways, and Mrs Keech returned to her former obscurity.

The project was important both for the insight it provides into the psychology of doomsday cults in general, and because in documenting the response of group members to the fact that the prophecies had failed to come true, it provided an unusual chance to test of the theory of cognitive dissonance under natural conditions.

Example 2 On being sane in insane places

Rosenhan's famous participant study of the hidden world of the psychiatric ward was carried out in order to test the idea that mental disorder is not so much diagnosed in terms of an objectively existing set of symptoms, as by the extent to which the behaviour of a patient matches the preconceptions of medical personnel about what mental disorder should look like. If this were true, Rosenhan reasoned, then it should be possible for anyone to fake insanity, and convince medical staff that they had a serious mental disorder when in fact no such disorder was present.

The research involved Rosenhan and seven other people each engineering themselves as patients into a different psychiatric hospital in the United States by claiming to have been hearing voices. (This was untrue, but it was the only deception practised on the hospital staff – all other questions were answered truthfully, and no symptoms were subsequently simulated by any of the researchers.) All eight of the research group were admitted to hospital for observation.

What happened next forms the substance of Rosenhan's research. His report paints a disturbing picture, from a patient's point of view, of life in the locked observation wards of a large psychiatric hospital. Possibly the most telling finding was that while the medical staff found it impossible to tell the pseudopatients from the real ones, the genuine patients experienced no such difficulty. The whole project was extremely revealing about the hidden processes at work within the psychiatric hospital, and Rosenhan was able to show that it was indeed true that the diagnosis and treatment of the mentally ill was determined more by the preconceptions of the medical staff about the nature of mental illness than by the objective presence or absence of symptoms.

REFERENCES

Festinger, L., Riecken, H. W. & Schachter, S. (1956). *When prophecy fails*. Minneapolis: University of Minnesota Press.
Rosenhan, D. L. (1973). On being sane in insane places. *Science, 179*, 250–8.

Doing Participant Observation Research: Some Practical Guidance

The aim of this section is to provide some guidance on how you might set about doing a piece of participant observation research of your own. However, because this approach to doing research directly involves the researcher as a participant there is a sense in which the skills involved can be learned only by direct experience. The research situation is more fluid, less predictable and more demanding, and the method needs to be learned through actually trying it out. This makes it difficult to offer clear guidelines about how to go about research which will be applicable to every situation. What follows, therefore, is not so much a set of instructions as an outline of some of the key issues to confront a researcher in the course of doing a participant research project. More detailed information on these matters can be obtained from any of the specialist texts dealing with field research, such as Burgess (1984).

Reading any of the published accounts of participant research is also a useful form of preparation for fieldwork. The previous section of this chapter provided two examples, and a browse through any fieldwork text will lead you to others, though they will not necessarily be directed towards the kinds of research questions which concern psychologists.

Despite the earlier warning (which I reiterate now) about the incredibly time-consuming nature of participant research, and the need to take careful account of any deadlines you may have to work to, you should also be aware that you don't necessarily have to commit all your time for months on end to being a participant observer. It is perfectly possible to do interesting and worthwhile participant research in a situation you enter only periodically, such as an evening class, which will probably meet for only a couple of hours once a week. The important factor, which determines whether the effort is likely to produce a worthwhile result, is whether you are able to be a member of the group over a sufficient period of time to allow relationships with the other group members to develop and thus to permit you to collect detailed qualitative data about their social worlds. However, even though this is an essential requirement of research by this method, it can be satisfied in ways that don't need the full-time involvement of the researcher. If you decide to do research in a milieu where new groups form regularly such as the evening class already mentioned, or perhaps where the nature of the group is to have a fairly fluid membership, such as a church, or a pre-natal class, then you can find it relatively easy to gain the acceptance of the other group members, at least on a fairly superficial level.

The processes involved in undertaking a participant research project can be divided into three distinct phases:

Entering the field   The first task is to gain access to the information which the field contains, so that data collection can begin.
Being in the field   Once in the field the researcher participates in the on-going social activity of the group, and can begin to record observations.
Leaving the field   The researcher extricates herself from the network of relationships which have been formed during the course of the research.

Entering the field

Identifying an appropriate research problem

As always, research begins with the identification of a specific problem which is to be addressed. Some types of research question for which this approach to

---

Box 4.3   *Types of research problem for which participant observation is appropriate*

The kinds of question for which the participant observation method is particularly appropriate are:

- Those where the aim is to study interactions between people at close range and where the role of the overt or detached observer might inhibit or alter the natural behaviour of the participants, e.g. at a party
- Those where the aim is to gain a participant's eye view of events, and to see things from an insider's perspective, particularly where the 'field' is a social institution such as a school, or shop, or prison
- Those where the aim is to acquire a direct appreciation of people's experiences, and the meanings which attach to those experiences, such as when a researcher wishes to know what the experience of physical disability is like to those who have a disability.

---

research has been found to be particularly effective are listed in box 4.3. As you can see from the information there, deciding whether to use the participant observation method is not so much a question of the particular topic which is to be researched as of identifying clearly the kinds of question which the research requires to be answered.

For example, while it is possible to study (say) family relationships by a variety of methods, including questionnaires, interviews and case studies, if the research requires the interaction of family members to be observed at close range over a period of time, then a participant observational study would be an appropriate choice (always assuming there is a family willing to accept a researcher into their household).

Identifying the place/environment for the research

Once the research problem has been identified, the environment which will constitute the 'field' of the research will usually suggest itself without much difficulty. It will, simply, be the place where one can meet the people whose behaviour and experience is the focus for the research. Obviously enough, to conduct participant research into (say) the experience of being a student, the researcher has to go where students are normally to be found – to schools colleges and universities.

From one point of view, 'entering the field' appears not to pose much of a problem. One simply finds an appropriate environment and places oneself within it. However, there is more to it than simply putting yourself physically in the same space as those who are being researched. It is also essential to be accepted as a full participant in their activities, and to be able to interact with them freely as a taken-for-granted part of the situation. Depending on the nature of the group involved, it may take anything from a few hours to several months to reach this point. And to complicate matters further, even after you have been allowed to become part of the group, you will find that your welcome will almost certainly vary from person to person, ranging from a ready willingness to talk to you, to extremely grudging. Whatever you encounter, unless some minimal degree of acceptance is granted to the researcher by the members of the group being researched, the participant research process cannot be said to have begun.

Getting into the field: passing the gatekeeper

Often success in entering the field depends crucially on passing the scrutiny of one individual, who occupies a position of power in the social structure which is to be investigated, and who is thus able to grant or deny access to the field, depending on the research milieu. Such people are known as 'gatekeepers' because, metaphorically (as well as occasionally in the literal sense) they guard the gateway to the research environment and can open or close the gate, thus allowing or preventing the researcher from gaining access. The headteacher of a school is an example of such a gatekeeper, because it simply isn't possible to do participant research in a school (unless one is already a member of staff or a student, and possibly not even then), without the consent of the head. This usually means convincing the head of two things. First, that the research will pose no threat to the established order, either internal or external. No head is likely to sanction research which is at all likely to cause problems inside the school, or threaten existing relationships with external bodies. Secondly (and quite a long way behind), the head will need to be convinced that the research has value. If there is value to the school, or other organization, even better. But the minimum requirement is probably that the research is perceived to answer some question which someone somewhere thinks is worth answering. In general, gatekeepers are unlikely to grant access to a researcher working on a project which appears to lack reasonable justification.

The gatekeeper is not necessarily someone who occupies a formal position in an organizational structure, such as a headteacher, a managing director (or a gang leader). There are also gatekeepers who, while they occupy relatively subordinate roles in the organization, are nevertheless powerful enough in informal terms to block your research. Such a person will be an influential person in the group you are studying, whose views carry weight with the other members and who, therefore, is another person who will need to be convinced that the presence of the researcher will not have any undesirable consequences. For example, in addition to convincing the head of a school of the potential value of the intended research, a researcher might, depending on the nature of the research, also have to win over the longest serving member of the teaching staff, or the school caretaker, if these are people whose opinions are regarded as significant. The problem here is that often, without inside knowledge, it is impossible to identify these individuals in advance.

However you achieve it, whether by letting your project speak for itself, or by putting on a convincing sales pitch, once you are through the 'gate', you

may find that a previously obstructive gatekeeper is almost magically trans-
formed into someone who will sponsor you and your research to the other
members of the group. This can obviously be very helpful indeed, not only in
terms of having your path smoothed as you enter the research milieu, but also
because the gatekeeper is frequently someone with a great deal of inside knowledge, who is able to give real help by pointing you towards sources of information which you might otherwise have missed.

Presentation issues: gaining acceptance

As we noted earlier, gaining acceptance by the people in the field, and especially by the individual who has the role of 'gatekeeper' is a major concern to
a participant researcher. The key factor in gaining acceptance is the way in
which a researcher presents herself and her research. This is what decides
whether or not the research gets off the ground, because if you don't present
both yourself or your research in a way which is acceptable to the 'gatekeeper',
and to other members of the group as well, you may never even get started.

Unfortunately, this is an extremely difficult topic on which to say very much,
since it is concerned with the question of how one individual is likely to be
perceived by another. Some discussion of self-presentation issues has already
been provided in chapter 2, so for our present purposes, we simply need to
make a few basic points.

Presenting yourself

The key issue here is the need to present an image or identity which meets the
expectations of the gatekeeper and the other individuals in the field. This not
only means paying careful attention to the way you dress, your personal adorn-
ment, or your grooming to ensure that you 'fit in' with the environment, but
it also means adopting an appropriate demeanour, and forms of behaviour.
You may know what these are already, but it is equally possible that some
preliminary research may be necessary to establish exactly what forms of dress,
behaviour and attitudes are likely to be required. The closer you can get in
these matters to your target group, the more easily you are likely to find
yourself accepted by group members. You are, for example, unlikely to get far
in a participant study of a group of churchgoers unless you are prepared to
behave in a subdued manner in church.

Presenting your research

The issues around research presentation include, how much or how little one
should tell the gatekeeper and other members of the group about the nature
and purpose of the research, and at what point in the project one should reveal
this information. In some cases you may judge that a straightforwardly direct
approach is best, in which you simply announce all the aims and goals of your
research to anyone who will listen. In other situations, and particularly, perhaps

where you believe that gaining access to the research field may be difficult, you will obviously want to be a lot more circumspect, at least until you feel that you have gained a degree of acceptance from the people you are researching. One strategy used by a number of field researchers, is simply to allow the fact that you are doing research to emerge by degrees as your relationship with those you are studying develops. This has the advantage that your informants' knowledge of your research aims will develop alongside their knowledge of you as a person, and is therefore less likely to stand out, as it would if it were presented before you had established some relationship with group members. If you use this approach, you will, of course, need to decide what kind of cover story you are going to present to account for your presence in the group during the early stages of the research.

In the field

Maintaining relationships in the field

Once entry to the field and a degree of acceptance by the people there have been achieved, the task is now to try to maintain those relationships in order to collect information for the research.

Part of this is simply the same process of managing relationships with others which occurs all the time in non-research situations and, because it involves exactly the same set of skills as are employed in everyday life, little needs to be said about them.

In addition, though, the researcher has to try to maximize the probability of collecting the data needed for the research. The key to this is probably to try to reduce, as far as possible, any really obtrusive differences between oneself and the people who are being researched. Although some of the personal characteristics of the researcher, such as age, or gender, may make it difficult, the researcher should try to 'blend in' with the surroundings – to become a taken-for-granted part of the scene by making sure that his clothes, mannerisms and appearance do not attract excessive attention.

Managing the observer and participant roles

Possibly the most problematic feature of participant observation research is that it requires the researcher to manage what are, in effect, two incompatible roles. On the one hand, the role of observer requires the researcher to stand back and simply record what occurs, while on the other, the role of participant requires the researcher to be continuously immersed in the stream of events, with little opportunity to stand back and record what is happening in an objective fashion. The researcher in the field can thus find herself being pulled in two directions. Successful participant research requires the researcher to maintain a precarious balance between the very different demands of the two roles.

There are penalties attached to any failure to maintain this balance. A researcher who fails to maintain a sufficient degree of detachment and who, consciously or unconsciously, becomes so involved in the group being studied – becomes, in effect a 'complete participant' – will have lost the essential ability to see things as an outsider and, to use the expressive phrase, will have 'gone native'. The result will be research which is partial, one-sided, and lacking in both objectivity and perspective.

Equally damaging to the research enterprise, too great an emphasis on asking questions and acquiring information in pursuit of the observer role may make it difficult, even impossible, for the researcher to be accepted as a participating member of the group. The result then may be a swift withdrawal of access to the research field, and the consequent scuppering of the whole project.

There is, ultimately, no solution to this problem, partly because it is intrinsic to the method itself, but more particularly because it also reflects the fact that a participant researcher is almost wholly at the mercy of the flow of events, to a much greater degree than researchers who employ any of the alternative methods.

Sometimes difficulties with maintaining an effective separation of the two roles can arise from the nature of the relationships which are formed in the field between the researcher and the members of the group being studied. You need to be aware of the distorting effect which relationships in the research environment can have on a researcher's judgement and behaviour. Relationships with other people in any situation can exert a powerful pull on the behaviour or ideas of any individual, and those who are trying to do participant research are certainly not immune from this. In fact, the literature of participant research is littered with accounts of how even the most experienced researchers have had to struggle to maintain objectivity and detachment under the impact of the expectations of the people they are studying in the field. All that a researcher can do in this situation is to try to maintain a constant scrutiny of the balance between the two roles, and to endeavour to take corrective action if it appears that one role is dominating the research to an undue degree.

Keeping records

Participant research is always a labour-intensive activity, and particularly so in the recoding and analysis of the data. If you are even moderately successful at your research, you should find that you are acquiring large quantities of highly detailed information about the social interaction of the people whose lives you are studying. This somehow has to be recorded in a way that permits you to retrieve specific items of data when you need to, relate one piece to another, and at the end of the project to analyse and make sense of all the information you have gathered. Not to put too fine a point on it, this can appear to be an extremely intimidating task as the data mounts up. How can you best approach it? Some researchers, particularly the professionals, for whom it is their main job, and who have books to write, develop vast archives of data from their research, consisting of multiple sets of cross-referenced notes on every aspect of the research field. However, this is scarcely realistic for people who are doing research with assessment, rather than publication, in mind, and a rather more modest approach is likely to be just as effective.

The following is a somewhat compressed account of a three-stage method of collecting and analysing participant data, which you should find both workable and effective from the point of view of turning out a research report for assessment. Bear in mind, though, that it does only represent the bones of a recording system, and you will have to work out for yourself the details of how you are going to proceed, in the light of the needs of your own particular project. The book by Burgess (1984) already mentioned, will give some help, as will most other fieldwork texts.

The three-stage method to be described here consists of: first, the initial recording of data as field notes while you are in the field; secondly, turning those notes into an entry in a daily research diary; and finally, weaving the information in the diary entries into a research report which describes and analyses your data and provides some conclusions on your research. We'll now examine each of these stages in more detail.

Field notes are notes made while the researcher is actively participating in events in the field. They hold a purely temporary record of all the different forms of information which are collected, including descriptions of events or people, transcribed conversations, copies of letters or other documents, or even quantitative behavioural data which might contribute to the research. The basic rule is that everything and anything which is thought at the time to be relevant to understanding the life experience of the people being studied should be included in these notes. This, of course means that you will have to exercise some degree of selectivity – but its aim should be inclusive rather than exclusive. You want to collect all possibly relevant information to which you have access: the process of choosing among these data comes later.

The six main categories of raw information which you will be aiming to collect in your research are listed in box 4.4. From this you can see that one of the main challenges of this kind of research lies in trying to attend to all the complexities of a situation in order to record a complete picture of the research milieu. Achieving this (or even holding the different categories of information in your mind at once) naturally requires practice, and to begin with you may find it easier to concentrate on attending to and recording the simple details of a situation. If you start your career as a participant observer by trying to provide straightforward answers to basic questions, such as, who said what? who did what? where did the action take place? who was present or absent?, you should find that you gradually become able to provide more complex accounts of the events you have been observing.

Finding a way of recording data in field notes is a crucial part of the research, and, in many cases it can represent a major problem for the researcher. This is because, somewhat paradoxically, taking notes on what is happening and being a participant observer are activities which do not easily mix. If the researcher is continually slipping off to one side in order to make notes on

---

Box 4.4   Six key categories of information in participant research (see Lofland, 1971, 1976)

Acts   Actions of relatively short duration, such as making a phone call, or reading a newspaper.

Activities   Actions which may last days, weeks or even months, such as attending a college course, or decorating a house.

Meanings   The participants' accounts of the reasons for their actions, such as 'having a laugh'.

Participation   A description of the range of activities in which the participants are involved. For example, someone might be a family member, but also be involved in a number of activities outside the home. The participation of that person in those external activities would also be of interest, even though the main focus might be on their role as a family member.

Relationships   Descriptions of the kinds of relationships which are observed among the individuals in the research setting.

Setting(s)   A description of the whole situation(s) in which the research is taking place.

---

whatever has just taken place, he is temporarily out of the action and may miss some vital piece of information. But staying in place in the on-going stream of activities may be just as unsatisfactory, since the act of taking notes is both obtrusive – people may stop what they are doing in order to watch you – as well as a very public reminder that you are not simply a member of the group, but a researcher who has joined it for your own purposes. This may be equally destructive to your research, since at the very least, the conversation is likely to dry up when you whip out your notebook.

However there are, fortunately, some solutions to the dilemma of how to record without seeming to do so. One possibility is to try to train your memory to hold the key points of conversations long enough to be able to make reasonably good notes some hours later, and those who have used this approach report that it becomes much easier with practice.

Another is to develop a convincing cover story which is capable of providing a rationale for note-taking in public. A keen interest in recording the details of bird behaviour might serve if the environment is outdoors and reasonably rural, but will obviously not do if your research field is indoors, in an amusement arcade. Trips to the lavatory (whether for real or simulated purposes) may likewise allow you to withdraw briefly from whatever is happening, in order to make notes, without calling undue attention to yourself, and with the added advantage of reasonable privacy.

The research diary, as its name indicates, is a record of the progress of the research which is written up every day from your field notes. The core of the diary will be a chronological account of the observed events written from your perspective as an observer. Lofland's categories, summarized in box 4.4, are a helpful guide to what you need to include.

Alongside this record of events, you could also include some preliminary analysis of the data from the point of view of any theory which may be relevant, perhaps as part of a daily summary of the research which you write. The analysis is the point in each day's write-up at which you try to stand back from the detail of the information. It gives an opportunity to distinguish any patterns, or identify correspondences or connections between different items of information, and to form the ideas which will eventually become the discussion section of your research report. Particular ideas or themes in each entry can also be cross-referenced to others as you go along to allow you to trace the history of different categories of information through the period of the research.

The research report

Finally after the conclusion of the research, and the withdrawal from the field, the diary forms the basis for a research report which gathers together the data and the interpretations which you wish to make of those data into a coherent whole. Typically, participant research reports take the form of an extended narrative description of the whole process of research, incorporating the information which has been gathered, together with analysis and discussion of the data from the perspective of the appropriate theory in order to provide an answer to the original research question. Such documents are, necessarily, rather long and complex, and are therefore almost certainly not an appropriate model to adopt if you intend to conduct your research for assessment purposes. If you are aiming to submit your report to meet the course work requirement of a programme of study, you will need to find out from a competent authority just what the requirements are as regards the length and format of your report.

Leaving the field

Just as there is more to entering the field than simply inserting oneself into the chosen situation, so too there is more to leaving the field than simply disappearing from the scene as soon as the research is complete. Before a piece of participant research can be said to have been brought finally to a close there are a number of tasks which must be completed. You should never just 'take the data and run'.

First, as an ethically aware approach to research demands, the people who have contributed information should always be given the opportunity to read and comment on your research and its conclusions. It is particularly important to do this following participant research because your report contains a qualitative record of their actions, conversations and relationships over a period of time, and in effect represents your commentary on their lives. You should therefore make sure that they have an opportunity to see what you have made of the information which they have provided, and this will almost certainly require return visits to the research setting after the fieldwork has been completed.

Secondly, in participant research perhaps above all other research methods, the other participants in the research have to be regarded as more than simply sources of data. The essence of the method requires the researcher to form relationships of different kinds with the informants and common courtesy and normal human concern alike therefore demand that the exit from the research environment should be conducted in a way which shows that the researcher places a value on the relationships which have been formed, irrespective of any value which the data may have. It is important, for all those concerned, and for the credibility of research in general, that relationships begun in the research setting should not be ended in a way which leaves the participants feeling that their goodwill has simply been exploited for narrow scientific ends.

Many of the awkwardnesses which can arise at the ending of a project can be avoided if you have been quite open from the beginning about the nature of the research, its aims, and its probable duration. All research projects have to come to an end sometime, and if the appropriate expectation has been built into the research from the beginning, then many of the difficulties of making an exit which is both ethical and graceful will be reduced, if not removed entirely.

Suggestions for Participant Observation Research

As we noted above, full-scale participant research requires a substantial commitment of time and energy on the part of the researcher which makes it difficult to contemplate if a project has to be completed under pressure of time such as happens when course deadlines have to be met.

The suggestions below are simply that – a few interesting questions which could be tackled by means of the participant method.

Participant research in one's own family was originally pioneered by researchers of the ethnomethodological persuasion, and it is still a relatively neglected field. It has the advantage that access is guaranteed, there are no gatekeepers who need to be negotiated with, and the construction of field notes can be easily accommodated by slipping out of the room for a few minutes.

Power is one of the fundamental variables in human relationships (a cynic would say that it is the *only* important variable). Using the privileged access you have to your own family, try to do some research on the processes by which power is managed in your family. How is power used in the decision making processes? Who holds the most power? What forms does that power take? How and when is it used? What happens when the power status quo is challenged by a family member? How are disagreements resolved? And so on.

Alternatively you could look at the basic processes of communication in the family, particularly at how communication depends on a set of shared knowledge and assumptions held by all family members. These are rarely, if ever, brought out into the open and discussed, but they form a kind of background against which everything else has to be interpreted, and they mean that what is said may be quite different from what is actually meant. Participant research is probably the most effective method of documenting and examining the nature of these assumptions.

You may feel that ethical, or other, considerations prevent you from using your own family as a object of participant research. As an alternative you could consider doing participant research on a group or organization such as hobby clubs, churches or sports organizations. These are readily accessible, and are generally very ready to accept new members. The best strategy is to find someone who is already a long-standing member of the social network in one of these groups who will be able to 'sponsor' you by introducing you to the other members. This will give you a much quicker entry into the group than would otherwise be possible. You can see the need for a sponsor if you consider doing research in a large rather formal group such as a church congregation. Churches exist in order to attract new members, and will probably not offer any formal barriers to someone who just turns up to services. However, without a sponsor, or someone who is 'in the know' about the network of relationships, it could take months before you can make any sense of the pattern of relationships you are observing.

Non-Participant Observation

This section of the chapter describes and explains the non-participant approach to research.

The concept of an observational system is described and examples are provided.

The key issues of the validity and reliability of non-participant observations are discussed.

The process of planning and implementing a piece of non-participant research is described, and examples of the method are provided.

Suggestions are given for research projects using this approach to observation.

Introduction

Non-participant observation lies at the opposite end of the continuum from participant research discussed earlier, and in its simplest form it involves no more than its name indicates. In non-participant (or 'pure') observation, the researcher's activities are devoted to watching and recording behaviour in a way which does not involve any kind of interaction with those being observed, and therefore, it is quite possible for research to be carried out without the subjects being aware of what is happening. This is, in fact, one of the reasons why this form of the observational method is widely used, especially in developmental research where very young subjects are being studied, since the behaviour of this group in particular is strongly influenced by the presence of adults.

The fact that the observational subjects may be unaware of the observer is important, since it permits the claim to be made that the observed behaviour has been unaffected by the process of collecting data, and thus that the problem of subject reactivity, mentioned earlier, can be avoided. It also, of course, raises important ethical issues which will be discussed once we have taken a closer look at what is involved in non-participant observational research.

Systematic observation

Systematic observation involves a data collection process which is organized by means of a clearly defined set of ideas and procedures. In contrast to unstructured observation, in which the researcher sets out to make observations of behaviour in a situation with few prior assumptions about what is likely to be of interest, systematic observation involves deciding what is to be observed, and under what conditions, before any actual observation is begun. These decisions mean that the researcher goes into a situation to collect data knowing that the purpose is to record a clearly specified range of behaviours under defined conditions, and that any other behaviours which may be present can safely be ignored. Systematic observation is therefore a much simpler, but at the same time much more rigid process than its unsystematic counterpart. Though it might appear to represent an easier task, it is in fact at least equally difficult, as we shall see. First, though, we need to take a look at the notion of systematic observation in a little more detail. To begin with we'll look at the main characteristics of observational systems in general, and then apply them to a specific problem to see how they work in practice.

The key elements which are required in order for a set of observations to be regarded as systematic are as follows:

1   **Systematic observation requires the selection of one type or form of behaviour for study.**   This must be isolated from the total range present in a situation to be the focus of the research.
2   **Systematic observation requires the construction of an observational system.**   This involves putting together a set of precise and (relatively) objective definitions of the various forms which the target behaviour can take and the situations under which observations are to be made.
3   **A sampling procedure for the collection of data must be specified.**   There is a range of sophisticated methods for sampling behaviour in observational research: box 4.5 lists some of these.

Box 4.5   *Sampling in systematic observation*

Continuous observation

In continuous observation, the observational field is observed non-stop for a given period of time and all instances of the target behaviour are recorded. The advantage of this strategy is that it provides a complete record of all occurrences of the target behaviours during the period of observation, no matter how infrequently these may have occurred. It also enables the sequencing or duration of behaviour to be recorded.

The disadvantages are that it is time-consuming, and may make considerable demands on the stamina and vigilance of the observer. The duration of the period of continuous observation should be set to ensure that a representative sample of the target behaviours can be obtained. When there are a large number of different types of behaviours to observe, or when behaviour changes rapidly, one of the following time-sampling methods should be used instead.

Time-interval sampling

Time-interval sampling is similar to continuous observation, except that it divides the period of observation into successive periods of a given length (say 60 seconds), and scores each observed occurrence of the target behaviour once only in each time interval, regardless of the number of times it actually occurred.

Time-point sampling

Time-point sampling provides a snapshot of behaviour at successive intervals through the observing period. The observer records any occurrence of the target behaviour at the end of successive time periods, say, every ten minutes. If the behaviour is visible at that point in time it is recorded, if not, not. Like time-interval sampling, the duration of the time periods has to be judged to provide a representative sampling of the behaviours of interest.

Random sampling

Random sampling of behaviour – not to be confused with random sampling from a population – is basically time-point sampling conducted on a random basis. To undertake random sampling, a sequence of integers from within the required range is taken from a table of random numbers. Each integer indicates the length of interval between one time point of observation and the next. When the research commences, the observer, makes the first observation, and records whether or not the target behaviour was observed, then consults the list of random numbers to determine how much time should elapse before the next observation is made, and so on.

The advantage of random sampling in this way is that it provides a surer estimate of the overall frequency of a given behaviour. If the same piece of behaviour is seen every time a random observation is made, then you can be confident that it is a behaviour which occurs consistently throughout the period of observation. This is in contrast to time-point sampling where the possibility always exists that the target behaviour is being produced at intervals which exactly match the observing intervals.

An example of systematic observation

As an example of how these criteria might be realized in practice, consider a researcher who decides to look into the possibility that there are gender differences in risk-taking behaviour. Suppose, further, that the specific aim of the research is to observe the behaviour of people at pedestrian crossings in order to see whether, in this situation, women are more or less prone to take risks than men. That is, whether they are more or less likely to 'jaywalk' – cross the road when the pedestrian signals are against them.

Systematic observation requires the selection of one particular form of behaviour for study.

Many forms of behaviour can be observed at a pedestrian crossing – standing, talking, eating, quarrelling, as well as walking. To meet the first criterion of systematic observation, the research will need to focus only on one part of the total behaviour which might be observed, namely the activity of crossing the road (whether by walking, running or trotting). Everything else that people might do will be ignored.

Systematic observation requires the construction of an observational system.

This criterion requires the construction of exact definitions of the forms or categories of the target behaviour. Crossing the road is a straightforward category of behaviour in itself, but it contains a number of sub-varieties which also need to be specified before the research begins. First of all, we need to define the difference between the behaviour we are interested in – jaywalking, and the other main way of getting across, namely crossing safely. Hence:

1   Crossing safely (non-risk-taking behaviour) is defined as crossing when the pedestrian signal is green.
2   Jaywalking (risk-taking behaviour) is defined as crossing when the pedestrian signal is red.

(Note that these are completely objective definitions: anyone with approximately normal vision could apply them to any sample of behaviour from any pedestrian crossing and categorize the behaviours into jaywalking and non-jaywalking without any uncertainty. Note also, that these definitions are purely behavioural, and are not at all concerned with the intentions or other mental states of those crossing.)

However, although these simple categories describe the basic forms of behaviour in which we are interested, they are not yet nearly precise enough to enable useful research to be conducted. We need to develop them further, and to do this we need to look more closely at the jaywalking category. Specifically, we need to subdivide it to take into account of the different levels of danger involved in crossing when traffic is either approaching, or not. In addition, some provision needs to be made for recording aborted crossings where a person begins to cross, but fails to complete the process. Thus, the basic categories become:

1   Crossing safely (non-risk-taking behaviour) is defined as crossing when the pedestrian signal is green.
2   Jaywalking (risk-taking behaviour), defined as crossing when the pedestrian signal is red and when traffic is approaching.
3   'Safe jaywalking' (non-risk-taking behaviour) is defined as crossing when the pedestrian signal is red, but when no traffic is approaching.
4   Abortive crossing (non-risk-taking behaviour) is defined as a crossing which is begun but not completed.

These four categories provide the basis for an observational system which defines in objective terms the main categories of behaviour which we can expect to meet on a pedestrian crossing, and which can be used to test a hypothesis about gender and proneness to take risks. However, there is still the need for a little more work to be done on the definitions, and in particular on the last one concerning abortive crossings. The problem is that while we can say quite exactly what constitutes a completed crossing (this is obviously that a person reaches the other side of the road), what constitutes an aborted one? This is rather harder, because in order to be quite clear about whether an aborted crossing has taken place it is necessary to have a behavioural definition of whether the decision to cross has been taken, in order to distinguish it from the kind of dithering which can also be observed at crossings. I leave it to you to decide finally, but one possibility would be to say that a crossing has begun when two or more steps have been taken in the road, and an aborted crossing occurs when a person leaves the pavement, takes two or more steps towards the other side, but then subsequently returns to the pavement from which they set out. You could also, if you wished take into account other (possibly) critical variables such as traffic density, or whether a person is crossing alone or with others, in defining safe and unsafe crossing behaviour.

However you continue to work at refining the sub-definitions of the main categories, once they have been identified and defined, they constitute the main part of the observational system to be used.

A sampling procedure for the collection of data must be specified.

Finally, the researcher has to make a decision about how the behaviour is to be sampled. In this case, the sequencing and duration of behaviour are not of interest, but it will be important to try to capture as many examples of risk-taking behaviour as possible. This indicates that a time-based sampling method should be used, with longish periods of observation (say thirty minutes in every hour of an eight-hour observing day). If the observations could be spread over a number of days (the more the better), and among a number of crossings, then confidence in the representative nature of the sample would obviously be greatly enhanced.

You can probably see by now some of the advantages (and possibly the dis-advantages also) of using this approach to observation. In the main, these are:

1   Systematic observation focuses on events and processes which can be precisely and objectively defined. The observer's attention is directed towards a limited part of the scene, and this permits the fine detail of behaviour to be studied in a way which would not otherwise be possible.
2   It generates clear and objective quantitative records which can be compared with each other. This, in turn, permits estimates to be made of the reliability of observations.
3   It permits the framing of very precise research questions and the testing of hypotheses.

On the other side of the scale, the disadvantages include:

1   The behaviour to be studied must be capable of being objectively defined. Those aspects of behaviour or experience which cannot be pinned down in this way are not accessible by this method.
2   By focusing concentration on relatively small-scale and finely detailed pieces of behaviour there is the risk that systematic observation will lead the researcher to lose sight of more large-scale elements of behaviour.
3   The emphasis which systematic observation places on the collection of quantitative data about behaviour ignores the importance of understanding the mental world of the subject, which includes the meanings with which particular pieces of behaviour are invested, and which can only be studied through the collection of qualitative data.

The question of how you use observational systems like these in research must already have crossed your mind while you have been reading, and this will be dealt with shortly in the section headed 'Doing non-participant observation research' on p. 179. Before we get there, however, I first want to introduce another example of an observational system, and then look at the issues of reliability and validity in observational research.

A further example of an observational system: Robert Bales's Interaction Process Analysis

As well as the example already given, you may find it useful to have a further example of an observational system to hand. Robert Bales's system has been chosen for two reasons. Firstly, because it is interesting in itself as a particularly successful attempt to provide the basis for the observation of communication behaviour and secondly because it is a system which has been widely used in variety of research contexts, and you may well find useful if you decide to do some non-participant research of your own.

Bales's system, called Interaction Process Analysis (IPA), (Bales, 1950a, 1950b), was designed to provide a method of observing and recording the communication between people in situations where they are engaged in a joint task. As you can see from the specimen IPA protocol in figure 4.1, the IPA system defines twelve types of utterance, which in turn are divided into four broad categories. These types cover the range of possible utterances which could be

	Member no.			
	1	2	3	4
Emotional responses of a positive kind				
A Shows solidarity: raises other's status, gives help, rewards				
B Shows tension release: jokes, laughs, shows satisfaction				
C Agrees: shows passive acceptance, understands, concurs, complies				
Task responses				
A Gives suggestion: offers direction, implying autonomy for other				
B Gives opinion: offers evaluation, analysis expresses feeling or wish				
C Gives orientation: offers information, repeats, clarifies, confirms				
Task questions				
A Asks for orientation: asks for information repetition, confirmation				
B Asks for opinion: asks for evaluation, analysis, expression of feeling				
C Asks for suggestion, asks for possible ways of action				
Emotional responses of a negative kind				
A Disagrees: shows passive rejection, withholds help, shows formality				
B Shows tension: asks for help, withdraws from field				
C Shows antagonism: deflates others, defends or asserts self				

Figure 4.1   An Interaction Process Analysis protocol. A simple IPA protocol for use with a four-person group might look something like this. The members of the group are each identified by a number, and each time a member of the group says something, a tally mark is entered in the column under their identifying number and against the type of utterance which was observed.

expected to occur between group members when they are engaged in a joint task. For example, one person might ask another group member for help in understanding the task – in the IPA system that would be classed as 'Asks for orientation'. The protocol also provides space for a tally to be made of the number of times each type of utterance is observed in a given observing session.

**Box 4.6   Discussion task for use with the IPA protocol –
'Survival in the desert'**

It is a mid morning in July, and the light plane carrying you across the Great Salt
Lake Desert in south-west Utah, USA, has just crash landed, killing both the pilot
and co-pilot, and causing the plane to catch fire. None of the passengers was
injured, however, but the pilot was unable to radio your position to ground
control before the accident occurred.

From remarks made by the pilot shortly before the crash you believe that you
are some distance off-course from your original flight plan, but you also recollect
him saying that there is a mining outpost about 70 miles away from the crash
site in an approximately northerly direction.

The temperature at ground level is already well over 100°F, and will continue
to climb until the sun is quite low in the sky. The area of the crash is flat and
featureless, except for numbers of large cacti. You are dressed in light clothing,
including good shoes, and you have approximately $50 and some cigarettes, as
well as personal items in your pockets.

Before the plane caught fire, you were able to salvage the following fifteen
items. Your task is to rank them in order of their importance to your survival
giving 1 to the most important, 2 to the next most important, and so on, until
all the items have been ranked.

Large torch (with batteries)	Magnetic compass
Large plastic raincoat	.45 calibre pistol (loaded)
1 large sterile dressing	Jack knife
Parachute (red and white striped silk)	Air map of the area
Bottle of 1000 salt tablets	2 pints of water per person
Pair of sunglasses per person	1 overcoat per person
A cosmetic mirror	4 pints of vodka
Book entitled *Desert Ecology*	

To use the IPA system to research interaction, a group has to be found or
created. The size of the group is not particularly important, although it should
be small enough to be easily observable – typical sizes range from three to eight
people. Once formed, the group is given a task which will necessitate discussion: any task will do – see box 4.6 for an example – and their communication
with each other about the task is observed. As each person in the group says
something, the observer decides which of the available categories the utterance
falls into, and then logs it in the appropriate section of the tally chart.

At the conclusion of the discussion, the tally marks are converted into a
count of the number of times each type of utterance is observed. A test statistic
such as chi-squared can then be employed to determine whether the pattern of
communication within the group is significantly different from what would be
predicted under the null hypothesis. (If you need to, you can find out more
information about the chi-squared test statistic, and when it can be used, in
chapter 9 (p. 419). The concepts of null and alternate hypotheses, and their

role in the process of data analysis is described in the latter half of chapter 7, pages 341–60).

Using Bales's scheme, it is possible to ask, and maybe begin to answer, questions about the nature of the communication among members of a group which could only be answered with difficulty if a less structured method of observation were to be used. For example, the following can all be answered to some degree by using this approach:

- What types of utterance do individual members of a group produce? Do they produce types of utterance from across the whole range of possibilities or do they tend to produce only a few types, and if so which?
- Do different people tend to produce characteristic kinds of utterance? Are all the questions asked by one person, say, and answered by another?
- Do particular types of utterance tend to be always directed towards the same people?
- How do utterances interact with the task in progress? Do all the questions come at the beginning of the task? What kinds of utterance are produced when the group is experiencing difficulties with the task, and by whom?

It is also easy to customize the basic IPA protocol so that more varied information can be collected and this will, in turn, allow more complex research questions to be addressed. For example, a modification to the protocol would allow extra data, such as the temporal order in which different types of utterance are produced, the identities of the speaker and of the individual to whom an utterance is addressed, to be collected. This, in turn, would allow one to see whether any pattern can be discerned in the temporal relation between speakers and types of utterance. For example, one could see whether certain types of questions are answered immediately, or only after an interval of time, how this interacts (if at all) with the identity of the person asking and answering the question, as well as how long the interval might be.

Validity and reliability in non-participant observation

Validity

The question of the validity of observational research is concerned with the extent to which an particular observational process can really be said to provide a representative sample of the variables which are sought by the researcher.

As we have seen, systematic observation requires the identification of a set of precisely defined categories of behaviour which are to be observed in the research, and it is here that the main sources of invalid observational research can be said to lie. First, there is the question of the definitions themselves. Do they represent valid ways of conceptualizing the forms of behaviour which the research seeks to examine? For example, look back at the earlier definitions of risk-taking and non-risk-taking behaviour at pedestrian crossings. How confident is it possible to be that they represent the best ways of capturing those notions both in terms of a general theory of risk-taking (perhaps part of a more general theory of gambling), and in terms of that situation? Furthermore, are the definitions complete in the sense that they do not omit any form of risk-taking or non-risk-taking behaviour which might occur in that situation? Perhaps there might be other forms of risk-taking in that situation which the definitions ignore, and if this is the case, then the data which are collected can at best represent only a partial sample from the total range of behaviour which occurs, with a consequent undermining of the validity of any conclusions which are drawn.

To some extent then, the validity question can be dealt with by ensuring (1) that the observational system can be justified in terms of any theory which it purports to provide a means of testing, and (2) that it is complete, i.e. it provides a description of all the categories of behaviour which are of interest. Apart from this, the main source of invalidity in observational research is simply inadequate sampling of the situation, and this can occur for any one of a number of reasons. It may, for example, simply be a matter of allowing too short a period of time in which to conduct the observations. The more complex the situation which is being observed, the larger the sample of instances which is needed, and hence the longer the observation process needs to be in order to be sure that the full range of instances of the variables have been obtained.

There is also the question of the complexity of the observational system. The more complex observational systems (of which Bales's IPA is one), require the observer to be fully familiar with it before it can be used in research. Even small-sized groups can generate a great deal of communication between their members, and a single observer can have to work very hard to keep track of everything which is going on and simultaneously make a record of the data. Important data may therefore be lost if the observer is less than familiar with the system, or is unable to handle the pressure of the observing situation.

Using more than one observer goes some way to reducing the possibility of data loss from this source, but the basic requirement is that the observer has to be able to provide a virtually instantaneous identification of the different types of behaviour required by the system, and to do this under possibly difficult research conditions.

Reliability

The reliability of observations depends on how consistent and accurate they are, and how free of random error. Accuracy simply refers to the extent to which the measures made of a variable actually reflect the real quantity of that variable which was present. For example, if an observer claimed to see ten examples of a particular behaviour on a single occasion, then accurate observation would require that there were actually ten examples of the behaviour. Consistency, on the other hand, is concerned with the extent to which the same standard of accuracy is obtained throughout the observing period.

One way of assessing the reliability, both as regards accuracy and consistency, of a set of observations is to determine inter-observer reliability. Independent observations of the same events are made by two or more observers, and the

extent to which their observations agree provides an index of the overall reliability of the observing process. This seems straightforward, but in fact is less
so than it seems, for two reasons. First, assessments of reliability using this
method have to take into account the nature of the observing task. Observers
who have to make few inferences, or who have relatively few variables to
watch for in the course of their observing will produce higher levels of inter-
observer agreement, than those who do not. This suggests that the exercise of
an observer's judgement across a range of possible choices may be the important source of error, rather than the observing process as such. Both reducing
the number of alternatives, or improving the training of observers in the use
of the observing system will therefore improve the reliability of research.

Secondly, there is the problem of 'observer drift'. This is the tendency for
independent observers to gradually lose their independence if they are able to
communicate with each other about the task. Their observations, in line with
the conformity effect, though initially independent of each other will show a
tendency gradually to converge. Multiplying the observers, with the intention
of taking an average of their separate observations is, therefore, not itself an
answer to reliability problems in observational research unless you can be sure
that each observer (and each observation) is truly independent from the others.

Doing Non-Participant Observation Research

The design and planning of a piece of non-participant observation can be
divided into the following three main processes:

- **The construction of an observational system**
- **The planning of the observations**
- **The collection and analysis of the data.**

Preliminary matters

The non-participant observational method is likely to be the method of choice
when the aim is to establish the frequency, context, outcomes or other objectively observable features of the behaviour of interest, and/or when the researcher is anxious to influence the data gathering process as little as possible.
In what follows, it will be assumed that a research problem has been identified
which matches these criteria. Since non-participant observational research generates numerical data which can be analysed using an appropriate test statistic
such as chi-squared, it can be used to test precise hypotheses about the frequencies of given items of behaviour.

Constructing an observational system: general principles

Putting together the observational system forms the first stage of the research
process. An observation system consists of a listing of all the different categories

or forms of the behaviour which are to be observed (see above for examples). Obviously, if your project replicates or extends another piece of research, then you can simply take over the observation system which was used in the earlier work, although you may wish to modify it to fit in with your own ideas.

Some of the general principles which lie behind the construction of an observation system have already been discussed earlier in this section of the chapter:

1   **Each of the categories of behaviour in the observational system must be uniquely defined.**   What this means is that each must be described in such a way that it enables any example of observed behaviour to be assigned to one, and only one of the categories.
2   **The system must be comprehensive.**   That is, in order to be effective the listing must include all possible forms of the behaviour of interest so that the researcher can be confident that no behaviour which is of interest will be observed which cannot be placed in one of the categories.
3   **The system must be usable in the field.**   In other words, the attempt to provide clear and unique definitions of the behaviour to be observed should not lead to descriptions which cannot be differentiated from one another in a real observing situation. They must be capable of being readily distinguished from each other by an observer.

Constructing an observational system in practice

With these principles in mind, how does one set about constructing an observation system in practice?

Establishing the categories

The first step is to **list the different categories** within the general behaviour of interest as fully and precisely as you can. Any theory which exists in relation to the problem will help here since it will probably suggest a number of categories into which the behaviour can be divided.

For example, if you intend to do some observation of social touching among males you will need to produce a set of categories which identify the different ways and contexts of touching and the different bodily regions which may be touched.

Similarly, to conduct observational research on play among pre-school children, you would need to identify different types or forms of play which you could expect to observe, and then provide a definition of each form so that they can be clearly and easily distinguished from each other.

Some preliminary observation of the target behaviour may be useful at this stage, in order to confirm that the identified categories of behaviour do in fact occur, and to see whether any have been overlooked. This also serves as a check on the ease with which the categories can be operated when the research is in progress.

Then **review the list.** It is possible that there may be some ambiguity in the definitions of different categories so that effectively there is overlap between one category and another. You need to refine the descriptions/definitions of each category to ensure that they really are distinct from each other. One way of doing this is to ask yourself how – by what behavioural signs – you would recognize each category of behaviour. Unless you can link each category to a distinctive and different behaviour in this way, they are not sufficiently distinct.

The last step is to **run a pilot test** using the preliminary list in order to check that it is both exhaustive and workable, i.e. that it contains all the types of behaviour of interest, and that these have been defined in a way which can be operated in the real observing situation. This will also suggest whether there is a need for training the observer(s) in the use of the protocol before the main data collection begins. The more categories of behaviour there are in the observing system, the more likely it is that some training, or at least careful familiarization with the categories will be needed.

Designing the observation process

Pilot testing, however, cannot begin until the question of the observation process which is to be used has been settled. This involves making decisions on:

- The location or environment where the observations are to be made
- Whether to observe overtly or covertly
- Whether to use continuous, time-interval, time point or random sampling.

Choosing the environment

The choice of environment in which observational research is to be carried out depends on a number of factors:

- **The availability, or general frequency, of the behaviour of interest.** Does it occur almost everywhere, or only in specific locations or situations? Is it public or private behaviour?

     In some cases, the choice of the place or situation where the research is to be done is made at this point. A researcher wishing to make a study of children's play will naturally head towards those places where play occurs, in playgroups, school playgrounds, parks, and even quiet side streets.

     If you plan more than one observing session beware of environment-specific 'time of day' effects. These occur if sampling the same situation at different times of day can produce different results. Morning playtime in a school playground, for example, may generate very different forms of behaviour from the afternoon playtime, which may be different again from after school or weekend play.

- **The presence of a special quality.** Sometimes in addition to this a researcher will be looking for an environment in which the behaviour has a particular quality, and this may further narrow the range of choice among the available possibilities. A researcher whose main interest lies in observing rough and tumble play, for example, will be likely to find better examples in an urban adventure playground than (say) in a playgroup, where if it occurs at all it is likely to be stopped by the adults present.

- **The need for clear measures.** It may also be that the choice of environment in which to conduct observation is influenced by the need to have behavioural measures of hidden (psychological) processes which are as clear and unambiguous as possible. In these cases, the environment selected for the research provides the researcher with a way of defining the hidden process in terms of a clear behavioural measure.
- **A manageable number of variables.** Situations can obviously vary in their complexity, and in the number of variables which they contain. Any which appear capable of influencing the behaviour of interest, will obviously need to be incorporated into the observational system and therefore, in order to limit the observational system to a reasonable size, it may be necessary to choose to observe in a situation which has as few variables as possible influencing behaviour which is being observed.

Overt or covert observation?

The planning for observational research includes the need to decide whether to undertake observation overtly or covertly. In overt observation, the observer does not hide the fact that observations are being carried out from those being observed, while in covert observation, some degree of concealment is involved, so that those being observed are unaware of the fact. Both forms of observation can raise the problem of whether, and how, to obtain the informed consent from the research participants prior to the research being undertaken.

Sometimes the problem is easily dealt with. If research is planned to take place in a laboratory, or similar setting, where those who are participating are aware from the beginning that they are to be observed, then this clearly meets the requirements of the ethical guidelines concerning informed consent.

However, if observation is planned to take place in a natural environment, such as a street, shopping mall or similar non-laboratory environment, then serious consideration of the ethical issues is required, which should be resolved at this stage before the project continues.

First, the decision to undertake overt observation in such situations may raise the problem, discussed earlier, of the reactivity of the research participants. Clearly, from the point of view of doing good research, it would be unwise to make observations in such a way if the presence of an observer is likely to have a major effect on the behaviour of those being observed. In such a case, covert observation may be seen as an easier and, from the point of view of doing effective research, better option to take, since it permits the reactivity problem to be avoided altogether.

However, as should be clear already, covert observations by definition are those made without the knowledge or consent of those being observed, and therefore involve a clear violation of the requirement to give informed consent. What is perhaps less clear is that the same difficulty can also arise when overt observation of behaviour in public is planned. This is because it is often impossible to ask every potential research participant for consent. Consider the example of someone conducting an observational study of behaviour in a shopping mall. Clearly it would be impossible to ask every single person whether they consent to their participation in the research, especially if you were unsure whether they would be required to contribute data to the sample.

The way forward from this dilemma is to recognize that there is a distinction to be drawn between observing behaviour in public places, like shopping malls, as opposed to private environments, such as private homes or in semi-private places like restaurants where behaviour can normally be viewed by a small number of others. The key difference between these two types of situation is the extent to which the people in them would normally expect their behaviour to come under the scrutiny of others.

When observation is planned to take place in a public place, where behaviour is normally open to view, and can be seen by anyone passing, then there can be no objection to undertaking observational research, even if informed consent hasn't been obtained. The reasoning here is that the researcher is simply doing, in a more systematic and concentrated form, what the other members of the public are already doing themselves, namely observing behaviour. The issue then becomes one of whether concealed or open observation is more likely to assist the purposes of the research.

On the other hand, if observation is planned of behaviour in private or semi-private situations, when people would normally expect themselves to be shielded from the gaze of the public at large, then clearly the informed consent of those to be observed must always be obtained before the research begins.

Finally, to see how each of these considerations can operate, consider the earlier example of the researcher into risk-taking behaviour. In this case, the choice of the pedestrian crossing as an appropriate place for research into risk-taking could have been a result of looking for an environment in which (a) mildly risky behaviour of an everyday nature takes place, (b) in which there would be reasonably clear behavioural evidence of the decision to take a risk, (c) in which relatively few, but objectively observable, variables would be likely to influence the decision-making process, and (d) where overt observation could be undertaken in a public place without any risk of changing the observed behaviour.

When each of these factors has been taken into account, it becomes clear that pedestrian crossings offer a better research milieu than (say) a rock-climbing school.

Continuous, time-series or random observation?

Finally, you need to make a decision about how your observations are to be distributed over time, the alternatives being: continuous, time-interval, time point or random sampling. These have all been described earlier, in box 4.5, and there is no need to repeat the discussion given there.

Designing the data collection sheet

The results of each of these decisions become part of the data collection sheet, or observation protocol. Having identified the categories of the target behaviour which are to be observed, and decided exactly how the observations are to be carried out, this is now a relatively straightforward matter of devising a simple tally chart which takes into account the following:

1   The different categories of behaviour to be observed
2   The number of sources of behaviour which are to be observed
3   The range of variables which may influence the behaviour
4   The type of observation schedule which is to be used.

The aim here is to provide a space in which each instance of the target behaviour can be logged as it is observed. It is also very important to provide a space in which the basic details of the observation such as the date, times and place of observation can be recorded. If more than one observer is used, the identity of the observer must also be recorded. See the earlier section on Bales's Interaction Process Analysis, or the suggestions for non-participant research using examples of observation protocols on p. 187.

Data collection and analysis and hypothesis testing

The main process of data collection follows from any adjustment to the observational system or procedure which has been shown to be necessary by the pilot study.

The data obtained from non-participant observation research can be of two types. First, quantitative data consisting of the frequencies (counts) of the number of times the target behaviours are observed. Provided the hypothesis has been specified before the data are gathered, these data can be used to test predictions about whether the behaviours have been observed to occur with significantly greater frequency than would be predicted by chance alone, or, alternatively whether there is a significant association between two variables which have been observed. If you need more information about how this can be done you can find it in chapter 9, where the two forms of the chi-squared test for these purposes are described and computational instructions are provided (pages 418–28).

Secondly, qualitative, descriptive data may also be collected to supplement the information provided by the purely quantitative data. For example, a study of family interaction would almost certainly be designed not only to gather data about the frequency of certain sorts of target behaviours by individual family members, but also about the way in which such behaviours manifested themselves – how they were performed. Such data can often be converted into numerical form and analysed, again by using one of the two forms of the chi-squared test described in chapter 9.

Finally, specify the hypothesis if one is to be tested, i.e. if this is not to be a purely descriptive research project. (If you are uncertain about any aspect of writing or testing hypotheses, you should read the latter part of chapter 7 before going much further). Unless there are particular course requirements which you need to satisfy, the writing-up of a non-participant project should follow the standard format for psychology reports, with appropriate modifications, as described in appendix 2.

That completes the review of the process of planning end executing non-participant research. To finish off this chapter on observational research, there is a checklist of tasks which will help you in the process of planning your observational research. After that, there is an example of a piece of research which uses the simplest possible observational system, and then some suggestions for this form of research which you may wish to pursue for yourself.

An example of non-participant observation

An interesting example of observational research, which demonstrates that it is not necessary to use a complex observational system in order to carry out worthwhile research, is provided by the work of Jenni and Jenni (1976). Their research, using non-participant observation is about as simple and straightforward as it could possibly be.

They were interested in the question of the sex-typing of posture – that is, whether a consistent difference exists between males and females in the way in which they locate the movable parts of the body, such as arms, in relation to the trunk. Specifically, they wanted to find out whether a difference exists between the sexes in their preferred method of carrying books and similarly shaped objects.

In their research, Jenni and Jenni first distinguished between two different ways of carrying books (see figure 4.2).

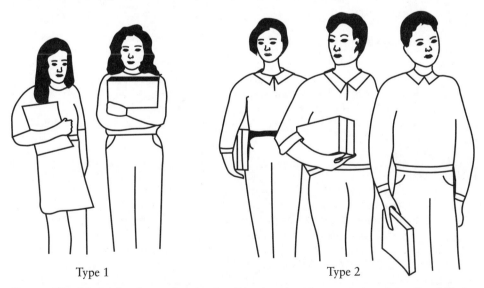

Type 1   Type 2

Figure 4.2 Methods of carrying books. Reprinted with permission from Jenni D.A. and Jenni M.A. (1976) Carrying behaviour in humans: Analysis of sex differences. *Science*, **194** 859–60. Copyright 1976 American Association for the Advancement of Science.

Box 4.7   *Non-participant observation – a checklist of design tasks*

This checklist provides a summary of all the issues and tasks which have been discussed earlier in this chapter. It can be used both as a guide to tasks which have to be completed during the process of design, or as a post-design check, to help ensure that nothing critical has been omitted from consideration.

1   The preliminary tasks

Have you
- Clearly described the research problem?
- Stated the precise aim of the research?
- Developed an explanation which either links your research to a theory or says why the observations should be made?
- Stated the hypothesis (if any) to be tested?
- Identified the appropriate test statistic, (if needed), using the test decision table on p. 386 and the descriptions of the tests in chapter 9?

2   The observational system

Have you
- Identified the type(s) of behaviour to be observed?
- Developed clear and objective definitions of each category of behaviour?
- Checked that the categories are complete, and cover all the target behaviours?
- Checked that each category is clearly distinct from the others?
- Checked that the differences between each category are easily seen in the observing situation?

3   The observation process

Have you
- Identified an appropriate location to make your observations?
- Decided which data sampling procedure to use?
- Decided whether to use overt or covert observation?
- Decided whether to use one or more observers to collect observations?

4   And finally . . .

Have you
- Designed the data collection sheet?
- Reviewed the ethical standards of the investigation?
- Run a pilot study and made any necessary amendments to the observational system, or procedure?
- If more than one observer has been used, made a preliminary assessment of inter-observer reliability?

Type 1   The books are held on the front of the body with one or both arms wrapped around the books and the forearms on the outside of the books supporting them.

Type 2   The books are supported by one hand and arm at the side of the body with the hand either above or below the books.

Their research simply involved observing a sample of males and females who were carrying books while going about their everyday activities at the University of Montana. Each person observed carrying books was placed into one of three categories – Type 1, Type 2 or 'Other', and it was found that 92% of women observed carried books using the Type 1 posture, while 95% of the males observed used the Type 2 posture.

The finding of such a striking difference between the sexes in the preferred method of book-carrying provides support for the idea that there may exist a number of general postural and gestural differences between males and females and clearly it raises the interesting question of whether such differences are innate or learned through imitation.

REFERENCE

Jenni, D. A. & Jenni, M. A. (1976). Carrying behaviour in humans: Analysis of sex differences. *Science, 194*, 859–60.

Suggestions for Non-Participant Observation Research

Suggestion 1   Gender effects in intra-group communication

Use the IPA protocol (Bales, 1950a, 1950b) described earlier, in order to study some aspects of the verbal communication within a group. Note that some prior practice in using the IPA scheme is desirable before embarking on data collection.

The aim of this project is to examine the question of whether gender has any effect on the processes of interpersonal interaction in a group. That is do male and female members produce the same number and types of utterances? Do they direct their utterances equally towards members of both sexes? What does this imply about the functioning of the group, and in particular the way in which gender influences the role which each group member plays?

A group of four or six people, evenly divided between males and females is needed for this investigation. Provide them with a discussion task, such as the one in box 4.6 above, and observe the resulting interaction continuously until the task is completed. The headings for the data sheet needed to log the utterances in each of the twelve IPA categories is provided in figure 4.3. Note that this is concerned only with the identity of the *producer* of the utterance

Bales's categories	Source of utterance					
	Females			Males		
	1	2	3	1	2	3
Shows solidarity						
Shows tension release						
etc. . . .						

Figure 4.3   Data sheet headings for use in an investigation into gender effects in intra-group communication

A similar sheet could be used by a second observer to log the *receiver* of each utterance.

Suggestion 2   *Play in captive chimpanzees*

The aim of this project is to use structured observation to investigate the play behaviour of a non-human species – the chimpanzee – under captive conditions. If you don't have easy access to a zoo, or do not wish to visit one for ethical reasons, the same project can be turned to the study of human play behaviour.

This study is patterned closely on the work of Maple and Zucker (1978), who investigated social play, that is, play which involves more than one individual in each of the great ape species (gorilla, gibbon, chimpanzee, orangutan) under captive conditions. They found that all instances of play could be accounted for using a set of 27 categories of play. Among the chimpanzees, they found that 81% of all play could be accounted for by twelve of the 27 categories (see figure 4.4).

The aim of this project is to carry out observation of a group of captive chimpanzees in order to determine whether Maple and Zucker's findings concerning the distribution of play activities can be replicated.

Planning the observation

You need to conduct the observation in a zoo which has a good colony of chimpanzees containing, if possible, some younger individuals who will be more active and playful than fully grown adults. A preliminary reconnaissance is a good idea in order to check that the chimpanzees are readily observable.

Type	Definition	%
Climbing	Jumping, swinging on apparatus	14
Pushing	Pulling, movement to free self from other animal	11
Mouth-fighting	Reciprocal contact with another's face with an open mouth	9
Jumping to ground	Jumping or dropping to ground from a climbing structure	9
Grabbing	Rapid movement to hold another animal by putting arms around other or gripping with hands	6
Object stealing	Grabbing or pulling an object away from another animal	5
Jumping over other	Jumping, swinging around, or over another animal	5
Hand contact	Touch contact with any part of another animal's body	5
Hair grasping	Holding on to hair and hair pulling	5
Hand grappling	Reciprocal grabbing and pulling at the hands of another animal	4
Dangling	Holding on to a structure with arms or legs, hanging unattached to the apparatus	4
Non-aggressive biting	Contact with other's body with open mouth, teeth visible	4

Figure 4.4   The twelve categories of behaviour accounting for 81% of all observed play in chimpanzees (Adapted from Maple & Zucker, 1978)

These days most zoos have an education department which may be able to provide information, or other help.

You will need to make your own decision about how to organize the periods of observation. The raw data from the observation will consist of a tally of every observed occurrence of any of the twelve target behaviours together with (if possible) the identity of the individual who produced it (so you can see whether one individual is more 'playful' than another). Any additional information which you can also record – vocalization, duration of individual play episodes, time of day, use of objects in play, will obviously be useful when you come to write up your research. A collaborative effort with a second observer can be useful provided you take steps to guard against 'observer drift'. The raw data can be analysed using a test statistic such as the chi-squared test in order to determine (1) whether the observed distribution of frequencies differs significantly from the chance expectation, and (2) whether it differs significantly from that found by Maple and Zucker.

Include in your write-up full information about the observations, including, if possible, the ages and sexes of the animals being studied; the size and layout of the enclosure (include a diagram); whether indoors or outdoors, and if outdoors, the weather at the time; the time and duration of observing periods; and any significant events such as feeding which take place while you are observing.

The observational system developed by Maple and Zucker for the study of play in non-human primates can also be applied to human play in order to find out whether the pattern of play activities observed in chimpanzees is also found in humans. You will need to carry out the observation in an environment containing opportunities for swinging and jumping, such as an adventure play-ground, in order to maximize the chance of observing as many of the behav-iours as possible, and some of the observational categories (such as the third and the last), will have to be dropped, but otherwise the human version of the project is the same as that for chimpanzees.

REFERENCES

Bales, R. F. (1950a). A set of categories for the analysis of small group interaction *American Sociological Review, 15*, 257–68.
Bales, R. F. (1950b). *Interaction process analysis: A method for the study of small groups*. Reading, Massachusetts: Addison-Wesley.
Maple, T. & Zucker, E. L. (1978). Ethological studies of play behaviour in captive great apes. In E. O. Smith (Ed.), *Social play in primates*, (pp. 113–42). New York: Academic Press.

Summary of chapter 4

Reduced to its essentials, observational research consists simply of a re-searcher carefully watching what occurs in a particular situation or part of the environment, recording those occurrences as accurately as possible, and then subsequently subjecting the record to analysis in order to obtain a clearer understanding of what has taken place. At least part of the value of this method of research to psychologists lies in the fact that, in its non-participant form, at least, it offers a way of studying behaviour which does not require the researcher's active intervention in a situation. This, in turn, means that as a method, it is well adapted to facilitate naturalistic research, in which natural behaviour (people's normal everyday activities) can be studied in the situation in which it normally occurs, and in a way which leaves the behaviour unaffected by the presence or activities of the researcher.

Participant observation, also known as 'field' research, is a form of observational research in which, as its name indicates, the researcher is both an observer of the on-going stream of events, and a participant in them. To do this it is necessary to be accepted as a group member by the people who are to be studied, who might be a family, a school class, or a criminal gang, or any other social unit, depending on the aims of the research. By living in close daily contact and by engaging as fully as possible in all their normal daily experiences, while simultaneously recording the details of events and interaction as they occur, the participant researcher aims to develop an intimate understanding of peoples' lives from an insider's perspective. As well as offering the possibility of insight into the normal experience of the people being studied in this way, the participant method also provides a way of researching the lives of marginal groups in society, such as criminals or drug addicts, who might otherwise be extremely unwilling to co-operate in more conventional forms of research.

The process of carrying out participant research is complex, and requires a considerable range of skills, including the ability to negotiate a way into the chosen research milieu, the presentation of oneself and one's research in a way which engenders co-operation, and the ability to manage the sometimes stressful relationships which may be found in the field. There is also, not unexpectedly, very strong tension between the two component roles of the participant observer, and a researcher who chooses this approach will find herself required to be constantly alert for signs that one role is becoming dominant at the expense of the other.

The alternative way of doing observational research is to adopt a 'fly on the wall' technique, that is, to conduct research by viewing events or the interactions between people from the perspective of a non-participant. This reduces the probability, which is always present in participant research, that the presence of the observer could influence the behaviour of those being studied.

This form of observation is, in general, based on some kind of observational system, consisting of a set of categories which can number anything from two in the simplest systems to several dozen in more complex ones, which are intended to provide an exhaustive description of every form of the behaviour which is to be observed, One well-known and widely employed observation system was devised by Robert Bales (Bales, 1950), for the recording and analysis of the verbal interaction between the members of a group who are engaged in discussion about a task. The construction of an appropriate and effective observational system represents a vitally important task for the researcher who uses this method, since it is the instrument used in the research environment to record the occurrence of each of the different types of the target behaviour which may be seen. Much of the success of a project will therefore be decided by whether the observational system is complete, concise and, most important, usable in the field.

The planning of non-participant observational research obviously requires decisions to be made about where to observe. In addition, the researcher has to decide whether to sample behaviour continuously, or by means of one of the time-sampling methods, and whether observations are to be conducted overtly (in which case there is always the risk that the behaviour will be contaminated by the presence of the researcher), or covertly, by a hidden observer. If covert observation is chosen, then careful consideration will need to be given to the ethical issues which arise, since the requirement of informed consent is clearly breached whenever people are observed without their knowledge. In general it is acceptable to observe behaviour without prior consent being given in those situations where a person would expect their behaviour to be seen by everyone, but if observation is planned in semi-private situations, such as a restaurant, then the advice of a more experienced researcher should be sought.

5 The Method of Experiment

This chapter provides a detailed introduction to the experimental method, and gives information and guidance on the planning and implementation of experiments in psychology.

- It reviews the reasons for, and the logic of experimental research, distinguishing between 'true' and 'quasi' experiment.

- It describes and explains the main options in experimental design, including the 'n = 1' design.

- It explains the concept of experimental error, and reviews the main strategies for reducing error in an experiment.

- It discusses the process of designing an experiment in detail, and provides a commented design to illustrate the process.

- It looks at three of the key ethical issues which arise in an experiment, and provides an ethics checklist for experimenters.

- It describes illustrative examples of experiments from published research and makes suggestions for project work.

(Note: In order to keep the explanations as succinct as possible, and to avoid needless duplication of information, much of the explanation about experiment in this chapter assumes that you have either read, or are also in the process of reading chapter 7 on hypothesis testing and can use the test statistics in chapter 9.)

Introduction: what is an experiment?

Before we look at the mechanics of the experimental method in any detail, we should perhaps begin by clarifying exactly what an experiment is, and what it is intended to achieve. As you will remember from chapter 1, scientific research in general involves the repeated gathering of data, by any method, in order to test hypotheses – tentative, low-level predictions which express the relationship between variables. The example from physics of the relation between temperature and pressure was given in chapter 1; another example, this time one of more interest to psychologists, would be the relation between, say, the number of words which can be remembered from a list and the length of the interval between reading the list and its subsequent recall. These relationships between variables can be of different kinds, but the most powerful, and therefore the most interesting to science, are those in which one variable is linked causally to another, so that any changes to the value of one *causes* a change to the value of another.

The identification of the relationships between variables is a fundamental aim of science because it enables more accurate predictions, and hence better theories to be generated. The problem, as you may have already realized, is how to ensure that causal relationships between one variable and another can be reliably identified when either or both may also be subject to a multiplicity of other influences. While non-experimental methods of research, such as the correlation method, can identify *regularities* in the relations between one variable and another, which may *suggest* the existence of a causal link, it is nevertheless always possible to suggest alternative reasons for the findings.

Here, in a nutshell, lies the reason for the dominance of the experimental method in psychology over the past hundred years or so. The experiment is the *only* research method which is, in principle, capable of excluding all explanations other than that which says that the changes to one variable *caused* the observed changes to the other. Whether or not such an inference can be made in the case of any particular experiment depends, as we shall see shortly, on how carefully the experiment has been designed and executed. Specific cases aside, the general point is that the experiment is the only method to permit the identification of causal relations between variables. The reason why it is able to do this lies in the concept of intervention. Consider the following definition.

> **An experiment is a method of research in which the researcher deliberately intervenes in order to introduce changes into a situation, with the intention of observing the effects of those changes on the process being studied.**

The defining characteristic of an experiment lies in the notion of intervention: the idea that a researcher acts to produce certain changes in a situation. The reason for this is tied up with the fact that the aim of the experiment as a method of research is to identify causal relationships between variables.

To see why this is so, consider again the case of the researcher who wishes to investigate the reason why people are unaccountably able to remember more of a list of words on one occasion and than on another.

Now it is obviously not possible for the researcher to reason backwards from the observed effect (i.e. differential remembering) to its cause because there are no clues in the observation itself as to what the cause might be. Nothing in the simple observation that people remember different amounts from a list on different occasions directs attention to any particular phenomenon which might act as a cause – the cause could lie in any one of several variables.

The only alternative, then, is to reason forwards, that is, to try to reason about what a potential cause might be, and then to test out the supposition in order to see whether it is correct. But here again there is a difficulty. While a potential cause for observed phenomena can be pulled out of thin air, so to speak, there is still the problem of obtaining confirmation that it has, in fact, acted on another variable to produce the observed phenomenon. This, as you have no doubt already seen, is where the concept of intervention becomes important.

Suppose our hypothetical experimenter has somehow guessed that the interval between memorization and recall is implicated in the phenomenon of differential remembering. How can it be determined whether it is really a cause and effect relationship? The first step to obtaining an answer is that such relationships can only be identified through the direct action of the experimenter. It is only if the experimenter acts deliberately to vary the interval between memorization and recall, and then subsequently observes whether recall undergoes any changes, that it is possible to even begin to infer the existence of a causal relationship between the variables. Only if observed changes to a variable can be traced back to known antecedents, is it possible to conclude that there may exist a causal link between them. The importance of the experimenter's intervention lies here, since without action to change the value of one variable one cannot begin to identify the source of any observed changes to another.

Of course intervention by itself cannot provide positive identification of a causal relationship between variables. As we will see shortly, it is also necessary to exclude all alternative possibilities by controlling other variables out of the experimental situation. Nevertheless, intervention provides the necessary condition on which the rest of the experiment is founded.

Independent and dependent variables

The first step towards an experiment is to limit to two the variables with which the research is to be principally concerned. These two variables, called the 'experimental variables', represent operational definitions of the specific psychological concepts in which the researcher is interested. (See chapter 1 for more about these concepts.)

The independent variable (hereafter referred to as the IV) is the variable which has been identified, from theory or elsewhere, as a possible cause of the phenomenon being researched. In the experiment, the value or level of the IV is changed by the experimenter in order to observe whether any consequent changes occur to the dependent variable.

The dependent variable (hereafter referred to as the DV) is the variable which is thought to be causally linked to the IV, and which is therefore expected to change its value in response to any changes induced to the IV. During an experiment this variable has its value measured in order to detect any such changes in response to manipulations of the IV. It is these measurements which constitute the data of the experiment.

The logic behind naming the variables in this way is that the IV, although it is controlled by the experimenter, is an independent force in the experiment, while the value of the DV will, if the causal link exists, be *dependent* on the changes which are made to the IV.

Controlling other variables

The aim of the experiment designer is to allow one IV to act on a single DV, so that any changes to the value of the DV can be measured. However, there are always more variables in an experiment than just the IV and DV, and many of these are potential influences on the value of the DV. These are sometimes called the 'extraneous variables' since they include all the other variables in the experimental situation, apart from the IV and DV.

The main categories of extraneous variables with which the designer of an experiment needs to be concerned are:

1 **Participant (or subject) variables**   Those variables, such as intelligence, motivation, expectations, manual dexterity, handedness, and so on, which constitute the differences between one research participant and another.
2 **Treatment variables**   Variables which arise from the way the participants are allocated to different treatments, or conditions in an experiment. For example, the order in which tasks are taken in an experiment is one kind of treatment variable.
3 **Task variables**   Those variables which arise from the procedures which the participants are required to perform in an experiment. They include such things as the degree of difficulty of the task, the time allowed for its completion, or the nature of the instructions given to the participants.
4 **Situation variables**   This is a large and varied category which contains all those variables found in the environment in which the experiment takes place. It not only includes the physical characteristics of the space, such as the temperature, noise level, and so on, but also features such as the demeanour of the experimenter, the presence or absence of other people.

Experimental error

The basic problem which faces a researcher engaged in designing an experiment is that unless extraneous variables are controlled, they may influence the outcome of the experiment. Without control, any changes which are observed to the DV could be due to the effect of one or more of the extraneous variables instead of, or as well as, the IV, and it will thus be impossible for a researcher to be sure that the IV has been the sole influence on the DV. When this occurs the extraneous variables are said to have become 'confounded' with the effects of the IV in the experiment.

A researcher has therefore to consider carefully the nature, and possible effects of the extraneous variables in the design of an experiment, because if they are not dealt with they may prevent the IV from acting on the DV in the desired fashion. The skill in successful experiment design comes from knowing which variables can (and must) be fully controlled, because they are certain to influence the DV, and which can be allowed to remain uncontrolled because they are unlikely to exert significant influence on the DV. Much more will be said about sources of error and methods of control later in this chapter.

Experimental and control conditions

The goal of experiment design, then, is to create a situation in which any causal relationships between variables may be identified by causing the value of an IV to change while recording the value of a DV. At the same time, the control of appropriate extraneous variables ensures that any changes to the DV which may be observed are attributable only to the effects of the IV.

In many experiments, the different levels or values of the IV are provided by the existence of separate **experimental** and **control** conditions.

(Note: The word 'condition' is being used here in a rather specialized sense. In the context of the design of an experiment a 'condition' refers to any of the different categories of experimental treatment within which data are collected, as the following should make clear.)

The **control condition** is the 'nil intervention' condition in the experiment, and is created when the value or level of the IV is such that the research participants effectively have received no treatment at all (apart, that is, from any procedures which are intended to *disguise* the fact that no treatment has been given). The measures of the DV which are obtained in this condition therefore provide the standard or baseline performance of the participants.

The **experimental condition(s)**, of which there may be more than one, are 'intervention' conditions. That is, they represent *changes* to the values or levels of the IV *away* from the level set in the control condition in order to see whether there occur any consequent changes to the value of the DV.

The important role played by the control condition in an experiment can be best appreciated by constructing, in imagination, different versions of the same experiment, as follows.

First, the basic scenario. Imagine a researcher interested in the effect which listening to music while studying (the IV) has on the comprehension of information (the DV). An experiment could be set up to look at this in which subjects, matched for academic ability, were required to study a standard passage from a textbook for a standard period under three conditions. The control 'no music' condition in which they study in silence, and two experimental conditions, each of which hears a different type of music (say, rock music and string quartets) being played while they study. All three groups are subsequently tested for their understanding of the test passage.

Suppose, first that the results indicate that comprehension is significantly worse in both the experimental groups compared to the control, but that there is no significant difference between the two experimental groups themselves. What can we conclude? It appears that listening to music of either sort has an adverse effect on the comprehension of information, since those subjects who listened to music while studying in general did worse on the test than those who studied in silence.

Now imagine, first, that there had been no control group in the experiment, and secondly, that a significant difference had been found between the two experimental conditions. What could be concluded from this? Certainly not that listening to music adversely affects the studying process, since there is no baseline condition against which to measure the performance of the subjects. In fact, as you can see, the character of the experiment has subtly changed in the second version. It is now not the presence of music while studying, which constitutes the IV in the experiment, but the character of the music itself. We have to conclude from these results therefore that if music is present when a person is studying, the type of music which is played may affect how much is learned. We are not, however, in a position, as we were before, to make a clear causal assertion about the effect of the presence of music as such.

Now, in your imagination, reinstate the control condition which, as before, produces results which are significantly different from either experimental condition, and retain the significant difference between the two experimental conditions. What might be indicated by this pattern of results? Since, once again, there is a baseline condition against which to gauge the results, we are now able to say again that the presence of music while studying *does* affect comprehension and in addition, that the effects of the music depend on what kind of music is played. In other words, we are able not only to make the simple assertion that music affects learning, but that its effects depend on the kind of music which is played.

The point of these mental exercises has been to demonstrate the role of the control group in experimentation, and to show how the presence of a 'nil-intervention' control group affects the nature of the IV and thus changes the kind of inferences which can be made about the results. These considerations should play an important role in influencing the decisions made at the design stage of an experiment. When the research is concerned with whether or not a particular variable produces a predicted effect, then it will clearly be necessary to include a control condition in the design. In other cases, such as when the general effect of a variable has already been established, and the aim of research is to determine whether different values or levels of the IV produce equal effects, then a control condition will be less vital (though still useful).

'True' and 'Quasi' Experiments

We are now in a position to make the important, but sometimes overlooked, distinction between 'true' experiments and 'quasi', or 'near' experiments. Understanding the difference between these two forms is crucial to ensuring that the results of experiments are correctly interpreted.

'True' experiments

A 'true' experiment is one which is capable, by virtue of its design, of identifying a causal relationship between an IV and a DV. That is, by choosing a 'true' experiment design, and ensuring that it is implemented effectively, the researcher can argue that any changes observed in the value of the DV have *really* occurred in response to the manipulation of the IV.

To qualify as a 'true' experiment the following are required:

1 **Random assignment to conditions** The research participants are *randomly* assigned to each of the conditions in the experiment in order to ensure that the conditions are equal to each other before the experiment begins. Random assignment provides the *necessary* condition for making causal inferences about the relation between IV and DV.

2 **Equal treatment of subjects** The treatment of research participants in the experiment is equal in every way *except* in relation to the variable being investigated as the IV. That is, in the experiment, participants are treated differently in different conditions in respect of only one variable, and the different treatments given them in the conditions constitute the different levels or values of the IV.

And, possibly, depending on the aim of the experiment (as mentioned above):

3 **Presence of a control condition** A control 'non-intervention' condition provides a baseline measure of the DV against which the values of the DV in the experimental condition can be compared. The confidence with which a casual relationship can be identified is strongest if there is a control condition.

'Quasi' experiments

A 'quasi' experiment is one which lacks one or more of the first two features from the list above. Therefore, it will not permit the conclusion to be drawn that an IV *caused* any observed changes to the value of a DV. It *may* be possible to conclude that a causal relationship is *suggested* by the data obtained from a 'quasi' experiment, but because the researcher cannot be sure about either the equivalence of groups, or the control of extraneous variables, it follows that is not possible to claim with certainty that the relationship is a causal one.

Nevertheless, 'quasi' experiments occupy an important place in the psychology researcher's cupboard of methods, because they often enable data to be gathered which could not be acquired by means of 'true' experiments.

One particularly useful application of quasi experiments is for questions where the IV cannot be directly manipulated by the researcher. For example, research on the effect of levels of self-esteem on another variable cannot, for ethical reasons, be pursued by directly manipulating people's views of themselves. However, it is possible to design a quasi experiment in which the participants provide indirect measures of their self-perceptions by means of a questionnaire, and are subsequently allocated to different conditions in the experiment on the basis of their answers. In this case, the research design involves a quasi rather than a true experiment because the assignment of participants to conditions is non-random, and there is no untreated baseline condition against which a comparison can be made.

Note that all but one of the designs in the following sections can provide *either* a true or a quasi experiment: only the single sample design is intrinsically a quasi experiment.

Field experiments

The discussion so far has tended to assume that the laboratory is the natural place for carrying out experiments, and that this is particularly so of 'true' experiments which seek evidence for the existence of causal relations between variables. The reasoning is that a researcher who is seeking to create a situation in which only a single variable is capable of influencing the value of the variable being measured is likely to be most successful if the experiment can be conducted where control can be exerted over the situation in which the measures are made. Thus, experiments in psychology have largely been carried out in the relatively controlled environment offered by laboratories. (Note, that in psychological research, the term 'laboratory' doesn't indicate a room of any specific size, shape or equipment. It simply means any environment over which some basic level of control can be exerted, and in which any equipment needed for the experiment can be set up.)

However, although psychology has historically been a laboratory-based discipline, it is not essential to work in a lab in order to do experiments. It is also perfectly possible to design and carry out experiments, both true and quasi, in more natural situations than the laboratory can provide. Experiments of this type are called 'field experiments' because they take place outside the laboratory. The 'field' is any non-laboratory environment in which people are engaged in the normal tasks of everyday life – working, studying, playing and so on.

The value of the field experiment as a research method is that it avoids at least one of the criticisms which have been levelled against laboratory-based research in psychology. This points out that laboratory research typically requires the participants to undertake tasks which are often difficult for them to comprehend under conditions which are highly constrained and very different from those to be found outside the laboratory. Inevitably, it is argued, the data produced under such conditions is a **laboratory artefact** rather than real information about human behaviour and experience.

Unlike laboratory research, the method of field experiment offers a way of studying behaviour and experience in the environment or situation in which it would normally occur. Doing a field experiment involves the researcher in *sampling* behaviour in natural situations rather than *producing* behaviour in the laboratory.

That last point may need explaining. Basically, the argument is that, in general, a laboratory experiment is designed to obtain a particular form of response from the research participants, even though that piece of behaviour might not be what the participant would normally choose to do. For example, a memory researcher might require participants to memorize a list of words, and then recall as many as possible, but the memorizing and recall of the list is clearly behaviour which has only been produced at the request of the experimenter. It might be quite different from what people would normally do when given a list of words to read.

In field research on the other hand, each research participant remains free to respond as they wish to a particular situation or environment. The researcher defines the situation in which the data are to be gathered, but the research participants are then simply allowed to behave as they normally would, without the researcher setting them a task, or requiring them to produce any specific form of behaviour. In such a case, the researcher is obtaining a sample from the whole range of behaviours which are possible in that situation. Field research into memory, for example, might be interested in how much people can remember about sequences of events – whether, for example, they can generally get the sequence right, or whether they tend to rearrange it to fit in with their assumptions about what is going on. A researcher on this topic might cause several different kinds of sequences of events to occur at different times in a busy street (a fight, for example, or someone falling off a bicycle), and might then ask onlookers what they could remember about the event and the setting. Some will remember quite a lot with some accuracy, some will remember a little, and possibly some will remember nothing. The important point is that, unlike the participant in a laboratory experiment, they have not first been instructed to remember by the researcher, and are, therefore, simply producing their natural behaviour in that situation.

The basic idea of field experiment, then, is to collect data about people's behaviour and experience by allowing them to respond to a situation in the way which is natural to them, rather than by requesting a particular kind of response in the constrained situation provided by a laboratory.

True and quasi field experiments

It is probably safe to assume that field experiments are more likely to be quasi experiments than true experiments for the obvious reason that it is likely to be extremely difficult to exert the same degree of control over the data gathering within a field experiment as is possible in a laboratory. This obviously weakens the extent to which causal inferences about the effect of an IV on a DV can be made. In a field experiment, for example, it may be impossible, to devise a true 'non-intervention' control condition, or to assign participants to conditions on a truly random basis, both of which are required to identify causal relations. Moreover, the extraneous variables in a field experiment almost always have to be allowed to change at random during the data gathering process, which further raises the possibility of confounding the IV.

This is not to say that true field experiments are completely unknown. In some situations it is possible for a researcher to exert a sufficiently high degree of control over key variables for a true field experiments to be carried out. One well-known example, mentioned elsewhere in this chapter, is the study by Rosenthal and Jacobson (1968), on the effects of teacher expectations on children's educational performance.

Experiment Designs

The aim in listing the ten different experiment designs which are in the following section is not to overwhelm you with choice, but to let you see how experimenters have risen to the challenge of designing different experimental situations in which useful data can be collected. Each different design has its own advantages and disadvantages, and as we note elsewhere, part of the challenge in designing good experiments lies in selecting the design which is most appropriate for the needs of a particular investigation. You will also find, if you have already read chapter 3, that some of these deisgns are familiar to you. This, as we noted there, is because they represent basic ways of organizing an investigation which are essentially the same whether data are to be collected by survey, observation or experiment.

The independent subjects design

In its simplest form, this design (which can also be called the independent samples design), is arrived at by taking a single sample of individuals, and

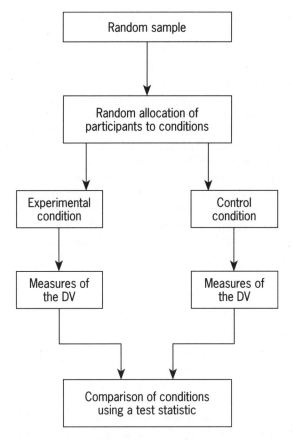

Figure 5.1   The independent samples design

assigning each participant *at random* to either one of two conditions. One of the groups constitutes the control (untreated) condition, and the other the experimental (or treatment) condition. Because under most circumstances, each participant is tested separately, and contributes data to only one of the conditions, each individual piece of data can be considered to be completely independent of every other piece. Figure 5.1 provides a summary of the key features of the design.

The aim of the independent subjects design is maximize the ability of the researcher to argue that any changes to a DV were caused by changes to the IV. Hence the use of randomized assignment to the conditions which tries to ensure that the two groups are as equal as possible before the experiment begins.

However, because each item of data comes from a different individual, all the various differences which exist between people are *not* controlled, and may therefore operate as a source of error in the experiment. For example, participants may differ from each other in terms of their motivation to co-operate with the experimenter, in their manual dexterity, or in their ability to follow instructions.

It follows then, that if this design is used, any difference between the two groups which is found in the data will be a reflection of the mingled effects of the experimental treatment *and* of the naturally occurring differences between individuals. However, the process of randomly allocating participants to conditions ensures that the effect on the data of such interpersonal differences is not systematic and it can almost certainly be disregarded.

If the independent subjects design is employed *without* random allocation of participants to conditions, then the experiment fails to meet the necessary criterion for a true experiment, and should be regarded as a quasi experiment. In such a case, the possibility exists that the interpersonal differences may favour one condition over the other, and this is enough to limit the extent to which a causal relationship between the IV and the DV can be argued.

Two commonly used variations which extend the basic two-group independent subjects design are the before–after two-group design and the multigroup design.

The before–after two-group design

In the before–after form of the basic two-group design the randomized assignment of participants to the conditions in the experiment is followed by administration of identical pre-treatment tests in order to establish the baseline values of the DV in each condition. The experiment is then run, with different treatments for participants in each condition and both groups are tested again. Subsequent comparisons of data are made between the results of the pre- and post-tests *within each condition*, rather than between conditions (see figure 5.2). This approach has the advantage that it offers additional control over inter-subject differences compared to the basic two-group version because it enables subjects to act as their own controls.

The multigroup design

The multigroup version of the design, as its name suggests, simply increases to two or more the number of experimental conditions in the basic design, thereby enabling the effect of more levels of the IV on the DV to be tested (see figure 5.3). This version can also be combined with the before/after design, described above, in order to obtain control over inter-subject differences.

The repeated measures design

The simple repeated measures (or correlated samples) design consists of a single group of participants which acts as its own control in the experiment. Each participant is tested twice: once as an untreated control, and then again, as a member of the experimental treatment condition (see figure 5.4). The aim in this design is to control for the possibility of experimental error due to the

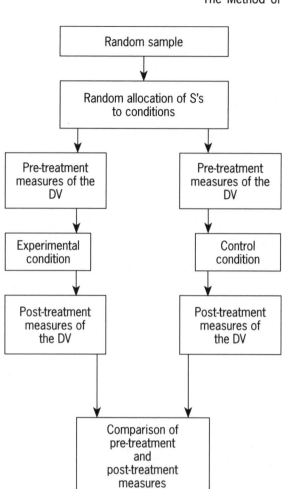

Figure 5.2   The before–after two-group design

individual differences between participants by using the same persons as the sources of data across the different conditions of the experiment.

It might be thought, in the light of what was said earlier, that an experiment using the repeated measures design cannot be a true experiment, since it is impossible to assign participants to the individual conditions at random. However, in this case, the critical feature of the design is the *order* in which the two or more conditions are taken (since each participant contributes data to all conditions). As long as participants are directed to take a particular order of conditions (either A–B or B–A) by means of a random procedure, then the repeated measures design *can* support causal inferences concerning the effect of the IV on the DV.

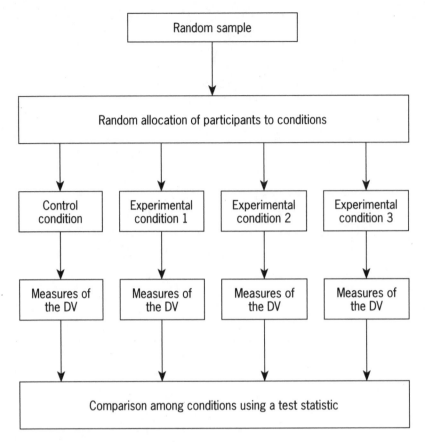

Figure 5.3   The multigroup design

If you use this design you should be particularly aware of the need to control for error due to the effects of the same participants appearing in more than one condition in the experiment. The effects on the participants of using this design will include fatigue if the experimental task is lengthy or boring, and 'practice effect' – enhanced performance on a second task as a result of completing an earlier first task – which occurs if the experimental tasks are similar or too closely spaced in time. Techniques which help to neutralize the possible effects of these sources of error are described later in this chapter.

The matched subjects design

The matched subjects design is a variation on the independent subjects design, which at the same time provides some of the advantages of the repeated measures design (see figure 5.5). It aims to improve the comparability of the conditions in the experiment by trying to control at least one of the interpersonal differences which otherwise would be a source of error in the experiment.

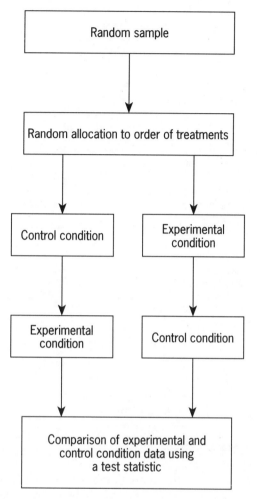

Figure 5.4   The repeated measures design

In this design two (rarely more) different groups of participants are involved. Each individual is given a pre-test, and then matched, i.e. paired up, with another individual on the basis of their pre-test scores. One participant in each pair is assigned at random to the control condition, and the other member of the pair becomes a member of the experimental condition. This arrangement means that although the participants contribute data independently to their conditions, each has at least one point of similarity with one participant in the other condition. Random assignment to conditions is, therefore, not achieved in this design.

It is also important to note that the matched subjects design may provide only partial control over the variable on which participants are matched. The effectiveness of the matching process is limited by the reliability and validity of the measuring technique used for the pre-test. Use of an unreliable method

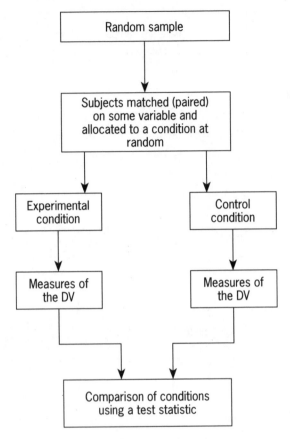

Figure 5.5 The matched subjects design

undermines the accuracy of the matching process, while an invalid measure simply renders the whole design ineffective. Moreover, unless a relatively large pool of potential participants can be drawn on, it may be impossible to achieve even a reasonably close match for every individual. Some participants may effectively be unmatched on the key variable, with undesirable consequences for the reliability of the data which are obtained.

The yoked controls design

The standard form of the first design we considered here, the independent samples design, aims to treat the control and experimental independent groups identically in every respect except, crucially, in relation to the independent variable. Typically, the experimental participants receive a particular treatment intended to produce a given effect, while the control individuals do not. However, sometimes it is not enough to define the control condition in terms of ensuring that the IV has a value of zero, but instead it is necessary to take the more subtle approach provided by the yoked controls design.

In the yoked controls design, each member of the experimental group is first paired with a member of the control group, and the two are then run together. The experiment is arranged so that as the experimental member of the pair receives the treatment appropriate to the experimental condition, the behaviour of that individual simultaneously determines the nature of the experience of the control. In effect, therefore, the two individuals are 'yoked' together since they each receive identical treatment in every respect except in relation to the single variable which constitutes the IV in the experiment.

For example, in an experiment into the effect of reward on self-image in a learning task, a yoked controls design would require that every time the experimental participant is rewarded for a correct response, the control must also be identically rewarded whether or not a correct response, or indeed any response, had been produced. Both are rewarded, but in only the experimental case is the reward linked to performance. Subsequent testing can then determine whether the rewarding of task performance has any effect on self-concept.

The single blind design

Because participants can be adept at figuring out the aim of an experiment from the clues in the experimental task, they may well be able to guess which is the experimental and which the control condition and tailor their behaviour accordingly. If this is likely to affect the outcome of the experiment, the single blind design can be used. This makes it harder for the participant to find the clues because it involves setting up the experiment so that the participants are unaware of whether they are contributing data to the control condition or to the experimental condition. Single blind conditions can be achieved if participants are allocated to conditions in the experiment at random and if care is taken to prevent participants from seeing anything which could provide a clue to the identity of the different conditions.

The double blind design

The double blind design extends the restriction on information to include the person running the experimental session. In the double blind experiment both participant *and* experimenter are unaware of whether any particular trial is an experimental or a control trial. This can be difficult to arrange, since to use it in psychological research generally requires a naive experimenter who is unlikely to guess the nature of the trial from the task. It is, however, a design worth considering if it seems likely that the participants in an experiment will be able to guess the purpose of the experiment, or the nature of the conditions from the behaviour of the experimenter.

The single sample design

The single sample design is also called the 'one-shot' design because it consists only of a single sample of participants who generate one set of scores (see

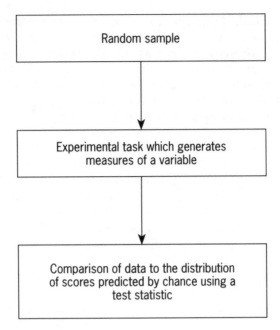

Figure 5.6   The single sample design

figure 5.6). The weakness of the design lies in the lack of a control condition
to provide a standard level of the DV against which the result can be measured,
so that the question of whether the IV caused the value of the DV cannot be
answered. However, the design can still be used to answer interesting questions
even though a control condition is unavailable. For example, given a single
sample of data, questions such as whether a set of scores are likely to be typical
of the population from which they were taken can be answered, and goodness
of fit tests exist which allow data to be evaluated against a theoretical distribution in order to determine whether a significant difference exists between
observed and predicted results.

The n = 1 design: Experiments involving a single subject

In all the designs mentioned above, experimental research involves collecting
data from a number of individuals who constitute a sample drawn from a
specified population. However, data collection from a group of subjects is not
essential to carrying out an experiment. As we discussed in chapter 3, the
function of sampling is simply to make it possible to generalize the results of
the experiment back to the population from which the sample was taken but,
as a number of examples from the history of psychology show, that may not
always be necessary. It is also possible to carry out interesting and valid investigations using what is, in effect, a sample of n = 1 consisting of only a single
individual. Herman Ebbinghaus (1850–1913) made pioneering use of this approach when he made the first systematic approach to the study of human

memory using only himself as the experimental subject. A further example, the case of 'Little Albert' (Watson & Rayner, 1920), is also described below.

Much of the interest in n = 1 experiments lies in the fact that they straddle two different approaches to research. On the one hand they take the rigorous, controlled approach to identifying causal relations which is the hallmark of the experiment, while on the other their clear focus on the behaviour and experience of a single individual give them clear affinities with the more qualitative approach taken by the case study method. A fuller discussion of the n = 1 approach to research can be found in Dukes (1965).

When might an n = 1 experiment offer an appropriate research strategy? If there is only one unique case to be studied then it clearly represents the only approach which can be taken. Although it is not strictly experimental, the case of the person known as 'SB', mentioned in chapter 2 is an example of such an approach, since there is only one person with SB's particular set of life experiences, (though there are certainly others whose experiences have been similar).

n = 1 research is also an option when the researcher believes that she is dealing with an aspect of behaviour or experience which is so general that data from a single case is expected to be typical of a wider population. The study (see below) of the classical conditioning of a fear arousing stimulus in an infant known as 'Little Albert', by Watson and Rayner (1920) is a case in point. Once it had been shown that the fear response could be conditioned (and generalized to other stimuli), further demonstrations were clearly redundant since repeating the basic experiment would not have added anything to what had been learned from the single case.

Finally, n = 1 experiment is useful as a method of exploratory research, which can be used in order to clarify issues, or to enable a new research strategy to be tried out. Its advantage lies in the fact that it can provide an economical way of starting a line of research, since it does not require the effort needed to draw a representative sample from a population. Obviously, though, if an interesting result is obtained, then further work involving a full-scale sampling procedure should be the next step.

Choosing a design for an experiment

Choosing a design for an experiment involves selecting one particular balance of advantages and disadvantages in relation to a particular research problem, and it is therefore difficult to give further guidance without also knowing the nature of the research problem to be addressed. As we have seen, interesting work can be done using the single sample and n = 1 designs, but the basic designs which will satisfy most ambitions are the three listed below. They are in order of preference, determined by their ability to support causal inferences about the relations between variables:

1　The before–after design (two or more groups)
2　The independent subjects design (two or more groups)
3　The repeated measures design.

The next section of this chapter takes us on from the basic questions of experiment design, to look at the various ways in which error can creep into the process of doing experiments. Before we do begin to look at this crucial concept, though, we'll first consider some examples of experiments drawn from the vast psychological literature. These are all 'classic' experiments which you can find discussed in virtually any introductory text. However, textbook descriptions tend to emphasize the result of the investigation, and only rarely dwell on the details of the research design, so it is easy not to notice what kind of an experiment you have been reading about. The purpose of this short selection is to provide living examples of some of the designs we have just been looking at and, I hope, also to demonstrate how the rather dry and abstract descriptions you were given earlier become much more interesting when you can see them in their natural surroundings.

Some Examples of Experiments

A simple two-group true experiment

Examples of this form of experiment abound in the psychological literature, and a good one can be found in the work by Gordon Bower et al. (1969) on the effect of the prior organization of information on memory. In this experiment, Bower and his co-workers show that reminding people of the way in which sets of nouns (such as the names of metals) can be organized into categories (common metals, precious metals, and so on), enables them to recall the nouns more easily.

The control group, who were not reminded of the categorization were able to recall significantly fewer nouns on the recall test, thus enabling Bower et al. to conclude that prior organization of the information *causes* better retention to occur.

A multi-group true experiment

An interesting example of this design is provided by the work of Schachter and Singer (1962) on cognitive influences on the experience of emotion. The experiment contained four different conditions, of which three provided the participants with different levels of information about the physiological effects of an adrenaline injection. After the injection, each participant's response to emotional behaviour by a confederate of the experimenter was rated by observers as well as by the participants' own reports in order to provide the measures of the dependent variable. A fourth 'placebo' group who received a saline injection instead of the adrenaline was included to control for the effect of receiving the injection.

The full results of the experiment can't be described here in detail, but the key conclusion drawn by Schachter and Singer is that the behaviour of some of the participants in the experiment was caused by a 'cuing' effect in which the participants used the behaviour of the confederate in order to make sense of physiological events caused by the adrenaline injection.

A yoked controls design

The famous 'kitten carousel' experiment of Held and Hein (1963), offers a particularly clear view of the workings of the yoked controls design. In the experiment, which was designed to investigate the effect of free movement on the development of perception in kittens, the control kitten was allowed to move freely within a patterned environment – actually a circular enclosure with a pattern of lines painted on the side of the inside wall. The yoked experimental kitten was restrained in a basket which ensured that it was not allowed free movement. However, the yoking ensured that the 'restrained' kitten received exactly the same set of visual experiences as the control kitten because the free movements of the control kitten were translated by the apparatus into movements of the basket, and hence into passive experience for the experimental kitten.

Later, when tested, the perceptual abilities of the control kitten were found to be superior to those of the experimental kitten, leading Held and Hein to draw the conclusion that free movement within a patterned environment was essential to the development of normal perception in these animals.

A quasi experiment

Detailed accounts of Stanley Milgram's (1963) investigation into obedience are easy to find, since it is one of the most famous pieces of research work in psychology, as well as possibly one of the most ethically notorious. Although it is often referred to as 'Milgram's experiment', it is not, in fact, a true experiment. The design consists of a number of different groups of participants, each of which is treated in a somewhat different way, but because there is no untreated control group, it has to be regarded as a quasi experiment.

The aim of the research was to determine whether participants would obey an instruction to deliver a painful shock to another person and, secondarily, whether they would continue to do so until the maximum voltage was reached, despite having many opportunities to stop doing so. The study was presented as an experiment on learning, and participants were required to deliver graded levels of electric shock to an individual, designated as the 'learner', whenever he failed to present the correct answer. In fact there was no current, and the 'learner' was a confederate of Milgram. The research found that people were generally willing, to an unpleasant degree, to deliver painful shocks to another person simply on the instruction of the experimenter.

Although there was no control group as such, many of the variables in the situation were carefully controlled, and Milgram was able to sift out some possible confounding variables, such as the reputation and prestige of the university in which the original experiment took place. However, the extensive use of deception in order to control the participants' understanding of what the experimental procedures were really about has been strongly criticized, and is now generally regarded as unacceptable.

A field experiment

An example of a field experiment which also possesses the essential characteristics of a true experiment is the study of Rosenthal and Jacobson (1968), into the effects of teacher expectations on academic performance. In this study, following the administration of a standard intelligence test, about 20% of the students in each of a number of classes were identified to their teachers as potential academic 'spurters'. In fact, they had been chosen entirely at random. After a year the children were tested again, and it was found that those who were believed by their teachers to be 'spurters' had made greater intellectual gains than those who were not. The conclusion which Rosenthal and Jacobson draw from this research is that the identification of some children as 'spurters' generated different expectations for those children in their teachers. These expectations then caused the teachers to interact with such children in a way which produced positive effects on their intellectual growth. The study is particularly worth reading for the care with which Rosenthal and Jacobson try to rule out alternative explanations for their findings.

A single sample design

We have already seen an excellent example of the single sample design described in box 1.4 of chapter 1. As well as providing a fascinating case study of the military funding of research, Philip Zimbardo's study of behaviour in a simulated prison (Haney, Banks & Zimbardo, 1988) also offers a particularly clear example of the application of the single sample design (or from a slightly different angle, the method of doing research through simulation).

   The conclusion which Zimbardo and his team draw from this investigation is that poor relationships between prisoners and guards in real penal establishments have more to do with the nature of the prisoner and guard roles, and the kinds of behaviour which such roles sanction, than with the personalities of the people who become prisoners or guards. This is plausible, but you should note that the nature of the design of the investigation – and especially the lack of controls – makes it very difficult to decide just what the causes of the participants' behaviour might be.

An example of n = 1 research: the case of 'Little Albert'

In this experiment, Watson and Rayner showed that it was possible to condition a fear response to a previously innocuous object by pairing it with a fear-inducing stimulus, using an 11-month-old child, 'Little Albert', as the experimental subject. Having established that Albert responded with fear when a 4-foot iron bar was struck with a hammer just behind his head, Watson and

Rayner carried out a series of conditioning trials in which they showed Albert a white rat and simultaneously struck the bar. Albert responded by showing fear on every occasion. On subsequent testing, when the rat alone was shown to him without the bar being struck, Albert again showed evidence of fear, thereby demonstrating that a conditioned response had been created through the repeated pairing of the rat and the noise. This was shown to persist for up to a month after the initial conditioning. Moreover, the conditioned fear response to the rat was found by Watson and Rayner to extend to furry objects in general, since Albert also showed fear at the sight of stuffed toys.

REFERENCES

Bower, G. H., Clark, M., Lesgold, A., & Winzenz, D. (1969). Hierarchical retrieval schemes in recall of categorised word lists. *Journal of Verbal Learning and Verbal Behaviour, 8*, 323–43.

Haney, C., Banks, C. & Zimbardo, P. (1989). A study of prisoners and guards in a simulated prison. In E. Aronson, (Ed.), *Readings about the social animal* (pp. 52–67). New York: Freeman.

Held, R. & Hein, A. (1963). Movement-produced stimulation in the development of visually guided behaviour. *Journal of Comparative and Physiological Psychology, 56*, 872–6.

Milgram, S. (1963). A behavioural study of obedience. *Journal of Abnormal and Social Psychology, 67*, 391–8.

Rosenthal, R. & Jacobson, L. F. (1968). Teacher expectations for the disadvantaged. *Scientific American, 218*, no. 4, 19–23.

Schachter, S. & Singer, J. E. (1962). Cognitive, social and physiological determinants of emotional state. *Psychological Review, 69*, 379–99.

Watson, J. B. & Rayner, R. (1920). Conditioned emotional reactions. *Journal of Experimental Psychology, 3*, 1–14.

Experimental Error

This section of the chapter examines the concept of experimental error.

The difference between random and constant error is explained.

The sources of error in an experiment are reviewed and the main methods of preventing or reducing it are discussed.

Introduction

The experimental method, as we have seen, aims to reveal the existence of causal relationships between pairs of variables by providing a controlled situation in which one variable (the independent variable, or IV) is allowed to act on one other (the dependent variable, or DV). In an experiment, the other variables in the situation apart from these two are held constant (are prevented from varying), and any changes to the value of the DV are measured. The assumption is that if the measurement process succeeds in detecting any changes to the value of the DV, then those changes were caused by the changes to the value of the IV.

However, for this assumption to hold, it has also to be assumed that all unwanted influences have been completely screened out of the experiment, so that the measurement process is able accurately to record a true value for the DV. Sadly this is always far from being the case. In psychological research any measure of any DV in an experiment will always represent some combination of the true value of the variable together with the effects of what is known as **experimental error**.

> **Experimental error is the effect on the DV produced by any factor or variable in an experiment other than the IV.**

Given that a psychology experiment is the complex and delicate process which it is, the measurement of the values of a DV are neither a simple nor an error-free process. In fact, the ability to design experiments so as to minimize the effects of error is a major part of the skills needed by a competent experimenter: the control of experimental error is crucial to doing successful experiments which can generate usable knowledge.

In the next few pages we look at this vital aspect of the experimental method from several different angles, from the important distinction between random and constant error, to the consideration of some of the main strategies available for the removal and control of possible sources of error, and finally to some of the most important sources of error in an experiment.

Random and constant error

The two fundamental forms of experimental error are **random error** and **constant error**.

Random error is error which sometimes affects one condition in an experiment and sometimes another, causing the measures of the DV to be sometimes greater and sometimes less than their true value in an entirely random fashion. **Constant error** is error which has a consistent character throughout an experiment, producing the same degree of over-estimate or underestimate of the true value of the DV. Constant error may affect only one, or more, of the conditions in an experiment. Constant error is often called bias.

Random error affects the sensitivity of the experiment, obscuring the true picture and making it harder to see the any effects which the IV may be having on the DV. Constant error, on the other hand, actually distorts the information obtained in the experiment. A useful analogy is that random error is like dirt on a windowpane: it makes it harder to see out of the window, but the view itself is undistorted. Constant error on the other hand, is like a pattern worked into the glass which makes it impossible to obtain a true view, no matter how clean the glass may be.

Clearly, of the two forms of error, constant error is much more of a problem for an experimenter. This is because while the presence of random error makes it harder to *detect* a causal link between an IV and a DV (if one exists), constant error may make it impossible to determine what *really* caused the DV to change.

How can these forms of error be dealt with? The basic aim of experiment design is to try to reduce *both* types of error to as close to zero as possible, and the following general methods are available for achieving this.

If a potential source of **constant error** is identified, the best strategy is to try to remove or neutralize the variable which is responsible. If neither of these alternatives is possible, then try to take steps to randomize its effects; (for example, in a memory experiment, by placing the words in a list in a different random order for each subject rather than using the same order throughout), thereby converting possible constant error into the less serious random error.

If this is not possible, two other strategies for dealing with random error can be used. First, try to increase the separation of the values of the IV (for example, in an investigation into the effect of list length on remembering, it would be better to use lists which are 10, 20 and 30 words long, rather than some which are 10, 14 and 18 words in length). The effect of this is to widen the difference between the conditions and thus weaken the obscuring effects of the random error on the measures of the DV. If the IV *is* influencing the DV, this will make the effect show up more clearly. The second way is equally simple, and involves reducing the significance level of the test statistic, say from $p = 0.05$ to $p = 0.01$. This reduces the probability of making a type 1 (false positive) decision error, which in turn means that the possibility that random error might cause the incorrect acceptance of the experimental hypothesis is likewise reduced. (As you can see, this strategy requires you to be informed about such key matters such as significance level, and the kinds of decision errors which can occur when hypotheses are tested. More infomation about these topics can be found in chapter 7, p. 328, which deals with the process of hypothesis testing in general: a discussion of significance level can be found on p. 346, and decision errors on p. 357 onwards.)

Box 5.1   Control strategies – specific approaches to controlling error

The following is a list of the main ways in which it is possible to control some of the error which exists in an experiment. Note that, as error can enter an experiment from several different sources, it is almost certain that you will have to apply all these techniques simultaneously whenever you design an experiment.

Design

The first step towards controlling error from extraneous sources in the experiment is to select the experiment design which minimizes the possible effects of some kinds of error, while still enabling the research problem to be pursued. If the effects of taking repeated measures of the DV are likely to be problematic, then choose an independent samples design. If, on the other hand, interpersonal differences are of concern, then the repeated measures or matched subjects designs should be considered.

Standardization

Standardization involves ensuring that the value of a variable does not change throughout the experiment and is the same for all participants within a condition, and perhaps across conditions as well. For example, the environmental conditions under which the experiment takes place should be, as far as possible the same for all participants in all conditions, while the instructions and experimental procedures should both be the same within each condition.

Randomization

Randomization is the process of distributing the probable effects of a variable at random through an experiment, or through a particular condition. For example, in the independent subjects design, participants should be allocated to the conditions in the experiment at random in order to control for the variable of inter-subject differences. Briefly, to do this you need to give each individual in the experiment a unique identifying number, using the random number table, place them in order and then assign equal proportions of the list to each condition. So, if you have a two condition experiment, you could make the individuals in the first half of the list the control condition, and the second half the experimental condition. (See also the page opposite table 1 in the Appendix for information about the random number table).

Counterbalancing

Counterbalancing ensures that error from one possible source is neutralized by being balanced (as far as possible) by an equal amount of error from another, similar source. For example, the order in which two tasks are performed is a possible source of error every time a repeated measures design is used. If all participants in the experiment perform the tasks in the same order, their scores on task 2 may be depressed (or enhanced), by having already completed task 1. Either way their scores on the task 2 will not accurately reflect their ability to do the task.

The solution is to counterbalance the order in which the tasks are taken, so that half the participants complete task 1 before task 2, while the other half take the tasks in the reverse order. Thus, any error due to taking task 1 before task 2 will be balanced by the equal but opposite error caused by taking task 2 before task 1. Note, however, that in order to ensure that a causal inference can be drawn, participants must be allocated to one of the task orders entirely at random.

The Main Sources of Error in an Experiment

While it is not possible to identify all possible sources of error without knowing quite a lot about the research in question, one can, nevertheless, indicate some of the principal routes by which both random and constant error can find their way into an experiment. The following section describes the four main possible sources of error in an experiment, together with some indications of what counter-measures can be taken.

You should be aware that no list, however comprehensive, can ever replace the careful scrutiny of your experiment design, whether by yourself, or by someone else. Often, allowing someone else to review a planned experiment can reveal unsuspected flaws in the design.

Sampling error

Sampling error is error which arises out of the failure of the sampling procedure to generate a sample which is representative of the population of interest. The only way in which error from this source can be avoided, therefore, is when every member of the population is included in the sample. In all other situations some degree of sampling error is inevitable, and the researcher's tactic has to be to try to minimize its effects as much as possible.

Constant error due to sampling can be converted into the much less serious random error through the use of a random sampling procedure. However, it may be difficult to achieve a random sample. In psychological research, the target population is often too large or too dispersed to permit all its members to be accessed, and therefore a non-random sample, such as a volunteer or opportunity sample has to be obtained. The assumption is usually made in such cases that the sample will not differ significantly from that which would have been obtained had random sampling been used. This may be true, but it needs to be justified by the researcher in every case.

The possibility of random error due to sampling can be dealt with by increasing the size of the sample and by increasing the sensitivity of the test so as to reduce the number of tied scores in the data. (More information about sampling procedures can be found in chapter 3.)

Error due to the differences between participants

Participant-related error is error which arises from the existence of uncontrolled differences between the experimental participants themselves, which confounds the independent variable in some way. Such differences include sex, handedness, visual acuity, motivation, general educational attainment, and manual dexterity, as well as many others. Not all of them need to be controlled in any one experiment, however. Although the individuals who participate in an experiment may differ one from another in all kinds of ways, only *some* of the possible differences are likely to be capable of influencing the DV, and will thus be a source of error. The other differences will be present, but because they are not able to confound the effect of the IV will not need to be controlled for.

Dealing with participant-related error

In the independent Subjects design, inter-participant differences exist both within and between conditions, while in the repeated measures design, inter-participant differences exist only *within* conditions, since the same subjects appear in each of the conditions.

In **independent subjects designs** the strategy for dealing with error due to inter-participant differences is to assign the participants to the conditions in the experiment at random. This converts any constant inter-conditions error into error which is distributed randomly between the conditions. If an inter-participant difference is known to correlate highly with the DV (and is thus suspected as a confounding variable), then the matched subjects design could be considered.

If participant-related error is suspected in **repeated measures designs**, the best strategy, having first identified the variable in question, is to try to equalize the number of participants in the sample who have different levels of the suspect variable (by, for example, making sure that there are equal numbers of right-handed, left-handed and ambidextrous individuals), and then to counterbalance the order in which the experimental tasks are taken so as to ensure that it does not interact with the task variable. Obviously, though, this procedure can only be carried out if the variable which is thought to be a possible source of error has been identified and can be measured in some way. If this is not possible, the best thing to do is to randomize the task order across the sample, so as to destroy any possibility of a systematic interaction between the experimental tasks and the inter-subject differences.

Task-related error

This is error arising out of the failure to control all the variables in the actual experimental situation which are capable of exerting some influence on the performance of participants. The way to deal with this is standardization to ensure that the experience of all participants is as far as possible identical, with the sole exception of the difference between the experimental and control condition. For example, you should:

- standardize instructions and explanations about the experiment to ensure that the task is presented in a uniform way
- standardize the number of practice, control and experimental trials
- standardize the interval between trials
- standardize the feedback to the participant during the experiment

and so on through every detail of the experiment which could affect the DV, and therefore act as a source of error.

However, there are some variables which cannot be controlled by standardizing the procedure without generating more experimental error. For example, in a repeated measures design, standardizing the order in which the participants perform the experimental tasks will itself generate error. Because the participants always perform task A before task B, their performance on task B may be affected by having just completed task A either by the effects of fatigue (if task A was tiring or boring), or by the effect of the practice (if task A was similar to task B). The technique in this case is to counterbalance the order in which the tasks are taken , so that half the subjects take task A before task B and the other half take the two tasks the other way round. This ensures that the effects of taking one task before the other are shared equally between the two tasks.

Error due to measurement

Ideally, the process of measuring changes to the DV should be perfectly accurate and reliable in order to register precisely all changes which may occur, no matter how small. However, no matter how carefully it may be approached, the measurement process in an experiment may be a source of both constant and random error.

Constant error due to measurement occurs when the measuring process produces a consistent overestimate or underestimate of the true value of the variable being measured in one or more of the conditions of the experiment.

A simple (but a little unlikely) example of this form of constant error can be obtained if you imagine an investigation into interpersonal distance which involves measuring the forehead-to-forehead distance between pairs of conversing individuals. Suppose that due to some freak accident back at the tape factory, the metric measuring tape which the researcher is using is defective, so that each centimetre on the tape is really only 0.9 of a true centimetre. Clearly, when the tape is used, it will be a source of constant error in the data since every measurement made will underestimate the true interpersonal distance by 10 per cent. Similarly, if the defective tape is used to measure distances in only one condition in the experiment, while an accurate tape is used for the other, the result will be constant error affecting only one condition.

The basic counter-measure against the possibility of constant error due to measurement is to ensure that the DV is measured by the exactly identical procedure in all conditions in the experiment. Where possible you should also take steps to check the accuracy of the measuring procedure against a known standard, in order to assess the possibility of a systematic overestimate or underestimate of the value of the DV, although, for obvious reasons, this is somewhat less serious than error affecting only one of the conditions.

As you will by now expect, experimental data can also be affected by random error from the measurement process, and this can come from several different sources.

The first possibility is that the measuring instrument itself is unreliable, so that it produces unpredictably different readings when it is used to measure the same true value of a variable on different occasions. While it is true that random error from this source is unlikely in an experiment which uses standard laboratory equipment such as a tachistoscope (a device for presenting a visual display for very brief intervals of time), it is nevertheless a real concern to all researchers who use questionnaires or similar pencil and paper based measuring instruments in their research.

These techniques are subject to some degree of random measurement error because they depend upon the individual respondent making a response to written statements or questions, or similar verbal material. However, questionnaires and attitude scales are constructed on the assumption that a given statement or question is capable of meaning exactly the same thing to every person who reads it, and that consequently the answer produced by any respondent will reflect only the particular variable which the test seeks to capture. Despite these hopes, some degree of random error inevitably enters the data because the same set of words can mean different things to different people, and hence generate unpredictably different responses.

The only effective approach to dealing with error from this source is to try to use measuring instruments whose reliability is known. All major psychometric tests, such as the Eysenck Personality Questionnaire (Eysenck & Eysenck, 1975), have undergone evaluation for reliability, and the extent to which measurement error can be attributed to this particular source has been estimated. Many pencil and paper instruments, however, are used without previously having undergone reliability trials, and the data obtained from these needs to be interpreted with caution. (See the section in chapter 3 dealing with questionnaire design for information on carrying out reliability trials of pencil and paper instruments.)

Random error can also enter the data if the measuring instrument is used inconsistently and, as you would expect, the greater the degree of inconsistency, the greater the error which results. For example, if some participants are allowed to read and write their own answers to a questionnaire, while others have the questionnaire read to them and have to dictate their answers, then this could be a source of random error due to measurement, since some people's answers will be affected by their mode of response, and some will not, with the effect occurring at random. The remedy in this case, which is also the general counter-measure applicable to all similar situations is to try to ensure as far as possible that absolute consistency is achieved in the use of the measuring instrument.

Finally, as a general strategy, random error due to measurement procedures can be reduced by the simple process of averaging each participant's performance across several trials. The greater the number of individual trials which contribute to this average, the more the effect of measurement error on the final score is reduced.

The Experiment as a Social Situation: Some Further Sources of Error

The participants in an experiment do not simply function as passive, neutral experimental 'objects' dispensing clean and accurate experimental data on demand. An experiment is a social situation of some complexity, and the participants in an experiment actively use the techniques and strategies which they use in their lives outside the laboratory in order to make sense of the (often) novel experiences provided by the experimental environment. As a result, in any experiment involving human participants, a number of interesting and subtle effects come in to play, which an experimenter has to understand and try to control.

The 'demand characteristics' of the experiment

The participants in an experiment will almost invariably wish to know the aims of the research, and if other sources of information are not available (and sometimes even if they are) they will probably to try to infer the hypothesis from cues provided by the experimental situation.

The importance of these cues was discussed by Martin Orne, who called them the 'demand characteristics' of an experiment, and defined them as 'the totality of cues which convey an experimental hypothesis to a subject' (Orne, 1962). Demand characteristics include all those verbal and non-verbal hints about the purpose of the experiment which are present in the experimental situation, including of course, those which are provided by the researcher herself.

The idea that an experiment constitutes a set of demand characteristics is a recognition that the participants in an experiment are always actively engaged in making inferences about the nature of the experimental processes and environment, which are then used by the participant to shape their behaviour.

The importance of demand characteristics to the researcher is not just that they exist, but the fact that the inferences which a participant may draw from the situation may seriously compromise the integrity of the experiment. For example, researchers have documented instances of experiments in which the participants have consciously tried to generate data which confirms what they believe to be the experimental hypothesis, as well as some less common examples of experiments in which they have tried deliberately to produce data which is negative, i.e. which disconfirms the hypothesis (Argyris, 1968). Either way, the data produced are the result of the social environment of the experiment, rather than simply a response to the experimental task.

How is a researcher to deal with the problem of demand characteristics? In this as in much else, honesty is the best policy. The more you communicate fully and openly with a participant about the aims and goals of the research, the less likely it is that demand characteristics will be used by a participant in order to draw inferences. Conversely, if a participant suspects that the experiment is not as it has been represented, then it is probable that the demand characteristics may be used as a source of information about what is going on.

The bad news for experimenters is that it is impossible to know whether and what kinds of inferences are being drawn from the available cues, nor what their likely effect on behaviour may be. This makes it impossible to deal with the problem with any degree of certainty. In fact, while some of the effects of demand characteristics can be reduced if the researcher is honest about the aims of the experiment, they can probably never be eliminated entirely. Even if you are entirely open with the participants about the goals of your research, participants will still make up their own minds about what is going on, and may arrive at a different conclusion on the basis of their perceptions of the situation.

As well as following a policy of openness about the purposes of the research there is one further strategy which can be used to keep track of any effects of demand characteristics in an experiment. The post-experimental debriefing can be used in order to check participants' general perceptions of the experiment, and it is a simple matter to ask whether they felt that the experiment was represented to them honestly, and whether this had any effect on their behaviour in the experiment. The answers may give some clues to whether or not that participant's response to the demand characteristics influenced the data.

The least acceptable solution to the problem, for both ethical and practical reasons, is to try to mislead participants about the real nature of the experiment. This is not only because the use of deception of any kind in an experiment is ethically unacceptable, and should not be undertaken unless independent advice has been sought, but also because it is ineffective. Not only can an experimenter never be sure that a deception has worked as planned, because there is no way of checking without revealing the existence of the deception, but also the effects of deception are unpredictable: there is no guarantee that the cover story will influence the participants' inferences in the expected way.

The 'social desirability' effect

Many of the forms of behaviour which particularly interest psychologists, such as conformity, altruism or aggression, are governed by strong social norms, which define certain forms of behaviour as more acceptable than others, so that altruistic behaviour is generally regarded as more socially desirable than selfishness, conformity than non-conformity, and so on. The social desirability effect is a reflection of the desire of research participants to be seen to conform to such general social norms. Participants may, for example, be unwilling to report negative feelings, to criticize others, or to engage in certain sorts of behaviour such as pronouncing words with sexual connotations. The general effect of social desirability is to limit the extent to which research participants are willing to respond to the requirements of the experimental situation in a way which accurately reflects their true beliefs or feelings. (For a little more on the subject of social desirability you many like to look back to chapter 2, page 78.)

One form of the social desirability effect which occurs particularly if participants feel they are being tested or evaluated in some way, is the 'faking good' already discussed in chapter 2. This involves a person falsifying or suppressing any information or behaviour which might be interpreted in negative or unfavourable ways in order to present a positive image to the experimenter. For example, research participants asked to express a preference for one of a range of different forms of sexual expression might choose the one they judge to be most 'average', rather than expressing their real preference.

In order to try to get round this problem some psychometric tests incorporate lie scales – test items which are designed to assess the extent to which a person's responses are likely to reflect attempts to 'fake good'. However, in the nature of things, the reliability of such scales is very difficult to establish.

Given that the urge to fake good is likely to be strongest when little information is provided about an experiment or when participants are uncertain about the eventual destination of their data, it follows that the best strategy for dealing with social desirability issues is, as always, to ensure that participants are fully informed. They should not only be told about the nature and purpose of the research, but should also know exactly how their data is going to be used, and should be reassured about its confidentiality.

Experimenter effects

In addition to the effects of those sources of error already mentioned, the data produced by the participants in an experiment can also be influenced by the behaviour of the experimenter herself. 'Experimenter effect' is the name given to the error which a researcher unconsciously introduces, often in the form of non-verbal cues, into the research situation. For example, an experimenter may have low expectations that a given experiment will produce a confirmation of the experimental hypothesis, and this can be picked up by participants from her general demeanour and influence their motivation and behaviour in the experiment. After all, it is unrealistic to hope that participants will give their best to an experiment if they sense from the experimenter's manner that the results are not expected to be of interest.

However, the problem of experimenter effect it is not simply due to negative behaviour on the part of the researcher. It has also been shown that experimenter effect can be produced by the personal characteristics, such as sex and age, as well as by the perceived competence and authority of the researcher (Rosenthal, 1966).

Experimenter effects can be reduced, but probably never completely eliminated from an experiment. The general strategy is to reduce the interaction between participants and experimenter to a minimum, and to ensure that when it does occur it is standardized and its nature is determined in advance, so as to minimize the opportunities to 'read' the cues provided by the experimenter.

Additionally, specific measures may be used to meet the needs of particular research projects which are judged to be particularly vulnerable to experimenter effect. One such is to use as a substitute for the researcher someone who is completely uninformed about the experiment (and possibly also about psychology in general), who is coached to act as the experimenter in place of the 'real' researcher.

The Process of Experiment Design

This section of the chapter sets out a detailed approach to experiment design.

A three-stage model of the design process is presented and the tasks required at each stage are described and explained.

A checklist of experiment design tasks is provided.

A commented experiment design is provided which explains the process of design step by step.

Three areas of particular ethical sensitivity for experimenters are discussed.

Some suggestions for research projects using the experimental method are given.

Introduction

Despite the impression which you may have gained from the preceding part of this chapter, designing a successful experiment in psychology is not in itself a particularly difficult or testing process. It lies well within the reach of the average person. The main quality required, in addition to a grasp of the basic issues, is to be prepared to take a systematic and careful approach to the task. Given that, competent experimental work lies within reach of anyone who wants to do it. And, as in most activities, practice makes perfect.

The critical issue is the amount of care and thought with which the business of design is approached, since this is the key to being able, eventually, to draw valid inferences from data. This may seem an obvious point, but it needs to be made, because it is all too easy to convince yourself that simply because you have designed an experiment and collected some data then those data *must* be capable of throwing light on the research question. Obviously, this is not invariably the case. Assuming that the question being researched is meaningful in the first place, the amount of useful information which can be extracted from a set of data is determined solely by the extent to which the researcher has been able to anticipate and solve the problems involved in measuring the effect of a single IV on a DV. If you try to run an experiment without having first carefully worked through all the various issues of design and implementation you are likely to end up with data which, at best, may not enable any clear conclusions to be drawn about the research question and, at worst, may be virtually meaningless.

Among the most commonly experienced, but avoidable, sources of difficulty and frustration for the experimenter, are the following:

1   Going ahead with the design or data gathering without being sufficiently clear about the precise problem or question which you wish to answer. This often only reveals itself at a later stage in the design process, when difficulty is experienced in writing hypotheses or identifying the variables which need to be controlled in the experiment. Often this situation is result of an entirely laudable and understandable desire to get on with the actual work of running the experiment and gathering data. However, it is essential to think through the research problem several times before any design activity is begun. If you are relatively new to doing research in psychology you simply need to take a little extra time to make sure that make sure that the ideas on which your research is to be based are completely understood.

2   A second major source of discouragement to the researcher is to realize, after data have been gathered, that a key variable was left uncontrolled so that the IV was allowed to become confounded. If this happens, sadly, the data are likely to be virtually useless, and the experiment must be re-run under more controlled conditions.

To some extent this difficulty disappears as you become more experienced as a researcher: the more experiments you carry out, the better you become at spotting the possible sources of confounding. However, you can speed up the process by ensuring that you give careful consideration to this aspect of the design at the planning stage and it is always a good idea to talk through your design with someone else, in order to check that the most obvious sources of error have been pinpointed and, as far as possible, controlled.

3   Finally, it is surprisingly easy to find yourself running an experiment without adequate preparation of all the supporting materials. It is possible to find that one is halfway through processing the first experimental participant only to find that there is no data sheet ready on which to write down the results. Again, this is often due to the desire to simply get on with the experiment rather than to poor organizing ability as such, but the possible repercussions on the participant and on oneself should not be underestimated. The participant obtains an impression of experimenter incompetence, which may affect her attitude and performance in the experiment, while the experimenter's self-esteem also takes a nosedive. It doesn't need saying that is better to avoid these possibilities by preparing the experiment thoroughly before any kind of data gathering is begun.

The three-stage design process

As we have seen, designing an experiment in order to generate usable data which are capable of answering a question of interest, requires a careful and systematic approach to the process of design. The purpose of this section is to provide a framework within which such an approach can be developed. The description which follows is organized around a three-stage model of the design process:

Stage 1   Defines the problem to be researched
Stage 2   Establishes the basic design of the experiment
Stage 3   Refines the basic design into a workable experiment and ensures that all essential preparations are completed

Within each of these stages are a number of key tasks which have to be completed by a researcher in order for the design process to be complete, and for the researcher to have confidence that the data will provide insight into the research question. These have been placed into order so as to form a logical progression through the design process, from the first dawning of a research question to the pilot study preceding the main experiment.

Although it is recommended that this order should be followed, at least for the first few experiments, what follows is intended to provide the researcher with support rather than constriction – a corset rather than a straitjacket. As you become more experienced in the business of doing experimental research, you will probably find that you have developed a system of your own, and can then dispense with this one.

Stage 1   Defining the problem

1.1   Identify the specific problem you wish to pursue
1.2   Research the background to the problem and identify the specific theory(s) or ideas with which the experiment will be concerned
1.3   Develop an explanation linking the theory to the proposed experiment
1.4   Make a preliminary identification of the experimental task.

Before the actual process of experiment design begins you obviously need to have developed in some detail ideas about the research question which you wish to pursue.

However, there is more to the process than just spotting an interesting question, and then going ahead with designing an experiment. If the experiment itself is to be a fruitful one, you need to spend some time thinking in detail about the problem you wish to research. This is important for at least two reasons. It ensures that the main part of the design process goes as smoothly as possible and it also gets out of the way much of the thinking which will be needed anyway when you come to write up the results of your research.

This preliminary part of the process of putting together an experiment involves the following tasks:

1.1 Identify the problem

For anyone who is a relatively new experimenter, a psychology textbook of some description is likely to be the most generally available source of research questions. However, you always need to read a text critically. Remember that the most worthwhile research is research that provides a test of a theory. Therefore, ask yourself questions as you read, such as: Do the experiments cited really test the theory under discussion? Does it seem likely that replication would produce the same result? How might they differ? How could the experiment in question be improved so as to provide a better test of theory?

You may find it rather difficult to quarry an introductory psychology text for workable ideas. The problem is that usually too little information is provided about an experiment to permit an exact replication of the research, and you therefore have to aim for partial replication. In this the key features of the earlier work are preserved, but the new version differs from the old in relation to such things as the instructions given to the participants or the precise questions of a questionnaire used to measure changes to the DV.

At some point, where there is little original detail available, a partial replication ceases to be replication at all and becomes instead an extension of the earlier research. This means that while the basic question which is being researched is the same in both cases, the approach and the methods used differ quite significantly, and the work may contain original thought to a significant degree. Extending earlier research is the only approach possible if you find an interesting idea in a textbook which lacks supporting detail about the original research.

1.2 Research the background

Once you have identified an appropriate problem or question to pursue, the next thing to do is to investigate what the context of the research might be. This involves using the resources available to you to find out about:

- The specific theory(s) which try to explain the phenomena in question. The aim is to find out what theory(s) have been proposed in relation to the phenomenon you are interested in, or if you already have that information, to clarify what it is that the theory(s) have to say. As you will see very shortly, it is important that every experiment constitutes a test of a theory of some kind, no matter how limited (or just plain wrong), that theory may seem to be.

- Published research which describes the results of experiments which bear some relationship to the research project which is currently taking shape in your mind. These may be of two kinds. First, it will probably be the case that there has been research explicitly directed at testing the theory(s) which you have identified as important to your problem. If there is, you need to find out as much as you can about these within the limits of the resources available to you, especially if you aim to replicate a piece of prior research.

Alternatively, previous research work may suggest methods, approaches or ways of thinking about the problem which you want to incorporate into your research.

Unless you have access to a university library you are unlikely to be able to read about research in its original place of publication, and will have to rely on secondary sources for your information. It is a good idea to use a number of different books for this, as even accounts of classic research in introductory texts can differ in the kind of information they provide and the emphasis they place on different aspects of a particular problem. The aim must be to try to build up as complete a picture as you can of the context of ideas and previous research within which your research will be located. This takes time, but it is never wasted effort.

1.3   Link the theory to the proposed experiment

By now, the experiment you want to do should be becoming much clearer in your mind. It may be so clear, in fact, that you may feel that it is high time to get on with the more exciting business of drawing up the experiment design in detail.

However, it is very important that before you get much further into the experiment you write down exactly how (or why) your experiment will act as a test of the theory. If everything so far has gone well you may find that this is little more than a formality. On the other hand any misunderstanding of the theory will be swiftly revealed by the attempt to explain the connection between theory and experiment. If there is any doubt on this point, you should of course return again to your sources and think further.

1.4   Make a preliminary identification of the experimental task

By now you will probably have some ideas about the nature of the experimental task which you will want to use in the experiment. If you haven't, you should start to consider the question now, as you will begin to work more closely on defining exactly what part it is to play in the experiment very soon, at step 2.2 below.

With at least one idea in mind for the experimental task, you are now ready to plunge into the business of designing the experiment itself, which, as has already been pointed out, consists of two further stages.

Stage 2   Establishing the basic design

2.1   Specify the aim of the experiment
2.2   Identify the independent and dependent variables and decide how the variables are to be operationalized

2.1   Specify the aim of the experiment

Your first thought might be that this simply involves repeating information you have already gathered in putting together a description of the background of the experiment. Not so. What you have already is likely to consist of a longish piece of writing, and it is important to begin work on the design with a clear and succinct statement of the aim of the experiment. The virtue of this is that the very act of writing such a statement ensures the clarity of the ideas which are being tested, and will reveal any flaws in the chain of reasoning which has led to the experiment. If you find it difficult to write a clear statement of your aims it probably means that you need to think more about what your experiment is trying to achieve.

2.2   Identify IV and DV and decide how they are to be operationalized

Identifying the IV and DV is unlikely to give any difficulty as long as you are sure about the difference between them. If in doubt consult the definitions given elsewhere in this chapter.

By this point in the process, you may have begun to develop ideas about how the variables in the experiment are to be operationalized. (Operationalization refers to the process by which psychological variables, such as stress, which cannot be accessed directly, are turned into variables which can be manipulated or measured in an experiment.)

If your experiment is to be a replication or adaptation of someone else's work, then the appropriate operationalizations of the IV and DV will probably be suggested by the work of other researchers. However, to avoid simply repeating another person's mistakes, it is a good idea to take a careful look at the previous work, and to ask a few critical questions along the lines indicated below.

You need to ask yourself what kind of task will provide an adequate operationalization of the IV in which you are interested. For example, if the IV in an experiment happens to be 'mild stress', then you have to determine exactly how you are going to produce mild stress, rather than, say, severe stress in the participants: how you are going to ensure that it is done reliably, (i.e. to approximately the same degree to all participants in the experiment), and how you are going to monitor the process so you can demonstrate that you are sure that the required level of stress was in fact produced.

Secondly, you have to consider by what means you will measure the effect of the stress on the DV. To some extent this is determined by the nature of the DV itself: clearly, if the purpose of the experiment is to investigate the effect of mild stress on eye–hand co-ordination, then you will need a task which demands eye–hand co-ordination. However (and this is where thought is required), it also has to be a task which is susceptible to mild stress *and* is sensitive enough to register the differences in the effect of the mild stress on each of the different research participants. Moreover, it must do so reliably and accurately. There is clearly no point in using a task which generates measures which are either lacking in consistency or which do not accurately reflect the true effects of stress on eye–hand co-ordination.

Finally, at this point you should consider the question of how many observations are to be made from each participant. In some experiments one only will be sufficient, or possible, while in others it may be necessary to collect several, and use the mean as the raw data. This latter approach has the advantage that it enables variation in the data due to changes in a participant's attention or motivation to be smoothed out.

2.3 State the experimental and null hypotheses

You must have a clear and succinct statement of these hypotheses, since, formally speaking, the experimental hypothesis is what the whole experiment has been set up to test.

The primary consideration in writing hypotheses is that they *must* be precise enough for there to be no doubt about which of them is to be accepted once the data have been collected and analysed. It is surprisingly easy to write hypotheses which are so loosely written that you are unsure after the experiment which you should accept. You can guard against this problem by carefully writing and rewriting your hypotheses until you are sure they are precise enough.

If you haven't already covered this, a detailed explanation of the part played by null and alternate hypotheses in an experiment is to be found in chapter 7. You should ideally have read most of that chapter (but especially between pages 341 and 346, before attempting to write hypotheses of your own for the first time. Examples of both types of hypotheses, which you can use as templates for your own can be found in the commented experiment later in this chapter as well as in the worked examples of the test statistics in chapter 9.

2.4 Decide the basic experiment design

The choices are laid out for you earlier in this chapter. The important point, as well as choosing the right design for your needs, is to make sure you are clear about why one particular design is the one you need. Remember you will need to be able to justify your choice in the report you write on your research.

2.5 Determine the test statistic and significance level

It is essential that the right test statistic is selected using the basic design and the nature of the data as guidelines at a very early stage in the design process.

The most logical point at which to do this is after the experimental and null hypotheses are written.

Consult chapters 7 and 9 for information to help with the decision about the test statistic and significance level.

2.6 Decide whether a one- or two-tailed test is needed

When you turn to the table of critical values of the test statistic you will almost always need to have decided whether your alternate hypothesis requires a one- or a two-tailed test. Briefly, if you are testing a directional hypothesis (i.e. one which predicts the direction of a difference), then you can use a one-tailed test, otherwise a two-tailed test can be used. See the section of chapter 7, p. 354, on directional and non-directional hypotheses if you need fuller information on this.

2.7 Decide the sampling procedure

The decision on sampling procedure is important because it determines the extent to which the results of an experiment (or indeed any research) can be generalized from a sample to a larger population. Chapter 3 provides information on the choices available to you and the procedures which need to be followed in different types of sampling.

At this point, the main outlines of the experiment are becoming apparent, and certain key decisions such as those concerning the statistical treatment of the results have been taken. It is now necessary to refine this broad outline into an effective experiment, and to complete the additional tasks which are necessary before the experiment can be run.

Stage 3 Refining the basic design and completing preparations

3.1 Review control of subject variables
3.2 Review control of task variables
3.3 Review control of the test environment
3.4 Construct or otherwise obtain any apparatus required
3.5 Write the instructions to participants and design the data collection sheet
3.6 Design the post-experiment debriefing interview
3.7 Read through the ethics checklist
3.8 Run a pilot study and assess the results

The main sources of experimental error, and the appropriate counter-measures (3.1, 3.2 and 3.3 in the list above) are discussed earlier in this chapter and do not need much more comment. The key to dealing successfully with this task is to ask yourself which variables are most likely to confound the IV by exerting an unwanted effect on the DV, and this will be easier if you take a systematic approach, and think about one set of potential sources of error at a time. Some possibilities will probably spring to mind straightaway, but others may need more careful thought.

The essential point is that while you can never guarantee control of all variables, it is possible, in most cases, satisfactorily to pin down those which are most likely to act as a source of error. However, this takes time and thought, and therefore this stage of the design process should never be hurried: otherwise you will be bound to miss something crucial. You should only proceed to the final stages of the design once you are reasonably certain that you have control over all major confounding variables, either by excluding them from the experiment altogether, or else by converting them from sources of constant error into random error.

Because it is easy to develop a blind spot about one's own research, it is always an excellent idea to discuss your proposed experiment with someone else, preferably with someone who is a more experienced researcher than you. Often a second pair of eyes will spot a major flaw in the design which, if left unattended to, could have completely wrecked the experiment.

This completes the central design processes for your experiment. However, there are still things which need to be done before the experiment is finally ready to roll.

3.4　Construct or obtain apparatus

The nature of the apparatus required by the experiment will almost certainly have become apparent at an early stage while you were clarifying the research question you wished to investigate. This is the point at which it should be obtained, and if you are intending to use anything which is at all complicated and/or unfamiliar you should take time now to make sure that you can operate it without a hitch. It is a good idea to practice, using a friend or acquaintance, if you have any doubts about your ability to operate the equipment easily and efficiently.

3.5　Write instructions to participants and design data collection sheet

The **instructions to the experiment participants** make up a kind of detailed script for the experiment written from the researcher's point of view. Everything about the conduct of the experiment which the researcher needs to say to the participant should be included. In fact, it should be so comprehensive that it could be used to run the experiment by anyone with no knowledge of psychology.

There are two advantages to having a script like this. Firstly, it ensures that the treatment of each participant is absolutely standardized. Reading from a script reduces the possibility that some participants will receive slightly different instructions from others, with the consequent possibility of experimental error entering the results. Secondly, having things written down in detail enables you to show clearly that you have tried fully to meet the ethical requirements of psychological experimentation. You can, for example, point to a section of the script which makes it clear that a participant can withdraw from the experiment at any time.

The instructions themselves should be written in a way which deliberately avoids the use of technical terms. This is to ensure, as far as possible, that participants are not intimidated by technical language, and all of them understand what the experiment is about. If a participant wants to know more about the experiment you can introduce technical terms to your explanation if you judge that they will be appreciated, but it is important that a participant's first encounter with the experiment is one in which she feels as comfortable as possible. The commented design which follows this provides an example of instructions which have been written in this way.

The time taken in getting the instructions for an experiment as clear and as complete as possible is always a very worthwhile investment. Inadequate or unclear instructions, or a less than complete script can not only be a major source of experimental error, but also of embarrassment.

An otherwise immaculately professional approach to the business of experimentation can be fatally undermined if your **data sheet** is a scruffy piece of paper. Participants will simply find it difficult to accept your assurances that the data they have generated – their data – are at all important to you. More crucially, if you use just any old piece of paper to record your results it may later be impossible to make sense of what you have written.

The best solution, from both angles, is to prepare specially formatted data collection sheets on which you can record your results. These should enable you to distinguish easily between data obtained from different participants and different conditions in the experiment, and may include spaces for recording the results of descriptive statistics such as the mean and standard deviation.

Prepare sufficient copies of this for the whole experiment before you begin, and clearly label the sheet on which the pilot data are to be recorded in order to distinguish it from data obtained from the main experiment. It is a good idea to photocopy your completed data sheets as soon as the experiment is completed in case the originals become mislaid. There is probably no more depressing experience than having to re-run an experiment because the original data have been lost.

3.6 Design the post-experiment debriefing interview

Every participant in an experiment should be given a short debriefing, during which you have a further opportunity to acquire useful information from your research subjects. The interview need not necessarily be long or detailed, but it will require some prior thought and planning as it should attempt to provide answers for your questions on at least the following topics:

1 Can you be reasonably sure that the participants have correctly understood the nature and purpose of the experimental task, and have tried to complete the task to the best of their abilities?

2   Have any design defects identified by the pilot study been rectified?
3   Do the participants feel that, as far as possible, the experience of being a research subject has been a positive and enjoyable one? If not, in what respects do they feel it has not, and – most importantly – how has this affected their responses?

The debriefing is also your opportunity to thank the subjects for their help with your research, and to offer to let them have a copy of the results after your data are collected. Very few participants are actually likely to avail themselves of this opportunity, but the offer should none the less always be made.

3.7   Read the ethics checklist

The importance of an ethically aware approach to the process of experimentation has been stressed elsewhere. Although you have probably done your best to maintain high ethical standards in the design of your experiment, it is still good practice to run a final check before you approach any potential participants. Use the checklist in box 5.2 to make sure that you have considered the main ethical issues which are likely to arise. If it gives the all clear you can then carry on to run the pilot study, but otherwise, you should go no further until you have attended to whatever aspect of the design or procedure the checklist has flagged up.

3.8   Run a pilot study

The pilot study is a dress rehearsal for the main experiment. It involves carrying out all the experimental procedures, and gathering data exactly as you would in the main experiment, only with a small number of participants rather than from a full-scale sample. Half a dozen participants would be about right for most purposes, though at the lower end of the scale it is perfectly possible to obtain useful information from a pilot study involving only a single individual.

The purpose of the pilot is to check that an experiment is as near perfect as it can be, and this has three aspects. First, it enables the procedures of the experiment to be tried out in a 'real' but not 'crucial' situation, so that anything which might prevent the main experiment from running like clockwork can be identified. Secondly, it provides information on the kind of data values you may expect to find when you run the main study. If those obtained in the pilot are very different from what is expected, then that may be a broad hint that the basic design of the experiment needs to be looked at again.

Finally, the pilot provides an important opportunity, which should be seized, to observe the experiment through the eyes of the participants. As well as looking to see whether the pilot trials can run without a hitch, and so on, you should also ask the pilot participants about their experience of taking part. They may have vital information which they will only share with you if you ask them. Box 5.3 lists the main questions you will need to ask.

Once the pilot has been run, it is essential to review the information obtained

Box 5.2 *An ethics checklist*

This checklist is not intended to substitute for a careful reading of the BPS Ethics guidelines (in appendix 1). If you have any doubts on what the ethically correct approach may be on any issue, check back with to the guidelines, or seek the opinion of a more experienced researcher who, in most cases, will be a lecturer at an educational institution.

Can you answer 'yes' to the following?

1 Full information about the purpose or aim of the experiment has been provided.
2 The consent of the participants has been explicitly sought and has been given.
3 The right of the participants to withdraw from the experiment at any time (along with their data) has been clearly explained.
4 The confidentiality of all data can be demonstrated. Apart from the experimenter, no one could identify any data with any particular research participant.
5 The experimental procedure has been carefully reviewed (if necessary with the help of a more experienced researcher) to ensure that participants will not suffer physical or psychological harm as a result of their participation in the experiment.
6 All participants will be debriefed after their participation, and will be questioned to check whether they have suffered any psychological ill-effects from participation in the experiment.
7 The experiment does not involve deception of any kind which has not first been discussed with a more experienced researcher.
8 The experimental procedure does not unnecessarily emphasize the passive nature of the participant role nor similarly expose participants to an experience of failure.
9 The consent of any third parties who may unwittingly be involved in the experiment, such as bystanders, or the people depicted in photographs, has been sought whenever possible.
10 The participants will be thanked for their help after the experiment, and will be able to receive details of the results of the experiment if they wish to do so.
11 In any case of doubt or uncertainty, the advice of a more experienced researcher has been sought and has been followed.

and make any necessary adjustments to the design or procedure before proceeding with the main study. Needless to say all the data obtained from the pilot study must be discarded.

Finally, to round off this section, box 5.4 contains one more checklist, which this time covers the whole experiment design process. This can be used as a guide to the process of designing your own experiments, and is probably the way in which you will wish to use it at first. Later on, as you become more

---

Box 5.3   *A checklist of questions for a pilot study*

(Note: This list does not aim to provide a comprehensive questionnaire for all pilots, but tries only to indicate the main areas which you should consider before moving on the main data gathering. You will need to customize this for your own experiment.)

Procedure
- Did the experiment run smoothly?
- Were there any hitches or gaps in the procedure caused by a failure to prepare materials or a failure to anticipate?
- Is the experiment easily runnable by the number of experimenters who will be used? (Solo experimentation can sometimes be difficult.)
- Were all the instructions easily understood by the participants?
- Did any ask for them to be repeated or otherwise show evidence that they found them unclear?
- Did the experimental task take the expected time to complete? If not, does the task need to be redesigned to make it longer or shorter?

Data
- Was the data sheet easy to use?
- Do the data values lie roughly within the range expected? If not, is there an obvious reason for this – for example, is the task too easy or too hard for most people?

Participants
- How did the participants feel when they were engaged in the experiment?
- Did they enjoy the experience?
- Did they understand that they could withdraw at any time?
- Are there any points in the procedure where the pilot participants suggest that changes should be made? What are they?
- Did the participants feel the experimental task was too easy or too hard for them?

---

expert, you can use it to run a post-design check on your work to make sure that nothing vital has been missed before you begin your experiment.

The next section of this chapter aims to show how this design process looks when it is applied to a real research question. It consists of a research problem which is worked through from beginning to end with comments added at appropriate points in the process. The aim is to provide a model of the design process, and to clarify some the issues involved in each design decision. Many of the matters mentioned in the next section are dealt with in more detail elsewhere in this chapter or in chapter 7 (especially from p. 340 onwards). If you haven't already worked through that background material, you will probably find it better to delay aproaching the commented experiment until you have done so. You will also need to understand something about how and

Box 5.4 *A checklist of experiment design tasks*

Stage 1 Define the problem

Have you
- Clearly identified the research problem or question?
- Researched the background?
- Developed an explanation linking the experiment to theory?
- Identified an appropriate experimental task?

Stage 2 Establish the basic design

Have you
- Stated the aim(s) of the experiment?
- Identified the IV and DV?
- Decided how to operationalize the variables?
- Decided how many observations to make of the DV?
- Stated the experimental and null hypotheses?
- Decided the basic experiment design, and the reason for the choice?
- Decided which test statistic and significance level to use and the reason for your choices?
- Decided whether a one- or two-tailed test is needed?
- Identified the population of interest, sampling frame, and decided the sampling procedure and sample size?

Stage 3 Refine the design

Have you
- Identified which participant, and task variables you need to control, and decided how to control them?
- Decided how to allocate participants to the conditions in the experiment?
- Identified and dealt with any possible order effects between conditions?
- Checked for any other confounding variables which may exist?
- Decided the location for the experiment and checked the environment for possible confounding variables, such as noise?
- Constructed or obtained the apparatus, and checked that it works satisfactorily?
- Written the instructions to participants and designed the data collection sheet?
- Designed the post-experiment debriefing interview?
- Checked that the experiment conforms to ethical guidelines?
- Carried out a pilot study, evaluated the results and made any necessary changes to the design or procedure?

why the t-test is used, and more information on this can be found in chapter 9.

The problem chosen for the commented design, which concerns Richard Gregory's theory of illusion perception, has been selected so as to make it as easy as possible to find further sources of information. Gregory's theory is discussed in virtually every introductory text, and there should be no difficulty in finding more information if it is needed.

That aside, the experiment poses exactly the same set of general problems of design and control as would arise in relation to virtually any other research question. The context within which such problems present themselves changes from experiment to experiment, but the basic issues and challenges confronting the researcher remain the same.

A Commented Experiment Design: Impaired Depth Perception and the Muller-Lyer Illusion

Stage 1   Defining the problem

1.1   Identify the problem

Visual illusions have long been of interest to psychologists because they represent the response of the visual system to an abnormal input. By studying these responses it is possible to obtain some clues about how the visual system may function when dealing with normal (i.e. non-illusory) input. Furthermore, as the experience of a visual illusion generally represents an involuntary response it offers particularly reliable material for use in experimental work.

In perceptual research, two of the basic research questions are, 'Why do we perceive visual illusions?' and 'What are they able to tell us about visual perception in general?' However questions like these, though they raise fundamental issues, are unfortunately far too general to be dealt with by means of a single experiment. To be at all tractable a research question needs to be much more specific. Accordingly, we shall confine ourselves to researching one issue connected with one particular form of visual illusion – the Muller-Lyer illusion (see figure 5.7).

The Muller-Lyer illusion figure consists of a pair of horizontal lines, each of which possesses a pair of fins at either end which point in different directions.

Figure 5.7   The Muller-Lyer illusion

The illusion is that the horizontal lines, which are objectively equal, are perceived to be of different lengths. When viewed under normal conditions, the line with the outward pointing fins (a) is invariably experienced by Europeans as shorter than the one with the inward pointing fins (b).

The basic research question with which we began therefore becomes the much more tractable question of 'Why do we perceive the Muller-Lyer illusion (and what, if anything, does the explanation suggest for visual perception in general)?'

1.2   Research the background

One explanation for the perception of the Muller-Lyer illusion is provided by Richard Gregory's 'constructive' theory of perception (Gregory, 1972), which argues that perception is largely a 'top down' process, involving the unconscious generation of inferences from raw sensory information.

Gregory argues that we experience the Muller-Lyer illusion because the two types of fins on the horizontals each cause the brain to make a different inference about the line between them. Because the horizontal lines are really the same length, they produce identically sized retinal images. However, the inward-pointing fins provide cues which the brain interprets to mean that the horizontal line between them is further away from the viewer than it really is, while the outgoing fins similarly suggest that the horizontal is nearer than it really is. Under normal conditions (i.e. when viewing objects which are not illusion figures), identically sized retinal images of objects which are perceived to be at different distances from the viewer can only be obtained if one object is larger, or in this case, longer than the other. The human perceptual apparatus therefore concludes that one of the horizontals of the Muller-Lyer figure is longer than the other, and that is how it is perceived.

1.3   Link the theory to the proposed experiment

Gregory's explanation of the Muller-Lyer phenomenon rests on the argument that the two halves of the illusion figure, because of their shape, generate different impressions of depth in the viewer. However, there is also another possible source of information available in the form of binocular disparity – the information available about depth which arises from the fact that each eye has a slightly different viewpoint on the external scene. (Other possible cues to depth are provided by motion parallax and superposition, which can both be discounted as sources of information when a subject views a stationary, unobstructed Muller-Lyer figure.)

When a Muller-Lyer figure is viewed under normal conditions, binocular disparity can be expected to inform the perceptual system that the two parts of the illusion figure are the same distance from the retina. Since this is contrary to the information which Gregory claims is extracted from the illusion figure itself, the two should, at least partly cancel each other out when the illusion figure is viewed with normal binocular vision.

It follows from this that if Gregory's theory is correct, the effect of viewing with only one eye should be to increase the Muller-Lyer effect, since the information from the figure itself will provide the only available cues to depth. If, on the other hand, no difference is found in the magnitude of the illusion when the effects of viewing under monocular and binocular conditions are compared, or if the illusion is greater when viewed with both eyes, then that would suggest that Gregory's explanation for the Muller-Lyer phenomenon is mistaken.

1.4   Make a preliminary identification of the experimental task

In this case, the experimental task selects itself. The obvious way of removing binocular disparity cues from the perceptual input is to make subjects use only one eye to view the illusion. A test of the theory will thus be provided in the experiment by comparing the perception of the illusion under two conditions: a 'binocular' condition in which the illusion figure is viewed with both eyes, and a 'monocular' condition, in which it is viewed with one eye only.

Stage 2   Establishing the basic design

2.1   Specify the aim of the experiment

The general aim of the experiment is to provide a test of Gregory's 'misapplied constancy' explanation for the Muller-Lyer illusion. The specific aim is to see whether evidence can be found for the existence of a causal relationship between the ability to perceive depth and the magnitude of the Muller-Lyer illusion.

Comment
The purpose of writing a statement of aims has been discussed already, and does not need to be repeated. Note that the statement above distinguishes between the general aim of the experiment, which is to test a theory, and the specific aim, which is to determine whether there exists a particular relationship which has been hypothesized on the basis of the theory. It is a good idea to do this because it reinforces the idea that there is an important logical distinction to be drawn between a theory itself and any predictions or ideas which have been derived from it. The reason for this is clear enough, but is often overlooked: theories are general statements which need to be related to concrete situations before they can be tested. For this reason a single experiment which disconfirms a theory is rarely likely to be sufficient to discredit that theory. Instead, it is necessary to test the theory across a range of situations in which predictions have been made.

2.2   Identify the IV and DV and decide how they are to be operationalized

The independent variable in this experiment is the extent to which the participants are able to use normal cues to depth in their perception of the Muller-

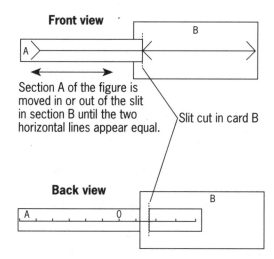

The scale on the back of the apparatus is calibrated in millimetres and measures the extent to which the perception of the relative lengths of the two lines differs from their actual lengths.

The scale should be read against the edge of the larger of the two pieces of card, and the zero point on the scale should be so placed that it indicates when the lengths of the two halves of the illusion figure are objectively equal.

The extent to which the illusion is perceived is indicated by the points on the scale to either side of the zero.

Figure 5.8   Apparatus to measure the magnitude of the Muller-Lyer illusion

Lyer figure. Two levels of the IV will be employed, each of which constitutes a different condition of the experiment, and because the experiment will be testing a hypothesis of causal relations between the IV and DV, a true experiment with a real control condition will be required.

Control condition (level 1)   Perception of the illusion figure under conditions of unimpaired depth perception (i.e. using binocular vision).
Experimental condition (level 2)   Perception of the illusion figure under conditions of impaired depth perception (i.e. using monocular vision).

The dependent variable in the experiment is the *magnitude* of the perceived illusion, i.e. the difference between the apparent length and actual length of the arms of the illusion figure. The data in the experiment consists of measurements of this variable made under the two conditions.

Comment
The experiment requires a method of measuring the magnitude of the illusion. One way of doing this is to construct the apparatus shown in figure 5.8, which combines both halves of the illusion figure. One half of the figure can be moved relative to the other half and a millimetre scale on the back enables the magnitude of the illusion to be measured.
    Note that the nature of the illusion is such that the same horizontal should always be perceived to be the longer of the two. However, the apparatus allows for the possibility that some individuals will report the reverse relation, but any such data should always be discarded as unreliable, and a new participant run as a replacement.

Six observations will be made of the DV for each participant under each condition, making twelve observations in total from each person. Analysis, using a test statistic will be performed on the mean of each person's performance in each condition.

Comment
In this experiment, the accuracy with which the magnitude of the illusion is measured depends on:

1   *The ability of the participants to report their own perceptions accurately*
2   *The accuracy with which the scale on the apparatus is read by the experimenter.*

There is no way of knowing how accurately the subjects may be reporting what they see, and so there is always the possibility that error from this source will creep into the experiment. The best solution to this problem is the one adopted here. Participants are required to generate several responses in each condition, the mean of which provides a score for the test statistic. In effect the experiment samples from each person's range of possible responses, and then takes the mean of the samples as a typical value.

2.3   State the experimental and null hypotheses

The experimental hypothesis   The one-tailed experimental hypothesis is that a significantly smaller magnitude of the Muller-Lyer illusion will be experienced when it is viewed with one eye compared to when it is viewed with both eyes.
The null hypothesis   The null hypothesis is that no significant difference in the magnitude of the illusion will be observed when the illusion figure is viewed with only one eye compared to when it is viewed with both eyes.

Comment
The experimental hypothesis is one-tailed because it predicts that scores in the experimental condition will be significantly lower than those in the control condition. Had the direction of difference between the conditions not been specified then the hypothesis would have been two-tailed.

2.4   Decide the basic experiment design

The experimental hypothesis will be tested by means of a repeated measures design in which all subjects contribute data to both the experimental (monocular view) and control (binocular view) conditions. The randomized ordering of the treatments will enable a causal relation between variables to be validly inferred if the experimental hypothesis is accepted.

Comment
The decision about which design to use for this experiment involves a straight choice between the independent subjects and repeated measures designs.

As the experiment is concerned with manipulating perceptual processes which are not under conscious control (it is not possible to choose not to experience the Muller-Lyer illusion), any error that may result from taking repeated measures from the same participants is likely to be less than error arising from using an independent samples design which has different individuals in each condition. The repeated measures design is therefore to be preferred in this case because it offers protection against the possibility of constant error due to interpersonal differences. (It also offers a more economical use of participants.)

2.5 Determine the test statistic and the significance level

The data will be analysed using the t-test for repeated measures, with a significance level of $p = 0.05$. See chapter 9 p. 401 onwards.

Comment
The considerations behind this choice are as follows:

1 **A statistic is required which provides for a test of significant difference between data in two conditions.** *The t-test is appropriate since it provides a test of significant difference between the means of two sets of data.*
2 **On what scale has the DV been measured?** *In this experiment the data consist of linear measures in millimetres, which represent measures on an interval scale. Although there are problems in assessing the accuracy of the measures themselves, this suggests that a t-test would be the appropriate statistic.*
3 **Are the values of the dependent variable likely to be normally distributed within the population of interest (in this case the general population)?** *For the purposes of this experiment the expectation is that this will be the case, on the ground that the distribution of the degree to which the illusion is perceived is unlikely to differ significantly from the distribution of other interpersonal differences, many of which are approximately normal in shape. Again, the t-test is indicated as the appropriate test statistic for these data.*
4 **Have the data been obtained from a random sample drawn from the population?** *Given the nature of the experiment, it is a reasonably safe assumption that even opportunity sampling will not produce a sample which differs significantly from that which would be produced by a true random sample. Again, the t-test is indicated.*
5 **Is the variance of the dependent measure likely not to be significantly different between the two conditions in the experiment?** *Because the dependent measures consist of measures of similar involuntary behaviour, the answer to this point is 'yes'.*

This final point means that all the assumptions behind the t-test can plausibly be assumed to have been met. The t-test is a robust test, which means that even if some of the assumptions are less well-founded than others (such as the homogeneity of variance assumption mentioned at point 5 above), it is still capable of allowing a valid decision to be made about hypotheses.

The choice of the significance level of $p = 0.05$ is the conventional level of significance for experiment in psychology , and represents an acceptable risk of making a type 1 decision error about the hypotheses.

A reminder: more detailed information on the t-test can be found in chapter 9, p. 389 onwards. The topics of hypotheses, significance level and decision errors are all covered in chapter 7.

2.6   Decide the sampling procedure

The population of interest in this experiment is the general population for which no sampling frame exists. The sample will be an opportunity sample of at least twenty people drawn from the students attending a large educational institution.

Comment
The experiment is concerned with measuring a form of involuntary behaviour under two different conditions in order to draw conclusions which apply to human beings in general. Although good experimental practice would dictate that data should be collected from a random sample drawn from a subset of the general population, it is almost certainly unnecessary to do so in this case. The nature of the Muller-Lyer illusion is such that it is likely to be perceived to approximately the same degree by all individuals with normal vision, so it can be assumed that, providing they meet the age and vision criteria mentioned below under 'subject variables', a volunteer or opportunity sample will not differ significantly from a truly random sample of the general population.

As always, the sample should be as large as possible and, for reasons concerned with the need to control task variables (see below), should ideally consist of a multiple of four. Somewhere between twenty and forty subjects represents a reasonable compromise between ensuring enough participants for the test statistic to generate a valid result, and avoiding the practical problems raised by having to work with large numbers.

At this point, the first stage of putting together the experiment design is complete. Decisions have been made about each of the key features which form the basis of the design, and the outline of the finished experiment, though lacking in detail, is nevertheless quite clear. The process now moves on to consider all the refinements which will turn the rough design into a finely tuned and effective, research instrument.

Stage 3   Refining the design

In order to ensure as far as possible that any changes to the DV are only caused by changes to the level of IV, the following variables will need to be controlled during the experiment.

3.1   Review control of subject variables

Age: The sample will consist of people aged 16 to 60.
Vision: The sample will consist of people who do not wear spectacles or contact lenses to correct their vision.

Comment
The intention is to collect data from people who are approximately equal in their ability to perceive the illusion: normal binocular vision is all that is needed for this. The upper and lower age boundaries for the sample are simply there to ensure that the sample is reasonably homogeneous in other respects such as general health.

3.2 Review control of task variables

Each participant is to be tested using the same illusion figure and the conditions under which the figure is viewed should contain the following controls:

1 Counterbalance the order in which participants take each of the conditions, so that half of them take the experimental condition first, while the remainder take the control condition first. Participants are assigned to their first condition at random.

Comment
Counterbalancing the order in which the conditions are taken ensures that any error due to some participants taking one condition before the other is neutralized by the fact that an equal number take them in the reverse order. The purpose of the random assignment to conditions is to enable a causal inference be drawn if the data indicate that the experimental hypothesis is eventually to be accepted. To do this, a number from one up to the number of participants is given at random to each participant when they arrive to take part in the experiment. All even numbered participants then contribute data to the experimental condition before the control condition, while the odd numbered ones take the conditions in the reverse order.

2 Counterbalance the left–right orientation of the illusion figure across both conditions and all trials in order to control for any error arising from the participants having been presented with the figure consistently in one orientation.

Comment
The illusion figure can be presented in either one of two orientations in the horizontal plane – with the moveable section to a participant's left or to her right. Because eye-movements from left to right are used for reading, they are more highly practised than right–left movements, and therefore it is possible that participants may find the task of tracking left–right movement slightly easier. To control for possible error arising from this, the illusion will be presented to each participant an equal number of times in both orientations. This can be achieved by having odd numbered participants see the left-biased figure on odd-numbered trials, and the right biased figure on even numbered trials, while even numbered subjects see the left-biased figure on even numbered trials, and the right-biased figure on odd numbered trials.
  However, this will interact with the counterbalancing already set up to control the effect of taking one condition first. Unless steps are taken to prevent it,

Box 5.5   *Experimental treatments log*

Participant no.	Condition taken first in the experiment	Direction in which the moveable section of the apparatus is pointing	
Place a tick against each number below as the trials are completed		Trials 1, 3, 5 in both conditions	Trials 2, 4, 6 in both conditions
1	Control	To left of participant	To right of participant
2	Experimental	To right of participant	To left of participant
3	Control	To right of participant	To left of participant
4	Experimental	To left of participant	To right of participant
etc. . . .			

participants will always see the figure in one particular orientation on the same trials in the same condition, which could act as a source of constant error. This can be avoided by changing the rule about the orientation of the figure. Instead of having all odd numbered participants see the left-oriented figure on all odd numbered trials, they need to see it only on half of the odd numbered trials. On the others, they see the right facing figure. Similarly, the even numbered participants need to be divided evenly between those who see the right-facing figure on even numbered trials and those who see it on odd numbered trials.

This has become complicated, as it is now necessary to be able to keep track of two types of counterbalancing keyed to the participants' identifying numbers. To achieve this, a memory aid like the one in box 5.5 can be constructed. This makes it clear that subject 1 takes the control condition first, and is presented with the apparatus with the moveable section pointing to her left on the odd numbered trials in both conditions, and so on. The table gives the assignment of the first four participants, and repeats itself for every group of four participants. During the experiment, it is helpful to have an assistant to check that the table is being followed correctly.

3 Standardize the movement of the adjustable section of the illusion figure either to inward or outward movement, so that all subjects see the movement as either increasing or decreasing the length of the figure.

Comment
It is conceivable that the participants' ability to identify when the two arms of the illusion figure are equal could be affected by the direction, (inward or outward) in which the adjustable section of the apparatus is moved. One solution would be to counterbalance the two directions of movement across subjects and trials in the same way as the effects of right–left orientation are to be counterbalanced. However, this adds a further level of complication to the experiment, and would necessitate extra manipulation of the illusion figure which may distract the participant. The alternative of standardization is therefore preferred in this case.

4 Standardize the distance between the illusion figure and the participant. On each trial, the illusion figure is to be presented at participant's eye-height at a standard distance of 2 metres from the participant.

Comment
The figure–participant distance has to be standardized because viewing the illusion figure at different distances produces differently sized retinal images, and it is possible that these could lead participants to make errors in their judgements about the relative length of the horizontal lines.

5 Standardize the method used to obtain monocular vision in the experimental condition. This can be obtained by having all participants wear a blindfold entirely covering the non-dominant eye, and lightly secured to the surrounding skin to prevent it slipping.

Comment
The whole experiment rests on the restriction of experimental condition participants to monocular vision, so it is necessary to ensure that this aspect of the experiment is very tightly controlled. There must be absolutely no possibility of any participant in the experimental condition using both eyes to view the illusion. Allowing participants to 'black out' one eye using a hand is particularly unwise as it is may be construed as an invitation to cheat. To be certain that only one eye is being used there is no alternative to the researcher blindfolding them herself, and using surgical tape to secure the blindfold lightly to the skin of the forehead and cheek in order to make sure that it doesn't move during the experiment.

6 Standardize the test environment, so that all participants as far as possible experience exactly the same environment on all trials. All participants will view the illusion figure from a seated position; the level of illumination under which the figure is viewed will be constant from trial to trial and from person to person; each participant will receive identical instructions; and all distracting stimuli such as noise will be excluded from the experimental situation.

Comment
Establishing a standardized test environment is a relatively straightforward process providing the situation in which the experiment takes place can be screened

from potentially distracting stimuli such as road drills, low-flying aircraft or people passing by. Unless it is part of the experiment it is rarely a good idea to attempt to run an experiment in a public place: there are likely to be too many distractions for participants to be able to concentrate fully on the task in hand. Nor is it good practice to try to run participants in batches of two or three, since this merely introduces an additional source of error into the experiment in the form of a social influence effect. Most damaging of all is the practice of mixing data from individual testing with that obtained from batch testing. No conclusions can be drawn from the results of merging different sets of data in this way because they were obtained under significantly different conditions.

3.3 Review control of the test environment

The experiment will take place in a secluded room which cannot be seen into by anyone outside, and which is not likely to be subject to intrusive noise. To ensure that no one enters the room and disturbs the concentration of the participants, a sign 'Experiment in progress. Please do not disturb' will be placed on the outside of the door.

Comment
These probably represent the minimum conditions needed for conducting a successful experiment.

3.4 Construct or obtain apparatus

The experiment requires the construction of a Muller-Lyer illusion figure from stout paper or cardboard, as illustrated in figure 5.8.

Comment
The construction of the apparatus is straightforward providing reasonably stiff card is used. None of the dimensions is critical, and the only thing to watch is that the moveable section of the apparatus doesn't waggle around too much and make it difficult to obtain an accurate reading from the scale.

3.5 Write instructions to participants and debriefing interview

'Thank you for coming to help me with this experiment. This is an experiment on visual perception designed to provide information about the mental processes involved in seeing. It will involve you in looking at a set of lines and making some judgements about them, and that is all.'
'Before we begin I need to know whether one of your eyes is stronger than the other.'
'Can you tell me which of your eyes you feel you see more clearly with?'
'Can you tell me which hand you prefer to use for tasks such as writing?'

Comment
If the answer to the first question is indeterminate (i.e. does not indicate clearly which eye is the stronger), then the answer to the second question can be used:

right handed people tend to be right eye dominant, and left handers to be left eye dominant.

'This experiment is trying to find out whether it is harder for you to see a visual illusion when you look at it with one eye or with both eyes. In a moment I am going to ask you to look at this figure, and while you are looking I will gradually move one side of the figure like this [the researcher demonstrates how the illusion figure can be adjusted]. I would like you to tell me when you think the line labelled "A" is the same length as the line labelled "B". When you think they are the same length I want you to say "stop". It is important that you say "stop" as soon as you think the lengths are the same.

'That's all you have to do. After you have said "stop" I will write down how far the adjustable section of the apparatus has moved, and we will repeat the procedure a number of times. For some of the times I will need to cover your weaker eye with this blindfold which will be lightly taped it down so it won't move. Is that OK with you?

'If you want to change your mind about taking part in this experiment at any time you just have to say and we'll stop immediately and your results will be destroyed or returned to you.

'Would you like to ask any questions about the experiment before we continue?

'Before we begin here are two practice trials for you to get used to the apparatus, and the general situation. Tell me to stop moving the apparatus when you think A and B are of equal length . . . OK. And again . . . OK.

'Are there any questions you want to ask before we begin?

'Now here are some more trials.

[1 *Instruction for monocular condition trials*]

'Now I'm going to cover up your weaker eye with this blindfold, and tape it down so it can't slip. Is that comfortable? Now look at the figure and tell me when you think A and B are of equal length . . . OK. And again . . . OK . . .

[2 *Instruction for binocular condition trials*]

'Now look at the figure using both eyes equally and tell me when you think A and B are of equal length . . . OK. And again . . . OK . . .

'That was the last trial. Thank you very much for your help with this experiment. As I said earlier, I'm interested in finding out whether viewing the figure with one eye makes any difference to how you see it. Your results will help answer that question, which may in turn provide some clues as to exactly what the brain does with the information coming in from the eyes.

'Before you go, is there anything else you would like to know about what we've been doing? Is there anything about the experiment that made you feel uncomfortable that you would like to mention?

'If you would like to have a copy of your results, or would like to know how the experiment eventually turns out could you write down how you can be contacted on this sheet of paper?

'Thank you again for your help'.

Design the data collection sheet

Comment
Data from each participant are entered on a single line of the record, and the mean of the six scores in each condition is computed and entered in the

Box 5.6   Data collection sheet

Experiment   The effect of impaired depth perception on the perception of the Muller-Lyer illusion

	Experimental condition (monocular vision trials) Magnitude of perceived illusion in mm								Control condition (binocular vision trials) Magnitude of perceived illusion in mm						
	1	2	3	4	5	6	mean		1	2	3	4	5	6	mean
1															
2															
3															
4															
etc. . . .															

appropriate column. It is important to note that the random numbering of participants referred to earlier as part of the process of assigning people to conditions means also that the lines of the data sheet will be filled in random order rather than from the top down. The number assigned to a participant at random is also the number which appears in the leftmost column of the data sheet.

Note that the title of the experiment, the difference between the conditions, the number of trials, and the units of measurement of the DV are all clearly indicated. Each half of the sheet could be prepared on a separate page, and this might make it easier to remember where data have to be entered, particularly as it will be necessary to keep track of two sets of counterbalancing (order of conditions, and the orientation of the apparatus) during the experiment.

3.6   Read the ethics checklist

See box 5.2, page 237.

3.7   Run a pilot study, and evaluate the results

See the box 5.3, p. 238, for the pilot study checklist.

I hope that if you have managed to work right through this design to the end you will feel you have acquired two things: not only a fairly complete and detailed understanding of how to set about the business of designing an experiment, but also a completely planned project which is virtually ready to run. All you need to do is a little research in an appropriate textbook, make your apparatus, draw up the data sheet and find some subjects. Why not do it?

Ethical Issues in Psychological Experiments

In an experiment, the participants enter a situation which is highly structured, almost wholly under the control of the researcher, and in which there may be little or no scope for independent behaviour. An experimenter, who may see the situation from only one perspective, and who anyway possesses concerns which are not shared by the participant, may also fail to appreciate the extent to which that situation is capable of making the participant feel uncomfortable, or worse.

From the point of view of doing ethical research, this is clearly a cause for concern, and the purpose of this section is to highlight three aspects of an experiment where, for this reason, particular sensitivity is called for.

1   The passive nature of the participant role

In an experiment virtually the entire situation is controlled by the researcher. Decisions about such things as the procedure to be followed, and how the research is to be conducted will have already been taken before the first participant arrives, so that the role provided for a research participant – the 'subject' of the research – is largely a passive one.

Although this is generally accepted as a natural feature of experimental research, it is still necessary for a researcher to take care to manage this situation in a way which shows regard for the participant's feelings. In particular it is important to ensure that a concern to project an 'efficient' or 'professional' image doesn't spill over into a tendency to treat a research participant simply as an insensate source of data rather than as a human person. Ordinary politeness and warmth, allied to a sensitive awareness of others' feelings can do much to ensure that the participant feels at ease throughout the experiment.

2   The situational pressure to continue

The fact that the experiment is a situation which the researcher controls may also make it difficult for the participant to disengage from the experimental situation if she wishes to do so. In effect, it is possible for someone to become 'locked in' to the situation, so that they continue with the experiment when, for whatever reason, they are not willing to do so.

Among the reasons for this, apart from the fact that they feel they are there to help the researcher anyway, is the fact that a participant will certainly be aware of the pressure of an expectation that people will continue in the experiment until all data needed have been collected. When added to the essentially passive nature of the participant role, these factors may make it hard for someone to disengage themselves from the situation, and for many participants it may require a considerable effort to transgress what they feel are the norms of the situation. Again, a sensitive awareness of the issue on the part of the experimenter, when coupled with clear information to the participant that withdrawal from the experiment is possible at any time, will almost certainly be sufficient to prevent any problem arising.

3   The effects of 'failure'

Finally it is also possible, because of some earlier experience which is nothing to do with the experiment, that some people may be sensitized to failure. Effectively, this means that they may be more ready to identify themselves as 'failures' and, more importantly from the point of view of the experiment, may also experience the negative effects of failure more keenly than the average person.

When an experiment includes the possibility that a subject will perceive himself to have 'failed' at the task, the researcher needs to be alert to effects that this can have on the participant's self-esteem. In such cases, careful debriefing may be necessary in order to help the person put events into a better perspective. If you feel that providing such help is beyond you, you should enlist the aid of someone with the appropriate skills.

Suggestions for Experiments

One of the best ways of developing your skills as an experimenter is to try replicating the work of other, more experienced researchers. This has the advantage that it takes care of much of the work involved in deriving testable hypotheses from a theory, and instead allows you to concentrate instead on the details of the design and procedure. However, a major difficulty is that to undertake a full replication of a particular experiment you need to have access to a complete account of the original research, and this may not be readily available.

A way round this is to attempt instead what might be called 'creative replications'. Many textbooks provide enough information to enable you to plan an experiment which, while it follows the broad outline of the original research, nevertheless differs from it in some details. The textbook provides the idea, and you then elaborate on it on the basis of whatever other information you have available. The following suggestions will give you the idea – you have some basic information about the experiments, but you will also notice that in each case, a considerable amount of design work still remains to be done before you have a runnable experiment.

Figure 5.9   The nine-dot problem

Experiment 1   *The effect of hinting on the solution of the nine-dot problem*

The nine-dot problem consists simply of nine dots arranged to form a square, as in figure 5.9.

The task is to draw four continuous straight lines to connect all the dots, without lifting the pen from the paper. Surprisingly, most people appear to be unable to solve this puzzle. Repeated experiments have consistently obtained success rates of close to zero because people seem not to notice that they have to extend the lines beyond the boundaries of the square to achieve a solution, as in fig 5.10. In terms of the Gestalt theory of perception, it appears that people become fixated on the overall shape of the pattern of dots and so cannot take into account the possibility that the boundaries of the square could be crossed by the lines.

One might expect that it would only take a small hint about the nature of the solution to enable someone to solve the puzzle, but again, this apparently doesn't happen. Even when a clear hint is supplied with the puzzle (Weisberg & Alba, 1981), the success rate only reaches about 20%. Four out of five people are still unable to arrive at the solution.

Several interesting experiments suggest themselves from this. One would be to compare a hinting condition with a no-hint condition, in order to see whether the solution of the basic nine-dot version of the puzzle does in fact present a difficulty. If you find that this is really the case, you could go on to see whether hinting is in fact as ineffective as Weisberg and Alba suggest. Could the *kind* of hinting make a difference? To test this possibility you could compare the effects of hints of different kinds such as verbal (e.g. 'don't limit yourself to the inside of the square'), versus visual (presenting a drawing of a partial solution as in figure 5.11).

Experiment 2   *Cue-dependent remembering in two environments*

Tulving's (1974) theory of cue-dependent remembering argues that the recall of memorized information is determined by a set of retrieval cues which are encoded in memory at the same time as the material is learned, and which are used in recall to facilitate the retrieval of the memorized information.

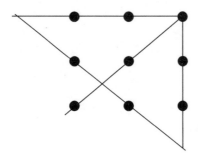

Figure 5.10   Solution to the nine-dot problem

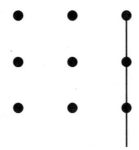

Figure 5.11   Partial solution to the nine-dot problem

An experiment by Godden and Baddeley (1975), provides an unusual test of this theory. They had members of a sub-aqua club learn lists of words in one of two conditions – either on dry land, or underwater, and subsequently tested recall either in the same or in the different environment.

They found that those people who were asked to recall in the same environment as that in which the words had originally been memorized generally were able to recall about 30% more of the words in the list than the people who were remembering it in a different environment. The conclusion, in line with Tulving's theory, is that recalling in the same environment as memorization enables the recall cues to be used, while recalling in a different environment prevents access to those cues, and hence results in poorer recall of the material.

This experiment could be subjected to a creative replication without a great deal of difficulty, since it is basically a standard memorization-and-recall test using a word list. However, since you are unlikely to have access to a group of experienced divers for your experimental participants, you will need to try to find a different approach. Basically, you need to design the two environments on land so as to ensure that there is maximum contrast between them on as many variables as possible. If you can use two different rooms, you could vary the level of illumination, ambient temperature, ambient noise, quality of furnishings and so on between them. Alternatively, you could use an interior and an exterior location (say a classroom and a garden). The important point is that there must be sufficient separation between the characteristics of the two environments to maximize the probability of obtaining different levels of recall when you come to compare recall in 'same' and 'different' conditions.

REFERENCES

Godden, D. R. & Baddeley, A. D. (1975). Context-dependent memory in two natural environments: On land and under water. *British Journal of Psychology*, 66, 325–31.
Scheerer, M. (1963). Problem-solving. *Scientific American*, 208, 118–28.
Tulving, E. (1974). Cue-dependent forgetting. *American Scientist*, 62, 74–82.
Weisberg, R. W. and Alba, J. W. (1981). An examination of the alleged role of 'fixation' in the solution of several insight problems. *Journal of Experimental Psychology (General)*, 110, 169–92.

Summary of chapter 5

The goal of science in general is to try to understand why things are the way they are, and this means trying to understand the influences which cause various phenomena to occur. The importance of the experiment as a way of doing research in psychology lies in the fact that it is the only method available which can answer questions about causes with any certainty.

Stripped to essentials, an experiment consists of a situation in which two variables – called the independent variable (IV) and the dependent variable (DV) are allowed to interact, while at the same time any other variables which could possibly influence them are either excluded from the situation, or controlled in some way. When an experiment is run, the values to be taken by the independent variable are also controlled by the experimenter, and measures of the effect of different levels of the IV on the DV are measured. When this is done, it becomes possible, in principle, to say whether the changes to the IV have caused any changes to the DV, since any alternative explanations for changes to the DV have been removed. A comparison of the effects of the IV under different conditions of the experiment will therefore allow clear conclusions to be drawn about whether a causal relationship exists between the IV and DV.

Not all experiments, however, permit such clear causal inferences to be made. 'True' experiments are those in which the design of the experimental situation, in such matters as the random allocation of subjects to conditions, is such that alternative explanations for changes to the DV can be confidently ruled out; but there is also a large class of 'quasi' experiments in which other, non-causal explanations for experimental results are also possible.

Both true and quasi types of experiment may be carried out either inside or outside the laboratory. In the latter type of environment, 'field experiments' – carried out in natural surroundings – can help to remove the criticism which is often made of psychology that laboratory-based research lacks vital 'ecological validity', i.e. the results represent a reflection of the artificial environment of the laboratory rather than the natural tendencies of the human subjects.

The question of experiment design deals principally with the issue of how the key elements in the experiment are to be arranged, and here several options present themselves, depending on the nature of the variables which are to be controlled. The basic choice lies between the independent subjects design, (either in the simple or before–after form), in which each experimental subject contributes data to only one condition in the experiment, and the repeated measures design in which each subject contributes data to all conditions. Other designs include the single sample, (one shot) design in which there is only one group of subjects who generate a single sample of data and the 'n = 1' design in which data are collected from only a single individual.

The fundamental problem facing the designer of an experiment is posed by experimental error caused by the existence of uncontrolled influences on the DV. These can creep in to an experiment from a range of sources, such as the experimental task, the research subjects, or from the measurement process, and recognized techniques exist for reducing the amount of error which may be present from each possible source. Less obviously, perhaps, the experiment itself can be regarded as a social situation of some complexity, and is also capable of acting as an important source of error. Particularly, the actions and demeanour of the experimenter play a significant part in influencing the behaviour of the subjects. Research has shown, for example, that the experimental subjects are not merely to be regarded as passive sources of data but are, on the contrary, active in their attempts to figure out the 'real' purpose of the research from the verbal and non-verbal cues provided by the experimenter. Sometimes the conclusions they draw lead them to try to 'help' the research by providing the data they believe the researcher is looking for, rather than simply behaving naturally, with the consequent injection of a considerable amount of experimental error into the data.

The lack of balance in the power relationship between experimenter and subjects places a significant responsibility on the former to scrutinize every experiment from the ethical perspective at the design stage. As well as the more obvious issues such as the need to obtain the informed consent of all subjects, the experimenter needs to be aware of, and prepare for less obvious matters such as the possible effects of repeated failure at an experimental task.

Experiment design can be seen as a three-stage process, encompassing problem definition, the construction of the basic design, and then the subsequent refining of the design.

Problem definition is not only concerned with the sometimes difficult process of identifying a problem to be researched, but also with locating the problem, when found, within existing theory and previous research.

Devising the fundamental structure of the experiment requires decisions to be made about sampling – how the subjects are to be drawn from their parent population; which design provides the best control of the variables which have been identified as significant potential sources of error, and the choice of a test statistic.

The third stage of refining the experiment builds on these decisions to deal with the identification and control of error variables and the practicalities of managing the data collection process, such as the design of the sheet for logging the raw data. If possible, it is good practice to conduct a small-scale pilot study of the experiment in order to test the procedure and recording system, and to make an assessment of any aspects of the experiment which may be causing concern for ethical reasons.

6 Working with Numerical Data

This chapter provides information and guidance on the analysis of numerical (quantitative) data in psychology.

- It introduces the task of measurement in psychology, describes the different scales of measurement, and reviews the basics of working with quantitative data.

- It explains the difference between a statistic and a parameter and looks at the reasons for using statistics.

- It introduces and describes the measures of central tendency, dispersion and correlation and explains how these can be used to provide concise descriptions of data.

- It reviews the different kinds of graphs by which data can be represented and gives a detailed description of how to construct and interpret a box and whisker plot.

- It makes suggestions for small projects in data analysis using descriptive procedures.

Introduction

You will remember from what was said in chapter 1 that the results of any scientific investigation consist of data – information – which can be of either the qualitative or quantitative type. Qualitative data consist of verbal descriptions of behaviour and experience resulting from processes of observation, interpretation and analysis. By using a qualitative approach, a researcher can capture information which it might otherwise be difficult, or impossible, to express by quantitative means. Descriptions of an individual personality, the details of subjective experience and the detailed analyses of patterns of behaviour are all examples of topics which require a qualitative record, although there are, of course, many others.

Quantitative data, on the other hand, consist of information represented in the form of numbers which represent the results of a (more or less precise) measurement process applied to the psychological variables (e.g. reaction times) in an investigation. Of the two types of data, quantitative data has wider use within the scientific community, for reasons which we will look at in a moment.

This chapter, and the three which follow, are intended to provide the information you need in order to analyse any quantitative data which you generate through your research. (This means basically that you use the numbers to find answers to the questions which interest you.) You will find the techniques which are presented in chapter 9, though rather formidable at first sight, to be particularly useful in that task.

Before we progress further, we should perhaps pause to remind ourselves of some of the advantages to be gained by using numbers rather than words to represent information.

First, numbers offer a way of representing information in a precise and unambiguous way. There is no doubt, for example, exactly what magnitude of temperature change is indicated by the difference between (say) 10°C and 20°C. Now compare two possible verbal equivalents – 'coolish' and 'warmish' – and ask yourself whether you can say anything about the actual temperatures those words designate, or about the difference between them. Of course, you find that very little, if anything, can be said beyond the fact that one represents a state of greater warmth than the other. (I should also point out that the greater precision offered by numerical data is not solely due to the difference between numbers and words. As we shall see very shortly when we look at the different scales of measurement, there are some situations in which data in the form of numbers are no better than words. However, this does not affect the general point being made, that the possibility of precise measurement can only exist if numbers rather than words are used to represent the information.)

Secondly, when numbers are used to represent information, the data, once collected, can be analysed (again in ways which are precise and unambiguous) by means of various statistical procedures which we will encounter later in the book. The value of these procedures lies in the fact that they permit us to go beyond the surface appearance of any information which we may have to hand and to draw conclusions about its significance and meaning. That is, by using statistics we can pass beyond the simple description of the set of numbers we have collected, and say something about what those same numbers imply about the situation in which they were collected; and of course this, in psychology as in other sciences, is what we are really interested in all the time – not the numbers themselves, but what they are able to tell us about the ideas they represent.

Of course, although numbers clearly offer significant advantages as a way of representing information, not everyone, for any one of several different reasons, finds it equally easy to think and reason numerically. Some people, indeed, think of themselves as so lacking in numerical ability that the thought of working with numbers is aversive, and so they try to avoid those situations, such as the pursuit of interesting questions in psychology, which look as though they might lead on to anything remotely mathematical.

Unfortunately, it is difficult, in a book of this kind, to make helpful suggestions for meeting this situation. The problem is that although the presenting symptom of numerical incapacity seems simple and straightforward, the underlying causes may vary from person to person, and so the advice which meets one situation may not do for another. Probably all that can (or should) be said is that the difficulty is unlikely to be as large or as formidable as it may appear. Many people seem to leave school with a poor image of their own numerical competence which is not at all justified by their actual abilities or performance, and they often turn out, after a little practice, to be better at working with numerical data than they would ever have believed possible. The two basic requirements needed to enjoy a reasonably successful career in numerical analysis at this level are simply perseverance and practice. You need the determination to hang in there while you master the techniques – and then lots of practice at using those same techniques to make sense of your data.

Assuming that any qualms you may be feeling about working with numbers have been somewhat quietened by the foregoing remarks, we'll begin the approach to the business of working with numbers in psychology by looking first at the different scales of measurement on which numbers can be used to represent information.

Scales of measurement

First, we need to recall that in essence, the process of measuring involves representing some quality of an object, such as the length of a piece of wood, or the temperature of a glass of water, as a position on a scale of values – on the scale calibrated in centimetres, say, in the first example, and on the scale of degrees Celsius, or one of the other temperature scales, in the other. It is then possible to use numbers to describe the magnitude of whatever quality is being measured. Thus a piece of wood can be 1100 or 1000 centimetres long (or some other value), while the temperature of water in a glass may be 5°C, or 10°C or 20°C or (again) some other value. This ability to describe a particular quality of something as a number on a scale is particularly useful because it permits one piece of wood, or glass of water (or anything else) to be compared with some precision to any other of the same kind.

The problem in psychology is that one is usually trying to measure mental processes such as intelligence, recall from memory, or reasoning ability, which are not directly accessible to the investigator, unlike physical qualities such as length or heat or gravity which generally are much easier to get at and measure.

This in turn means that a psychologist, depending on exactly what it is she wishes to measure, may have to employ one of several different approaches to measurement.

There are, in fact, four distinct ways in which numbers can be used to make measurements and support comparisons between different measures. These are known as 'scales [or levels] of measurement', and the most important thing about them for psychologists is that they permit measurements to be made under a range of different situations, including even those from which it might be thought impossible to extract numerical data. As usual, though, there is a price to be paid for flexibility, and in this case it concerns the precision with which measurements can be made.

Ranked in ascending order according to the precision of the measurements which they support, the scales are:

- **The nominal scale**
- **The ordinal scale**
- **The interval scale**
- **The ratio scale.**

The nominal scale

Measures on the nominal scale offer the lowest level of precision, since the numbers simply act as identifiers – names – and have no significance other than making identification possible. This way of using numbers is very widely used, but is occasionally misunderstood. The way to get it clear in your mind is to ask yourself whether the numbers represent a measure of any particular quality of the individual. If they don't, then the numbers are acting as names.

For example, the numbers on soccer players' shirts represent measures on the nominal scale, and are only used to identify particular individuals, just as a name would be. If we apply the test mentioned above we can see that, clearly, no quality of the individual is being represented. The wearer of a number 9 shirt is not necessarily a better player (nor is he likely to earn more money, or be a faster runner) than the individual in the number 3 shirt (and still less is he likely to be three times better, richer or faster). So the shirt numbers represent nominal scale values.

In psychology, the nominal scale is used when you simply wish to identify different individuals who can each be placed in one of several different categories. Suppose you are observing the behaviour of people in a supermarket in order to determine whether a particular display is more effective at stimulating purchases among male or female customers. You might decide to divide your observations into 'look but fail to purchase' and 'look and purchase' categories, and then record the sex of each individual under one of the two categories.

Using the nominal scale you could represent each male shopper by a 1 and each female by a 2, which might give the following results of the first ten observations:

Look but fail to purchase	Look and purchase
1	1
1	2
2	2
1	2
1	2

Note that each number is being used as the name of the sex of each shopper, and you could, if you wish, replace the digits by the words 'male' and 'female' without any loss of information. However, if verbal labels are given they will still have to be converted into numerical form before a test statistic can be used, and clearly it is more convenient for the subsequent computation if the data are represented as numbers from the beginning.

The ordinal scale

An ordinal scale is one step up in precision from the nominal scale because measures made on this scale can be compared with each other and their relationship described, albeit in rather simple terms. The measures made on an ordinal scale preserve the presence or absence of differences in scale value (and the sign of the difference), but not other information such as the magnitude of the difference. With data representing measures on an ordinal scale, therefore, it is possible to say whether any two values are equal or whether one is greater than the other. That is, the values can be ordered (hence the name) in relation to each other, although no further conclusions can be drawn about the relation of different values.

For example, if you take a group of ten people, line them up in order of height and give the shortest the number 1 and the tallest the number 10, the resulting numbers will provide measures of height on an ordinal scale. That is, the differences in the numerical values assigned to each person will reflect actual differences in height but the reflection will not be exact. So, although number 8 in the line will certainly be taller than number 4, it cannot further be inferred that he or she is twice as tall.

In psychology, ordinal scales are used whenever more precise measures are impossible, and especially where the aim is to provide a measure of purely subjective variables such as likes and dislikes. For example, if subjects are asked to assess, using a 10-point scale, the extent to which they perceive five prominent show-business figures to be supporters of the Conservative Party, the variable being measured is the perceptions of the subjects, and not the actual strength of the political support for the Conservatives in the minds of the celebrities. The outcome would be a collection of scores, ranging between 0 and 9, representing measures of subjects' perceptions on an ordinal scale. It would, therefore, be possible to infer that a score of 3 (say) indicates that an individual is perceived to be a less enthusiastic Conservative supporter than an individual who scores a 4, but NOT that the difference in perceived support between a 3 and a 4 is equal to the difference between scores of 7 and 8.

The interval scale

Like the ordinal scale, the interval scale also preserves the magnitude of relations, but additionally, it possesses equal intervals. That is, the intervals between values on the scale represent equal-sized differences in the variable being measured.

To take the Celsius scale of temperature as an example, suppose we have measured the temperature of two objects and have found that the temperature of one is 10°C while the other is 25°C. These two points on the Celsius scale, or any other two points for that matter, represent a difference (in this case measured as 15°C) in the 'hotness' of the objects. Clearly, one object is hotter than the other – they stand in an ordinal relationship. However, because the Celsius scale is an interval scale we can go further and say that the difference in temperature which this 15°C represents will be equal to the heat difference between any other two points on the scale which are also 15°C apart (such as 3°C and 18°C, or 9°C and 24°C, or whatever). This is what 'equal intervals' means, and it is a characteristic of all other interval scales in addition to the Celsius scale.

But it is still not possible to say that the temperature of an object which is measured at 15°C on the scale is 15 times hotter than something which measures at 1°C. In order to make that inference, you need to measure on a ratio scale, which is dealt with next.

In psychology, measurement on the interval scale represents the most powerful and precise form of measurement which can be attained with any certainty, although even this is probably not achieved as frequently as claimed. Some variables, such as reaction time, do represent measures on an interval scale, and may possibly even represent measures on the even more powerful ratio scale, though this is debatable – see below. Others, however, such as psychometric test scores, while they are often treated as interval scale data, probably are not, since the crucial characteristic of equality of intervals can only be assumed rather than demonstrated.

The ratio scale

The ratio scale is the most powerful of the four scales of measurement, since in addition to possessing all the attributes of the other three scales it also has one which they don't, i.e. a true zero point. This is important, because, as the name of the scale indicates, it means that any measure of a variable made on a ratio scale can be described in terms of its ratio to other measures. For example, a metre stick calibrated in centimetres is a ratio scale because it has a true zero: that is, there is a point on the scale which represents a total absence of the variable – length – which is being measured. Possession of the zero point means that it is possible to say that a piece of wood which is 30 cm long is twice as long (ratio 2:1) as one which is 15 cm long, or four times as long (4:1) as one which is 7.5 cm in length.

To illustrate the concept of the true zero more clearly, consider the difference between the Celsius and Absolute scales of temperature. The Celsius scale, as we have just seen, possesses equal intervals, but it does not have a true zero. That is, 0°C does not represent a complete absence of the variable (heat) which is being measured. To obtain temperature measures which do possess a true zero point you have to use the Absolute (Kelvin) scale on which 0°A (the freezing point of helium, Celsius equivalent –273°C) does indicate the total absence of all heat.

In psychology, the existence of the ratio scale emphasizes the difference which exists between directly and indirectly measured variables. All psychological variables (that is, those which are a result of some mental activity – such as holding an attitude, liking someone, remembering, or solving a problem) can only be accessed indirectly by measuring other, related variables which can be measured directly. Thus, the ability to recall information (the psychological variable) may be measured in terms of the number of items recalled from a list. The problem for psychologists arises because although the directly measured variable (the number of items recalled) represents a measurement on the ratio scale, it isn't possible simply to assume that the underlying psychological variable is also being measured on a ratio scale. To put it another way, the issue is one of interpretation: recall scores (or any similarly directly measured variable) may represent measures on a ratio scale in themselves, but they cannot simply be read as straightforward ratio scale measures of a psychological variable. They invariably need to be interpreted to some degree, and in practice this means treating them as scores on no more than an interval scale.

Two further examples may help clarify this. First, in the field of psychometric testing, an intelligence test score of zero is certainly possible, but cannot be interpreted to mean the complete absence of intelligence in the individual being tested. For one thing he or she may simply have failed to answer any of the questions in the test – arguably in itself an intelligent act. Or, if the test has been attempted, it may be that it is badly designed, and unable to discriminate effectively between people with below average intelligence. Either way, a zero score on the test cannot be treated as indicating a complete absence of the quality being measured, and so measurement on an interval scale is the best that can be assumed.

Similarly, interpreting reaction times (RT) obtained in response to a stimulus signal may be equally problematic for the psychologist. In general the measurement of elapsed time involves measuring on a ratio scale, since it is always possible to observe a time interval of zero duration. (All that is necessary is for two events to occur simultaneously, and for measurements to be made using a very accurate timepiece.) However, when psychologists measure RT, they are using it as a way of measuring the time taken for the mental processing of information and, although they are clearly measuring elapsed time on a ratio scale, it cannot be assumed that the mental processes involved can also be measured on the same scale. Consider the case of the reaction time of zero.

Box 6.1   Check your understanding of scales of measurement

On the left is a list of different situations in which numbers are used to represent the values of a variable; on the right is the name of one of the scales of measurement on which it *could* be considered that the variable is measured. Do you agree with the scale identified in each case? Can you say why?

A National Insurance number	nominal scale
The index number on a train ticket	interval scale
A reading on a thermostat dial	interval scale
A telephone number	nominal scale
The total on a supermarket till receipt	ratio scale
The *Financial Times* 100 Share Index	interval scale
An entry on a train timetable	interval scale
A reading of 60 mph on a speedometer	ratio scale
A car registration number	nominal scale
Third place in the Top 40 record chart	ordinal scale

Although very short reaction times may be reliably obtained and of considerable interest, a reaction time of zero can only mean that the experimental subject anticipated the stimulus, and (presumably by chance) made the required response just as the signal occurred. So, although a zero result may say something about a person's ability to anticipate an expected signal, it does not represent information about the speed of mental processing in response to a stimulus simply because no reaction to a stimulus took place. The scale on which the speed of mental processing is measured therefore cannot have a true zero and so measurements of that variable (but not RT itself) are at best made on the interval scale.

Data, statistics and parameters

Numerical information, on any scale of measurement, belongs to one of the following three general categories. It is important to have these quite clear in your mind, because they define differences between types of data which will be encountered again throughout the remainder of the book.

Raw data

Raw data consist of the measurements of a variable as collected directly from source during an investigation, and before any statistical processing takes place. For example, the scores achieved by a group of students on a psychometric test or measures of the perceived magnitude of a visual illusion will be raw data until they are subjected to further treatment. The results of such treatment are values which are either statistics or parameters.

Statistics

A statistic is a value computed from a sample. The items of raw data obtained from any group of subjects can be used to calculate the value of various descriptive variables such as the mean or standard deviation of the data, which we will be encountering shortly. When, as is often the case, the group of subjects represents a sample taken from some larger population, then any value computed from those data is a statistic. (You may find it helpful to turn to chapter 3 to clarify the sense in which the words 'population' and 'sample' are being used here.)

Parameters

Like a statistic, a parameter is also the value obtained for any of several descriptive variables, but with the difference that the value is computed from a whole population rather than from a sample. Two commonly encountered examples of parameters are the population mean and standard deviation. Usually parameters cannot be obtained directly from a set of raw data (unless the sample comprises the whole of a population), and thus they have to be estimated from statistics. The way in which this can be done – a process called, logically enough, 'parameter estimation' – is described in chapter 8.

Why use statistics?

One question which may have occurred to you at this point, especially if you are relatively new to the business of doing research, is: Why is it necessary to use statistics at all? Surely the result of an investigation can be determined simply from carrying out a careful inspection of the raw data?

The short answer to that last question is that no, it can't. Taking a long, hard look at a set of raw data (so called because at this stage they are in an unprocessed state) is certainly to be recommended as a preliminary before you do anything else, but it is unlikely to generate any very satisfactory answers to the research question you happen to be pursuing, for the following reasons.

Often in psychology, the results of an investigation will be a set of scores – quantitative (numerical) data which represent some aspect of the research participants' behaviour. Such sets of raw data may be quite large and the larger they are, the more unwieldy they are to work with and the harder it becomes to develop a view of the data as a whole. For obvious reasons, this problem rapidly becomes more and more acute as the size of a data set increases, so that even with quite moderate quantities of raw data, it is impossible to develop an accurate view, let alone to draw any useful conclusions. A typical situation in which this problem might occur is when a researcher needs to compare two or more sets of data in order to ask whether the differences between them are too great to have occurred by chance, or whether the values in two sets of data vary consistently with each other. As you can test for yourself, it is only necessary to have a handful of values in each of two groups of scores before the technique of 'just looking' starts to run into difficulties. What is needed is an approach which will enable us to 'see the wood for the trees'; to begin to extract the essential information from the raw data, and to permit us to begin to figure out what it is the numbers might *mean*: that is, to say something about their significance for the problem which is being pursued.

This, then, is the reason why the statistical procedures exist, and why they occupy such an important place among the psychology researcher's skills. They have been developed because researchers need to get answers from numerical data which simply cannot be reliably or efficiently obtained in any other way. The meaning of data is almost *never* revealed by a quick visual inspection. It is *always* necessary to dig beneath the surface appearance, using the procedures of statistics, in order to find out what implications may be there for the question being researched.

Approaching numerical data

This section focuses exclusively on the task of working with quantitative data. The rather different problems raised by the analysis of qualitative data are considered in chapters 2, 3 and 4.

Working with quantitative data requires a particularly methodical approach. Without it, the sheer mass of numbers which may have to be processed after a data gathering exercise can be difficult to organize and control, and the statistical calculations, although not difficult in themselves, can involve several stages, so that it is all too easy to lose track of what you are doing.

Not everyone necessarily feels confident about their ability to work successfully with numbers, and there are several possible reasons for this. You may be lacking in recent practice or have unhappy memories of maths lessons at school, or just be rather uncertain about how best to organize yourself to begin. The important thing at the beginning is not to allow yourself to be intimidated. Using statistics can feel awkward at first, but like all developing skills, will feel more natural and easier as you become more practised.

It is virtually certain, anyway, that you already have the basic mathematical skills needed to carry out all the statistical calculations in this book. As long as you understand the principles of simple mathematical notation (such as multiplying the values in parentheses), and can use a calculator to work out squares and square roots, then you almost certainly won't find statistics to be too much of a challenge.

This section on working with data begins by offering some suggestions on the organizational aspects of working with numbers. This is followed by some detailed guidance on how to carry out two basic procedures in statistics which you will need to use over and over again.

Organizing your work with quantitative data

The best approach to working with quantitative data when you come to it for the first time is consciously to try to develop a set of routines – set ways of dealing with the numbers which you can use in order to ensure that you stay in control of the process. The following are suggestions for ways of working which can be applied to every statistical procedure you encounter from here onwards:

1 Always transfer raw data (that is, the data before you apply any statistics) onto a new sheet for the statistical calculation. Never try to work out a statistic in one corner, or on the back of the sheet on which you collected the data.

2 List the raw data in column format, and label every column clearly.

3 Begin each computation on a new page every time and put the brief title of the investigation at the top of the sheet. This enables you to set out each computation relatively spaciously, and readily identify the project to which a computation belongs. The latter is essential if you have more than one project in progress – it is astounding how easy it is to mix up the working notes for different projects.

4 Place the data in order. Unless there are good reasons otherwise (such as the need to preserve the relationship between two sets of data), you should *always* begin by doing this. Arranging data in ascending order from left to right across the page, or from top down in a column, always seems the most natural approach to me, though there is no reason why you shouldn't also use a different way of ordering data if you want to. In case you are uncertain how to proceed when data contain mixed positive and negative values, some guidance is given below.

5 Create additional clearly labelled columns for those stages of the calculation which have to be applied to all the items of data (such as squaring). The instructions for calculating the statistics in this chapter, and in chapter 9, tell you when it is appropriate to do this.

6 Make a clearly labelled space for such vital information as the number of items of data you are working with (that is, the size of the sample) and their mean and standard deviation. It is a good idea to transfer this information to the raw data sheet as well.

7 Always write out each stage of each calculation in full. This will make it much easier for you to pursue any errors you may happen to make.

8 Train yourself to use correct statistical symbols, especially the ones for the statistics you use most frequently, such as the mean and standard deviation. A full list of the statistical symbols used in this book can be found in appendix 4 at the end of the book.

9 If your raw data consist of whole numbers and you are using a calculator, you can ignore all decimal places beyond the second when you read off an answer. Psychology is not (yet) an exact science, so although giving a statistic to six places of decimals looks impressive, only the values in the first two places are at all likely to matter. You can safely round up (all

values above and including 0.005), or down (those below 0.005), in order to get rid of the excess numbers. If the raw data are not whole numbers, then, of course you may have to use more decimal places.

Obviously, following these suggestions won't guarantee that you never make an error in working with your data. However, if you do try to put them into practice, you should find you make fewer 'mechanical' mistakes.

A note on electronic calculators

Though not essential, a calculator will help you enormously in the task of working with data. All you need in order to work with the statistics in this book (and most of the other statistics you are likely to need in the immediate future) are the four functions: addition, subtraction, multiplication, division, and a square root facility. However, there are now many calculators on the market which offer considerably more than the basics, and many students will already own one which possesses automatic routines for calculating the mean, standard deviation and correlation.

My feeling is that your understanding of the logic behind a statistical procedure (i.e. the reason why it is *able* to provide information about the data) is actually helped if you begin by working your way through the calculation by hand, tedious though this may often be. Then, once you are clear about what the procedure is doing with the data, you can switch to using the automatic routines in your calculator.

Many students will also have access to a computer running statistical software, and this can be particularly useful if you have a large data set to analyse. The best examples of such software, such as MINITAB® (1991) permit data analysis to be carried out either 'by hand' – for example, as they are laid out step by step in this book – or automatically. Again, it is best to use 'manual' methods, in the early stages, and only move on to using the automatic routines when you are reasonably clear about what it is that they are doing.

Two key procedures: ordering and ranking data

There are two key procedures which you will find you need to use again and again in the course of dealing with quantitative data. These are: the placing of the data into ascending or descending order, and the assigning of a rank to each item. They are important because they represent the very first stage of the process by which an unorganized mass of data can be made to yield a coherent picture.

Ordering data

Ordering data involves placing a set of numbers into either ascending (from lowest to highest) or descending order (from highest to lowest).

To place data in ascending order, and if the data all have a positive sign, you simply write down the lowest value in the data (the one closest to zero), then the next lowest, and so on, until you have worked through all the scores.

If the data have mixed positive and negative signs, or are all negative, you begin with the lowest negative value (the negative value furthest from zero), and work through them in order until you arrive at the one closest to zero. If you then still have some positively signed scores to be ordered, you continue to work up through the positive values until you arrive at the highest one.

To place data in descending order, you simply reverse the instructions above. Begin with the positive value *furthest* from zero if the data are all positive (or mixed positive and negative), or with the negative value *closest* to zero if the data are all negatively signed. When you've finished, you should run a quick check to make sure that you haven't missed a score, or unintentionally written the same number down twice.

Ordering data is a deceptively simple procedure which gives you access to a number of powerful descriptions of the data. Once you have placed your data in order you can easily go on to develop a more detailed description. You can, for example:

1   Determine the range of the data.
2   Identify the median and modal value(s).
3   Make a reasonable guess about the value of the mean.
4   Obtain an idea of the shape of the distribution. For example, you can see whether there is any clustering of values anywhere in the data. This is useful to gain a preliminary idea of the shape of the distribution without the necessity of actually drawing a graph.

Ranking data

Ranking data is a complementary process to placing the data in order. It involves taking an ordered set of data and assigning a numerical value or rank to each item which identifies its place in the order.

Ranking data is very straightforward in principle. Once a set of scores have been ordered (see above), the first value in the order (whether it is the lowest or the highest value) is given the rank of (1), the next lowest (or highest) is given the rank (2) and so on. (Note: To avoid confusion, it is good practice to place all rankings in parentheses (brackets), so as to differentiate them clearly from the data.)

Dealing with ties

When you come to rank data you are quite likely to discover that some of the values occur more than once, and that you have therefore to deal with 'tied' rankings.

For example, suppose you wish to rank the following data, in which two values each occur more than once:

0   14   **18**   **18**   **18**   23   29   **30**   **30**   35

The values of 18 and 30 are tied. To deal with situation like this, you do the following:

Step 1   Assign each value in the ordered set of data a raw rank which takes no account of the presence of tied values. That is, you simply give every value a different rank from lowest to highest. Thus:

Data   0   14   18   18   18   23   29   30   30   35
Raw rank   (1)   (2)   (3)   (4)   (5)   (6)   (7)   (8)   (9)   (10)

Step 2   Now focus on the two groups of scores with the same value: in each case, to find the rank adjusted for the presence of tied scores you simply find the mean rank for the group, i.e. add together the ranks of the tied scores and divide by the number of tied values in that group.

Thus, taking first the three tied scores with a value of 18, finding the mean rank gives $3 + 4 + 5 = 12$. Divide by the number of tied values in the group, 3, and you get $12 \div 3 = 4$. So the adjusted rank for each of the members of that group will be 4.

The same process is also applied to the tied pair of value 30. In this case, finding the mean rank gives the result of 8.5. The complete set of ranked data, with the rankings adjusted for ties, therefore becomes:

Data   0   14   18   18   18   23   29   30   30   35
Raw rank   (1)   (2)   (3)   (4)   (5)   (6)   (7)   (8)   (9)   (10)
Adjusted rank   1   2   4   4   4   6   7   8.5   8.5   10

If these ideas are new to you, you may find it helpful to go over them again sometime soon, as you will almost certainly be needing to use them once you begin to collect data for analysis. For now, though, having reviewed these basic procedures, and established some guidelines for working with numbers, we can begin to put this information to work by turning to the useful area of statistical knowledge called 'descriptive statistics', and in particular to the key notion of 'distribution', which has already been mentioned several times.

Distributions of data

A distribution is the name given to any collection of data once the values have been organized in a way which enables the 'shape' of the data to be seen. One way of doing this is simply to range the scores from lowest to highest to produce a 'raw score' distribution. For example, consider the following collection of scores:

17   25   28   29   33   35   38   45   46   48

Simply putting these scores in order gives an immediate impression of the data. We can see that the range of the distribution (the difference between lowest and highest) is 31 units, that no value occurs twice, and also that the

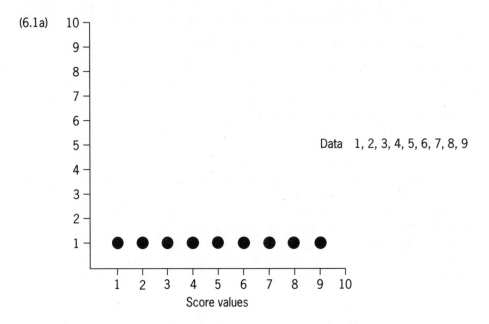

(6.1a)

Data   1, 2, 3, 4, 5, 6, 7, 8, 9

Score values

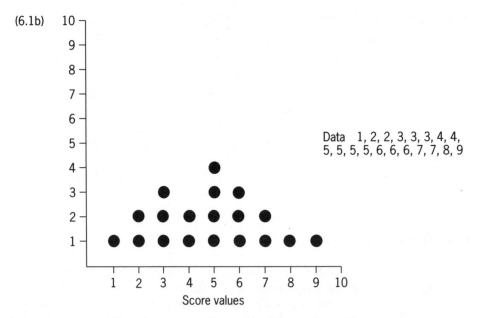

(6.1b)

Data   1, 2, 2, 3, 3, 3, 4, 4,
5, 5, 5, 5, 6, 6, 6, 7, 7, 8, 9

Score values

Figures 6.1a, 6.1b & 6.1c   A simple method of graphing frequency distributions

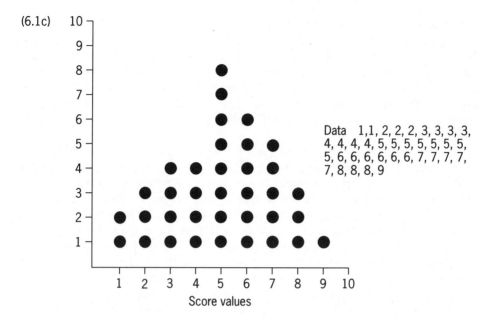

(6.1c)

Data 1,1, 2, 2, 2, 3, 3, 3, 3,
4, 4, 4, 4, 5, 5, 5, 5, 5, 5, 5, 5,
5, 6, 6, 6, 6, 6, 6, 7, 7, 7, 7,
7, 8, 8, 8, 9

Score values

score values appear reasonably evenly distributed between the lowest and highest. However, this approach really only works when the number of scores is relatively small. For larger groups of data we need a better approach to describing a distribution, and this exists in the form of the frequency distribution.

The frequency distribution for any set of data is obtained very straightforwardly by counting the number of times each of the possible values occurs in the set of scores. The result might simply be recorded on a tally chart, but more usually, it is represented on a graph in which the horizontal (x) axis carries the range of score values of the data, while the vertical (y) axis of the graph represents the number of times each value occurs. The advantage of the frequency distribution is that it gives a simple way of examining a whole collection of data, even when this involves dealing with a large number of scores.

The simplest kind of frequency graph identifies each item of data individually. Figure 6.1a shows the frequency graph for a set of scores (which could, say, represent the performance of a sample of schoolchildren on an attainment test of some kind), to help illustrate how a graph can assist with the analysis of data by representing the shape of the distribution. Because we are dealing with only a small sample, there is almost no gain in information obtained by drawing the graph. We have simply confirmed what we already knew from looking at the scores themselves, namely that no score has a frequency greater than one. However, if the size of the sample is doubled (and as long as the range of the data remains the same), it becomes harder to see the shape of the distribution from the scores alone, but easier to see it from the graph. The graph of the distribution now looks as in figure 6.1b.

Notice that we can see at a glance which score values have the highest and lowest frequencies, and can also identify where they are located in the range of scores. To emphasize the point that drawing a frequency distribution yields significant benefits when large numbers of scores are involved, we double the number of schoolchildren yet again for figure 6.1c. As you can see, it is now rather difficult to pick out score values with the highest and lowest frequencies from the raw data at a glance, although they are easily spotted on the frequency graph.

Providing the sample is not large, a dot diagram can easily be combined with a box and whisker plot, as in figure 6.13. However, if the number of scores to be dealt with is large the most convenient way to represent frequencies is by means of a histogram. This is a type of bar graph in which the height of each bar indicates the frequency of one or a group of score values. More information on these graphs can be found towards the end of this chapter.

There is one further piece of information you need on this topic before you can draw frequency distributions for yourself. It is that if the range of the data is larger than about twelve units it will be difficult to fit scores individually onto the x axis as in figures 6.1a, 6.1b and 6.1c. For wider ranges of data it is necessary to proceed by dividing the range into a set of 'class intervals', counting the number of data items which fall into the various classes, and then drawing a graph of the result. For example, consider the following set of 66 test scores:

```
27  35  35  38  43  19  31   8  30  38  38
41  18  22  34  10  32  24  42  45  21  25
37  13  36  26  21  21  23  28  40  16  27
29  24  23  25  31  43  19  30  32  26  26
34  48  22  33  35  29  28  31  37  15  25
28  33  33  30  38  32  32  34  40  17  28
```

The first point is that clearly, there is a lot here to take in; in fact, without looking carefully, nothing much can be discerned, beyond the fact that a good proportion of the scores occur more than once. However, as we have seen, it is possible to expose the shape of the data if we draw a graph to represent the distribution. In this case, the range of the data is quite wide. The lowest score value in the sample is 8, and the highest is 48, which gives a range of 40 score units – too many to accommodate individually on the x axis. So, we have to organize the data into groups called **class intervals**, before going on to draw the frequency distribution of those classes.

To group data into class intervals:

Step 1   Find the difference between the highest and lowest scores (the range). In this case, as we have seen, the range is 48 − 8 = 40.

Step 2   Decide the number of class intervals. There should be not less than 10 and not more than 20 of these, and their preferred size is 1, 2, 3, 5, 10 (or multiples of 10) score units. A simple rule for deciding the number of class intervals is to divide the range by the preferred size of classes, and add 1. If

Table 6.1 Exact limits of classes and frequencies for 66 test scores

Score limits	Exact limits of classes	Tally	Frequencies
46–48	45.50–48.49	/	1
43–45	42.50–45.49	///	3
40–42	39.50–42.49	////	4
37–39	36.50–39.49	///// /	6
34–36	33.50–36.49	///// //	7
31–33	30.50–33.49	///// /////	10
28–30	27.50–30.49	///// ////	9
25–27	24.50–27.49	///// ///	8
22–24	21.50–24.49	///// /	6
19–21	18.50–21.49	/////	5
16–18	15.50–18.49	///	3
13–15	12.50–15.49	//	2
10–12	9.50–12.49	/	1
7–9	6.50–9.49	/	1

this results in too many or too few classes, simply adjust the size of the interval.

In the case of these data, the range of 40 divided by a preferred interval size of 3 gives 14 intervals ($40 \div 3$ is approximately equal to 13 and then $13 + 1 = 14$). This means we have to divide up the range into 14 equal-sized groups, each of which contains three units of score. So the first interval will contain scores of 7, 8 and 9 (with 7 to 9 called the score limits of the interval), the next interval holds scores of 10, 11 and 12, and so on up to the 14th interval, which has score limits of 46 to 48.

It is important to note that all that this does is to say in 'whole-number' terms which score values belong in which intervals. It is true that when the data themselves consist of integer values, as in this case, this approach is enough to permit the scores to be sorted accurately into groups. However, if the data do not consist of integers, it is necessary to say exactly where the boundaries or 'exact limits' of each interval lie, since otherwise, it may be impossible to deal with the scores accurately. This is easily done. The convention is to regard the lower boundary of each interval as lying 0.5 units below the lowest integer value, and the upper limit as 0.49 units above the highest integer value. By applying this principle to the example, the exact limits of the lowest interval are found to be 6.5 and 9.49, those of the next 9.5 to 12.49, and so on up to the last interval where the exact limits are 46.5 and 49.49. You can see how this arrangement works out in table 6.1.

The next step is to draw up a table which identifies each interval, and provides a space for tallying the scores and computing the frequencies for each of the class intervals. Note that the table follows the convention of placing the lowest score values at the bottom of the table and the highest at the top. Place

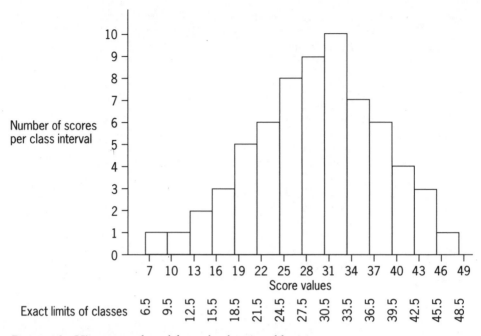

Figure 6.2   Histogram plotted from the data in table 6.1

a check mark in the table for each item of data, and when all items have been tallied, count the frequencies.

Now we draw the graph of the frequencies. Although we could equally have chosen to draw a line graph by connecting the frequency values at the mid-point of each interval, in this case we shall represent the distribution by means of the more usual histogram. The result can be seen in figure 6.2. In this graph both the score limits and the exact limits of the classes are shown on the horizontal axis. (Note: the exact limits are given purely to help explain the construction of the graph and must always be omitted from any histograms you draw for your own data.)

What more does this representation of the data tell us than could have been obtained from studying the raw data? The whole point is that although no new information has been added to the original data, by drawing a histogram of the frequency distribution we have made the information in the data much more accessible. It is now easy to compare the distributions of different collections of data – something which would have been impossible while the data remained in raw form. We can also now see the overall shape of the data much more clearly. For example, we can now see which are the most and least frequently occurring values as well as how these values are located in the overall range of the data.

Finally, before moving on, we should note that the process of drawing the graph for these data has revealed a frequency distribution with a distinctive near-symmetrical appearance. Its shape is significant because it approaches the form of another, particularly interesting, frequency distribution called the normal distribution, which provides the foundation for most of the statistical techniques discussed in the remainder of this book. You will find much more information about the normal distribution and its uses in chapters 7 and 8.

Cumulative frequency

The simple frequency distribution described above can easily be extended to give even more useful answers. As well as wanting to know how frequently a particular value or set of values appears, one might also like to know where a particular value stands in relation to the sample as a whole. Specifically, one might ask what proportion of the data values lie above or below a particular score value. Finding the answer requires the construction of a **cumulative frequency distribution**.

To see how this can be done first look back at table 6.1. To construct that table, the number of scores in each interval was tallied, and then the frequency value for each of the 14 intervals was computed. These values, when drawn as a graph, provided a histogram (figure 6.2), which described the distribution. The notion of cumulative frequency takes us one step beyond this list of simple frequencies, by adding together (cumulating) the simple frequencies into a running total. This running total is the cumulative frequency.

Now, clearly, it is possible to begin to cumulate the frequencies from either end of a distribution – from the highest or the lowest value – and unless the distribution is perfectly symmetrical, the result will be different in either case. The direction of the cumulation also affects the kind of question that can easily be asked of the results of the process, and we shall need to return to this point in a short while. For the moment, to demonstrate the computation of cumulative frequencies we return to the data in table 6.1 and compute the cumulative frequencies from lowest to highest score values, displaying the result in table 6.2.

Table 6.2 displays most of the information earlier seen in table 6.1, except that the column carrying the tally marks has been omitted, and a new column for the cumulative frequencies has been added on the right. Note that the last cumulative frequency must always equal the total number of scores: in this case n = 66.

Having computed the cumulative frequencies in this way, we can use them to answer questions about what number of scores lie below a given point on the scale. For example, how many scores in the sample are equal to or less than a score of 27, the approximate mid-point of the range? (Note that the reference point in this case is the upper limit of the class interval.) The answer, which is easily read off from the table, is that 26 out of the 66 scores lie below that point: this can very easily be converted into percentage form in the following way:

$$(26 \div 66) \times 100 = 39.39\%$$

thus we can say that virtually 40% of all the scores are equal to or less than the score of 27.

Table 6.2   Exact limits of classes, simple frequencies and ascending cumulative frequencies of 66 test scores

Score limits	Exact limits of classes	Frequencies	Cumulative frequencies
46–48	45.50–48.49	1	66
43–45	42.50–45.49	3	65
40–42	39.50–42.49	4	62
37–39	36.50–39.49	6	58
34–36	33.50–36.49	7	52
31–33	30.50–33.49	10	45
28–30	27.50–30.49	9	35
25–27	24.50–27.49	8	26
22–24	21.50–24.49	6	18
19–21	18.50–21.49	5	12
16–18	15.50–18.49	3	7
13–15	12.50–15.49	2	4
10–12	9.50–12.49	1	2
7–9	6.50–9.49	1	1

Suppose, though, that instead of asking a 'less than' question (i.e. 'how many scores lie below point x on the scale?'), we need to ask the 'more than' version about how many scores lie *above* a given point on the scale. Clearly, we can't get an answer from table 6.2, since there the cumulative frequencies were computed to run from lowest to highest scores. Instead, it is necessary to re-compute the cumulative frequencies from the opposite end of the range, starting at the top scores and running down to the lowest; and – one other difference – we also have to use the *lower limit* of any class interval as the reference point. Apart from these two differences, though, the logic of the process is identical. Table 6.3 presents a recalculation of the cumulative frequencies from the opposite direction. Using this presentation of the data, we can now answer questions such as 'How many scores are greater than or equal to a score value of 19?' – the answer is 59 scores, or $(59 \div 66) \times 100 = 89.39\%$ of the total number of scores.

Centiles

In the discussion in the previous section the point was made that cumulative frequencies, whether computed 'top-down' or 'bottom-up', can be expressed in two ways – either as a simple cumulations or as a percentage of the total number of scores. When (and only when) the cumulation is ascending (that is, proceeds upwards from lowest score to highest as in table 6.2), the percentage of the total number of scores falling below a given point is known as a **centile** (also called a percentile). A centile is simply any point on the scale of score values below which falls any given percentage of scores. Thus, the 10th centile (also known as the first decile) is the score value below which fall 10 per cent

Table 6.3   Exact limits of classes, simple frequencies and descending cumulative frequencies of 66 test scores

Score limits	Exact limits of classes	Frequencies	Cumulative frequencies
46–48	45.50–48.49	1	1
43–45	42.50–45.49	3	4
40–42	39.50–42.49	4	8
37–39	36.50–39.49	6	14
34–36	33.50–36.49	7	21
31–33	30.50–33.49	10	31
28–30	27.50–30.49	9	40
25–27	24.50–27.49	8	48
22–24	21.50–24.49	6	54
19–21	18.50–21.49	5	59
16–18	15.50–18.49	3	62
13–15	12.50–15.49	2	64
10–12	9.50–12.49	1	65
7–9	6.50–9.49	1	66

of all the scores. In the distribution in table 6.2, the score of 30 is the point on the distribution below which lie 35 of the 66 scores. In centile terms, therefore, it is located just a whisker above the 53rd percentile ($35/66 \times 100 = 53.03$).

Note also that although one can discuss data in terms of any centile one chooses, such as, say, the 37th centile (the point below which 37 per cent of scores occur), or the 91st centile, particular points on a distribution such as the deciles are likely to be most useful in practice.

Three centiles are particularly identified by their own names. Of these, the most important is the 50th centile – the point below which exactly 50 per cent of all scores occur. This value is also known as the **median**, and, since it is widely used as a description of the central tendency of a sample of data, more will be said about it later in the chapter. The other named centiles are the 25th and the 75th. These are known as the **quartiles** in acknowledgement of the fact that, along with the median, they permit the sample to be neatly divided up into quarters.

Centiles are very useful for giving a quick fix on where a single value stands in relation to a larger mass of data. It is immediately informative to know that, for example, a particular score is located in the top or bottom quartile or decile of a sample.

Descriptive Statistics

In this section of the chapter we review in turn each of the three key types of descriptive statistic: the measures of central tendency, the measures of dispersion and the measures of correlation.

Introduction

Descriptive statistics are the traditional starting point for work with quantitative data not only because they are relatively straightforward to compute, but also because many of them form the basis of much of the subsequent analysis which you will need to do. Although some of them may seem to be so simple as to offer virtually negligible information about a set of data, it is important that they should not be underestimated. Despite their simplicity, they offer a set of powerful conceptual tools which you will be able to use in order to extend your understanding of data in a number of important ways.

The function of these particular statistics is to provide a **summary** of a set of data. They enable you to reduce any set of data, no matter how large and unwieldy, down to a single, precise, easily comprehended statistic, which represents a particular property, or relationship of the entire set.

The descriptive statistics fall into three groups:

The measures of central tendency are the descriptive statistics which provide a summary of a set of data in terms of its most representative or most typical value. **The measures of dispersion** summarize data in terms of the distribution of individual data items around a reference point – usually the mean of the data. **The measures of correlation** provide a summary of the relationship between the values in two different sets of data.

If these statistics should be completely new to you, it will be really worth your while to spend the time needed to become completely familiar with them. I suggest that you give yourself some practice by trying out each one several times as you come to it. You can either use some data you have made up for the occasion, or you can look around for a set of 'real-world' data which you can use. The important thing is to practise! These statistics don't take a great deal of effort to understand, and even a moderate amount of practice on artificial data will quickly enable you to get the feel for what they can tell you.

The measures of central tendency

Faced with the task of understanding a mass of data, most of us would probably start by asking the question 'What is the typical, or most representative score here?' In other words, our first response to the complexity of the data would be to wonder whether any single value could be found which could be used to summarize *all* the values in the data set.

This is exactly what the three statistics known as the **measures of central tendency** do. Called the **mean**, the **median** and the **mode**, they each provide a single, representative value which can stand for a whole mass of data. Each of them takes a slightly different approach to the process of identifying such a single, typical value, and they therefore each provide the user with slightly different information about the data.

Because they provide the basic information needed by so many other statistical treatments of data, you should always begin by using one or more of these measures as a matter of routine no matter what kind of analysis you intend subsequently to carry out.

The mean

The mean is the *arithmetic average* of a set of data. It is represented in statistical notation by the symbol $\overline{X}$ (pronounced ex-bar), and it is calculated by summing, or adding (represented in the formula by the symbol Σ) all the scores in the set of data, and then dividing by the *number* of scores. The formula for the mean is therefore $\Sigma X/n$ which reads as 'the sum (Σ) of the set of scores (identified by the X), divided by the number (n) of scores'.

To see how the mean is able to represent all the values in a set of data consider these below. This consists of a set of scores, which could represent, say, reaction times, measured in thousandths of a second (1/1000 sec), and placed in ascending order:

Data   105   110   128   130   154   164   171   173   176   179
n = 10

The sum of the data $\Sigma X = 1490$
The mean of the data $\overline{X} = 1490 \div 10$
                                     $= 149$

If you mark the approximate place in the order where it would lie, you can probably see that the value 149 seems a reasonable summary value for the whole set of data. It is about halfway between the highest and lowest values, and it does provide a good general impression of the whole set.

Note, though, that the mean does not lie *exactly* at the halfway point. This is because it reflects the magnitude of every one of the individual data items. Each piece of data contributes something to the mean. While this is clearly a good thing from one point of view (because all the items of data are represented), it is less good from another. The nature of the mean as a measure of central tendency is, as we shall see later, that it is sensitive to the presence of any particularly large or small values in data.

For example, in the following set of data, the mean is inflated by the presence of a single, exceptionally large, value:

Data   25   37   39   48   56   76   77   83   88   **487**
n = 10

The sum of the data $\Sigma X = 1016$
The mean of the data $\overline{X} = 1016 \div 10$
                                     $= 101.6$

You can see the effect immediately. The value of the mean obtained from these data is larger than nine out of the ten scores in the set, which means that the mean cannot really claim to be representative of the whole set of the data. What has happened, of course, is that the single large value has exerted a sort of gravitational pull on the mean and has attracted the mean towards itself. The effect is somewhat reduced by the presence of the other nine smaller values, but they are too few and too small to hold the mean within the limit of their range.

To check the effect for yourself, recalculate the mean after replacing that single large value in tenth place with a score which is of the same order of magnitude as the other nine, say 92. You will see that the mean returns to a value which is roughly central to the set.

The sensitivity of the mean is clearly not going to be a problem when all the data values are reasonably similar, but if any extreme values should occur, then it follows that the mean may not be the best statistic to use.

The median

The median is the *positional average* of a set of scores which represents their central tendency in a very literal way. If a set of data have been placed into ascending or descending order then the median is that value which occupies the precise mid-point of the order irrespective of the actual magnitude of any individual values. Exactly half the scores in any set of data will lie above the median and exactly half will lie below it.

Thus, in the following set of data (reaction times again, in milliseconds), the median value is the central one, namely 154:

Data   105   110   128   130   154   164   171   173   176
                                    ↑
                                  median

As you can see, the median value can be found very easily if you have an *odd* number of items of data. It is simply the central value in the set once you have placed the scores in order. (Watch out, though, if you have a large quantity of data: you may have to count carefully to find the central value!)

If, on the other hand, you have an *even* number of items of data, you will have to determine the value of the median by a slightly more roundabout method. In this case, once you have placed the data in ascending (or descending) order, the median value will lie *exactly* at the halfway point between the two middle values. To find it, you simply add the two middle values together and divide the result by 2, as in the following collection of 12 scores:

34   38   46   67   68   **74**   88   89   90   93   96   100

Here the two central values are 74 and 88. Summing them and dividing by 2 gives the median of the data:

$$(74 + 88) \div 2 = 81$$

Again, you can check visually to see that the value obtained really is a reasonable representative value for these data. In this case, it lies at the centre of an ordered set of data, of which the items are all of the same general magnitude, and can therefore be regarded as representative of the whole set.

The mode

The mode is the third of the measures of central tendency, which, because it is a less informative statistic, is used somewhat less often than the other two. However, it does have its uses, and, in fact, for one kind of data, it represents the only option (see the next section, on choosing a measure of central tendency).

The modal value is the easiest of the three measures of central tendency to find. It is simply that value which occurs most frequently in the set of data. Clearly, then, some sets of data will have no mode, because no one value in the data occurs more times than any other, but equally, some may have one or more modal values. Such data are called **bimodal** (if there are two modes), or **multi-modal** (if there are three or more). For example, in the data below:

    8   9   10   11   **13**   **13**   **13**   16   18   20

the modal value is 13, but:

    8   9   10   11   13   15   16   18   19   20

has no modal value, while:

    9   **9**   **9**   10   11   **13**   **13**   **13**   16   18   20

is bimodal, since it has two modes, 9 and 13.

Choosing a measure of central tendency

Although the mean will be the measure of central tendency which you find yourself using the most to summarize data, the decision to use the mean should *never* be automatic. It should always be the result of a conscious decision, and should take into account the following two issues.

First, as we noted earlier, the mean is highly sensitive to the presence of extreme values in the data. ('Extreme' in this context is a very imprecise concept which can refer to any value which is a lot bigger or smaller than most of the other items of data in a group.) If you have one (or more) of these in your data, you have to ask yourself whether it may be due to transcription error in copying data (check and correct, if this is so), or whether it is an 'outlier'. This is a value which for some reason is very different in magnitude from the remainder of the data. It may be that it reflects a one-off effect in the data, such as might occur when a student who is ill produces an unusually low score on a psychometric test compared to the other 'well' members of the sample. If it is suspected, or can be established that this kind of effect has occurred, then clearly the outlier should be discarded from the sample before any further statistical work is begun. If, on the other hand, no reason for discarding the extreme value can be found, it can be retained, but the mean will be unable provide a true representation of the central tendency of the data, and you should use the median instead. This will remove the effect of the magnitude of the extreme value while retaining it as a score.

If, even after a careful inspection of the data, you still aren't sure which measure would be the more appropriate, the best thing to do is to calculate *both* the mean and the median and use them both to express the central tendency of your data.

The second issue which you need to take into account when you are choosing a measure of central tendency concerns the scale of measurement of the data. As we saw earlier in this chapter, important differences exist between data which represent values of a variable which can be measured directly and with considerable accuracy (such as the passage of time, or temperature), and data which, say, consist of only indirect measures of a variable, such as are obtained from attitude scales, or intelligence tests. These, in turn, are different again from other data in which the numbers simply identify some gross difference, such as the difference between the sexes. These differences are such that you should always take the nature of the data into account when you are checking that you have chosen the right central tendency measure. In particular, you need to be aware that the median is usually more appropriate for summarizing the central tendency of **ordinal** data, and the mode is the *only* option available if the data represent measures of a variable on the **nominal** scale.

Measures of dispersion

The second group of summarizing statistics are collectively called the measures of dispersion. The dispersion of a set of data is a measure of its variability, or the extent to which individual scores differ from one another. Where a set of scores differ greatly from one another, then the variability will similarly be great. By the same token, a set of scores which all have the same value will have zero variability.

You may be wondering what knowing the variability of a set of scores can add to the understanding which can be obtained from having the measures of central tendency? The problem is that by themselves the measures of central tendency cannot give a full picture of the data. As you will shortly see, two sets of data can have identical means or medians, and yet be very different from each other in terms of their variability.

The measures of dispersion, then, are the statistics, which, in a sense, will help us grasp the 'shape' of any group of data we have to deal with. They tell us, in a very concise form, how similar, or different, the individual members of a set of scores are.

The variability, or dispersion, of a set of scores can be measured in three ways. These are:

- **The range**
- **The variance**
- **The standard deviation.**

However, the variance and the standard deviation are closely related statistics. Although they do differ from each other in one crucial respect, when you know one you can very easily get to the other.

The standard deviation is the most important of the measures of dispersion, since it is the one which you will need to use again and again in your analysis of numerical data, both by itself and also en route to the determination of several other statistics. However, we begin with the simplest of all the dispersion measures: the range.

The range

The range is the simplest, but the least informative of all the measures of dispersion. It is calculated by finding the difference between the lowest and highest values in a set of data.

It tells us the size of the gap between the top and bottom limits of the data, but says nothing about how the data values are arranged between those limits. As you have probably already realized, the difficulty with using the range as an indicator of dispersion is that, like the mean, it is affected by the presence of any extreme values in the data.

Although the range is a simple statistic, which tells us relatively little, the information nevertheless can make a valuable contribution to the task of building up a picture of the data. It does have its uses, though it always needs to be used in combination with more informative procedures.

The variance/standard deviation

The variance and standard deviation of a set of scores are, as we have already observed, closely related measures of the dispersion of a set of values around their mean.

Variance is the mean of the squared differences between each of the values and their mean.
Standard deviation is the square root of the variance (i.e. the square root of the mean of the squared differences).

(Note: The symbol for the standard deviation is either s or σ depending on the context. See pp. 290–1 for an explanation of why this is so. The variance has no generally recognized symbol, but may be denoted by the abbreviation 'var' or by s^2 or σ^2 as appropriate.)

Both measures, therefore, take the mean of a set of scores as their reference point, and determine the average of the differences between it and each of the scores. The close relationship between them, as we have noted above, lies in the fact that in the calculation of the variance the differences remain squared, whereas in the standard deviation the effect of that squaring is removed by taking the square root of the mean of the squared differences as the last step in the calculation. It is therefore accurate to say that the procedure for calculating the standard deviation *includes* within itself the procedure which is needed to find the variance.

You may be wondering why it is necessary to have two such closely related measures of dispersion at all. The reason is that the variance can be confusing when it is used on certain sorts of data. If you look at the computation procedure below, you will see that at step 6 the variance is calculated from the *squared* differences between the mean and each individual score. Because an answer in squared units is not always the most convenient form in which to have to think about the dispersion of a set of scores, the standard deviation is there to provide an alternative. It gives a measure of dispersion which, because it is expressed in the original units, can easily be interpreted. The variance *is* often used, however, when a measure of dispersion is required as part of a more complex statistical computation.

One final point. The variance/standard deviation measures are appropriate only if you have data measured on at least an interval scale. Neither of them should be used with nominal or ordinal data.

The importance of dispersion

As a demonstration of how important it is to take the dispersion into account when summarizing a set of data, consider the following.

Suppose two groups of athletes each run separate 100m events and record the following times (in seconds), listed in ascending order:

Group 1   18.3   22.0   22.5   22.9   23.1   23.5   24.2   24.2   24.5   24.8
Group 2   13.1   13.8   14.8   15.1   16.3   22.0   32.1   32.3   34.9   35.6

Now, it is possible to spot certain important differences between the two groups simply by inspecting the data. For example, the group 1 times are more homogeneous than group 2, since all but one lie in the lower half of the twenties, whereas group 2 contain data in the teens, twenties and thirties. Similarly, you can see that group 2 contains a number of athletes who are faster than the fastest and slower than the slowest in group 1. Descriptive statistics not only allow these differences to be pinned down more precisely; they also make it possible for features of the data to be identified which are hidden from the eye.

Group 1 $\overline{X} = 23.0$ range = 6.5   s = 1.78
Group 2 $\overline{X} = 23.0$ range = 22.5   s = 9.1

Both sets of scores have turned out to have identical means, but very different dispersions. As you can see, in group 1, the range of the data is less than a third and the standard deviation is only about a fifth, of the same statistics calculated for group 2. We can, therefore, not only see that the group 1 scores are less dispersed in relation to their mean than those in group 2 (something we could have determined fairly easily by inspection), but we can also place a precise value on the degree of dispersion, and thus make a precise comparison between one measure of dispersion and another.

The point is this. When you are evaluating data, for any purpose, you have to take into account all the information which is available to you. This means using the measures of central tendency *and* dispersion in combination in order to obtain a full picture.

(Note: The box and whisker graphing technique provides an extremely clear representation of the relationships between central tendency measures, and the dispersion of any set of scores, and can make it easy to see exactly what they are saying. It is particularly effective when, as in this case, two or more sets of data have to be compared. Instructions on how to set about drawing these useful graphs can be found later in this chapter.)

A computation procedure for the variance/standard deviation

The basic formula for the standard deviation of a set of scores is

$$\sigma = \sqrt{\frac{\Sigma d^2}{n}}$$ **Formula 6.1**

where:

σ is the symbol for the standard deviation
d is the difference between each score and the mean
n is the number of scores
Σ directs you to sum all the (squared) differences.

To compute a standard deviation using this formula you proceed as follows:

Step 1   Find the value of n, the number of items of data in the sample.
Step 2   Write the following headings across the page, and list the scores (symbol X in the computation) under column 1:

Column 1	Column 2	Column 3
Data (X)	Differences (d)	Squared differences (d^2)

Step 3   Sum the data in column 1 and divide by n, the number of items of data, to obtain the mean.
Step 4   Subtract the mean from each item of data, and enter each result (including the sign) in column 2.
Step 5   Square each difference in column 2 and enter the result in column 3.
Step 6   Sum the values in column 3 and divide by n. This value is the mean of the squared differences or variance of the data.
Step 7   Find the square root of the variance (in order to reverse the effect of the squaring of scores at step 5).

The result of step 7 is σ, the **standard deviation** of the data.

Standard deviations of samples and populations

To complicate matters slightly, you also need to know that there are two forms of the standard deviation. The difference between the two in terms of the actual calculation is minimal, but you do need to try to keep them separate in your mind, and to ensure that the version you use is correct for your data, and your intentions.

Although this may seem potentially confusing, you can keep things clear if you apply the following rules.

1   Formula 6.1 (using the symbol σ), in the previous section, gives the procedure for obtaining the standard deviation of a population when the whole population has been sampled. (The distinction between population and sample is crucial here: if you need to check your understanding of these concepts see chapter 3.) As an example, you might have a collection of scores obtained from the students in a class, and wish to do no more than describe how they are dispersed around their mean. That is, you are interested in the students in the class as an entire population of interest, rather than a sample from some larger population.

2   On the other hand, if you have obtained a sample (using a formal sampling procedure) which constitutes only part of some population and you wish to get behind those data to say something about the population (using the techniques described in chapter 8), you should instead use the following formula:

$$s = \sqrt{\frac{\Sigma d^2}{n-1}}$$

Formula 6.2

where:

s is the symbol for the standard deviation of a sample
d is the difference between each score and the mean
n − 1 is the number of scores in the sample minus one
Σ directs you to sum all the (squared) differences.

You would use formula 6.2 rather than formula 6.1 if, again, you had obtained a sample of test scores from a number of students, and wished to estimate the likely dispersion of scores within the population from which they had been taken. Note that the only difference between formula 6.2 and formula 6.1 is that whereas in 6.1 you divide by n before taking the square root to find σ, in 6.2 you divide by n − 1, then take the square root to get the value for s. That is the only difference. Running the calculation with n − 1 gives you the standard deviation of the sample, and this can then be used as an estimate (note the word) of the standard deviation of the underlying population. If you wish, you could then go on to use this estimate in various ways to make inferences about the population mean and standard deviation, using the techniques described in chapter 8.

It is a good idea to try to get the difference between the two versions of this statistic clear in your mind from the beginning. However, as researchers we are never particularly interested in describing the set of subjects who have provided the data. Instead we almost always want to get behind the immediate data to say something about the underlying population – in the case of the standard deviation, to find s rather than σ. Given this, it is virtually certain that formula 6.2 is the one you will need to use whenever you wish to compute a standard deviation. (Most computer software also calculates s rather than σ when asked to produce the standard deviation.)

Variance/standard deviation: a worked example

A psychologist with an interest in the factors affecting memory for everyday events tested a group of ten informants on their ability to remember a selection of twenty recent events, such as what they had for lunch on a given day. The data obtained represent the number of events correctly recalled out of the twenty by each subject, and the analysis begins by computing the standard deviation (s) for the sample.

Subject	1	2	3	4	5	6	7	8	9	10
Data	3	17	11	6	9	12	11	16	10	12

Computation procedure			
		Column nos	
	1	2	3
1 Find n, the no. of items of data: $n = 10$ 2 Insert the column headings across the page	Data	Diffs	Squared diffs (d^2)
3 Sum the data in column 1 and divide by n to obtain the mean: $\overline{X} = 10.7$	3	−7.7	59.29
	17	+6.3	39.69
	11	+0.3	0.09
4 Subtract the mean from each item of data and enter the result in column 2	6	−4.7	22.09
	9	−1.7	2.89
	12	+1.3	1.69
5 Square each difference in column 2 and ·enter the result in column 3	11	+0.3	0.09
	16	+5.3	29.09
	10	−0.7	0.49
	12	+1.3	1.69
6 Sum the squared differences . . .	$\Sigma X = 107$ $\Sigma d^2 = 156.1$		

. . . and divide the result by n − 1 to
   find the variance
	Var. (X) = 156.1 ÷ 9
	    = 17.34		

7 Find the square root of the variance to get
   the standard deviation
	$s = \sqrt{17.34}$
	   = 4.16		

But what does it mean?

A value for s of 4.16 is clear and precise enough, but what does it actually mean? Remember that we said earlier that the standard deviation gives a measure of the dispersion of scores about their mean. Also this version of the standard deviation computation provides an estimate of the population standard deviation. Putting those two ideas together (and assuming that the sample in question is representative of the population from which it was taken), we can say, first, that the mean number of memories recalled by these subjects approaches 11, with a dispersion of about 4 memories, and second, that these values estimate the values we would obtain if we were to test the entire population.

The Correlation Coefficient

This section introduces the concept of co-variation, and describes how the scattergraph and the correlation coefficient can be used as complementary ways of representing the relationship between two groups of data.

We also examine briefly the use of the correlation coefficient in psychological research.

(Note: If you only require the instructions for calculating a correlation coefficient you will find two procedures in chapter 9.)

Introduction

Often in psychology, it is very useful to be able to relate one group of data to another, and to measure how much the values vary in relation to each other. For instance, a researcher, suspecting that they are somehow connected, might want to find out how a group of scores representing performance on a verbal ability test are related to scores (obtained from the same individuals) on a test of ability to empathize with others. Is it the case that people who score highly on the verbal ability test also tend to obtain high scores on empathy? Or is the relationship the other way round? Or is there no discernible relation between them?

This relationship between two variables is called **co-variation**. It means that if we put two groups of data (from the same or, less usually, from different sources) alongside each other, so that each score in one is paired in a meaningful way with a score in the other, then the variables represented by the scores in each set will be found to co-vary with respect to the other, to a greater or lesser degree.

The statistic which provides a summary of this relationship is called the **correlation coefficient**. Its function is to provide a compact numerical representation of the degree to which any two variables, represented by two groups of data, co-vary. There is, however, one restriction on the use of this statistic which you need to bear in mind from the beginning. If the correlation coefficient is to give a reliable description of the data it can only be used if the underlying relationship between the two sets of data being correlated can reasonably be regarded as a *linear* one. (Linear means 'in a straight line'.) This doesn't mean that when you plot a graph of your data it always has to turn out to be a nice straight line. It means, rather, that you have to have a reasonable belief that the two underlying variables (but note, *not* the data which only represent measurements of the variables) are related in a linear fashion. That is, you have to be reasonably certain that increases or decreases to the value of one variable are accompanied by corresponding and parallel increases or decreases to the value of the other *throughout the whole range of possible values* of the variable. There is a very good reason for this which will be explained a little later.

Scattergraphs

The co-variation of any two groups of data can be represented visually by means of a simple graph called a scattergraph. Any point on the field of the graph represents two values, one on the vertical axis, and one on the horizontal. If you take each **pair** of scores (that is, one from each group of data), you can therefore plot the point on the field of the graph which represents them both. If this process is then repeated until all pairs of data have been plotted, then the extent to which the two sets co-vary is shown by the shape of the pattern made by all the individual points.

To see how this is possible, we need to look at some of the possible results of this process.

(Note: You will find detailed instructions for drawing a scattergraph towards the end of this chapter. If the technique of scattergraphs is unfamiliar to you, you may want to read through that section before continuing.)

Suppose, then, that there are two groups of scores representing measurements made of two different variables. Essentially, there are only three ways in which these sets of data can co-vary in relation to the other.

1   One possibility is that the values in each set of data are completely in step with each other, so that as the values in one set of data increase, so the values in the other set increase also by a proportional amount (or as one set of values grow smaller, so do the others). This relationship is called **positive co-variation**. If we plot the scattergraph for two such sets of data (called, for convenience, variable 1 and variable 2), the graph will look like figure 6.3. Note that the points on the graph run in a straight line from bottom left to top right.

2   The second possibility is that as the data values in one set *increase*, the values of the other *decrease*. This is **negative** or **inverse co-variation**. Again, if we had two sets of data where the relationship was perfectly linear in this

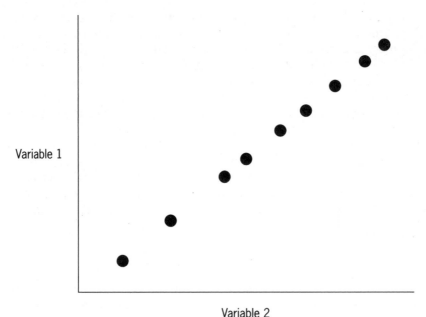

Figure 6.3　Scattergraph of a perfect positive correlation

way, we would obtain the following scattergraph from those data. This time the direction of the line of points is from top left to bottom right because every *increase* in the value of variable 1 is paralleled by an exactly proportional *decrease* to the value of variable 2, as in figure 6.4.

3　Finally, the third possibility is that there is *no* pattern of relation whatever between the two sets of values. This is **random co-variation**, and the scattergraph for these data would look like figure 6.5. Note that the points are scattered at random all over the field of the graph so that it is impossible to say whether they have a tendency to form any kind of regular linear pattern.

Of course, such clear-cut examples of co-variation between two sets of data are unlikely ever to be encountered outside the pages of a statistics text. What you *are* likely to obtain from real-world data are scattergraphs which look more like those in figure 6.6 (which we'll discuss in a moment).

Clearly, the scattergraph provides a useful tool for understanding the relationship between two sets of data, since it provides a readily comprehensible visual representation of the scores involved.

However, it does have a couple of disadvantages. The least important is that it can be a fairly tedious business to plot a scattergraph if you have large amounts of data. The much more important drawback is that while it contains a great deal of detailed information about the co-variation of the scores, this information is not presented in a form which is sufficiently succinct to permit it to be readily communicated. Nor does it allow for easy comparisons to be

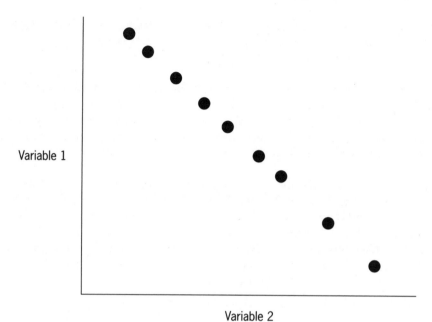

Figure 6.4 Scattergraph of a perfect negative correlation

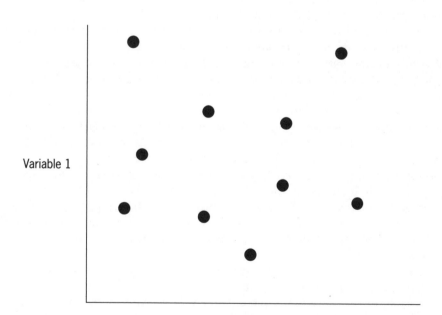

Figure 6.5 Scattergraph of a zero correlation

made between data in different scattergraphs – something which has to be possible if different pieces of research are to be compared.

This means finding an alternative approach, and this is what the correlation coefficient provides. The great advantage which this statistic has over the scattergraph is that as long as the underlying relationship between the two variables is a linear one, a reasonably simple computation (see chapter 9) gives a precise numerical value on the degree of co-variation between two groups of scores. It thus enables the relationship between them to be captured exactly and in a way which facilitates comparisons between different collections of data.

However, this is certainly not to suggest that drawing a scattergraph is a waste of time. Far from it! You still need the graph to provide you with an initial impression of the relationship between scores. That visual representation is essential to help you detect patterns in the data and interpret the correlation coefficient. There are some examples a little later on in this section which show why this is so. Before we get to them, though, we need to clarify exactly what is meant by the term 'correlation coefficient'.

The correlation coefficient

The correlation coefficient can be calculated from any two sets of data, and is a numerical value between –1 and +1. The sign of the value (+ or –) indicates the direction of the *relationship* between the variables, and the magnitude of the coefficient (that is, where the value lies in the range from 0 to 1) indicates the *degree* or *extent* to which the two sets of data co-vary in a straight-line fashion.

A number of different versions of the correlation statistic have been developed for working with different kinds of data. Instructions for computing two of these, the Pearson product-moment and the Spearman rank order correlation coefficient, can be found in chapter 9 of this book. Whichever version you use (depending on the kind of data you are working on), they both produce the same result: a numerical value in the range –1 to +1 indicating the degree of co-variation of two sets of data. What do these numbers mean?

To take the extreme possibilities first, a correlation coefficient of +1 indicates a perfect positive correlation – i.e. that the two sets of data co-vary in such a way that each increase in the value of one variable is accompanied by a proportional increase to the value of the other. This is perhaps a difficult relationship to visualize, so we need to turn to the scattergraph for help. The result of plotting two such groups of scores as a scattergraph would look like figure 6.3 above.

Conversely, a correlation coefficient of –1 indicates that the two sets of data co-vary perfectly in a negative or inverse direction, meaning that each increase in the value of one variable is accompanied by a proportional decrease to the value of the other. The scattergraph of that relationship would look like figure 6.4 above.

However, I should also mention again that the probability of obtaining a perfect positive or negative correlation from real data is so remote that it can be almost completely discounted. All 'real' measurements (as opposed to data which have been constructed to demonstrate a statistical idea) will almost certainly generate a correlation coefficient which lies somewhere *between* –1 and +1, rather than one which lies exactly at either extreme, with the sign of the coefficient, as we said earlier, decided by the direction of the relationship.

Given that the extremes of the possible range of values for the correlation coefficient are –1 and +1 respectively, it follows that the mid-point of the range lies at zero. So, the question arises, that if a coefficient of –1 or +1 tells us that there is a perfect relationship between the variables in question, what does a coefficient of zero indicate? You may remember that the answer was already hinted at in the discussion about the scattergraph. A coefficient of zero indicates that the degree of co-variation between the two variables is precisely nil: that is to say, it shows a situation in which the scores on one variable are entirely random with respect to the scores on the other. The scattergraph representing this relationship will therefore (depending on the number of scores to be correlated) contain a rash of points scattered across the entire field of the graph, as in figure 6.5 above.

What does a coefficient value between 0 and 1 mean?

As you have probably been able to see from the above discussion, when you come to calculate a correlation coefficient, you are most likely to finish up with a value which sits somewhere between 0 and –1 or +1, rather than neatly on any of those points. This means, of course, that you need to be able to offer an interpretation of such intermediate results. It's quite simple: essentially, those values of the coefficient which lie along the range of possibilities, rather than sitting at the extremes, or bang on the centre, indicate the extent to which the relationship between the two variables in question contains random-ness. Those variables which possess a high degree of co-variation will produce co-efficients close to –1 or +1, whereas those which co-vary little (i.e. whose relationship is largely random) will produce coefficients closer to zero.

When a scattergraph is drawn for pairs of variables with this kind of relationship, the points on the graph are found not to lie neatly along a straight line, but are more scattered across the field of the graph. The more random the distribution of points across the field of the graph, the closer the correlation coefficient will be to zero (and the lower the degree of co-variation between the two variables).

Once you have calculated a correlation coefficient, you have obtained a succinct numerical representation of the dispersion of your data about a straight line, and should also have a clear visual representation of this in the form of the scattergraph. However, there is still one further thing to do. You now have to translate the relationship between the variables into a form which permits it to be inserted into the text of a report. To help you do this, box 6.2 provides a set of very approximate translations. As long as you have already shown that a correlation is not simply due to chance (see chapter 9), these may be helpful

---

Box 6.2   Approximate translations of values of the correlation coefficient

Value of coefficient (+ or −)	Relation between variables
1.0	Perfect correlation
0.9	Very strong correlation: close straight-line relationship between variables
0.7 or 0.8	Strong correlation: reasonably close straight-line relationship between variables
0.5 or 0.6	Some degree of correlation: not a close relationship between variables
0.3 or 0.4	Weak correlation: very low degree of relationship between variables
0.1 or 0.2	Very weak correlation: virtually no relation between variables
0	Nil or random relationship

---

for interpreting the results of calculating the correlation coefficient of up to about 30 pairs of scores. They are not, however, intended to replace your own careful study of the scattergraph or the data itself, and it must be emphasized that they are an unreliable guide to interpreting collections of scores containing more than 30 pairs.

Scattergraphs and correlation coefficients

We are now in a position to return to a point mentioned earlier – that the scattergraph is an essential tool for assessing the co-variation of two collections of scores even when you have computed the correlation coefficient.

Consider figures 6.6a and 6.6b. If you were to calculate the correlation coefficients for the data represented on those scattergraphs you would obtain the same coefficients of $r = 0$ from each, and you would almost certainly conclude that there was only random co-variation between the scores. However, when the scores are plotted to produce the scattergraph in figure 6.6a we find a good line, indicating a strong positive correlation between the variables, spoilt only by the presence of one outlier (possibly due to a plotting error).

In figure 6.6b, similarly, the graph reveals that there are two, roughly parallel, lines of points, each showing a strong positive trend, and this is a result which requires further investigation. It may be that the two lines represent some clear division within the sources of data, for example, data obtained from male and female subjects, and if this should be so, each sub-set will need to be considered separately.

In both these cases, the correlation coefficient, if considered alone, would

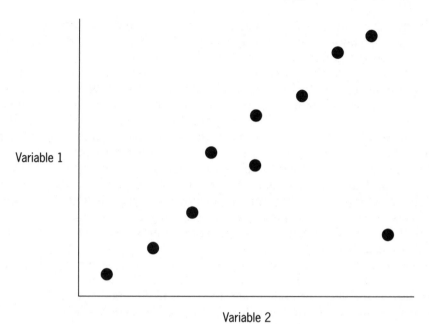

Figure 6.6a   Scattergraph with outlier

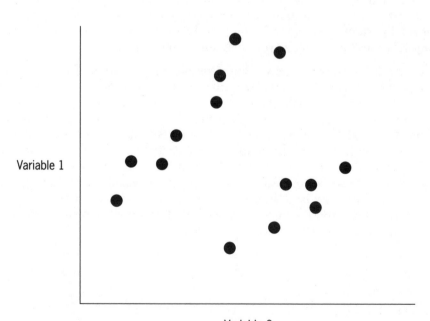

Figure 6.6b   Scattergraph showing evidence of two categories of data

have misled us into thinking that the relation between the variables was no more than a random one. It is only when we can actually see the distribution of points on the graph that we can see that in the first example (6.6a) there is a very strong positive relationship between the variables, and in the second (6.6b), similar evidence of strong positive relationships between the variables, coupled to a very clear hint to look more closely at the sources of data.

Two more examples make the same point from the opposite direction. If you were to calculate the correlation coefficients for the scattergraphs in figures 6.6c and 6.6d you would obtain r = −0.9 – a very strong negative correlation indicating an inverse 'straight-line' relation between the variables in question. However, in figure 6.6c the 'outlier' in the top left corner is probably influencing the calculation to produce the high-value coefficient. If that point were to be removed from the computation the remaining plots, grouped into a symmetrical blob in the opposite corner, would almost certainly generate a coefficient close to zero.

In figure 6.6d, the two groups of points may again represent separate classes of data, just as they did in 6.6b. If the coefficient were to be computed separately for the members of each group, then it is likely that a value close to zero would be obtained, a result which indicates, as we shall see below, that there is no relationship between the variables.

Two illustrations of the correlation coefficient

The following pair of examples will help clarify the idea of co-variation, give an indication of how to approach the interpretation of correlation data and, incidentally, show how the technique can be used in research to identify interesting relationships between variables for further investigation.

A positive correlation   A psychologist researching consumer behaviour for a well-known supermarket chain has collected ratings of 'shopping enjoyment', from 100 customers in each of ten stores on one particular day. Sifting through the records she notices that the highest mean rating for that day was achieved in the store which also had the highest number of staff on duty, and she wonders whether this relationship also exists for the other stores sampled. Noticing that the stores are comparable in most other respects, such as floor area, sales, and number of different product lines stocked, she decides to while away a few quiet moments by looking at the relationship between the mean enjoyment ratings and the number of staff on duty for the ten stores for which she has information. The data are as follows:

Store no.	1	2	3	4	5	6	7	8	9	10
Mean shopping enjoyment	8.4	2.7	5.7	4.7	7.6	5.1	7.5	6.8	8.2	4.6
Staff on duty	24	11	16	13	20	15	19	16	19	12

An inspection of the data suggests to the psychologist that the correlation will be a positive one, since it appears that every increase or decrease in the number

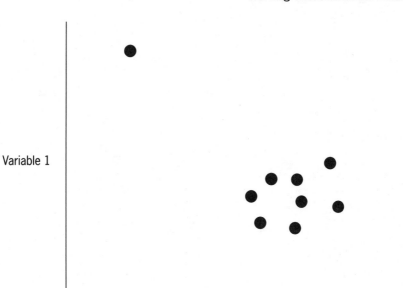

Figure 6.6c   Scattergraph with outlier

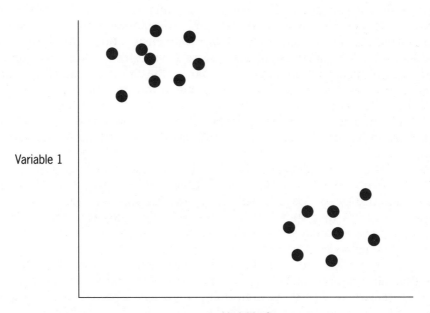

Figure 6.6d   Scattergraph showing evidence of two categories of data

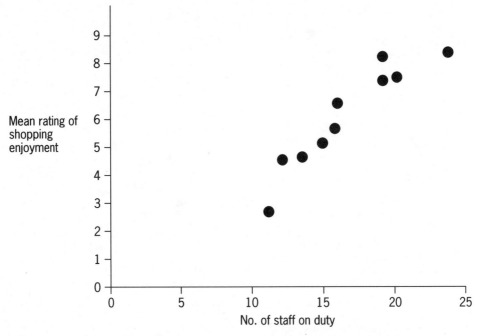

Figure 6.7a   Scattergraph of mean ratings of shopping enjoyment plotted against number of staff on duty: data obtained from samples of 100 shoppers at ten stores

staff on duty is paralleled by a corresponding increase or decrease in the mean rating of shopping enjoyment. For example, comparing store 1 with store 2, she can see that store 2 has both a lower enjoyment rating and fewer employees than store 1. Similarly, comparing store 2 with store 3, the values on both variables are higher in the latter store than in the former. In no case does the value of one variable increase while the value of the other decreases. She therefore decides to assume that the relationship between these variables is a linear one, and continue with the analysis. Her first impression, that there is a positive relationship, is confirmed when she draws the scattergraph of the data (figure 6.7a).

When she examines the scattergraph, it is clear that there is a strong positive relationship between the variables, since the general distribution of points shows a clear upward trend from bottom left towards the top right-hand corner. This pattern indicates that staff numbers and shopper enjoyment ratings have a strong positive tendency to co-vary, even though the points do not fall into a perfectly straight line on the graph.

The next step is to compute the correlation coefficient for these data, using the Pearson product-moment coefficient (see chapter 9). This yields a correlation coefficient of $r = +0.93$, confirming that, as suspected, there is a very strong positive relationship between the mean enjoyment of shopping and the number of store staff on duty.

However, the psychologist is aware that this does not necessarily mean that the two variables are directly connected. A correlation coefficient only describes the extent to which variables co-vary; it says nothing about the possibility of there being a causal connection between them, no matter how large the value of the correlation may be. Furthermore, a moment's thought suggests to her that the presence of large numbers of staff in a store is unlikely, by itself, to increase shopping enjoyment. In fact she finds it all too easy to imagine a number of situations in which high staff numbers actually reduce any enjoyment one might experience in shopping – if they are actually unhelpful, or otherwise fail to do their jobs, for example. A much more likely possibility, she feels, is that good staffing levels mean that all the things which can make shopping such a hassle – such as queues at the checkout, empty shelves, and trolleys scattered far and wide across the car-park – can be dealt with efficiently, thereby minimizing the possibility of frustration among shoppers. She therefore hypothesizes that the high correlation between staff numbers and shopper enjoyment occurs because of the hidden causal relationship between the speed with which the key tasks in a supermarket are performed and the ability of shoppers to get their shopping done with a minimum of delay. However, since none of these possible relationships between the variables can be explored by means of the existing data, she concludes that more research will need to be done.

A negative correlation   Suppose, though, that the data studied by the psychologist were rather different. The stores and the staffing levels are the same, but the mean rating of shopping enjoyment is plotted against the percentage of staff on duty who are part-time employees.

Store no.	1	2	3	4	5	6	7	8	9	10
Mean shopping enjoyment	8.4	8.6	4.3	4.9	3.0	6.6	5.1	7.3	6.1	7.5
Part-time staff on duty (%)	24	11	16	13	20	15	19	16	19	12

What kind of a scattergraph and correlation coefficient will these data produce, and, more importantly, what kind of a conclusion about the co-variation of the variables will they suggest?

A first inspection of the data suggests that, in this case, the relationship between the variables will be a negative one, since in all stores except the first, higher proportions of part-time staff are accompanied by moderate to low mean ratings of shopping enjoyment. The scattergraph (figure 6.7b) broadly confirms this interpretation. The points plotted on the graph are somewhat dispersed but it is nevertheless possible to discern a fairly clear line running from the bottom right towards the top-left corner of the graph, indicating an inverse relationship between the variables. Note, however, there is also one 'outlier' point on the right of figure 6.7b. This point, produced by the data from store 1, lies considerably apart from the main cluster, and will need to be taken into account in the further analysis of the data. We shall return to this in a moment.

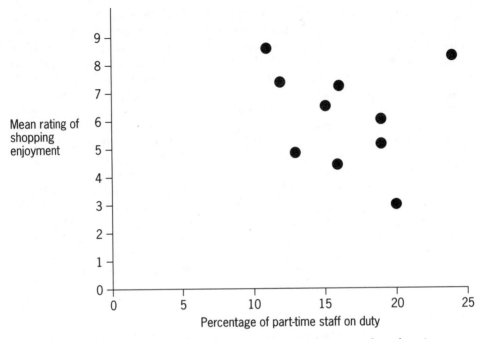

Figure 6.7b   Scattergraph of mean ratings of shopping enjoyment plotted against percentage of part-time staff on duty: data obtained from samples of 100 shoppers at ten stores

As in the previous example, the next step in the analysis is to compute Pearson's product-moment coefficient for the data. This gives a value of $r = -0.19$, suggesting, as expected, that there is an inverse relationship between the variables, but also (and contrary to expectation) that the relationship is a very weak one. In fact, the coefficient is so low as to indicate that the co-variation is not much more than random, indicating that there is virtually no consistency in the relationship between the variables, and thus that the relation between part-time staffing levels and measures of shopping enjoyment is of only negligible interest.

However, before finally writing these data off as uninteresting we should consider again the influence which the single 'outlier' from store 1 exerts on the coefficient value. This point on the graph represents the highest proportion of part-time staff and the second highest score on shopping enjoyment in the data, and therefore suggests that there is a strong positive relationship between these variables in store 1, in contradiction to the general negative trend in the data obtained from the other nine. This, in turn, suggests the possibility that the store 1 data may have been influenced by some factor not present in the others. For example, it might be that the manager at store 1 has trained his staff to be more customer-friendly than the staff at the other outlets.

Whatever the reason for the presence of the outlier may turn out to be, clearly the analysis and interpretation of the whole collection of data might be more accurate if the data from store 1 are removed from the computation. If this is done, and the Pearson product-moment correlation procedure is applied to the remaining nine pairs of scores, the recomputed value of the coefficient turns out to be $r = -0.67$. While this result still does not indicate that there is a very strong degree of co-variation between the two variables, it does provide a more accurate summary of the general trend of the data as revealed in the scattergraph.

As always, the final stage of analysis is to draw a conclusion from the result. In this case, with the outlier data excluded, we can see that there is evidence of a moderately strong, but inverse, relationship between the variables. That is, a high score on customer enjoyment of shopping tends to be associated with lower levels of part-time staffing, and conversely, higher levels of part-time staffing tend to be associated with lower levels of shopping enjoyment, although, as we have already noted, the relationship is not particularly strong. Nor is it possible to conclude from the study of co-variation that there is a causal link between the variables. The fact that the data generated an inverse coefficient does not mean that the staff at these stores were simply being horrible to their customers. As was suggested in the previous example, there could well be some other variable associated with staffing levels which caused the variation in customer reaction between stores. A psychologist who was given the task of interpreting these data and making recommendations to the management of the supermarket chain would report the results of both analyses (i.e. with and without the outlier taken into account), and might suggest taking a closer look at the relationships between staffing level and efficiency, in order to try to identify the variables which influence shopping enjoyment.

Correlation and causality

One of the things which was earlier said about the correlation coefficient was that the procedure can be applied to 'any' two sets of paired data. This is literally true. The procedure for calculating a correlation coefficient does not assume that a relationship of any kind necessarily exists between the two variables. A correlation coefficient, therefore, is simply the result of a procedure which takes any two sets of data and reports on the degree of co-variation between one and the other. However, since in psychology the aim of the whole exercise is almost always to permit a conclusion to be drawn about some aspect of human behaviour, the two sets of data do need to be connected in some way – for example by having been generated by the same individuals. Without this connection it is impossible to say anything beyond simply giving the value of the coefficient.

It is also sometimes easy to assume that because two sets of data produce a high value for the correlation coefficient, there must therefore be some kind of causal link between them. This is not so. No value of the correlation coefficient, no matter how high, permits a researcher to conclude that therefore one variable has influenced the other. The presumption must always be that the two variables are causally unconnected. In fact, there may be a link, either

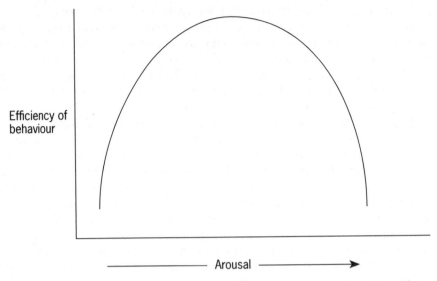

Figure 6.8   Graph showing the curvilinear relation between arousal and the efficiency of behaviour

direct, or indirect – as when, for example, one of the correlated variables exerts a direct causal influence on a third variable which then in turn influences the second correlated variable – but the existence of such causal relationships must always be regarded as hypotheses to be confirmed later by experiment rather than as conclusions from the correlation coefficient. As statisticians say, 'Correlation does not imply causation'.

Linear and curvilinear relationships between data

It was said earlier that the underlying relationship between the two sets of data being correlated should be a linear one if a correlation coefficient is to be used. To see why this is important we can look at an example from psychology – the Yerkes-Dodson Law. This 'law' describes the relationship between two variables: 'arousal' and 'efficiency of behaviour'. The Yerkes-Dodson Law says that the relationship between these two variables is a **curvilinear** one, so that if they were to be measured under ideal circumstances, the data would produce a graph (figure 6.8) with an upturned U shape. Let's pursue what this means for the correlation coefficient.

The graph shows that as arousal increases from zero, on the left, so the efficiency of behaviour also increases, until a maximum level of efficiency is reached at the top of the curve. If arousal does not increase any further, then all will be well and behaviour will continue at maximum efficiency.

However, if the arousal level continues to rise, then the efficiency of behaviour begins to fall, until at maximum arousal (represented by the extreme right-hand end of the curve), the efficiency of behaviour has fallen back to close on zero.

Now suppose we were to take measures of these same two variables, arousal and efficiency of behaviour, from a group of subjects, and calculate a correlation coefficient. What kind of answer would we expect?

The answer depends on the level of arousal shown by the subjects. If they were all functioning at low levels of arousal (i.e. on the left-hand side of the inverted U), high scores on arousal would tend to be associated with high scores on efficiency (and equally, low scores on arousal would tend to be associated with low scores on efficiency), and we would therefore expect to obtain a positive correlation of some kind. Similarly, if they were all rather highly aroused we could expect to get a negative correlation, since there would be an inverse relation between high scores on one variable and high scores on the other. However, if, as is also possible, half the subjects were highly aroused and half were not, then each of the different directions of co-variation would cancel the other out, and a correlation coefficient of around zero could be expected.

The point is, then, that although there *is* a clear relationship between the two variables, because it is a curvilinear relationship, the correlation coefficient is unable accurately to summarize it. The relationship *is* there, but what the correlation coefficient reveals about it will depend on the level of arousal in the subjects at the time the variables were measured, and not on the relationship between the two variables themselves. Because the correlation coefficient is intended for data which co-vary in a linear fashion, it is unable to express the curvilinear relationship, and instead is most likely to return a coefficient which hovers somewhere close to zero. In other words, it is able to see only random variation in the data when in fact a curvilinear relationship exists between the variables. To repeat, the correlational procedure is good only for summarizing the relationship between two variables where the relationship is fundamentally a **linear** one.

The practical point is this. Before using the correlation coefficient to summarize data you have to ask yourself whether there is any possibility that the relationship between the variables *could* be curvilinear. If the answer is 'no', then all well and good, but if the answer is 'yes' or 'maybe', then you should be very cautious about using a correlation procedure on your data.

How can you tell if a relationship between two variables is likely to be a curvilinear one?

There is no certain way. You should begin by plotting a scattergraph for your variables, although, for the reasons pointed out above, it will not necessarily indicate that you are dealing with a curvilinear relationship, since you may have data taken from one half of the curve.

The most effective approach is to apply your general knowledge of psychology to the variables in question. At least one variable – the age of your research participants – should be treated with great circumspection if you have a correlational procedure in mind. Very many variables of interest to psychologists, such as performance on cognitive and psychomotor tasks, show a curvilinear relationship with age, because performance levels start to decline in middle age. This is obviously not too much of a problem if your research participants are all around the same age. If, though, you have a sample of participants drawn from a wide span of ages, then you should be cautious about using a correlation coefficient because the underlying relationship between the variables *may* be a curvilinear one.

Statistical significance of a correlation coefficient

In addition to obtaining a value for the correlation coefficient, it is probable that you will also, at some point, wish to assess its statistical significance. Before you do, however, you are recommended to read the information on hypothesis testing which is contained in chapter 7. It is especially important to be clear about the concepts of the null and alternate hypotheses, and significance level, which you will find there.

Tables 3 and 4 in appendix 5 provide critical values for the two correlation coefficients described in this book at the $p = 0.01$ and $p = 0.05$ levels of significance. Using these tables you can tell, for any given size of sample, whether the correlation coefficient you have obtained is *so different from zero* as to be unlikely, at the probability of the significance level, to have been obtained if the null hypothesis is correct.

Using the correlational method in psychological research

Reduced to its barest essentials, carrying out correlational research in psychology simply involves collecting two sets of data, and determining the extent to which they co-vary, by means of the appropriate correlation statistic. However, if the results are to be at all informative, some care needs to be taken in planning and executing the research.

The role of theory

There is a temptation in planning correlational research simply to pick two likely-looking variables and then to collect data in order to find out whether or not they correlate highly. This, as suggested earlier, is not the best way to proceed. The two sets of data selected must be connected in some way, because although it is perfectly possible to compute the correlation coefficient for any pair of variables whatsoever, this does not necessarily convey any real information beyond the fact of the correlation coefficient itself. For example, the number of ships in the Royal Navy each year since 1945 can be correlated with the number of books owned by householders in the Birmingham area across the same period. However, the resulting correlation coefficient can hardly be said to mean very much because there is no necessary connection between the two variables – or, put another way, one would expect book ownership in Birmingham to be entirely independent of whatever factors influence the size of the British Navy.

A meaningful result from a correlation statistic can only be obtained if there are reasons for believing that there is a connection of some kind between the two sets of data. The most straightforward way of ensuring this is to collect both sets of data from the same group of individuals, possibly under different kinds of conditions, depending on the nature of the hypothesis being tested. Since they come from the same source, such data will at least have one thing in common. Note, though, that this is still not enough to be able to infer that one variable caused the other, but only that they *might* both be influenced by the same third factor, which could then be the subject of further research. However, the assumption of the existence of some connection between variables is not enough by itself. The connection must also be justifiable in terms of an underlying theory which justifies both the selection of the variables to be examined, and the reasons for the predicted direction of co-variation. Only if the theoretical underpinning is in place can correlational research generate meaningful results.

For example, one could correlate scores on a psychometric test of verbal fluency with scores on a test of general intelligence as long as both sets of scores have been generated by the same group of people. If the results of the correlation indicate that the two sets of data co-vary significantly in (say) a positive direction, it could be concluded that there is some overlap between verbal fluency and general intelligence. If, however, the scores came from different individuals, it would not be possible to draw any conclusion concerning these two variables, no matter how high the correlation coefficient might be. But even if the data do come from the same individuals, and do generate a high positive correlation, it is still necessary to turn to theory to explain what such a correlation may tell us about the structure of intellectual abilities, and why this information is of interest. Without an underlying theory, correlational research is a largely empty exercise producing results which could point to any number of possible conclusions.

Types of variables in correlational research

In designing correlational research it is sometimes useful to distinguish between two types of variables, predictor variables and outcome variables.

The predictor variable is so called because it enables a prediction of the value of the outcome variable to be made, and is the variable which in some sense comes before, or pre-dates, the other in the design.
The outcome variable, on the other hand, is the object of the research, the variable about which a researcher seeks to discover more information.

Sometimes this distinction has a basis in logic, as in the case of the research into the causes of lung cancer. In that research, smoking (strictly speaking, some measure of tobacco-smoke intake, such as the number of cigarettes consumed), was the predictor variable, and lung cancer the outcome variable. These two variables are identified by the fact that, in nature, one comes before the other. Although not all habitual smokers contract lung cancer, acquiring the smoking habit usually precedes the disease, and it is relatively rare among non-smokers.

Two real-life examples of correlational research

In the course of this section we have examined the use of the correlation coefficient in a number of hypothetical situations. Here, to show how useful this approach to research can be when practical or ethical considerations render alternative methods impossible, are two real-life examples taken from the psychological literature.

Murstein's research into perceived attractiveness

Murstein designed this investigation in order to provide a test of the 'matching hypothesis', which suggests that people tend to choose as partners others who are roughly equally as physically attractive as themselves. Previous investigations had involved collecting ratings of attractiveness by independent judges, and Murstein followed this approach initially in his research. However, he also wondered whether there was any relationship between a person's self-assessment of their own attractiveness and their ratings of their partner's attractiveness: between how attractive s/he believed him/herself to be, and how attractive s/he believed his/her partner to be.

The research involved a sample of 99 dating couples who were students at two US universities. The members of each couple were asked to rate themselves and their partner for attractiveness on a 5-point scale. They were also photographed in both smiling and unsmiling poses, and their photographs were rated for attractiveness by a panel of judges using the same scale.

In order to test the matching hypotheses, sample members' ratings of self-perceived attractiveness were correlated with their ratings of their partner's attractiveness. For men the correlation turned out to be +0.5, and for women, +0.45, both of which were significant at $p = 0.01$. The concept of statistical significance is explained in chapter 7, but the meaning of this result is that there is a stronger association than would be predicted by chance between how attractive a person believes themselves to be, and how attractive a partner is believed to be.

The Murstein research provided further support for the matching hypothesis, and, more distantly, for the Exchange Theory of relationships which says that people are likely to choose relationships with others which offer a balance between rewards and costs.

Dement and Kleitman and the relation between rapid eye movements and dreaming

During the 1950s, sleep researchers had established that sleep in which rapid eye movements occur (also called REM sleep) is qualitatively different from other nocturnal states and also that it appeared to occur at the same time as dreaming. However, the latter point had not, at the time Dement and Kleitman carried out their research, been established beyond doubt, and they therefore decided to try to demonstrate that there is an association between REM sleep and the experience of dreaming.

The research involved obtaining data from a sample of sleepers whose EEG trace was monitored continuously while they were asleep. They were wakened during both REM and non-REM sleep and asked to say whether they had been dreaming, and to estimate the duration of their dreams. The direction of eye movements in REM sleep was also monitored, and an attempt made to relate these to the eye movements which could be expected to occur in similar waking situations. The aim was to try to establish beyond doubt that dreaming did in fact occur during REM sleep episodes: not that REM sleep caused dreaming, but simply that the two sets of events occur together.

Dement and Kleitman found that people wakened from REM sleep tended to report that they had been dreaming immediately before wakening, whereas those awakened from non-REM sleep did not. From 191 episodes of REM sleep studied, from which the sleeper was wakened, 152 reports of dreams were obtained, whereas, from 160 episodes of non-REM sleep, only 11 resulted in dream recall. The researchers concluded that REM activity and dreaming did indeed co-occur. In addition, they attempted to obtain more objective measures of the strength of the relationship, and collected data on the duration of each of the REM periods and on the number of words which were used by members of the sample to describe each of their dreams (a crude measure of dream length). A high and statistically significant positive correlation was found between these two measures which confirmed the other findings.

REFERENCES

Dement, W. & Kleitman, N. (1957). The relation of eye movements during sleep to dream activity: An objective method for the study of dreaming. *Journal of Experimental Psychology*, 53, 339–46.
Murstein, B. I. (1972). Physical attractiveness and marital choice. *Journal of Personality and Social Psychology*, 22, 8–12.

Graphs: Presenting Data Visually

Descriptive statistics, as we have seen, provide simple but powerful methods of condensing large sets of data into a single representative value, which stand for some feature of the relationship between all the individual items of data. Undeniably useful though they are, such techniques do have a weakness as far as providing for the full comprehension of data is concerned, since they still present information in numerical form. Although numbers are fine for communicating information in a very concise and economical way, they do have the drawback that generally human beings find it easier to extract meanings from visual material – pictures of some kind – than from numbers alone. It can, for example, be very difficult to relate the result of a descriptive statistic back to the mass of data from which it has been calculated, or to draw together the results of different statistics to obtain an overall picture from the summaries which they provide. It is therefore generally necessary, particularly when writing up a research report, to translate the information from numerical into graphical form – that is, to change it from numbers to the visual image provided by some form of graph.

The basic rule for writers of research reports, then, is that at least one graph will almost always be required unless you are certain that the data are so simple that a graph is incapable of clarifying them any further. There is also the further advantage that a graph or two will not only help the reader of your report to understand your data more easily, it may also help you to do the same.

The purpose of this section is to provide a quick review of the more common types of graph you are likely to need to use, followed by more detailed information on one which, though it is less frequently encountered, is nevertheless one of the most useful of all for the psychologist.

Types of graph

The basic range of graphs which you are likely to need to use to describe the results of your research are:

- **Line graphs (straight line and curved)**
- **Bar graphs and histograms**
- **Scattergraphs**
- **Box and whisker graphs.**

Of these, only the fourth type, the box and whisker graph, is likely to be completely new to you, and will therefore be dealt with in more detail.

The line graph

A line graph is used to plot the changes in the relationship between two variables. If the values to be plotted represent the results of an experiment then the independent variable in the experiment is plotted on the horizontal (x) axis, and the dependent variable on the vertical (y) axis. All line graphs begin as a set of points on the field of the graph, but are of two main varieties. In one, the aim is to fit a straight line or a smooth curve to the pattern of points in order to indicate the underlying relationship between the variables, as in figures 6.9a and 6.9b. Note that it is not necessary for the line to pass through all the points plotted.

In the other form of line graph, each point on the field of the graph is connected by a short straight line which gives the graph a characteristically

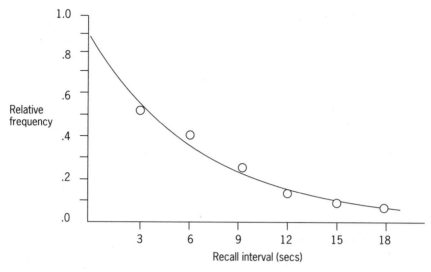

Figure 6.9a Example of a curved-line graph: correct recalls as a function of recall interval (Peterson & Peterson, 1959)

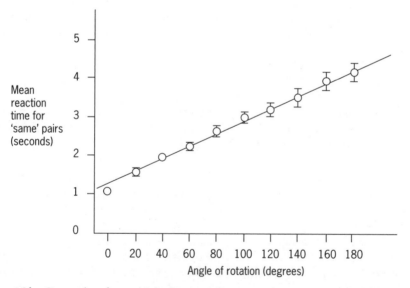

Figure 6.9b Example of a straight-line graph: mean reaction times to two perspective line drawings portraying objects of the same three-dimensional shape. Reprinted with permission from Shepard, R. & Metzler, J. (1971). Mental rotation of three-dimensional objects, *Science*, *171*, 701–3. Copyright 1971 American Association for the Advancement of Science.

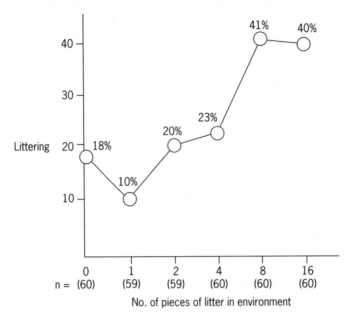

Figure 6.9c Example of a straight-line graph: percentage of subjects littering as a function of the number of pieces of litter in the environment. From Cialdini, R.B., Reno, R.R., and Kallgren, C.A. (1990). A focus theory of normative conduct: Recycling the concept of norms to reduce littering in public places. *Journal of Personality and Social Psychology* 58 1015–26. Copyright © 1990 by the American Psychological Association. Reprinted with permission.

jagged appearance, as in figure 6.9c. In this form of graph the aim is simply to guide the eye across the range of points, and to provide a visual representation of the differences between the points in terms of the x and y variables.

Sometimes you may wish to draw a line graph to represent the difference between the results obtained from different conditions in an experiment. Two things need to be borne in mind here. First, unless you wish to represent a difference between the conditions which can be measured as a continuous variable (such as, in figure 6.10, the difference in time of testing), a bar graph gives a much clearer result and is therefore always to be preferred. Secondly, a line graph of any kind should only be drawn if there are three or more points to be plotted. The reason for drawing a line graph in the first place is to show, through the slope of the line, the way in which changes to the value of one variable are reflected in the value of the other. If there are only two points plotted on the graph, however, the slope of the line – because it must be wholly determined by the scales chosen for the two axes – is unable to convey any information about changes to the values of the two variables which cannot already be obtained from inspection of the data. On the other hand, if there are three or more points plotted on the graph, then the slope of the line between the points carries information about the rate of change between those points relative to the others, even though the precise angle of the line still depends on the scales chosen for the axes. Again figure 6.10 illustrates.

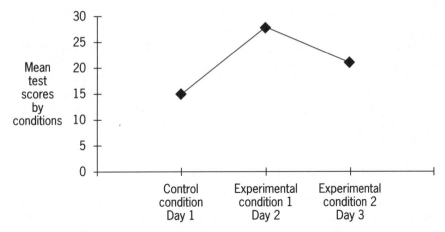

Figure 6.10   Example of a line graph: data from an experiment run on three different days

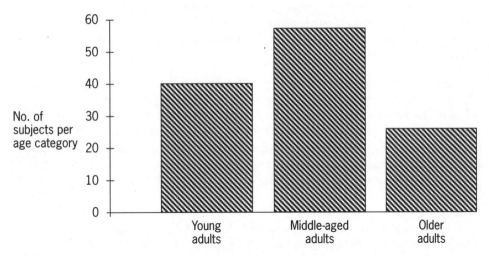

Figure 6.11   Bar chart of the age distribution of a hypothetical sample. Note that the bars represent discrete categories of age.

The bar graphs

The basic idea of the bar graph is to represent the data by means of a series of vertical bars running upwards from the horizontal axis of the graph, with the upper edge of the bars indicating the rise and fall of the value of one variable. There are two main types of bar graph:

Bar charts (figure 6.11) are the form of bar graphs in which the vertical axis (the y axis in a line graph) always represents the changes observed to occur to the DV, and the horizontal (x) axis represents the values of the IV. In a bar chart the bars should not touch each other, and it is therefore often to be preferred to a line graph, since the separation of the bars emphasizes the discontinuous nature of the independent variable.

Histograms are frequency bar graphs in which the vertical axis scale measures the frequency with which the values of a variable are observed, so that the area of each 'bar' is proportional to the frequency it represents. The key features of a histogram, as distinct from an ordinary bar graph, are that the horizontal (x) axis must have a proper scale and the bars must touch each other. (See figure 6.2 for an example.)

The scattergraph

Line and bar graphs are used to represent the changes in one variable in response to the influence of another. The scattergraph, as we have already seen, is used to represent the co-variation of any two continuous variables when we are searching for evidence of an underlying relationship between them.

The scattergraph is so called because each pair of data items is used to determine the location of a single point on the field of the graph, so that when two sets of data are graphed, the graph depicts a scatter of points, each representing one pair of data items. See figures 6.3 to 6.7 for examples of this type of graph.

To draw a scattergraph   To draw a scattergraph, list the two sets of data in parallel columns, and determine the limits (i.e. the highest and lowest values) of each. Draw up the two axes of the graph with appropriate scales. Now take the first pair of items of data and identify the intersection point on the body of the graph. This is the point at which a line drawn up from the appropriate point on the horizontal axis meets a similar line drawn across from the vertical axis. If it coincides with an existing point draw it slightly to one side. Mark the point clearly with a dot or cross. Repeat for all the other pairs of data: the result is a scattergraph depicting the co-variation of the two data sets.

Finally, determine the 'line of best fit' by drawing a straight line to pass as close as possible to the greatest number of points. The direction of the line (i.e. whether it is inclined from bottom left to top right, or vice-versa) indicates the direction of the co-variation (whether positive or negative), and the strength of the correlation is indicated by the closeness of the points to the line. The closer the points, the greater the degree of co-variation between the two sets of data.

The box and whisker graph

The box and whisker graph is likely to be less familiar than the preceding ones, and the procedure will therefore be described in a little more detail (see box 6.4). Essentially, a box and whisker graph offers a powerful yet very simple way of representing the relationship between the various statistics which summarize the features of a distribution. For example, it can show clearly the relationships between the standard deviation of a sample and its mean, median

---

Box 6.3   *Some general principles for drawing effective graphs*

1 Aim to make every graph you draw as simple and as clear as possible. Always use graph paper if it can be obtained.

2 Choose appropriate scales for the axes. The basic requirement is that the axes must be scaled to represent the magnitude of the variables involved in the investigation. The range of values of the scales needs to be only just longer than the range of values in the data. The vertical scale should generally start at zero so that the true magnitude of changes can be seen. A common error is to represent individual participants as points on one of the axes (i.e. the points on the scale represent different individuals rather than degrees of magnitude of a variable.) The result, though it can look seductively meaningful, rarely conveys much information beyond the obvious point that individuals differ, sometimes to a considerable extent. For psychologists, differences between groups of individuals are the main focus of interest, and the scale on the x axis should therefore represent the range of one of the variables on which the group has been measured, rather than identify the individuals themselves.

3 If you are graphing data obtained from an experiment, always plot the IV on the horizontal (x) axis and the DV on the vertical (y) axis.

4 Ensure that you label *both* axes *and* the whole graph clearly and appropriately.

5 Occasionally you may wish to plot two different sets of values against the scale on the x axis in order to make for easy comparisons – as when, for example, you want to look at the relationship of two different variables over a 24-hour period. You might be interested in, say, reaction time, which is usually measured in milliseconds, and in another measure such as, say, grip strength, measured in ergs. Clearly, you need a way of accommodating both of these quite different scales on the vertical axis if you are to get both sets of data on the same graph. The solution is quite straightforward. Give each variable a separate, carefully labelled vertical scale; one on the left-hand side, and the other on the right, and design them so that, if possible, the two lines do not cross at any point and cause confusion. In addition, colour the two lines differently to emphasize that they represent two different sets of data.

---

and range, and this is very useful because they can be quite difficult to visualize from the numerical data alone.

The basis of the box and whisker graph is the idea that any set of data can be summarized effectively by just a few values. These are:

- **The extreme values (highest and lowest)**
- **The mean and median**
- **The two 'hinges' – points above and below the mean, measured in terms of a particular unit such as the standard deviation, or a percentile.**

To see how these values can be represented on a box and whisker plot, consider the following ten hypothetical decision time scores:

15   69   34   42   48   49   54   38   39   27   (seconds)

Box 6.4   How to draw a box and whisker graph

1   From the range of values in the data decide the scale on which you intend to draw the graph. Draw the scale (a).
2   Locate the highest and lowest values in the data, (b) and (c), on the graph by drawing vertical lines at appropriate points above the scale.
3   Calculate the mean of the data and draw a longer vertical line, (d), at the appropriate position on the scale. Similarly calculate the median and draw the dotted line (g). (NB: For some data, it may be necessary to place the median *outside* the box.)
4   The hinges on the box and whisker graph can be defined in terms of any value which describes the distribution of scores around the central tendency. You can use either the mean or the median as the reference point for the hinges, and this decision will depend on your assessment of which of the two provides the best summary of the central tendency of the data.

    In the example graphs, the hinges are defined in terms of the standard deviation of the data, and their position is computed in relation to the mean, since this gives the best representation for our purposes. However, they could equally have been defined in terms of the variance, or in terms of the quartile points on the distribution above and below the median.

    When you come to draw the graph, you simply take whichever value has been selected, and locate the upper hinge, (e), by adding that value to whichever of the mean or the median has been chosen as the reference point, and then drawing a vertical above that point on the scale. Similarly, locate the lower hinge, (f), by subtracting the value in question from the mean (or median), and add it to the graph. (NB: In some cases one or both hinges may lie beyond the extremes of the range.)
5   Connect the hinges to form the 'box', and draw a line from each extreme to meet the hinges to make the 'whiskers'.
6   If there are not too many points to deal with, you may wish to plot the individual items of data on the box and whisker graph. Simply place a dot, or a small 'x' to represent each item of data, at the appropriate point on the scale in a line above the body of the graph, as has been done in figure 6.13.

This sample of data, which can be described by the following values, can also be represented by the box and whisker graph in figure 6.12:

Range	54.0 secs
Mean	41.5 secs
Median	48.5 secs
Standard deviation	14.1 secs

Interpreting the box and whisker graph

The box and whisker graph provides a particularly clear representation of a set of data in a way which numerical information cannot. However, even after the graph has been drawn, the meaning of the information still needs to be inter-

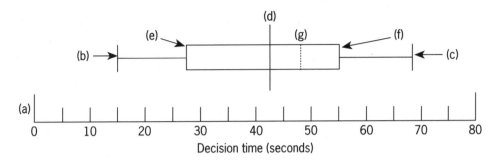

Decision time (seconds)

Key:

(a) The scale
(b) Lower value of range
(c) Upper value of range
(d) Median
(e) Lower hinge (mean minus 1 standard deviation: in this case, 41.5 – 14.1 = 27.4 secs)
(f) Upper hinge: (mean plus 1 standard deviation: in this case, 41.5 + 14.1 = 55.6 secs)
(g) Median

Figure 6.12   Box and whisker graph of a set of hypothetical decision times

preted if it is to be used to its full extent. Here are four ways in which you
can use the information in the box and whisker graph to make further inferences about the data:

1   Look at the distance between the mean and the median. The greater the
    distance the more the mean has been affected by the presence of relatively
    extreme (large or small) values in the data. Consider whether the distance
    is such as to indicate that the data are seriously skewed, taking into account
    the magnitude of the range and standard deviation.
2   Examine the relationship between the extremes and the hinges. If the box
    is centred on the mean and the hinges represent one standard deviation
    above the mean *and* either of the extremes lies *within* the box, it means that
    you have some extremely skewed data. If either the top or bottom range
    values are within one standard deviation of the mean, it suggests either that
    the standard deviation itself is singularly large, or that the mean is excep-
    tionally close to one end of the range, because of the presence of extremely
    large or small values in the data. You can resolve this by inspecting the data
    and the numerical values obtained from the descriptive statistics.
3   The question of whether a sample of data is normally distributed can also
    be answered if the individual data items are also plotted on the same scale
    as the graph (see figure 6.13). If the distribution of the sample *is* normal,
    then you will find that:

    •   The mean (and therefore the 'box' also) will be located in the centre of
        the range
    •   The median will be extremely close to the mean
    •   About 66 per cent of the data items will be located between hinges
        located at one standard deviation above and below the mean.

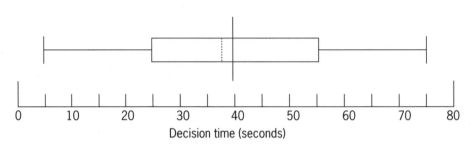

Figure 6.13   Box and whisker graph of a near-normal distribution of twenty decision times with a mean of 50 seconds and a standard deviation of 15 seconds (each dot represents one item of data)

4   You can also use the box and whisker graph to compare different sets of data with each other in order to estimate the likelihood of significant difference between them. While a simple visual inspection of the graph can never be a substitute for using a test statistic on the data, nevertheless it can suggest whether the computation of a test statistic is likely to reveal a significant difference.

   To do this, first construct a separate box and whisker graph for each set of data, one above the other, against the *same scale*. Now examine both graphs together with the following questions in mind:

- How far do the ranges overlap? If there is no overlap at all it is a good indicator that the two sets of data may be significantly different (depending on the significance level you decide to adopt).
- Are the means close together or far apart?
- How big are the boxes? Do they indicate that the distribution of scores around the means are much different? How great is the difference?
- Does the mean of one set of data lie within the box of the other? If it *doesn't*, this again could be an indication that the two means are significantly different.

Summary of chapter 6

Using numbers to represent information carries considerable advantages of precision and clarity over ordinary language and therefore the analysis of quantitative information in the form of numerical data is central to psychological research as it is to all other scientific disciplines.

   The numbers used in psychology represent measurements made on one of four different but related scales, representing the different degrees of precision with which measurements can be made. Only the lower three scales of the four are achievable in psychology. These are: the nominal scale, in which the numbers simply identify different individuals or events; the ordinal scale, in which the numbers indicate only relationships of 'equal to', 'greater than' and 'less than', and the interval scale, in which equal steps in the quality being measured are associated with equal steps on the scale of measurement. The fourth, the ratio scale, which is unique in possessing a true zero point to indicate the complete absence of the quality being measured, represents a level of measurement which probably cannot be achieved in psychology.

The foundations of the statistical treatment of data are provided by the three categories of descriptive statistics. As their name suggests, these give ways of describing and summarizing large quantities of data in a single value. The measures of central tendency, such as the mean or median, are concerned with the typical, or 'average' value in a set of data; and the measures of dispersion, principally the variance and standard deviation, describe the average distribution of scores around a point of reference, such as the mean. Used together these procedures can provide a useful and succinct description of any data set, whatever its size or complexity, and they also provide important contributions to the calculation of more complex statistics.

The third category of descriptive statistics, the measures of correlation, are used to describe the relationship between two variables, where this is known, or can be assumed to be linear in nature. The measure they provide, called the correlation coefficient, indicates the extent to which the values of one variable co-vary with those of the other, and is a value lying between −1 and +1, in which the magnitude indicates the strength of the relationship and the sign indicates its direction. Thus a correlation coefficient of −1 denotes a perfectly negative (inverse) relationship between the two sets of data (i.e. such that changes in value to one set of data are all exactly in inverse proportion to those in the other), and one of +1 represents an exactly proportional positive relationship. Values between −1 and +1 indicate the degree to which the relationship is proportional, with the mid-point of zero indicating a nil, or random relationship.

Drawing conclusions about data from the correlation coefficient is straightforward as long as you remember what its limitations are. First, and most importantly, the coefficient can be computed for any two sets of data whatsoever, however little connection there may be between them, and therefore is capable of representing nothing more than the relationship between two sets of randomly chosen values. By itself, no correlation coefficient, however impressive, can be interpreted as evidence of a causal connection between the two variables correlated.

Secondly, the correlation procedure is only appropriate if the relationship between the two sets of data is (or appears to be) a linear one. This means that the relationship must lie in the same direction (either positive or negative) throughout the whole range of the data. If there is a positive relationship among the lower values of one variable and negative among the higher ones (or vice versa), then the relationship between them will be curvilinear (i.e. can be represented by a curve rather than by a straight line), and in such a case the correlation procedure should not be used.

The correlation coefficient provides the statistical summary of the data in the correlational method of research, which examines the degree of co-variation between pairs of variables which are related in some way (for example, because they have both been obtained from the same group of individuals). The evaluation of the results of such research is aided by the fact that precise hypotheses about co-variation can be tested, since it is possible to determine whether the difference between an obtained coefficient and zero is statistically significant.

Various techniques exist for making data more accessible by putting the information in the form of a graph. Line graphs, either in their straight or curved line form, permit the changes in the relationship between two variables to be plotted with some accuracy. However, for some purposes, such as plotting data obtained from the different conditions in an experiment, a bar graph, in which the height of the bar represents the magnitude of the data values, may be preferable, since the discrete nature of the levels of the IV are thereby emphasized. Frequency data can be effectively represented by means of a histogram. The scattergraph, which consists of a plot of the points of intersection between two sets of data, is used to represent the co-variation between two variables. A 'line of best fit' drawn on the graph can provide a rough prediction of the direction and magnitude of a correlation coefficient.

The box and whisker plot permits a rather more detailed analysis of data to be made than is possible by any of the alternative graphing techniques, since it combines central tendency and dispersion data to provide an image of the distribution of values in a sample. Using this approach, for example, it is possible to represent precisely the relation of the standard deviation of a sample to its mean, median and range, and thereby to make a reasonable estimate of whether the data are likely to be normally distributed. Different sets of data can also be compared by plotting box and whiskers for different data against the same scale, and an assessment made of whether they are likely to be significantly different from each other.

Four projects: data collection and analysis using descriptive statistics

If you would like to test your skills in data analysis on some data you have collected yourself, you could try your hand at some of the following project suggestions. You can approach as small or as large a sample as you wish, and if you prefer you can confine your enquiries to members of your family and friends. However, it will be better, from the point of view of obtaining representative data, to be more adventurous and to try to collect data from members of the general public. (First, please read the section of the appendix dealing with research ethics.)

Projects 3 and 4 describe correlational research projects and represent rather more demanding pieces of work than the others. Before you embark on them you should also make sure you are clear about how to set about testing hypotheses. See chapter 7 for details.

Project 1   The accuracy of estimates of distance

The purpose of this mini-project is to try to assess how accurately people are able to estimate distance. If someone says, for example, that the distance between two towns is 'about 120 miles', it would be useful to have some idea of the amount of error which there might be in that estimate. If it is only accurate to within plus or minus 10 per cent, say, then the actual distance between the two towns could be anywhere between 108 and 132 miles. Given this, it is clearly useful to know, at least roughly, how accurate a distance estimate is likely to be.

You can approach this question quite straightforwardly by asking people to estimate the distance between two towns. The task becomes more interesting if you prepare a list of towns and pair them up at random in order to reduce the possibility that any of your informants actually knows the distance between them. You can then compare your informants' answers to the actual 'crow-flight' distance (which you work out from an atlas). A further variation would be to ask for estimates in both metric and imperial units (kilometres versus miles) and compare them for accuracy. You could also ask people to say how much confidence they are prepared to place in their estimates, by adding to it a margin of error. For example, do they think their estimate is accurate to within five miles? Ten miles? More?

When you come to analyse the data, you could examine the relationship between estimated distance and actual distance between any two towns, and the estimates of error in the following way.

Draw up the data in five columns thus:

Subject	Actual distance	Estimated distance	Difference between actual and estimated	Estimate of error
1				
2				
3				
etc.				

You can use all three types of descriptive statistics to make comparisons among these values. In addition, graphical techniques such as the box and whisker graph and the scattergraph may also be used to represent the data.

- First, find the typical value in each column. What does a comparison among these suggest? For example, how accurate, on average, are people in their estimates?
- Find the range and standard deviation of the scores in each column. What does the dispersion of scores suggest about the differences between the people in your sample?
- Using a correlation coefficient, explore the extent to which the data in any two of the columns co-vary. For example, you could look at the degree and direction of co-variation between the values in the last two columns. What does this suggest about people's estimates? Do people tend to over- or under-estimate the accuracy of their estimates? Does the magnitude of error increase as the estimated error increases? Or are the people who make the greatest errors likely to be those who most underestimate their errors?

To finish off, try writing two or three short paragraphs to summarize your findings as concisely as possible. What do you think your results suggest about the estimation of distance?

Project 2 Decision times in a card-sorting task

Card-sorting, in which someone is asked to sort one or more decks of cards into a number of piles, is a simple psycho-motor task which can be used to look at decision-making, and in particular at the way in which the number of alternatives affects the speed with which a decision can be made. Although common sense would suggest that decision times rise as the number of possible alternatives increases, the relationship is not a simple linear one as other factors such as manual dexterity also play an important role.

To carry out this investigation, you will need one or more ordinary decks of playing cards from which the jokers have been removed, and a number of people who are prepared to act as your experimental subjects. Shuffle the cards thoroughly and instruct each subject to sort the cards into one of the categories listed below at a steady rate, *and to try to make no errors at all*. If any errors should occur, you, as experimenter, must count them, but they must be ignored by the subject doing the sorting (i.e. the error should not be corrected and sorting should continue). Time the sort as accurately as you can, and record both time and the number of errors (if any). Give your subject a short rest (say, 30 seconds), and then obtain another sort using a different set of categories, repeating the process until you have data from that subject for as many different types of sort as you intend to explore: then repeat the process with as many subjects as you are able to obtain. You may like to explore the effects of the following different instructions:

Sorting into two alternatives	Sort by colour (red/black)
	Sort by type (i.e. court cards and others)
Sorting into four alternatives	Sort by suit
Sorting into eight alternatives	Sort by suit *and* by type.

(To obtain a baseline measure of the subjects' manual dexterity simply time how long it takes each person to 'sort' the cards into a single pile.)

When you have collected data from a number of individuals on sorting times and the number of errors for each type of sort, use the appropriate descriptive statistics to draw some tentative conclusions about the relationship between the number of alternatives presented by the task, and the speed and accuracy with which it is accomplished. Do differences in manual dexterity complicate the picture? What relation, if any, can be discovered between the number of sorting categories, decision times and manual dexterity?

Compare the errors made in each type of sort. Is there a relationship between the number of errors and the number of alternatives presented by the task?

A more complex decision-making situation (which combines a decision task with a vigilance task, and so may be regarded as being very loosely analogous to the position of an air-traffic controller watching a radar screen), can be made by inserting a single joker card into the pack(s) at random, and giving subjects a special instruction for dealing with it when it appears – for example you could ask them to sort the joker onto the left-hand pile. What effect does this variation on the task have on decision times in a two-alternatives task? Does it have more or less effect than on the four- or eight-alternatives tasks? What, if any, implications do you think your results may have for the air-traffic control system?

Project 3   Sleep duration and mood

The connection between sleep and mood disturbance is well established: severely depressed patients typically claim a greater need for sleep, and usually sleep for longer, than non-depressed people. Among people who don't feel depressed, however, the relationship between sleep and mood is much less clear. Everyday experience suggests that a belief that one has not slept for long exerts a lowering effect on mood, but many people seem to be able to sleep for relatively short periods without any noticeable effect. Margaret Thatcher, while Prime Minister, was well known to sleep for only four or five hours each night, with no obvious lowering of mood, or other impairment of efficiency.

The aim of this research is to try to determine whether, in non-depressed people, there is a positive correlation between how long a person sleeps and how s/he feels. This involves collecting the following two items of data from a reasonably homogenous sample:

1   An estimate of the duration of sleep on the immediately preceding night
2   A self-assessment of mood.

Obtaining an accurate estimate of the duration of sleep shouldn't pose any problems – most people have a fair idea of what time they went to sleep and what time they woke up. For simplicity, exclude from the sample any individuals who say they woke during the night, so that you are only dealing with people who believe themselves to have enjoyed an unbroken night's sleep. The assessment of mood is somewhat more tricky. One approach would be to simply ask the members of the sample to estimate how 'good' their mood is by rating themselves on the dimension sad–happy, using a 10-point scale in order to force them to make a decision in one direction or the other. Thus 'extremely sad' would rate 0 and 'extremely happy' would rate 9.

Making the assumption that these two variables are related in a linear fashion (that is, if they are related at all), the extent of co-variation can be measured using the appropriate correlation coefficient. Of course it is always possible that these two variables are actually related in curvilinear fashion, in which case the shape of the relationship might show up on a scattergraph, but equally might not. You will have to decide for yourself.

If you want to pursue things further, one or two refinements suggest themselves. The reliability of the self-rating of mood could be improved if a simple 'mood scale' employing a number of different questions were used rather than a rating on a single dimension. The scale should be organized so that a high score indicates a 'good' mood, and a low score a 'bad' mood, and ideally should be evaluated for reliability and validity.

Secondly, you could widen the scope of the inquiry to include insomniacs and people suffering broken sleep patterns. Is there any relationship between the duration of episodes of wakefulness and mood? How does age influence any relationship – try comparing sleep and mood relations in a group of young adults and a group of older people. Is there a time-of-day effect – do the results change when you collect data in the morning as against the afternoon or evening? How might this be explained?

Project 4 Self-liking and liking of others

Research into the factors which influence the formation of friendships has shown that we tend to like people more if we believe they like us (Walster, Aronson, Abrahams and Rottman, 1966). This well-attested finding concerning reciprocal liking in turn raises the interesting question of whether people who like *themselves* also show more liking for others. This seems on the surface to be quite possible, since one could make a good argument for saying that self-liking (and hence high self-esteem) would be likely to help a person to tolerate the idiosyncrasies of others more readily than might otherwise be the case. However, the experience of everyday life suggests that the reverse is the case. In other words we tend to believe, on the basis of folk psychology, that a high level of self-liking goes with a strong tendency to look down on others. This is something which it might be possible to settle by empirical research.

To undertake this project you need first to develop adequate measures of the two variables – self-liking and liking of others – and then collect data on these from a sample which can then be correlated. There are obvious problems here to do with the reliability and validity of the measures, which I will not attempt to solve for you. The self-liking variable could be measured by asking how far (on a 10-point scale) the members of the sample feel they like themselves (or feel comfortable with themselves). If this seems to them to be too difficult you could ask them to estimate how far their actual self-liking differs from their 'ideal' self-liking (i.e. how much they would ideally like to like themselves, given the opportunity) – and again a 10-point scale could be used. Alternatively, you could try to think of questions for a 'self-liking' scale in order to assess levels of self-esteem in more detail. See chapter 3 for more information on how to set about designing such a scale.

Measuring the degree of liking of other people by the members of your sample needs to be done in a way that avoids any 'friendship effect'. That is, you don't want to measure a person's liking of any particular individual, but only of other individuals in general. One way of doing this is to construct a brief verbal description (about 150 words) of an imaginary person. This should be as general and non-specific as possible, covering matters such as appearance, behaviour and interests, and should especially not contain anything which is particularly striking, bizarre or unusual. Sample members can then be asked to read the description and then estimate, again on an appropriate scale, how much they believe they would like that person if they were to meet him or her.

REFERENCE

Walster, E., Aronson, E., Abrahams, D. and Rottman, L. (1966). Importance of physical attractiveness in dating behaviour. *Journal of Personality and Social Psychology, 4,* 508–16.

7 An Introduction to Inferential Statistics

This chapter provides an introduction to the process of using inferential statistics in order to test the hypotheses which are often generated in the course of a research project.

- It introduces the important ideas of probability and chance and distinguishes each from the other.

- It introduces and describes the normal distribution, and explains its relevance to inferential statistics in general.

- It gives a detailed picture of the process of hypothesis testing, and explains how decisions about hypotheses are made.

(Before you read this chapter you may find it helpful to have read those sections of chapter 3 which deal with the concepts of 'sample', 'population' and 'random sampling'.)

Introduction

As we have already seen in chapter 6, there are a number of techniques for summarizing and describing the data which may be generated by a research project. Such techniques are mostly simple and easy to use, and are extremely helpful to the researcher as he tries to build up a picture of what the data are telling him. However, although they certainly provide a necessary and useful first step in data analysis, they are also limited in what they are able to reveal. Because they are descriptive statistics they are only able to deal with the data as they stand, and thus cannot give more information than is already present in the numbers themselves. In psychology, though, we almost always want to be able to do more than simply use descriptive statistics to make succinct statements about the central tendency or dispersion of a given set of data. Psychologists collect numerical data because it is one way of describing and examining psychological processes which are not themselves directly accessible. We are, therefore, not so much interested in the numbers themselves, as in whatever information they may contain about such processes. Another way of putting this would be to say that psychologists, once they have collected some data, are less interested (in fact hardly at all) in what the numbers *are*, than in what they might *mean*. And, as you may have already realized, although the task of saying what the numbers *are* is easily accomplished by means of the various types of descriptive statistics, to say anything about what they might mean requires a quite different approach. It requires, in fact, the techniques of inferential statistics which form the substance of this chapter and of the ones which follow.

What are inferential statistics?

First, it may be helpful to approach the subject of inferential statistics by clarifying the meaning of the key word 'inferential', since it is this which divides this class of techniques from those called 'descriptive'. By way of definition, we can say that an inference is a conclusion or deduction made on the basis of some evidence or information, and so it follows that inferential statistics are procedures which can be used – by psychologists and others – to draw conclusions from data. In fact, there are two general kinds of question about the meaning of data which psychologists often need to answer, and which can be addressed by using inferential statistics.

The first of these questions concerns the relationship between a single sample of data (of any size), and the population from which it was taken. If a sample of data is viewed as an imperfect representation of the population, the question arises of whether it is possible to use the information in the sample to estimate a parameter, such as the mean of the population. That is, is it possible to start from the position of knowing only the sample mean and sample standard deviation and go on to say something about the population mean and standard deviation? As you can probably see, this is an important question, because it represents an attempt to assess the wider significance of the actual data which have been collected, and to go beyond what can be said about specific instances in order to make general statements.

Can it be done? It certainly can, by applying the procedure known to statisticians as **parameter estimation**. You will remember from what was said in chapter 6 that a statistic is defined as a value calculated from a **sample**, while a **parameter** is a similar value calculated from a **population**. Parameter estimation, therefore, refers to the statistical technique by which sample data can be made to generate an estimate (the key word) of one or more of the underlying population parameters, with inferential procedures used subsequently to find the degree of confidence which can be placed in that estimate.

However, though interesting and extremely important, this technique is perhaps not one which is needed by everyone who reads this book, and therefore further explanation and discussion on parameter estimation will be held over until chapter 8. For now, we will concern ourselves with the second, and much more widely used, application of inferential statistics in research – the statistical testing of hypotheses.

This application is required when a researcher (generally but not invariably one who has collected data by means of an experiment) may wish to compare one set of data with another. Given that some degree of difference between the sets is inevitable anyway, due to sampling error, the question arises of whether they are *so* different from each other that the difference is unlikely to be the result of random influences, but is more likely to be caused by whatever conditions were established in the experiment. Usually this question about difference is posed in the form of explicit hypotheses, as part of the formal structure of an investigation. Once the data are in, these hypotheses must be evaluated, and it is at this point that inferential statistics play a crucial role.

If you have already read the sections on the experimental method (chapters 1 and 5), you will appreciate the importance of being able to assess the meaning of data. It is, clearly, one thing to conduct an experiment and collect the data, and quite another to be able to determine what kind of an answer the experiment has delivered to your inquiry. Without some method for determining whether the independent variable has really influenced the dependent variable in the way you expected, you are left with data about whose meaning you are uncertain. Inferential statistics provides just such a method.

To summarize the immediately preceding paragraphs, we can say that there are two main applications for inferential statistics in psychology – parameter estimation and hypothesis testing. However, it should be emphasized that both uses arise from the same circumstance: that the data obtained through the application of a particular research method represents a sample from a population, and it is invariably the population and not the sample which interests the researcher. This point will emerge again and again as we look at the two ways of using inferential statistics in more detail.

You may also be wondering how it comes to be that inferential procedures can provide valid answers to these questions about population parameters and hypotheses. The answer, or at least a good part of it, lies with the notion of random sampling. All inferential statistics are based on mathematical models which incorporate the assumption that the sample data are obtained from a population by the process of random sampling which was described in chapter 3. As long as this fundamental assumption is justified, and data are obtained by a random or near random procedure, then inferential statistics can be used quite straightforwardly in order to make inferences from the data. On the other hand, if the sample is not a random one, then the problem of assessing hypotheses or estimating population parameters becomes much more problematic, involving techniques which lie well beyond the scope of this book.

The reason why the assumption of random sampling is so central to the process of making inferences lies in the mathematics of sampling theory. During the nineteenth century it was found that, given the assumption that sampling was random, then the relation between a population parameter, such as the population mean, and all possible sample means could be expressed mathematically in a formula. In other words, the relationship between a parameter and the same variable computed for all possible samples could be described in a way which was true for all populations and all possible samples from those populations, given the sole proviso that the sampling process was always random. Subsequently, this insight provided the basis for the various test statistics which were developed, some of which are described in this book.

The remainder of this chapter is concerned with describing the process and logic of hypothesis testing, which, as we have noted, relies on inferential statistics. I hope that by the end of the chapter you will have a clear idea of how its various components fit together, and, more importantly, why they appear as they do. These are extremely important and powerful ideas, and it is scarcely possible to do research of any kind in psychology without holding them in a reasonably sound grasp.

Before we get on to the main business of the chapter, though, we need to address some of the core concepts which will be needed later. These are, principally, the notions of probability and chance and the important idea of distribution, particularly the normal distribution.

Probability and Chance

What is probability?

Probability is an important idea to psychology, since, as you will see, it is the hook from which all inferential statistics hang. Its usefulness lies in the fact that it lets us look at the range of different kinds of events which might possibly occur, and (as long as we know something about them), go on to say something quite precise and clear about each one.

The basis of the concept of probability is the obvious truth that not all possible events are equally likely to happen. There is a gradient of likelihood running from those things, like death and taxes, that *are* certain, on to those which are highly likely, down to others less likely, and so on all the way down to those occurrences which are so very unlikely as to be virtually certain not to occur. The scoring of (say) more than twenty goals by one player in a Premier League football match might be regarded as falling into this last category!

This continuum of probabilities, which runs from things which are certain to occur down to those which are certain not to occur, can be given a numerical scale. This allows the idea that some events are more probable than others to be expressed with precision, and also permits probabilities to be calculated. Thus, events which are certain to occur are given a probability of 1 (written as p = 1.0), and those which lie at the other end of the continuum, and which are certain *not* to occur, are given a probability of zero (written p = 0.0). All intermediate events, which are neither certain to occur nor certain not to occur, are assigned a value between 1 and zero, with the size of the value reflecting how likely it is that the event will occur. The more probable events have larger values attached to them, and the less likely events have smaller values, but all lie somewhere between the extremes of 1 and zero.

This means, then, that any event for which the probability is p = 0.75 is one which is more likely to happen than an event for which the probability is only p = 0.25. Similarly, an event with a probability of p = 0.50 has exactly a 50–50 chance of taking place, and the probability of p = 0.001 refers to an extremely small probability (of only 1 chance in 1000) that the event referred to will actually take place.

As we have demonstrated, this convention gives a way of expressing with any required degree of precision the probability of occurrence of any event, no matter how uncertain the actual event may itself be. The only proviso is, of course, that we should have sufficient information to be able to calculate the probability in the first place. After all, there is no value in assigning the (quite high) probability of p = 0.75 to winning a new car in a raffle, if that assessment of the probability is not based on information about how many tickets were sold, and the conditions under which the draw is to be held. If there are only four tickets for that draw, and you hold three of them, and, moreover, it is to be an absolutely fair draw, then the probability that you will win the car will indeed be p = 0.75. If, on the other hand, several hundred thousand tickets have been sold, and the draw is to take place somewhere in Central America, then I would say that the probability of your winning the car is not p = 0.75, but something infinitesimally small.

The key point is that the assessment of a probability must be based on information which enables the probability to be more than just a wild guess; otherwise it is simply worthless. In statistics, the basis of estimates of probabilities is largely provided by the normal distribution, which we will discuss in a moment. First, though, we need to spend a few moments to distinguish the concept of probability from the idea of chance, with which it is often confused.

Chance

The concept of chance is closely related to the idea of probability and is sometimes (and incorrectly) used interchangeably with it. However, although the concept of chance is, like probability, a key one in statistics, it is important to try to keep the two entirely separated in your mind. Essentially, the difference between chance and probability is this. As we have seen, the **probability** of an event refers to the likelihood, however remote it may be, of that event taking place. **Chance**, on the other hand, is that random influence on events which results in one event occurring rather than another.

For example, suppose you have a box containing equal numbers of black and white balls. If you close your eyes and pull out a ball at random, you have an equal probability of pulling out a black one as of pulling out a white one. The **probabilities** of both events are the same, i.e. $p = 0.50$.

However, if your eyes are closed, so that you cannot make a deliberate choice, what is it that influences whether you get a black or a white ball? The answer is that it is chance. If both possible outcomes were initially equally probable, and your choice is really completely undirected (because you have your eyes closed), then only chance (or randomness) could have influenced the result. Balls are not capable of jumping out of bags by themselves.

To sum up the discussion so far, while probability assesses the likelihood of any particular outcome (such as drawing a white ball) from the entire range of possibilities, chance provides an explanation of why only one from a number of equally possible events is actually observed. This explains why, in statistics, we sometimes link the two concepts and speak of the probability of something happening by chance (as in '. . . the probability of obtaining the results (of an experiment) by chance alone was $p = 0.05$'). In saying this we are simply assigning a numerical value to the probability that a particular event was the result of random (or undirected) influences.

Expressing the idea of a probability 'greater or less than'

In psychology we often want to express the idea not simply of an exact probability (such as, say, a probability of precisely $p = 0.8$), but of a probability which is greater or less than some limit. For example, it is often necessary in psychology to refer to a probability which is less than $p = 0.05$, while not being able to say exactly how much less. This can be done by using the signs $>$ and $<$ (the 'greater than' and 'less than' symbols), either alone or in combination with the 'equals' sign in order to express the idea of 'equal to or greater than', and 'equal to or less than'. Using these symbols, one can express the idea that, for example, the probability of an event is something less than one in a hundred by writing $p < 0.01$. Similarly, an event with a probability which is equal to or more than 8 chances in 10 can be written as $p \geq 0.8$, and so on for any other level of probability you need to express. Note, though, that when a probability is expressed in this way, it simply sets a boundary on the probability continuum, with the event in question lying above or below that boundary. The question of exactly how far above or below is always left open, often because it simply is not known. This indeed will be the case when you encounter this way of expressing probability again a little later in connection with significance levels and the region of rejection.

That is all we need to say about probability and chance for the moment, although as we have said the concepts underpin virtually the whole of the statistics in the remainder of the book. Now we need to move on to consider the normal distribution, which, as we said a little earlier, provides the basis for the assessment of probabilities in much psychological research.

The Normal Distribution

What is the normal distribution?

A **distribution** in statistics is, as we noted earlier, the name given to any set of data values or scores once they have been organized in a way which enables the 'shape' of the data to be seen. As we also saw in chapter 6, one useful approach to constructing a distribution is to count the number of times each different score value occurs in the data, and to use that information to construct a distribution called a **frequency distribution** (so called because it is based on the number of times, or frequencies with which, different values occur).

The idea of a distribution of frequencies provides the basis for an important theoretical distribution called the normal distribution. Before we move on to consider the very useful and intriguing properties of this distribution in any detail, let's look first at why it is so important.

First, the distribution of a great many variables in nature can be shown to approximate closely to the shape of this distribution. For example, the distribution of height in the human population, when plotted from a sufficiently large sample, turns out to be close to normal in form. And, although this cannot be verified with certainty because of the difficulties of measurement, this is probably also true of the measurements made of psychological variables, such as intelligence test scores, or reaction times. It seems that the concept of the normal distribution gives us a powerful way of describing the distribution of many variables in nature. (The reason it is said that they 'approximate to' rather than exactly match the normal distribution is that a normal distribution describes a very large population indeed, whose properties have been established on the basis of statistical theory. However, when 'real' data have been collected, they necessarily constitute a sample from the population. Consequently, even though the values in the population may be perfectly normally distributed, the distribution of a sample can only *approach* normality. The closeness of a sample distribution to the theoretical model is always influenced by, among other factors, the size of the sample and the nature of the sampling procedure employed. For the former, large samples produce better approximations to the underlying distribution, since there is a greater probability of including a fully representative set of values in the sample. For the latter, a truly random sampling procedure is needed in order to minimize the inevitable influence of sampling error on the sample data.)

Secondly, there is the rather more technical, but no less interesting, fact that so long as sampling is random, and the sample reasonably large, then even if the population from which the data are drawn is non-normal itself, and though the scores in the sample may include the effects of various sources of random error, the distribution of the mean of the scores (called the sampling distribution of the mean), will *still* be close to normality. Moreover, the *larger* the size of the samples, the *closer* that distribution will approach to normal. This fact provides (among other things) the basis for the technique of parameter estimation which is dealt with in the next chapter. It is also responsible for the very great interest which psychologists show in the normal distribution, since the data with which they have to work are often drawn from populations whose characteristics are only partly known.

Thirdly (and this remains to be explained fully), the unique properties of the normal distribution mean that it offers a way of assigning probabilities to score values, so that the relationship between sample data and their parent population can be clearly expressed. This, as we have already noted, is a major gain: particularly in psychology it is only rarely that a researcher enjoys access to an entire population of interest.

Taking these three points together, you may, I hope, begin to get a sense of why the normal distribution is so central to the statistics used in psychological research and why it is necessary to explore its properties in more detail, as we shall now do.

The normal distribution

The normal distribution is depicted by graphing probability against score value. However, it is important to keep in mind that the normal distribution is a *purely theoretical* distribution obtained by plotting theoretically obtained probabilities (rather than 'real' ones obtained by sampling) across the whole range of possible values from minus infinity to plus infinity along the horizontal (x) axis. This produces a graph which bears a family resemblance to the symmetrical bell-shape shown in figure 7.1.

As we shall see in a minute, the normal distribution is really a family of distributions (hence the reference above to the family resemblance among different normal distributions). However, each and every normal distribution, whatever its precise shape, always possesses the following four important features, two of which (nos 1 and 3) you can clearly see in the distribution in figure 7.1:

1   The distribution is perfectly symmetrical about its mean, which therefore divides the area under the curve exactly in half.
2   The mean, the median and the mode of the distribution are equal. The arithmetic average is equal to the central value in the distribution which in turn is equal to the most frequently occurring value.
3   The tails of the distribution extend out in both directions to touch the horizontal (x) axis of the graph only at infinity. This means that they should be thought of as continuing forever, growing closer and closer to the x axis without ever touching it, although, of course, it is impossible to represent this in any of the figures.
4   The total area under the curve is one unit (or, put another way, the area under the curve includes all the possible values which the variable may take.) Consequently, the area under the curve can be precisely subdivided, and any given proportion of the total area (such as 5%, 10% or 50%), can

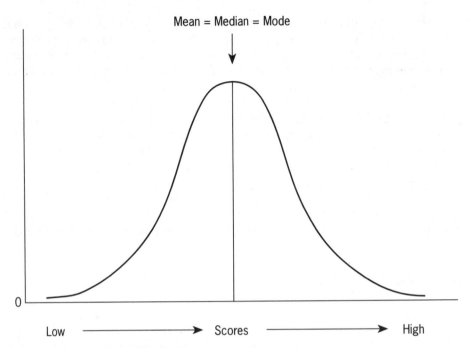

Figure 7.1 The normal distribution

be used as a statement of the probability (p = 0.05, p = 0.1 or p = 0.5) that a score value will be observed to lie within that area.

These features are responsible for much of the family resemblance among normal distributions which we noted above. However, there is one further point of similarity, which is found in all normal distributions, and which provides the basis for the determination of probabilities in inferential statistics. This arises out of the relationship between the shape of a normal distribution and the standard deviation of the data which it represents. (You will remember from chapter 6 that the standard deviation of a set of scores is a measure of the dispersion of the scores about the mean, measured in the same units as the scores themselves.)

Standard deviation and the normal distribution

Consider figure 7.1 again. There, the scale on the horizontal (x) axis of the normal distribution represents raw score values, with the mean, median and mode occupying the central point on the scale. However, the x axis can also be calibrated in units of standard deviation, each of which is equal to some number of raw score units. So, on a distribution with a mean of 100, and a standard deviation of 15 raw score units, 1 unit of standard deviation equals 15 raw score units, 2 standard deviation units equals 30 raw score units, and

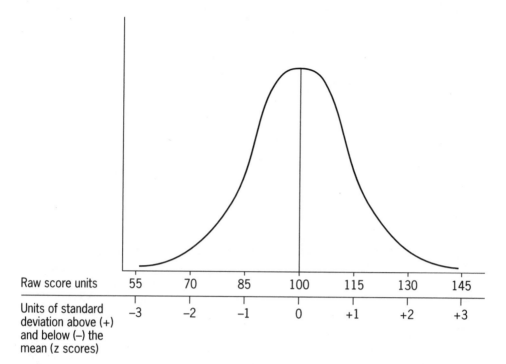

Raw score units	55	70	85	100	115	130	145
Units of standard deviation above (+) and below (–) the mean (z scores)	–3	–2	–1	0	+1	+2	+3

Figure 7.2   A normal distribution with a mean of 100 and standard deviation of 15

The horizontal (x) axis shows the relation of raw score units to units of standard deviation (z scores).

so on. To illustrate the relationship, figure 7.2 shows a normal distribution with the x axis calibrated in both raw score units, and in units of standard deviation (more usually called z scores) from the mean.

This relationship between raw scores values and standard deviation in the normal distribution turns out to be a very interesting and powerful one. If the x axis of a distribution is calibrated in terms of standard deviation (z score) units, rather than raw score units, we find that any given area under the curve (i.e. the area between the line of the curve and any two points on the x axis) can be determined easily if we use the z score to locate the boundaries of the area to be established. And – an even more powerful and useful feature – the area under the curve between any two points on the x axis is always the same from one normal distribution to another, no matter what the precise shape of any particular normal distribution might be. These areas under the curve are depicted in figure 7.3, which shows a normal distribution, with the various areas under the curve marked off by points on the x axis in increments of one unit of z score (standard deviation) above and below the mean.

From figure 7.3, you can see how the area under the normal distribution curve can be subdivided into fixed and predictable proportions in relation to the z scores on the x axis. So, the area lying from 1 z score below the mean

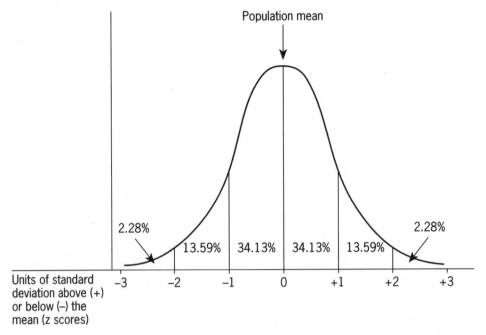

Figure 7.3 The normal distribution showing how the total area under the curve is divided in relation to units of standard deviation

up to 1 z score above is shown to represent 68.26% (2 × 34.13%) of the total area under the curve, and this is not only true for this particular normal distribution but also for all others, whatever their precise outline. Similarly, the area lying between 2 standard deviation units above and below the mean (from z score −2 up to +2) will always contain 95.44% (2 × [34.13% + 13.59%]) of the total, and the remaining 4.56% [2 × 2.28%] of the total area will always lie at the extreme ends of the curve outside, respectively, 2 units of z score above and below the mean.

What isn't immediately clear from the figure is that it is not necessary only to use the area under the curve which is bounded by any of the whole-number 'landmark' points on the x axis. In fact, the area between *any* intermediate values of standard deviation can also be found by reading the required value from the table of areas under the normal curve in appendix 5 (table 2). For example, suppose we wish to find the area of the region under the curve lying between 0.75 standard deviation units below the mean and 1.86 standard deviation units above it. How do we proceed? Consult table 2, noting that in the table the standard deviation units are referred to as 'z scores', and simply run your eyes down the column labelled 'z' until you come to the z score value you require to the first decimal place, then read across until you find the column headed with the value of the second decimal place. The value given in the cell at the intersection represents the proportion of the area under the curve lying between the point on the x axis indicated by the z score and the mean.

Thus, from the table,

Area from the mean down to 0.75 standard deviation units = .2734
Area from the mean up to 1.86 standard deviation units   = .4686
Proportion of the total area between these two points   = .7420 or
                                                           74.2%

The fact that the relationship between standard deviation units and proportions of area under the curve is a general property of all normal distributions, whatever their precise shape may be, renders the normal distribution an extremely useful tool for the researcher. Because, as we have seen, the different proportions of the area under the curve can be found by reference to particular points on the x axis scale of standard deviation units (z scores), and because that scale is the same for every normal distribution, it means that, given knowledge of the raw score values of the mean and standard deviation of the distribution, it is possible to say what area under the curve lies between any two values of z score. By itself, of course, this is not particularly interesting: the real pay-off lies in the next step. As we shall see in the next chapter, given the proportional area under the curve it then becomes possible to make statements of probability concerning the different values in the distribution. That is, we can say how likely it is that any given score value on the distribution will be achieved.

For the moment, we need to set this extremely useful idea to one side, and consider one final general truth about the normal distribution. It is that differently shaped normal distributions, no matter how different they may be, differ in only two rather limited respects:

- **They may differ in their mean value. This affects their position on the x axis.**
- **They may differ in their standard deviation. This affects their width, and because the area under the curve is fixed at one unit, their height also.**

Figure 7.4 shows three different (but equally normal) curves of different heights and different values of standard deviation drawn on the same x axis. The important point is that whatever their precise shape they are all equally normal, and therefore all possess exactly the same useful properties.

This completes our exploration of the properties of the normal distribution, at least for the moment. We return to consider its role in the process of parameter estimation (that is, relating sample data to its underlying population) in the next chapter, and if what has been said so far has whetted your appetite, you can certainly jump ahead to continue working on the normal distribution.

The next section of this chapter, however, takes us in a slightly different direction, into the field of hypothesis testing. This, as you will no doubt remember, was the second use for inferential statistics mentioned earlier. Here again, as you will see, some knowledge of the normal distribution proves to be absolutely central to seeing how the procedures of hypothesis testing work, and how the various test statistics which they employ are able to generate such useful insights into data.

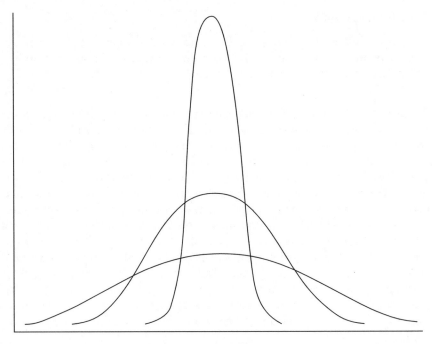

Figure 7.4   Three normal distributions with identical means plotted against the same scales to show the relationship between standard deviation and the shape of the curve

Hypothesis Testing Using Inferential Statistics

In this section of the chapter we look in some detail at the concepts and process involved in hypothesis testing.

The two types of statistical hypothesis – the null and alternate – are described, and their roles are explained.

The process of making a decision about hypotheses is presented from two perspectives: a surface level description which outlines the process, and a deeper level which explores the logic and rationale of the process.

Key terms and concepts including 'directional' and 'non-directional' hypotheses, 'significance level', and 'type 1' and 'type 2 decision errors' are explained.

Introduction

You will recall that the notion of hypotheses first made its appearance, in chapter 1, in the discussion on the process of scientific research, where it was said that they play a central role in process of generating new scientific knowledge.

Hypotheses are essentially predictions made about the outcome of an investigation before any data have been collected, and they therefore represent statements about what findings are expected. The fact that they are, in principle at least, formulated on the basis of what a theory predicts rather than descriptions of what has already been found, means that they play an important role in the testing and evaluation of theories. If the prediction in a hypothesis is shown to be correct, then that strengthens the theory on which it is based. Conversely, any prediction which turns out to be incorrect has the effect of weakening the theory, and this, if repeated sufficiently, can result in the theory eventually being discredited.

In chapter 7, we also said that hypotheses can be either non-statistical (associated with qualitative research and with general predictions derived from a theory), or statistical (making very precise predictions, and used in the analysis of quantitative data). It is with the latter type, which can be tested and evaluated by using inferential statistics, that we are now concerned.

To see why this is so, consider how the need for the testing of these precise statistical hypotheses comes about. As we have seen earlier, scientific research begins with the construction of hypotheses which predict, on the basis of theory, what the results of the investigation will be. Suppose, then, that an investigation (which might be an experiment, but need not be), is carried out in which two sets of data are collected, representing behaviour under two different conditions. The hypothesis, constructed before the collection of data, will assert that a difference is expected between the two conditions, and the whole point of the investigation is to see whether this prediction is upheld when the data are examined. After data have been collected the next step is, therefore, to decide whether or not the difference between the two sets of data can be attributed to the effects of the experiment, and thus whether the statement made in the hypothesis is correct or not.

However, the problem, as we pointed out earlier, is that a visual inspection alone will not be enough to permit a sound decision to be made. Because human behaviour is highly complex and variable, and because of the difficulties of attaining accurate measurement of variables by the techniques available, the possibility *always* exists, even in a tightly controlled experiment, that any differences which can be seen in the data merely reflect chance or random influences, rather than the straightforward effect of one variable on another. Moreover, to one person's eye such differences might appear quite large, while to another they might appear so small as to be insignificant. Clearly, then, if a sound decision is to be made, more needs to be done than simple inspection of the data. What is needed is some way of making more objective the process of determining whether the prediction is upheld by the data.

The hypotheses

The solution is to construct two hypotheses before the data collection begins. These are called the **null hypothesis** and the **alternate** (or **experimental**)

hypothesis, and their function is to express, as clearly and concisely as can be done, alternative statements about differences between parameters of the population from which samples are to be taken. (Note: The term 'alternate hypothesis' is the generic name for the hypothesis which acts as the alternative to the 'null hypothesis'. 'Experimental hypothesis' is the name sometimes given to the alternate hypothesis when the investigation in question is really an experiment. If in doubt, 'alternate hypothesis' is always correct.)

At this point, you may be wondering why hypotheses should concern themselves with the existence (or not) of differences between population parameters? Surely in the light of what was said earlier, they should really concern themselves with possible differences between the samples?

The reason why they don't do this is quite straightforward. Remember the point made at the beginning of this chapter, that we are generally interested in sample data only to the extent that it can tell us about the population from which it was taken. We are, as we said, really not very interested in the sample as such, but in the population which lies behind it. A difference between (say) the means of two sample sets of data is largely trivial considered in isolation. However, we wish to use that difference to say something about the population – specifically, to say whether the discovery of a difference between the means of the sample sets indicates that the same difference would be found in the population if it were possible to test it in its entirety. It follows from this that hypotheses must really be concerned with making statements about the population(s) lying behind the sample data rather than with the samples themselves although, of course, only the sample data are accessible to be worked on.

Consequently, when data analysis takes place in an investigation, such as a simple two-condition experiment, it is done in order to compare estimates of a population parameter obtained (in this case) under two different conditions. As you can probably see already, only two results of this comparison are possible. Either the two parameters will be found to be the same, or they will be found to be different. So, it follows that the hypotheses appropriate to this experiment need to be formulated to express both of these possibilities, stating on the one hand that there is no difference between the population parameters, and on the other, that there is such a difference. The former is, of course, the null hypothesis of the investigation, while the latter is the alternate (or experimental) hypothesis.

What exactly do these hypotheses look like? We have already said that they need to be concise and to express alternative possibilities about the parameters of the population. We need now to examine them a little more closely.

The null hypothesis

The null hypothesis always makes a statement of no (null) difference between the values of a population parameter. Very frequently, especially when data are to be generated by an experiment, the parameter in question will be the mean or median value of a variable. The null hypothesis in this case will state that there is no difference between the mean (or median) of the variable in the different populations sampled.

The comparison between population means or medians is, however, only one among several possibilities. Other methods of data collection may mean that a comparison between other parameters is required in the hypotheses, and in these cases also, the null hypothesis should similarly express a hypothesis of nil difference. For example, the null hypothesis appropriate for a correlational study might assert that no difference exists between the population correlation coefficient and a coefficient of zero. If, on the other hand, a chi-squared test of goodness of fit is contemplated, the null hypothesis should state that no difference exists between the distribution of frequencies in the population, and that predicted by theory. Whatever the statistic used, the null hypothesis should always assert that no difference is to be expected. Further examples of null hypotheses can be found in the worked examples of the test statistics in chapter 9.

The alternate (experimental) hypothesis

The alternate hypothesis, so called because it provides the alternative to the null hypothesis, is a hypothesis of difference. That is, it always makes exactly the opposite statement about two values of a population parameter to that made by the null hypothesis, by saying that there *is* a difference between them.

It is probably unnecessary to give a full list of examples of the alternate hypotheses since you simply have to reverse the sense of the null hypothesis, and it is quite difficult to get it wrong. As long as the null hypothesis is correctly expressed, the alternate hypothesis is likely to be correct also. However, to make quite certain this important point is clear we'll look again at an example. It was said earlier that if a correlational study is to be carried out, the appropriate null hypothesis might assert that no difference exists between the population correlation coefficient and a coefficient of zero. It follows from what has been said that the complementary alternate hypothesis for the correlation coefficient must be that a difference exists between the population value and zero. The same principle can be followed to produce the alternate hypotheses to match all other forms of the null hypothesis.

Hypotheses, then, always come in pairs – one null with one complementary alternate, with each making a very precise and unambiguous statement about the population values which can later be tested using the actual results obtained in an investigation. It follows that hypotheses, of both sorts, need to be written very carefully, as it must be possible to say with absolute certainty which of the pair is confirmed by the data and which is not.

To help you in the writing of your hypotheses, you may find it helpful to have the following examples available. Suppose you are designing a simple independent subjects experiment which aims to investigate the question of whether teenage males who succeed on an experimental task subsequently show greater self-esteem than those who fail. The IV in this case is the subjects' success or failure on the task (for the sake of the example we'll assume that an inconclusive result on the task is the equivalent of failure), and the DV is the level of self-esteem in the subjects as measured by an appropriate psycho-metric test. The population of interest, on which the hypotheses focus, consists of males aged between 13 and 20 years. The hypotheses appropriate to this investigation would therefore be:

Alternate hypothesis   Among teenage males, the mean level of self-esteem is lower for those who have failed at an experimental task than the mean level for those who have succeeded.
Null hypothesis   Among teenage males, the mean level of self-esteem is the same for those who have failed at an experimental task as for those who have succeeded.

Notice that the hypotheses above are expressed in terms of the variables with which the investigation is most directly concerned. In an experiment such as the example, both hypotheses should always be couched in terms of the possible effect of changes to the value of the independent variable (success or failure at the experimental task) on the dependent variable (self-esteem). Similarly, in other kinds of investigation, such as observational research, in which hypotheses are to be tested, the hypotheses themselves should always be formed around the variable(s) which are to be measured. This is important, because unless they are, the data will not be able to provide a basis for testing the hypothesis. You can certainly compute a test statistics, and make a decision about hypotheses, but it will be a largely empty exercise because the essential connection between the data and the hypotheses will not exist.

The hypotheses as a decision framework

The null and the alternate hypotheses are complementary in the sense that they express alternative possibilities which cannot both be true. One states that there is no difference between the parameters, while the other says that there is. However, it is important to realize that they do not have equal standing. For the purposes of a hypothesis test we start by assuming the null hypothesis to be true. We then build up the test on this assumption. If the experimental evidence shows this assumption was not well founded, we can reject the null hypothesis and accept the alternate hypothesis. If, however, there is not suffi-cient evidence to reject the null hypothesis, then we can only report that there was not enough evidence to permit the rejection of the null hypothesis and therefore the alternate hypothesis was not supported. Notice that strictly speaking we do not simply 'accept' the null hypothesis in this situation: rather, we are unable to accept the alternate hypothesis on the basis of the available data, and so we 'fail to reject' the null hypothesis. In other words, the null hypothesis represents the default position to which we revert if we are unable to find a clear reason for positively accepting the alternate hypothesis. To summarize, in deciding about hypotheses, the decision is made as follows:

- If, and only if, the evidence is sufficiently strong, the alternate hypothesis may be accepted, and the null hypothesis rejected.
- In all other cases (i.e. when the evidence is not sufficiently strong), the alternate hypothesis is not supported, and you 'fail to reject' the null hypothesis.

This seems straightforward but, as we have already noted, it is complicated by the fact that the various forms of error in the data almost always ensure that there is *some* difference to be seen between the values being compared. 'Just looking' under such circumstances will lead to the prediction of the alternate hypothesis being accepted as correct and the null rejected, when, possibly, the data do not really justify that decision.

An example may make this clearer. Suppose that in the course of research into the effect which different kinds of textual organization have on comprehension, it was found that the ability to comprehend text was not significantly affected by the two different ways of organizing information which were being studied. There was a difference between the data obtained from the conditions in the experiment, but the statistical test indicated that it was so small that it was very unlikely to have been the result of the experimental manipulations. The researcher therefore concluded that there was insufficient evidence to justify rejection of the null hypothesis (that no difference exists in the ability to comprehend text when it is organized in two different ways), and consequently the null hypothesis was retained.

The point of this is that the null hypothesis was not rejected even though some degree of difference existed between the data in the two conditions. Even though a difference was there, it was not large enough to justify accepting the alternate hypothesis, and so the null hypothesis could not be rejected.

You will probably have noticed that we have subtly changed the form in which the question is put to the data. Instead of simply asking whether there is a difference in the data (indicating a difference between parameters), we ask instead whether there is a difference which is *so large* as to justify the rejection of the null hypothesis (and therefore the consequent acceptance of the alternate hypothesis). If the answer is 'yes', we can accept the alternate hypothesis and reject the null, while if it is 'no' we fail to reject the null hypothesis on the ground that the difference, though present, is no greater than could be expected if it were due to random influences.

But we encounter a problem. Given that we have to make a decision about hypotheses, while focusing on the magnitude of the difference rather than on its presence or absence, we still need some kind of criterion against which the decision can be made. We need a way of deciding whether a given difference is large enough to justify accepting the alternate hypothesis. This is an important consideration because the size of a difference alone is not necessarily a good guide to whether the alternate hypothesis should be accepted. Even quite a large difference between two sets of data could still be due to random factors, and could therefore, if taken at face value, lead to the alternate hypothesis being accepted as true, when in fact it is the null hypothesis which is really correct.

The way around this problem, which provides the required standard, is to apply the concept of probability, in the form of a **significance level**, to the decision process. This enters the decision as part of a test statistic, and is only really meaningful in that context, although in what follows we will deal with the two parts of the process separately.

The concept of statistical significance

As we have seen, when we are testing hypotheses we are in the position of wanting to express the idea that a difference (for example between two sample means) may be so great that it is unlikely, at some level of probability, to have occurred by chance, but may instead be the result of one variable influencing another. The notion of statistical significance enables us to express just such an idea, since to say that a difference is 'statistically significant' is to say that it is so great as to be unlikely to have occurred by chance alone. Notice, though, that in referring to the statistical significance (or otherwise) of any particular difference it is not enough simply to say that it is 'unlikely' to have occurred by chance. For such a statement to be useful we also need to be able to assign to it a specific level of probability which says exactly how unlikely the difference might be: this is called the significance level.

The significance level enters the decision process with the test statistic and is that point on the scale of probabilities (ranging from 0 to 1), chosen by the researcher, which sets the risk of wrongly rejecting the null hypothesis due to sampling variability. You will remember that the two hypotheses in an investigation express the two alternative possibilities which could arise from a comparison between population parameters. We also said that it was inevitable, due to sampling error, that some degree of difference would be found, and this is exactly where the idea of significance level becomes important. What it does is to help with the decision about whether the observed difference is great enough to permit the alternate hypothesis to be accepted. It does this by specifying a probability of obtaining a misleadingly large difference in the data even though the null hypothesis is correct. Or more clearly, for any particular test, the significance level sets the maximum acceptable probability of rejecting the null hypothesis (because the difference in the data is large), *when in fact it is true and should not have been rejected.*

If this seems difficult, as well it may, I hope the following illustration will make things clearer. Suppose a researcher has decided to adopt a significance level of $p = 0.05$ for the analysis of some data. This indicates that *in this particular case* the researcher has decided that the maximum desired probability of making the wrong decision about the hypotheses and rejecting the null hypothesis when it is true should be no more than 5 in 100. Any lower probability of the incorrect rejection of the null hypothesis of, say, 4 in 100, *will* be acceptable, but a greater probability, even of 6 in 100 ($p = 0.06$) will not. The significance level sets the boundary between what is and is not an acceptable risk.

The level of significance which is to be used in any particular investigation can in theory take any value between 0 and 1. However, the values which are chosen will naturally lie close to zero, since the aim is always to have the smallest possible risk of wrongly rejecting the null hypothesis. The $p = 0.05$, or more exceptionally, $p = 0.01$ levels are therefore the most commonly used in behavioural research, although researchers in other disciplines, such as medicine, may routinely use even smaller values such as $p = 0.001$ (i.e. 1 in 1000 of incorrectly rejecting the null hypothesis) as their criterion. The important point is that whatever the level of probability chosen for the significance level, its function is always to specify the probability of the null hypothesis being incorrectly rejected.

You may be wondering at this point just how the important decision about hypotheses is made. True, we have said that there will be some kind of comparison involving the data, and, as we have just seen, the significance level chosen will state the probability of wrongly rejecting the null hypothesis, but there is still a gap in the picture to be filled. This space is occupied by information about the role of the various test statistics. How are these used to make decisions about hypotheses?

Decisions about hypotheses

We will approach the question of how decisions about hypotheses are made from two perspectives. The first, more general one, provides a description at the surface level, listing the different elements which make up the decision process. The second will look beneath the surface of some of those elements to explain the key principles on which a decision on hypotheses is arrived at. (Note that, in the interest of providing an overview which is as little encumbered by detail as possible, some of the ideas referred to, such as 'region of rejection', are not fully explained when they first appear. They are, however, dealt with later in the chapter, when the background ideas are explained. To get a full understanding of the process of hypothesis testing it is, of course, necessary to read both the overview and the more detailed explanations which follow. In addition, information about hypotheses and the role they play in the scientific process can be found in chapter 1, and information on test statistics in chapter 9.)

The seven stages of hypothesis testing

The process of hypothesis testing can be divided into seven separate stages. Note that all these stages up to, but of course not including the computation of a value for the test statistic, should always be completed before any data are collected. They are:

1 State the null hypothesis.
2 Specify the alternate hypothesis.

3   Select the test to be used.
4   Decide the significance level.
5   Determine the rejection region and find the critical value.
6   Calculate the test statistic.
7   Make a decision about hypotheses and draw a conclusion.

1   State the null hypothesis
The first step, before all others, is to specify the null hypothesis, since this describes the default result of the comparison. This, as we have seen, must assert that there is a relationship of equality (or null difference) between population parameters.

2   Specify the alternate hypothesis
The alternate hypothesis should state that there will be a difference between population parameters. If, as is likely, the direction of the expected difference is known (i.e. the theory says that one parameter will be greater than the other), then a one-tailed region of rejection is required at stage 5: if not, then a two-tailed region of rejection is indicated. See below for more information about the 'region of rejection', especially in the section headed 'The sampling distribution of the test statistic'.

3   Select the test to be used
Guidance on finding the right test for your data is to be found at the beginning of chapter 9: nothing more needs to be said about this now.

4   Decide the significance level to be used
As we have seen, the significance level sets the probability of accepting the alternate hypothesis when the null hypothesis is true. A level of $p = 0.05$ is generally regarded as appropriate, although exceptionally, a significance level of $p = 0.01$ may be used.

5   Determine the region of rejection and find the critical value
If the alternate hypothesis specifies an expected direction of difference between the two parameters, then the region of rejection is one-tailed, corresponding to that proportion of the most extreme end of the distribution of the test statistic identified by the significance level. Thus, a one-tailed significance level of $p = 0.05$ identifies a one-tailed region of rejection corresponding to the most extreme 5% of the distribution.

On the other hand, if no direction of difference is specified, then the region of rejection is two-tailed, and corresponds, for a significance level of $p = 0.05$, with the top 2.5% and the bottom 2.5% of the distribution.

Use the appropriate table in appendix 5 to determine the critical value for the required sample size and significance level and define the rejection region. Demonstrations of this stage can be found among the worked examples in chapter 9.

6   Calculate the test statistic
Once the data have been collected and the test statistic computed, compare it with the critical value to find out whether or not the computed value lies within the region of rejection of the distribution.

7 Make a decision about the hypotheses and draw a conclusion

Finally, make the decision. If the computed value of the test statistic turns out to lie in the rejection region, i.e. to be more extreme than the critical value in the appropriate table, you can reject the null hypothesis and accept the alternate hypothesis on the ground that the probability of obtaining the test statistic by chance is no greater than the significance level.

Another example will help show how this works out in practice. Suppose a researcher is interested in whether, when a particular test of creativity is used, male students can be shown to be more creative than female students, and having designed the sampling procedure and other features of the investigation, is almost ready to collect some data. First, though, she has to state her hypotheses, and run through the list of other preliminaries to hypothesis testing. (The numbers refer to the stages in hypothesis testing as listed above.)

1   The null hypothesis is that within the population of students, there will be no difference in the median creativity test scores of males and females.
2   The one-tailed alternate hypothesis is that within the same population the median test scores of males will be higher than those of females.
3   As the creativity test generates ordinal data, she correctly chooses the Mann-Whitney test as appropriate.
4   The significance level of $p = 0.05$ will be used.
5   The one-tailed rejection region consists of all values of U which are so small that their associated probability under the null hypothesis is $p = 0.05$ or less, corresponding to the extreme 5% of the distribution of the test statistic. The null hypothesis will therefore be rejected if the critical value of the test statistic falls within this region.
    The one-tailed critical values for the Mann-Whitney U at the $p = 0.05$ significance level can be found in table 6 in appendix 5.
6   Having completed these stages, the researcher collects the data and computes a value for the Mann-Whitney U statistic.
7   Finally, she makes a decision on the hypotheses. If the computed value of U is equal to or less than the table value then it lies within the region of rejection and she can reject the null hypothesis at the 5% level of significance. This means that the difference between the median creativity scores of males and females is so great as to be unlikely ($p \leq 0.05$) to have occurred by chance, and she may conclude that there is a significant tendency for males to score more highly than females on this creativity test.
    If, on the other hand, she finds that the computed value of U is greater than the critical value in the table, then because the computed value lies outside the region of rejection, she must fail to reject the null hypothesis, and reject instead the alternate hypothesis on the ground that the probability of obtaining the computed value by chance is greater than the significance level. Her conclusion in this case is that there is insufficient evidence to show that males and females differ.

To summarize, the process of making a decision about hypotheses rests on a comparison between the value of the test statistic (computed from data), and the critical value obtained from the appropriate table. The result of the comparison indicates whether the null hypothesis can be rejected. If the comparison indicates that the computed value is so extreme as to lie in an area of the distribution of the test statistic called the 'region of rejection' (and hence can be regarded as unlikely to have occurred by chance), then the null hypothesis can be rejected. Conversely, if this proves not to be the case, because the computed value lies outside the region of rejection, then the null hypothesis must be retained.

Decisions on hypotheses: the view beneath the surface

The description above is concerned mostly with what happens on the surface when a decision has to be made about hypotheses, and for many users of this book this may be enough information. There is, however, a further layer of explanation below this surface view which deals with how the tables of critical values of the test statistics (mentioned at step 5) permit a decision to be made. The explanation of this involves the normal distribution, which we encountered earlier, and which we now meet again in the form of the 'sampling distribution of a test statistic'.

The sampling distribution of a test statistic

You will see when you get to chapter 8 that a sampling distribution is obtained when a statistic, such as the mean or standard deviation, is computed for each one of a large number of random samples from the same population and then those values are plotted as a frequency distribution. Sampling distributions, however, do not only exist for descriptive statistics, such as the mean or standard deviation; they also exist, with known characteristics, for each of the test statistics. This means that providing that the assumptions underlying the test statistic have been satisfied in sampling, the features of the sampling distribution can be used to make various inferences about the data. Most usefully, it becomes possible to talk about the probability of observing any particular range of values of a statistic, because, as we said earlier, it is possible to translate the concept of areas under the curve into statements of probability about different ranges of values of a statistic. The logic of this process is described in detail in the section on the standard normal distribution in the next chapter, and if you are curious to know how it is done you should read that section before continuing. All you need to know at this moment to make sense of what follows is that it is not only possible to use the values on the horizontal (x) axis of a normal curve to work out intervals and their proportions of the area under the curve, but also to say that those same intervals have a probability of occurrence in the distribution which is the same as the proportion of the area under the curve which they identify. Thus, for example, the interval on the x axis which represents the top 5% of the area under the curve (that is, the most extreme rightward 5%) also has a probability of occurrence which is 5%, or $p = 0.05$. In other words, it is possible to assign a probability to any interval associated with a statistic (or indeed of any other variable), providing we know (as we do in the case of most test statistics) where it is located on its distribution. To see the practical application of this we now need to link the concept of the sampling distribution to one other important idea, namely, the table of critical values.

The sampling distribution and tables of critical values

The connection between the sampling distribution of a test statistic and its table of critical values is straightforward. Every entry in a table of critical values comes from a different sampling distribution of the relevant test statistic, and, for any given level of significance, the table values will have been taken from exactly the same point on each distribution. Thus, all that it is necessary to do to create a table of critical values for the significance level of $p = 0.05$ is to copy from each one of the sampling distributions that value which is located at the point on the x axis which divides the area under the curve in the proportion of 95% to 5%. Similarly, to construct a table of critical values for the $p = 0.01$ significance level, the values which divide the sampling distributions up in the proportions of 99% to 1% will be needed.

The critical values of a test statistic (such as those found in the tables in appendix 5) define intervals which have a known p-value. (This, you will remember, is the shorthand term for the rather cumbersome phrase 'the probability of obtaining the observed value, or one more extreme'.) Thus, the critical values for the $p = 0.05$ significance level define those intervals from the sampling distributions of the statistic which have a probability of being exceeded (or p-value) of $p = 0.05$. These values are used to assess whether the probability of obtaining the computed value of the statistic is greater or less than the significance level of the test. As we will see below, if we know which values of the statistic have a particular p-value (i.e. the critical values), it then becomes possible, by a simple process of comparison, to establish whether the probability associated with any computed value of the statistic exceeds the critical values.

You may be wondering why this does not result in tables consisting only of identical values: the reason is that the sampling distributions of test statistics are such that different sample sizes (for some statistics, expressed as degrees of freedom) generate different ranges of values on the x axis. The 5% critical value will, therefore, turn out to be different for different sampling distributions of the statistic.

The pay-off to all this is that once a researcher has decided on a significance level and has carried out the computation of the test statistic, the problem of determining the *meaning* of the obtained value for the test statistic can be dealt with by consulting the table of critical values for the statistic in question. We will look at an example in order to make the logic of that particular process clear, although as you will see, you need to understand how the areas under a normal distribution can be used to generate statements of probability before you can follow the example fully. If those ideas are completely unfamiliar to you, I suggest that you turn immediately to chapter 8, to work through the

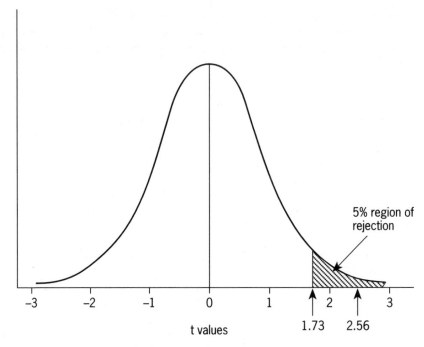

Figure 7.5 The sampling distribution of the t statistic for 18 degrees of freedom

sections dealing with the standard normal distribution and standard error before coming back to the next part of the argument.

Using the sampling distribution to make a decision about hypotheses

To see how the decision process operates, let us consider another example of a researcher who, having already formulated hypotheses, decided on a one-tailed significance level of $p = 0.05$ (the importance of 'tails' in this context is explained shortly) and specified the region of rejection, has computed a value for t in the independent samples t-test of 2.56 from samples of $n = 10$. She now needs to determine whether or not she can accept the experimental hypothesis at that level of significance. In effect, she needs to find out whether the value of the test statistic is so extreme relative to the other values on the sampling distribution that its probability of occurrence (its p-value) is $p = 0.05$ or less.

To find the answer the researcher could simply consult the table of critical values for the t-test, as is done in the worked examples in chapter 9. However, instead she chooses to use the theoretical graph of the 18 degrees of freedom sampling distribution for t, shown in figure 7.5. If she knows the mean and the standard error of the sampling distribution of t she can now find the answer to the question by locating the point on the horizontal x axis which divides the total area under the curve into two in the ratio of 95:5. The area beneath the curve to the right of this point corresponds to 5% of the total area, and thus the values of the 't' statistic which lie within this region must have a probability of occurrence of $p = 0.05$. The researcher can read off from the x axis that value for 't' which corresponds to the lower edge of the top 5% of the area under the curve. The graph in figure 7.5 gives the value for t which corresponds to that point as $t = 1.73$ and, because areas under the curve can be read as statements of probability, that value for t can be said to have a probability of occurring, or being exceeded, of $p = 0.05$.

Of course, the probability of obtaining a computed t value which is exactly 1.73 is vanishingly small. However, we are not interested in this, but rather in the probability of getting one which is 1.73 or more. The probability of this is no greater than $p = 0.05$. In this case, we have obtained a value for t of 2.56, and can see from figure 7.5 that the area beyond 2.56 is quite a lot less than 5% of the whole, and therefore we can say that the probability associated with $t = 2.56$ is less that $p = 0.05$ ($p < 0.05$).

To continue with the example, as the computed value for t of 2.56 exceeds the table value (i.e. lies further towards the extreme end of the distribution in the region of rejection), it follows that it must have a probability of occurring or being exceeded which is less than $p = 0.05$. That is, its p-value is less than 0.05 (p-value < 0.05). The implications of this result for the decision about the hypotheses being tested are described below.

Another way of expressing this is to say that $t = 2.56$ falls within the 5% **region of rejection** of the null hypothesis. That is, it lies in a tail region of the distribution (determined by the significance level), within which lie those values of the statistic which are so extreme as to require the rejection of the null hypothesis.

So, with the detailed mechanics of the decision on hypotheses finally exposed, a principled decision on hypotheses becomes possible. Given that a significance level of $p = 0.05$ was chosen by the researcher, a computed value of $t = 2.56$, since it is greater than 1.73, clearly falls within this rejection region and so the correct decision on the hypotheses is to reject the null hypothesis and accept the alternate.

At this point the value of having tables of critical values becomes apparent. It would clearly be a disincentive to using statistics if it were necessary to determine the complete sampling distribution of a statistic before any data could be analysed. Fortunately, the existence of tables of critical values renders this laborious process unnecessary, because they provide, for any required level of significance, a list of the critical values for a test statistic, across a range of sample sizes. These values represent the boundaries on their respective distributions between those values which have a p-value which is lower than the significance level, and those whose p-value is higher. If the table is for a significance level of $p = 0.05$, for example, then the critical values of the statistic are those which mark off the 5% rejection region: if for a significance level of $p = 0.01$, then they mark off the 1% rejection region, and so on for any desired level of significance.

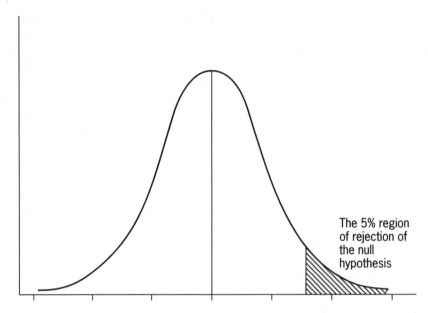

The 5% region of rejection of the null hypothesis

Figure 7.6   The 5% region of rejection for a one-tailed hypothesis (shaded area)

A one-tailed experimental hypothesis specifies at which end of the sampling distribution of the test statistic the rejection region will lie. In this case it is located in the upper tail of the distribution, but could, alternatively, occupy the corresponding area in the lower tail.

Directional and non-directional versions of the alternate hypothesis

There is one remaining piece of information which you need to know about the alternate hypothesis: it is that the alternate hypothesis comes in two versions, a directional form and a non-directional form.

The directional alternate hypothesis

A directional alternate hypothesis is one in which one population parameter is stated to be greater (or smaller) than the other. In other words, it goes further than just saying that there will be a difference (if the alternate hypothesis is true), by specifying in addition an expected **direction of difference**.

This form of the hypothesis is also called a **one-tailed hypothesis**, since by saying in which direction the difference will occur it also specifies the end of the sampling distribution of the test statistic at which the computed value is expected to lie if the alternate hypothesis is true. The **region of rejection** on the distribution in figure 7.6 is the area, *either* at the top *or* the bottom, within which lie those values of the test statistic which are so extreme (i.e. whose p-value is so low) as to require the rejection of the null hypothesis.

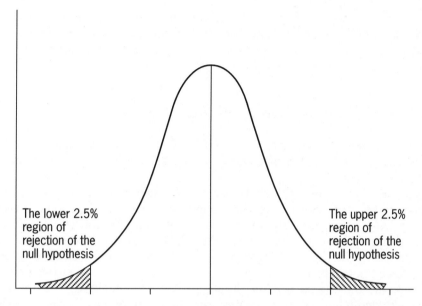

The lower 2.5%
region of
rejection of the
null hypothesis

The upper 2.5%
region of
rejection of the
null hypothesis

Figure 7.7   The 5% region of rejection for a two-tailed hypothesis (shaded areas)

A two-tailed experimental hypothesis does not specify at which end of the sampling distribution of the test statistic the rejection region will lie.

In testing a one-tailed hypothesis the computed value of the test statistic is compared to values at one end of the distribution. If a value has been obtained which is so extreme as to locate it at one end of the distribution, *and in addition* the direction of difference stated in the alternate hypothesis matches the difference in the data, then the alternate hypothesis may be accepted and the null rejected. In all other cases, including that when the computed value of the statistic is more extreme than the critical value, but the direction of difference stated in the alternate hypothesis is the *opposite* to the one actually found in the data, the null hypothesis cannot be rejected.

The non-directional alternate hypothesis

When an alternate hypothesis specifies a difference between two parameters but does not state which of the two is larger than the other, then this is a non-directional or **two-tailed hypothesis**. It is called two-tailed because the computed value of the test statistic is compared with the values in the regions of rejection at *both* ends (or tails) of the sampling distribution (see figure 7.7), each of which, in the case of the 5% significance level, constitutes 2.5% of the total area under the curve. The **regions of rejection** on the distribution in figure 7.7 are the areas at *both* the top *and* the bottom, within which those values of the test statistic lie which are so extreme (i.e. whose p-values are so low) as to lead to the rejection of the null hypothesis.

In testing a two-tailed hypothesis the computed value of the test statistic is compared with values at *both* ends of the distribution, and if a value has been obtained which is either so large or so small as to locate it in *either* region of rejection, then the null hypothesis may be rejected.

Which type of alternate hypothesis should you choose?

The fact that the alternate hypothesis comes in two versions means that it is always necessary to decide which should be used in any given piece of research. Which should you choose?

In general, psychologists tend to regard the non-directional version of the alternate hypothesis with suspicion, on the grounds that there are likely to be few situations in which it is genuinely difficult to predict the direction of difference. It is argued that in virtually all research there is an expected direction of difference implied by the theory being tested, even if this is only based on common-sense expectations. In order to preserve the purity of the decision process, therefore, the directional version should perhaps be preferred, and the non-directional two-tailed version reserved for those rather rare occasions when there is genuine uncertainty about the outcome of the investigation.

So far it seems straightforward, with the one-tailed hypothesis likely to be the usual choice. However, there is also another consideration to be borne in mind which complicates matters somewhat. It is always *harder* to find the evidence needed to accept a two-tailed alternate hypothesis compared to a one-tailed hypothesis at any level of significance. Consequently (and rather paradoxically in view of what was earlier said about preserving the purity of decision-making by preferring the one-tailed hypothesis over the two-tailed variety), the selection of the two-tailed hypothesis places a higher hurdle in the way before the alternate hypothesis can be accepted. As we shall see in a moment, it also means that the decision error called the type 1 error becomes less likely.

So, which type of hypothesis should one choose? Should you try to preserve the integrity of the decision process but set a lower standard for accepting the alternate hypothesis, or set a higher criterion, and ignore the implications which the two-tailed hypothesis may have for decision-making?

The critical question here is, when was the decision to use a one- or two-tailed test made? If you decide on the test *after* you have seen the data, then there is always the possibility that your decision could have been influenced by your assessment of the trend displayed there. For example, you might think that it 'looks significant' so you decide to try the less stringent test in the hope of confirming your hunch. Clearly what this does is to introduce an element of bias into the process which is undesirable: you are no longer carrying out a perfectly fair test of the hypothesis. Ideally, the form of the test should always be decided before the data are seen. However, this may not always be possible, and in such cases, the two-tailed test is always to be preferred. If you do wish to use the less stringent one-tailed test, you should always decide to do so *before* you have seen the data, i.e. before data are actually collected, and then there can be no suspicion of bias affecting the testing of the hypothesis.

Which level of significance should you choose?

As you will by now have realized, when a researcher sets the significance level she is deciding how cautious she wishes to be in making decisions about the hypotheses. A higher significance level (say p = 0.1, or a probability of 1 in 10) is *less* conservative than a lower one (say p = 0.01 or 1 in 100). This is because with a significance level set at p = 0.1 it is easier for the alternate hypothesis to be accepted even though the null hypothesis is true. The *lower* the significance level (i.e. the closer to zero), the more difficult it is for this to occur.

This suggests that the process of decision-making about hypotheses using the significance level is not an infallible process; and this, unfortunately, turns out to be the case. The decision about whether to accept or reject a null hypothesis actually involves the probability of making not one but two forms of error, neither of which can be completely avoided.

Types of errors in making decisions about hypotheses

The type 1 error

A type 1 error is a 'false positive' error which occurs when the decision is made to reject the null hypothesis when in fact it should not have been rejected – the equivalent in terms of the criminal law of assuming that people are innocent until proved guilty, but nevertheless finding guilty and imprisoning an innocent man.

In statistics, this type of error occurs when, even though the null hypothesis is correct, the test statistic falls in the rejection region by chance alone. Because, as we have seen, the decision process is a very tightly structured one, this leads to a rejection of the null and the consequent acceptance of the alternate hypothesis.

It follows that the probability of making a type 1 error in any particular investigation is set by the significance level which is being employed. A significance level of p = 0.05 means that the probability of making a type 1 error (and hence of incorrectly rejecting the null hypothesis) is p = 0.05 (5 in 100). Similarly a significance level of p = 0.001 means that the probability of incorrect rejection of the null hypothesis is p = 0.001 (1 in 1000), and so on.

The type 2 error

A type 2 error is a 'false negative' decision made when a researcher fails to reject the null hypothesis when it should in fact have been rejected. That is, the test statistic has returned a value which, by chance, lies outside the region of rejection indicated by the significance level, even though the IV has influenced the DV in the fashion specified by the alternate hypothesis. The decision is thus taken not to reject the null hypothesis, and to reject the alternate hypothesis, even though the latter is correct. To pursue the legal analogy, this would be the equivalent of holding a trial which acquitted a guilty individual.

The reason for the existence of type 2 errors lies in the fact that every attempt, by means of reductions to the significance level, to exclude the possibility of a type 1 error necessarily also means that the probability *increases* that a genuine effect of the IV on the DV will be rejected. Thus, if you try to reduce the probability of making a type 1 error by reducing the significance level of a test from $p = 0.05$ to $p = 0.01$, you also make it more likely that a genuine, though small, difference in the data will be identified as being due to chance or random factors.

Which is the more serious type of error?

The 'false positive' type 1 error is the more serious because it occurs when a researcher accepts that the IV has influenced the DV in the fashion predicted by the alternate (experimental) hypothesis when, in fact, it has not. This is potentially misleading because it suggests that there is a relationship between the variables which in fact does not exist. Moreover, because positive results are much more likely to be reported in the literature, it could lead to an entirely erroneous direction being taken by subsequent research.

On the other hand, the 'false negative' decision of the type 2 error is rather less serious. Although such a decision seems to close off an avenue of research by concluding that there is an unacceptably high probability that the differences are due to chance or random factors, it still leaves open the possibility that a later replication of the experiment will find a significant difference. And because failures to accept an alternate hypothesis tend not to be reported, no great harm is done.

It is also worth noting that both these types of error demonstrate how important it is to carry out replication studies in scientific research. It is good practice to repeat one's own work, as well as the work of other investigators, in order to test the possibility that a false (positive or negative) decision has previously been made.

Reducing the probability of type 1 and type 2 errors

The probability of making a type 1 error is set by the significance level which has been selected, and it can therefore be reduced simply by dropping to a lower significance level for the statistic employed, say from $p = 0.05$ to $p = 0.01$. The problem with doing this is that it desensitizes the test and increases the probability of making a type 2 error, making it *less* likely that the test will detect any effect which the IV has had on the DV.

Given that it is impossible to avoid making both type 1 and type 2 errors, the most usual strategy is to set the type 1 error to an acceptable level (via the significance level), having previously checked that the sample size is adequate to give sufficient power to ensure that the probability of making a type 2 error is as low as possible. More information on the power of statistical tests can be found in most advanced texts.

Summary of chapter 7

Inferential statistics – the techniques by which it becomes possible to move beyond simply describing or summarizing the information in the data, to say something about what the data might mean – are fundamental to research in psychology.

These procedures, in turn, rest on the twin concepts of probability and chance, which although they are sometimes used interchangeably should nevertheless be clearly distinguished. Essentially statements involving the use of probability represent an assessment of the likelihood of some particular event, while statements involving the concept of chance are statements about the role of random or unpredictable influences in determining events. To make a probabilistic statement is to assign a precise value (between 0 and 1) to an event. In inferential statistics, chance or random factors affecting the data are part of the problem which the statistical methods were devised to deal with, and the concept of probability is used to express the likelihood of given events, such as the probability of incorrectly rejecting the null hypothesis.

One key distribution used in inferential statistics is the normal distribution, which is a symmetrical bell-shaped curve describing the distribution of many variables in nature (including in psychology). Possibly its most important feature is the fact that if the curve is drawn for a normally distributed variable, then the mean and standard deviation can be used to give the proportion of the total area under the curve between any two points on the x axis. This means, in turn, that if we know that a distribution is normal, and also know its mean and standard deviation, it is possible to assess the probability of occurrence (p-value) for any range of values of the variable.

Hypotheses, which play a central role in the development of theories in science, are predictions made in the course of an investigation before data collection takes place. They come in two types. Ordinary or 'scientific' hypotheses are general predictions about what the likely shape of the data will be if the theory is correct; statistical hypotheses, on the other hand, are highly precise sets of paired statements about the population which express the general scientific hypothesis in a directly testable form, and which form a framework for making decisions about the results of the investigation. The experimental or alternate hypothesis specifies a difference between two population parameter values, while the null hypothesis is a hypothesis of no difference.

Once the hypotheses are stated and the data collected, inferential statistics can be used to determine which of the two possibilities represented by the hypotheses is correct. Clearly, they cannot both be right. To make the decision, a value for the test statistic is computed from the data, and that 'computed value' is compared to a 'critical value', obtained from the appropriate table. In general if the 'computed value' of the test statistic falls into the rejection region, the experimental (alternate) hypothesis will be accepted. If, on the other hand, the 'computed value' does not lie in the rejection region, the null hypothesis will not be rejected and there is insufficient evidence to support the alternate hypothesis.

These decisions on hypotheses cannot be error-free, and in fact two types of error, called the type 1 and type 2, are always present to some degree. The probability of making a type 1 error, which occurs when the null hypothesis is wrongly rejected, is set by the significance level of the test. The type 2 error is the mirror image of the type 1, since it is made by failing to reject the null hypothesis when it should have been rejected. Of the two, the type 1 error is the more serious, as it involves identifying a relationship between two variables which doesn't exist, and it may therefore lead research and theory in an entirely erroneous direction. The type 2 error is less serious because although it involves the failure to identify a relationship which does exist, there remains the possibility that the error will rapidly be corrected through replication.

Having set the probability of making a type 1 error, the probability of making a type 2 can be reduced by increasing the sample size, or by taking measures designed to increase the efficiency of the instruments used to make measurements of the variables.

8 Parameter Estimation: Inferring from Sample to Population

This chapter explains how it is possible to make inferences about the parameters of a population on the basis of sample statistics.

- It explains the problem posed by sampling error in reasoning from sample to population.

- It introduces the standard normal distribution and the concept of z score as a way of reasoning about probabilities in relation to sample data.

- It introduces the concept of the 'sampling distribution of the mean' and describes its characteristics.

- It shows how, using the concepts of 'sampling distribution' and 'standard error', it is possible to make inferences about the population mean on the basis of sample data.

- It introduces and explains the concept of the confidence interval.

Introduction: the problem with samples

This chapter deals with the solution to one of the more fundamental problems faced by many researchers in the social sciences, namely how to say something about the characteristics of a population from the evidence presented by only a single sample of data.

This problem arises because only very rarely is it possible for a researcher to gather data from the entire group of interest. Almost always she will be in a position of having to work with data which represent a sample from a much more numerous but largely inaccessible population, which constitutes the real focus of interest. One could say that researchers are not so much interested in the sample data as in what the data are able to reveal about the underlying population, and they are therefore extremely interested in finding ways of going beyond any sample in order to say something about the numbers in the background. This process of using sample data in order to infer some characteristics of a population is, as we have already noted in the previous chapter, called **parameter estimation**.

The function of any sample is to act as representative of its underlying population, and one possible way of dealing with the problem posed by reasoning from sample to population would be to assume that sample data are perfectly representative of the population. This means that the sample is assumed to be such that the values of all variables computed from sample data, such as their mean, are exactly those which would be obtained if the whole population were sampled and the same variables computed. That is, it is assumed that sampling has occurred with zero error. This is highly unlikely, of course, but if the assumption is made, then any variable computed from a sample which is taken as a straightforward estimate of the corresponding population parameter is referred to as a **point estimate** of that population parameter. So, if the assumption were true, then a sample mean (say) would have exactly the same value as the (unknown) population mean, and so, similarly, would other statistics such as the measures of dispersion have the same value as their corresponding parameters.

However, as we have noted, point estimation depends for its accuracy on one crucial, but unwise assumption. Though it may seem reasonable at first sight (especially, perhaps, if a random sampling procedure has been carefully implemented), the underlying assumption on which point estimation is based almost never holds true. The problem is that no sampling procedure can *ever* deliver exactly representative data. There will always be a difference between the set of sample data and what one would have obtained from the entire population. This difference is said to be due to **sampling error**, and it exists because of randomness in the method of selecting the sample. In the very nature of things an investigator never knows how individual data values are likely to be distributed within a population (that, of course, is why research is necessary in the first place); so no matter how impeccably conducted a sampling process may be, it always generates data which are unrepresentative to some degree. Furthermore, sampling error affects not only the raw score values but also the values of any descriptive statistics which are derived from them, so that in addition to the sampling error of the raw scores there is also a sampling error of the mean and other measures of central tendency and dispersion as well. (For the sake of simplicity, however, the following discussion will focus on the sampling error of the mean, though you will need to bear in mind throughout that in principle, the ideas apply also to the sampling error of the other descriptive statistics.)

The existence of sampling error means that although a statistic such as a sample mean may represent an accurate **point estimate** of the population mean, it is much more likely that it does not; and, more seriously still, this approach offers no way of assessing the size or the probability of difference between the two values. Point estimation offers a 'quick but dirty' solution: it gives a speedy, but possibly very inaccurate approach to assessing the possible value of a population parameter, and we need something better if we are ever to get behind sample data to make useful inferences about the population.

Clearly, then, what is needed is a way of circumventing the effects of sampling error on the accuracy of parameter estimates, and fortunately, a better technique called **interval estimation** is available. This approach applies ideas from statistical sampling theory and the normal distribution to the task of looking behind sample data. The process has two stages. First, starting from a set of sample data, interval estimation permits a precise estimate to be made of a 'confidence interval'. This is a statement of the range of possible values a given population parameter may take. This may not seem much of an advance over point estimation, but what makes it particularly useful and powerful from the researcher's point of view is the fact that it is also possible to attach a probability to that range estimate. This permits one not only to give the range within which a parameter may lie, but also to say how likely it is that it lies within the stated range. This, as you will appreciate, permits the value of a parameter to be pinned down with some precision, and represents an important advance on the point estimation technique discussed earlier. As you have probably realized, the notion of confidence interval is the key to the whole procedure, and we will return to it later in this chapter.

Before we can get down to considering the details of interval estimation, however, we have first to look at an important variant of the normal distribution which we met in chapter 7. This is called the standard normal distribution, and it is vital to understanding how interval estimation is able to deliver information about a population.

The standard normal distribution

As its name implies, the standard normal distribution (SND) is a normal distribution whose horizontal x axis has been calibrated in a standard way in order to enable actual score values from any normal distribution to be dealt with using just one standard table.

You have already met the key idea behind the SND in the form of the unit of standard deviation which was mentioned earlier in connection with the normal distribution. As we saw then, the x axis of a normal distribution can be calibrated in either raw score units or in units of standard deviation above and below the mean. The SND uses exactly the same idea, except that in this

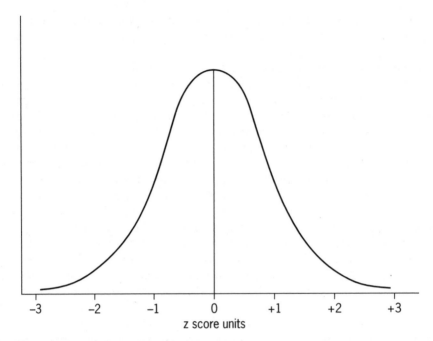

Figure 8.1   The standard normal distribution

case the units of standard deviation are called z score units. One unit of standard deviation (representing a number of raw score units) is equal to one unit of z score. The main difference between the SND and other normal distributions is that the mean of SND is standardized on zero. In formal terms, the SND is defined simply as a normal distribution, having a mean of zero and a standard deviation of 1, whose x axis is scaled in terms of z scores. The result looks like the distribution in figure 8.1.

As we saw from chapter 7, an important feature of any normal distribution (whatever the nature of the scores it represents) is the fact that the area under the curve falls into precisely predictable proportions in relation to the standard deviation of the distribution. Because it is a version of the normal distribution, it follows that this is also true of the SND. The only difference is that we will use z scores rather than standard deviation units to locate the boundaries of any area below the curve of the SND which we are interested in establishing.

You will also remember from that earlier discussion of the normal distribution that we only looked at the areas under the curve marked out by whole number values of the standard deviation units on the x axis, although it was also shown at that time that it is possible to determine the area under the curve for any values of standard deviation which may be desired. The time has now come to show more fully how this can be done, using one of the tables in appendix 5.

The table of areas under the normal curve (appendix 5, table 2) is based on the standard normal distribution (that is, it is based on a distribution which has its horizontal (x) axis calibrated in z score units having a mean of zero and a standard deviation of 1), and gives the areas under the curve between the mean, and any z score above or below the mean, in steps of one-hundredths of a unit of z score. This means that it is possible to determine the area under the curve between **any two points on the x axis**, either by reading the value required directly from the table, or by doing some simple arithmetic on the table values.

However, just knowing that different proportions of the area under the normal curve are related to different values of z, though interesting, is not exactly what we need in order to draw useful inferences from a set of data. Rather than simply finding what proportions of the total area are represented by different areas under the curve, a researcher will be much more likely to want to determine the probability of obtaining some value of the variable which is represented in the distribution, although it might not actually be present in the sample. An example of this might be when, given a set of IQ scores with, say, a range of 83 to 129, a psychologist wishes to find the probability of obtaining a more extreme score than those found in the sample, such as one greater than 140. Note that here she is interested in using the scores obtained by sampling to say something about a range of score values which are not actually in the sample, although, of course, they might have been. This can easily be done as long as the assumption can be made that the scores (in this case IQ scores, but in principle the values of any variable) are normally distributed. If the assumption holds, then the table of areas under the curve can be used directly as a table of probabilities to find the answer. The reasoning behind this is as follows:

1   The normal distribution (and hence the SND also) is a theoretical distribution which covers all possible values of the variable in question. Another way of putting this is to say that the area under the curve represents 100% of the possible score values.

2   Therefore, any proportion of the area under the curve will represent exactly the same proportion of all possible scores. For example, 25% of the area under the curve will enclose 25% of the scores; 10% of the area encloses 10% of the scores, and so on. Another way of expressing this point is to say that the probability of any individual score lying within a 25% segment of the area under the curve (NB *any* 25%), is p = 0.25, or 1 chance in 4. Similarly, the probability of any score lying within 10% of the area under the curve is p = 0.1 (1 chance in 10), and so on for *any* proportion of the area from 0 to 100%.

3   Given this, and if the mean and standard deviation of the distribution are known, it turns out that it is quite easy to go on to find the probability of obtaining any range of values in the raw scores.

For example, suppose a psychologist is working with a large sample of normally distributed raw scores with a mean of 80 and a standard deviation of 10. Suppose, further, that she wishes to find out, first, what proportions of the scores will lie between 75 and 85, and second, what the probability might be

Table 8.1 Translation of raw scores having a mean of 80 and a standard deviation of 10 into z scores

Raw score	50	55	60	65	70	75	80	85	90	95	100	105	110
z score	−3.0	−2.5	−2.0	−1.5	−1.0	−0.5	0	+0.5	+1.0	+1.5	+2.0	+2.5	+3.0

of obtaining scores greater than 100, and third, what value is exceeded by only 5% of raw scores. The procedure for obtaining these pieces of information is as follows.

Procedure

Begin by translating raw score values into z score units. This can most conveniently be done by writing out the z score values, and then adding the raw score equivalents above or below, working from the mean outwards in either direction (see table 8.1).

To find the z score equivalent of any raw score the general formula is:

$$z \text{ score} = \frac{\text{raw score} - \text{mean}}{\text{standard deviation}}$$ **Formula 8.1**

that is, subtract the mean from the raw score, and divide the result by the standard deviation. This gives the z score. However, if you simply wish to find the raw score equivalent of integer values of z score, the easiest approach is to start from the mean and successively add or subtract 1 standard deviation expressed in raw score terms. Table 8.1 shows the result of this process for the example data. There is no need actually to draw the curve unless you wish to do so, although many people find a sketch diagram to be a helpful aid to visualizing the distribution.

Having mapped the raw score values onto their z score equivalents, you can see that in terms of z score values the questions to be answered now become:

Q1 What proportions of scores will lie between z scores of −0.5 and +0.5?
Q2 What is the probability of obtaining a z score greater than +2.0?
Q3 What is the value of z score which marks the boundary between the topmost 5% of the distribution and the rest?

For Q1, once you have found the z score equivalents to the raw scores the rest is simple. It simply involves using the table of areas under the normal curve (table 2 in appendix 5). This shows that the area between the mean and a z score of 0.5 in either direction is .1915 (i.e. 19.15%) of the total. Since question 1 asks for the proportion under the curve between the mean and a z score of 0.05 in *both* directions, we simply *double* the table value. Since all possible score values are said to be included in the normal distribution, we can simply read the proportions of the area as proportions of scores. The answer to the first question is, therefore, that the proportion of raw scores lying between z scores of −0.5 and +0.5 is:

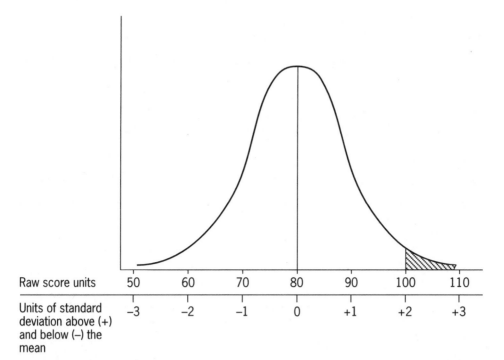

Raw score units   50   60   70   80   90   100   110

Units of standard   −3   −2   −1   0   +1   +2   +3
deviation above (+)
and below (−) the
mean

Figure 8.2   The area beyond 2 units of z score on a normal distribution with a mean of
80 and a standard deviation of 10

$2 \times 19.15\% = 38.3\%$ of the total.

Q2 requires essentially the same process except that the table of areas under
the curve must now be used as a table of probabilities. We consult table 2 in
appendix 5 again, this time to determine the area under the curve which lies
beyond a z score of +2.0 (see figure 8.2). This table shows that the area
between the mean and a z score of 2.0 in either direction is .4772 (47.72%)
of the total area under the curve. However, in order to find the area under the
curve which lies *beyond* that point, the area given in the table has to be
subtracted from 50%. This gives the proportion of raw scores lying beyond a
z score of +2.0 as:

$50.0\% - 47.72\% = 2.28\%$

and hence the probability of obtaining a z score greater than +2.0 is also:

$p = 0.5 - 0.4772 = 0.0228.$

(Remember that the mean, because by definition it coincides with the median
in the normal distribution, divides the area under the curve into two halves: the
table, however, only gives the areas under the curve on *one* side of the mean.)

   To answer Q3 we have first to find the z score value which divides the top
half of the distribution in the proportions 45% to 5%. Consulting table 2 gives

a z score value of between 1.64 and 1.65 – say, 1.645. Then we use formula 8.1 to convert this value into its raw score equivalent thus:

$$\text{mean} + (\text{z score} \times \text{standard deviation}) = 80 + 1.645 \times 10$$
$$= 80 + 16.45$$
$$= 96.45$$

(Note that if we had wanted to find the score which was so low that only 5% of the scores were lower, we would have *subtracted* rather than added the mean in the formula.)

The last stage of the process involves re-translating the z scores back into raw score terms to give the following answers to the original questions:

Answer 1   The proportion of all scores lying between raw scores of 75 and 85 is 38.3% of the total.

Answer 2   The probability of obtaining a score greater than a raw score of 100 is exactly p = 0.0228, or approximately 1 in 50.

Answer 3   The raw score value which is exceeded only by 5% of the scores is 96.45.

The more you engage in this process of reasoning about probabilities, the easier you will find it becomes. If you feel you would like more practice, some statistics texts include exercises on this topic which you could try. Alternatively, why not go out and collect some data and (perhaps after making some assumptions about the randomness of the sampling), practise working through these ideas for yourself?

By this time you may well be wondering where all this gets us, to which the answer is that it gets us quite a long way. As we have just seen, it is possible to use the characteristics of the normal distribution and the table of areas to express very precise probabilities of particular events in a way which expands our understanding of the raw data. Even more valuably we can, as we will shortly see, use essentially the same technique to go on to deal with the knotty problem raised by the existence of sampling error, with which we began this chapter. How is it possible to draw useful conclusions about the relationship between a set of sample data and the population from which they were taken? To see how this can be done, we need to develop the concept of a **sampling distribution**.

In order to try to make the following discussion as clear as possible, we shall deal in detail with only one of the range of possible sampling distributions, called rather formidably the **sampling distribution of the mean**. However, it is important to realize as we do so that each statistic computed from a sample – such as mean, median, variance and so on – can be related to a sampling distribution of its own in just the same way as the mean.

The sampling distribution of the mean

The sampling distribution of the mean is best approached by an example. Imagine that instead of taking a single, random sample of data, containing 20

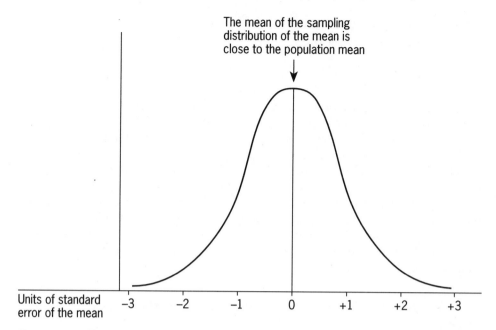

Units of standard error of the mean

Figure 8.3 The sampling distribution of sample means

scores, from an (unknown) population, you take many (say 10,000) such samples. Suppose also that you then calculate the mean of each sample and plot the frequency distribution of the means. The result, which will look very much like a normal distribution, will be the sampling distribution of the mean. (Figure 8.3 represents a perfectly normal model for the sampling distribution of the mean.) It turns out that this distribution has three important properties:

1   If random samples are taken from a normally distributed population, then the theoretical distribution of sample means will also be normal, with a mean which is exactly equal to the population mean. *This will always be true no matter what the size of the samples.*

2   For large-sized samples, even if the population from which the data are drawn is extremely non-normal, the distribution of the sample means will still be close to normality. In such cases, the *larger* the size of the samples, the *closer* the distribution of sample means approaches towards normal (this is known as the central limit theorem). Samples of n = 20, even if taken from a non-normal population, will give a distribution closely approximating to a normally distributed sampling distribution of the mean.

3   **The standard error of the mean** is the standard deviation of the sampling distribution of the mean (i.e. the standard deviation of all the means in the sampling distribution). Its value in any particular case tends to be equal to the population standard deviation divided by the square root of the sample size, and it is therefore calculated directly in the following way:

First, suppose that the parent population is normal and that we already know σ, the population standard deviation. Then, we can easily find the standard error of the mean (symbol $\sigma\overline{X}$) by dividing σ by the square root of the sample size. The formula for this is:

$$\sigma\overline{X} = \frac{\sigma}{\sqrt{n}}$$

Formula 8.2

This formula has considerable practical importance because it means we are now in possession of two essential pieces of information. First, we know from point 1 above that the distribution of sample means *always* tends to be normal in form, and second, by using formula 8.2 we have a way of finding the standard deviation of that distribution. By taking these, and adding the technique used earlier to explore the values which might be found in a sample, we can assess the probability of any given value occurring in the distribution, and, most usefully, can also 'zero in' on the population mean. We will, in short, have arrived at the goal we have been aiming for, which is to make a precise inference about the population solely on the basis of the characteristics of the sample. This is how it is done.

Making inferences about a population mean on the basis of sample data

Suppose a psychologist has the following group of 50 scores representing the number of items correctly identified in a visual recognition task. These represent a random sample from a population in which the distribution of scores is assumed to be approximately normal.

59	67	97	55	78
79	59	69	66	66
95	55	57	97	74
88	86	76	58	56
74	91	82	69	73
86	79	61	68	56
76	79	66	52	74
85	58	61	86	97
97	76	66	56	59
57	66	87	65	84

Mean of sample = 72.46 items

(For the sake of keeping the reasoning as clear as possible, we will also suppose that the standard deviation of the population from which the sample has been taken is $\sigma = 13.44$, and this is already known to the researcher. We will, of course, see later what needs to be done if this value is unknown, as it usually is.)

The general question which a researcher would wish to answer is whether this single sample of scores may be taken to represent the population. This is an important question, but it expresses the issue in far too general a way to be very helpful. The question needs to be posed more precisely so that statistical expertise can gain some leverage on the problem. A slightly better approach to the same question would be to ask whether the statistics obtained from the sample are the same as their corresponding population parameters. In this case, the possibility of finding an answer is blocked by the existence of sampling error. So we have to go one step further still, to an even more precise version of the question, and ask how close the mean of the sample may be to the mean of its population. As you may be able to see from the information already in your possession, this, at last, is a question for which we can find a clear answer. The procedure looks like this.

The first step is to substitute the value of σ (already known), in formula 8.2, to get the standard error of the mean (the standard deviation of the distribution of sample means). In this example the sample size, n, is 50:

$$\sigma \overline{X} = \frac{\sigma}{\sqrt{n}} = \frac{13.44}{\sqrt{50}} = 1.90$$

For this example, therefore, the standard error of the mean (the standard deviation of the distribution of sample means) is 1.90.

Since the distribution of sample means is known to be a normal distribution, it must include, by definition, *all* possible values of the mean for random samples of equal size drawn from the same population distributed around the population mean. Furthermore, given the shape of the normal curve, and in particular the fact that the tails of the distribution approach closer and closer to the horizontal (x) axis with increasing distance from the mean, it is possible to say that it is unlikely that any particular sample mean will lie further than 2.0 standard deviation units from the mean of the sample means in either direction. This relationship is represented in figure 8.4, which shows the relation between one sample mean and the population mean (still unknown) on a sampling distribution whose standard error is 1.90. From the figure it is possible to see that, as we said, the sample mean is unlikely to lie more than 3.8 units of raw score (i.e. 2 × 1.90) from the population mean in either direction. As this in turn means that the population mean is equally unlikely to lie more than 3.8 raw score units above or below the sample mean, we have therefore succeeded in identifying a possible range of values within which the population mean may lie – namely ± 3.8 units of raw score above and below the sample mean, or within the range 68.66 to 76.26.

This is clearly helpful, but we still need to determine the precise probability that it will actually lie within that range. As we shall see in more detail as we progress, these two variables are connected: the probability you select determines the size of the range of values on which the population mean can be located. (In this context the range of possible values and their associated probability is called, for obvious reason, the **confidence interval**; we shall return to it shortly.)

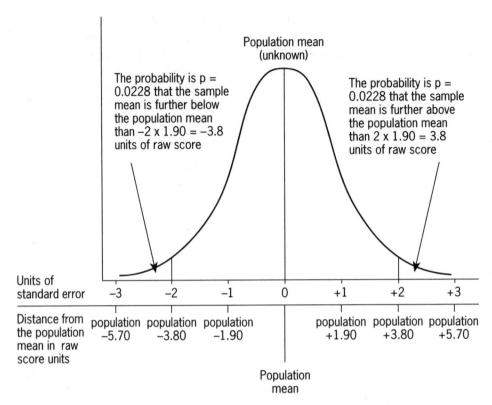

The probability is p = 0.0228 that the sample mean is further below the population mean than −2 x 1.90 = −3.8 units of raw score

Population mean (unknown)

The probability is p = 0.0228 that the sample mean is further above the population mean than 2 x 1.90 = 3.8 units of raw score

| Units of standard error | −3 | −2 | −1 | 0 | +1 | +2 | +3 |

| Distance from the population mean in raw score units | population −5.70 | population −3.80 | population −1.90 | | population +1.90 | population +3.80 | population +5.70 |

Population mean

Figure 8.4   Using the standard normal distribution to locate the sample mean in relation to an unknown population mean

The process really should begin with a decision about how confident (expressed as a probability) you wish to be that once you have obtained a possible range of values for the the population mean, it really does lie within the given range. However, in order to make the reasoning behind the process as transparent as possible we are going to approach it from a slightly different angle. We begin by finding a range of possible values for the population mean, and then go on to determine the probability that it lies within that range. Once we have reasoned it through in that way, you should be equipped to reverse the process and, starting from a desired probability, determine the associated range of possible values.

For now, let us continue to suppose that the sample mean is located at exactly the 2 z score mark (either above or below the mean; it doesn't matter which). Whichever it is, we can conclude, as shown in figure 8.4, that the sample mean and the population mean are unlikely to lie *more* than 3.8 units of raw score away from each other. We can also (and this is the key point) give the probability they are likely to lie closer to each other than 3.8 units of raw score. The reasoning is as follows. Recall that the range of values we have obtained is centred on the sample mean of 72.46, and the range of possible raw score values for the population mean is the equivalent of 2 z scores on either side. From the table of areas under the normal curve we can easily determine the probabilities associated with the raw scores which lie either inside or outside that range.

We begin by finding the z score value of 2.0 on the table and reading off the area lying between the mean and the 2 z score point in either direction (we'll assume that it is above the mean). The proportion of the total area under the curve between these two points is given as 0.4772, which you will remember can also be read as the probability of a score being located in that region. So, we can say that the probability of the population mean lying up to 2 z score units (= 3.8 units of raw score) above the sample mean is $p = 0.4772$. It should be clear that the same process of reasoning will give us exactly the same result for the probability that the population mean lies up to 2 z score units *below* the sample mean, and so the sum of the two probabilities gives us the answer we seek. The probability that the population mean is located within 2 z scores above and below the sample mean (i.e. in raw score terms within the range 68.66 to 76.26) is $p = 0.4772 + 0.4772 = 0.9544$ or 95.44%. Conversely, we can also say that the probability that it lies outside that range is the very small one of $p = 1 - 0.9544 = 0.0456$.

More generally, we can also say that given any sample mean from a random sample, the population mean will lie within ± 2 units of standard error of it 95.44% of the time. This is called the 95.44% **confidence interval** of the parameter estimate. We will return to the concept of confidence interval shortly.

Finally, we need to tie up one loose end. As we noted earlier, choosing a range of possible values (the confidence interval) for the population mean, and then finding the associated probability, is rather rare (although it is sometimes needed). Much more frequently, you will wish to find the range of values associated with a particular probability – most often $p = 0.05$ or $p = 0.01$. This is not difficult as the reasoning involved is exactly the same as that used above; you simply change the order of the various operations, and you can probably see for yourself how to proceed.

To help you, the following is a summary of the more usual sequence of operations:

- **Decide the probability required, and use the table of areas under the normal curve to find the z score value corresponding to that probability (remember that the table gives values for only half the distribution).**
- **Take the estimate of the standard error of the mean and convert the z score to a raw score equivalent.**
- **Add and subtract the raw score equivalent from the sample mean to give the interval associated with the chosen probability.**

To show how this works, consider the example of a psychologist who has obtained a sample of data with a mean of 25. In addition, she knows that the standard deviation is 40 and so can work out the standard error of the sampling distribution using formula 8.2. This gives a value of $40 \div \sqrt{25} = 8.0$. She now wishes to estimate the values of the population mean for the 99% confidence interval. Here's how it is done:

1　As the table of areas under the curve gives only values for half the distribution, she needs to seek the z score for half of 99%, or 0.4950. The table, however, has two possible values: 0.4949 or 0.4951, with associated z scores of 2.57 or 2.58. The solution is to use the mean value of these z scores, 2.575, as corresponding to a probability of 99%.
2　Next she converts this z score to its raw score equivalent by multiplying it by the standard error estimate: $2.575 \times 8.0 = 20.6$.
3　Finally, adding and subtracting the raw score equivalent from the sample mean gives the interval for the population mean: for the lower value, $25 - 20.6 = 4.4$, and for the upper value, $25 + 20.6 = 45.6$.

She can therefore say, on the basis of her sample, that the 99% confidence interval for the population mean stretches from raw score values 4.4 to 45.6. Put another way, she knows that the probability is $p = 0.99$ that the population mean will lie within that range of values.

So, by using our knowledge of the sampling distribution of the mean we have been able to improve on the earlier state of uncertainty regarding the relationship of the sample to its parent population. We have in fact found our way to an answer which almost exactly deals with the question from which we set out. We have not been able to say precisely how near the population mean lies to the sample mean, but we have done the next best thing: we have identified a range of possible values for the population mean, and using the notion of the 'confidence interval', have also been able to say how likely it is that the 'true' population mean lies within the given range. This, as you will appreciate, represents a significant gain.

The confidence interval

We have already met the idea of a confidence interval in the preceding section. As we saw there, the usefulness of this concept is that it permits a range of values to be stated for a population parameter and associated with a known probability. In fact, a definition of confidence interval is that it is a parameter estimate such as (but not only) a population mean consisting of the range of values known to include the parameter at a specified level of probability. Its importance lies in the fact that without it we would be able to do no more than state some possible values for a parameter, without having much idea whether or not they were correct, nor even how close they might be. Without the confidence interval we would, in fact, be no better off than if we had decided to employ the point estimation technique.

The purpose of this section is to explain the key ideas behind the confidence interval, although, as we have said, many of these have already been encountered in the explanation of parameter estimation in the preceding pages. However, this section takes a rather different approach to explaining the logic

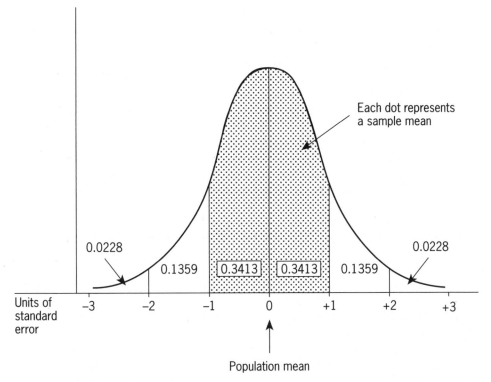

Figure 8.5 The sampling distribution of the mean with areas under the curve expressed as probabilities

underlying the use of the confidence interval, and it therefore provides a complementary treatment to that given earlier.

The starting point is the idea that a sampling distribution, such as that of the mean, represents the distribution of a very large number of individual sample means which (since this is a normal distribution) are clustered symmetrically about the population mean. Part of such a distribution is depicted in figure 8.5 in which the dense scattering of dots represents individual sample means. Of course, the very large number of sample means needed to construct this distribution will be spread with equal density right into the very ends of the distribution: for the sake of clarity only those lying between ±1 unit of standard error are shown.

The problem which the idea of confidence interval is intended to solve is this. Given that a particular sample mean may be identified with any one (but only one) of those dots in figure 8.5, how is it possible to arrive at a reliable estimate of the population mean? Some dots clearly lie on the line of the population mean, and thus have the same value, while others lie some considerable distance from it. We need some way of expressing the relationship between any one of the sample means and the population mean, which is the value we are really interested in.

The way forward, as we saw earlier, is to use the fact that the normal distribution permits a precise probability to be attached to any given range of scores. Using the table of areas under the curve, we can assign a probability to any range of score values (in this case to the possible values of the population mean) which we choose, and thus obtain a confidence interval.

Suppose, for the sake of a simple explanation, we choose for a confidence interval the probability associated with ± 1 unit of standard error about the mean: p = 0.6826. We will have more to say about this choice in a few moments, but for now we wish to estimate the range of values which may be taken by the population mean with a probability of p = 0.6826. Coincidentally, this is also the probability associated with the mass of sample means marked on the distribution in figure 8.5. To labour the point slightly, the probability that any particular sample mean will lie within the range of 1 unit of standard error above and below the mean is also p = 0.6826.

Now look at figure 8.6. This shows a few of the many sample means which were depicted in figure 8.5, with 'wings' added on either side to indicate the extent of 1 unit of standard error. Note that in the figure some of the 'wings' are crossed by the line of the population mean, while others, belonging to different means, are not. Where the line crosses a wing it means that the sample mean is located within 1 unit of standard error of the population mean. Our initial question was what range of possible values could the population mean hold with a probability of p = 0.6826, or, what are the values of the 68.26% confidence interval? A different but equivalent way of expressing this in relation to figure 8.6 would be to ask what are the highest and lowest values of sample mean for which the line of the population mean crosses one of the 'wings'? (Remember that the wings are 1 unit of standard error long.) As you can see, the answer is to be found among those sample means which are located exactly on the line of 1 unit of standard error above and below the mean, which, we have already said, have an associated probability of p = 0.6826. Those points represent upper and lower limits of possible values for the population mean for that level of probability. Here's why. Assume for the moment that you have a sample mean which lies dead centre to the distribution in figure 8.6. What is the furthest away from it in either direction that the population mean could lie and still have an associated probability of occurrence of p = 0.6826? The answer is, of course, is that it could lie no further away than 1 unit of standard error in either direction about the sample mean. So the values associated with the 68.26% confidence interval are those which lie 1 unit of standard error above and below the sample mean: all that remains is to convert the unit of standard error into its raw score equivalent to be able to state clearly the range of values of the population mean associated with that confidence interval.

This exploration has concerned only the 68.26% confidence interval. However, it should be pointed out that it is rather rare to find this confidence interval quoted. What you will find more frequently are the 95% and 99% confidence intervals. We will work out the 95% confidence interval of the

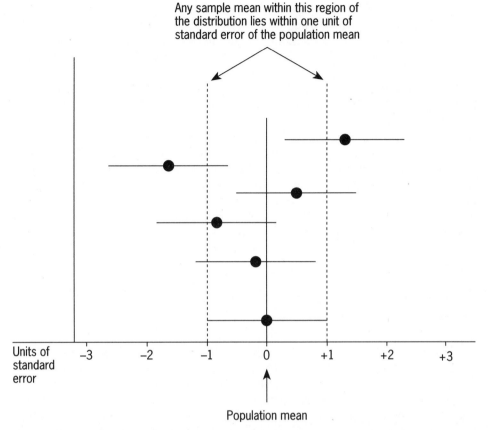

Figure 8.6 Six sample means from the distribution in figure 8.5 with 'wings' added showing the range of the 68.26% confidence interval

population mean together. Then, if you wish, you can work out the 99% confidence interval for yourself. As you will see, the process is simple enough.

The 95% confidence interval requires the finding of the raw score values which mark half of the central 95% of the area under the normal curve. This, as can be found from the table of areas under the curve (table 2 in appendix 5), is 0.4750 or 47.5% of the area on each side of the mean. From the table also, we find that the z score value indicating that proportion of the total area is 1.96. The 95% confidence interval for the population mean is therefore the sample mean ±1.96 standard errors. So we can say that we are 95% certain that the value of the population mean will lie within ±1.96 standard errors of the sample mean. Taking the sample mean and separately adding and subtracting 1.96 times the standard error then gives raw score values of 98.61 and 45.92 as, respectively, the upper and lower limits of the range of possible values.

You may now like to go back to the table and find the range of possible values of the population mean which lie within the 99% confidence interval.

There is an important feature of the confidence interval which was only briefly mentioned in the earlier description. As a confidence interval widens, and the probability that it includes the population parameter increases, so the actual estimate of the population parameter becomes less and less precise. Eventually, with very wide confidence intervals (such as the 99%), we can be close to certain that we know the range within which the population mean must lie. However, at the same time, its range of possible values has widened, so it becomes less easy to be definite about the actual value. In other words, there is a trade-off between the precision with which an estimate of a population parameter can be made and the probability that an estimate is correct. This means that although we can, if we wish, generate a very precise idea of the value of the population mean from any data, we also have to take into account the fact that a very precise estimate has a higher probability of being incorrect. In general, statistics users prefer to choose the second option and deal with relatively imprecise, but highly probable (typically at the 95% or 99% level) estimates of population parameters.

Estimating the population mean when the standard error of the mean is also unknown

You may remember that at the very start of the discussion of parameter estimation we used an example in which it was said that the standard error of the mean was known to be $\sigma = 13.44$. However, what happens if, as is much more likely, we do not have this information readily available? How can we proceed, since, as we have just seen, having a value for the standard error is crucial to the computation of the confidence interval? The answer is that even if we do not know the standard error of the appropriate sampling distribution we can nevertheless estimate its value and then carry on to estimate the parameter we are interested in.

To do this, you first need to calculate s, to estimate the standard deviation within the population from the sample data using formula 6.2 in chapter 6. Next, insert that value in formula 8.3 to find $s_{\bar{x}}$, an estimate of the standard error of the mean:

$$s_{\bar{x}} = \frac{s}{\sqrt{n}}$$ **Formula 8.3**

Then, instead of using the normal distribution table to ascertain the z score value identifying the desired area under the curve, it is necessary to use the t distribution. This is because we are dealing with sample values rather than population values and we must therefore compute s rather than σ, for the reasons already explained in chapter 6. However, s gives only an *estimate* of the population standard deviation, and this is not sufficiently precise to permit the use of the SND, which requires an exact value to be known. So we turn instead to the t distribution. Like the standard normal distribution the t distribution has a mean of zero, but as the x axis is calibrated in t values above (+) and below (−) the mean, and since t distributions are similar to normal rather than exactly normal, the t values stand in different relationships to the areas under the curve from the z score. If needed, the complete set of t distributions may be found in advanced statistics texts, but for our purposes, the table of critical values for t in table 9 of appendix 5 will provide the values to compute both the 95% and 99% confidence intervals.

To use the t distribution, first calculate the number of degrees of freedom which is 1 less than the number of items of data used to calculate the standard deviation (n − 1) and then turn to table 9 in appendix 5. From either the p = 0.05 or p = 0.01 columns of two-tailed critical values (depending on whether you want the 95% or 99% confidence interval), read off the t value for the desired degrees of freedom. This value demarcates either the 5% or 1% area under the curve at the extreme ends of the distribution and can be used to determine the confidence interval for a parameter, such as the population mean, in exactly the same way as the z score was used earlier.

To clarify how this is done, consider the following example. Suppose you have collected a set of IQ scores from a random sample of 20 individuals. The sample has a mean of 58, and a standard deviation, s, of 15 (note that in this case s rather than σ is used: see pp. 290–1), and you wish to determine from these sample data the 95% confidence interval for the population mean. Here's how you set about it.

First, obtain an estimate of the standard error of the mean, using formula 8.3.

$$s_{\bar{x}} = \frac{s}{\sqrt{n}} = \frac{15}{\sqrt{20}} = \frac{15}{4.47} = 3.35$$

Now, apply this value for the standard error of the mean to determine the range of possible values for the population mean. To do this you need to identify the point on the t distribution which marks the boundaries of the 95% confidence interval. If you consult table 9, the table of critical values of t, and look at the columns containing the two-tailed values you will find there are two of them, one for p = 0.05 and the other for p = 0.01. In this case you need the former, because you are interested in obtaining an estimate with a 95% confidence interval, and this gives the value for t of t = 2.093. (If you had been trying to obtain the 99% confidence interval you would, of course, have used the latter column.)

Now for the final piece of reasoning. The 2.093 represents the value of t which demarcates the central region of the distribution containing 95% of the area from the remaining 5% located in the tails (i.e. 2.5% at each end). Therefore 95% of the area under the t distribution lies within t = −2.093 and t = +2.093, and this constitutes the 95% confidence interval which you seek. All that remains, then, is to convert these values into raw score values to find the range of possible values for the population mean. This is easily done by multiplying the standard error of the mean by the t values obtained from the

---

Box 8.1   *Estimating the population mean from sample data when the population deviation also has to be estimated*

To obtain an estimate of a population mean from sample data, when the standard error of the mean is estimated from the data:

1   Estimate the standard error of the mean sampling using formula 8.3:

$$s_{\bar{x}} = \frac{s}{\sqrt{n}}$$

2   Determine the number of degrees of freedom using $(n - 1)$.
3   Consult the table of critical values for the t distribution. Use the column giving the critical values for the $p = 0.05$ two-tailed significance level for a 95% confidence interval and the $p = 0.01$ two-tailed significance column for a 99% confidence interval. Obtain from the table the critical values for the appropriate number of degrees of freedom.
4   Convert the t value to its raw score equivalent by multiplying it by the standard error.
5   Add and subtract the result from the sample mean to find the confidence interval for the population mean.

---

table, and adding and subtracting the result from the mean of the sample. Thus, the upper limit of the 95% confidence interval will be

$$58 + (2.09 \times 3.35) = 58 + 7 = 65 \text{ units of raw score}$$

and its lower limit will be

$$58 - (2.09 \times 3.35) = 58 - 7 = 51 \text{ units of raw score.}$$

Therefore, on the basis of the sample data from which we began it is possible to say that the population mean will lie within the range of 51 to 65 units of raw score, with a probability of $p = 0.95$ (95%).

Throughout this chapter we have concentrated on finding an estimate for the mean of a population, although, as we noted earlier, any population parameter, such as the population median, variance or standard deviation can also be estimated using this technique. If you wish to do so, however, it will be necessary to use the correct sampling distributions for those parameters and, as such matters are beyond the scope of this book, you should seek guidance from a more advanced statistics text.

This is an appropriate point at which to end this introductory excursion into parameter estimation. In this chapter we have seen how, beginning from a random sample of raw data, it is possible to arrive at accurate assessments of key descriptive values for the underlying population. Here, for me, and perhaps for you too, lies much of the power, and fascination, of statistical reasoning. Perhaps you will want to continue your exploration of these ideas.

Summary of chapter 8

The process of collecting data always raises the problem of sampling error, which can be defined as the difference between the picture obtained from the data collected from a sample, and that which would have been obtained from the whole population. In all cases of sampling (except when a complete population is sampled), the existence of sampling error means that initially at least, the relationship of a sample to its parent population is uncertain. The fact that in research one is not so much interested in the sample as in the population from which it is taken means that some method of dealing with this problem is required so that it will be possible to draw conclusions about the population on the basis of sample data.

One approach to saying something about their relationship is to use the sample statistics as straightforward estimates (called 'point' estimates) of the population parameters. However, this approach simply ignores the possibility of sampling error, and is not therefore entirely satisfactory. A better approach is to use the technique of parameter estimation, which represents the second major area (hypothesis testing is the other) in which inferential statistics are used in psychology.

Parameter estimation sometimes uses a version of the normal distribution called the standard normal distribution. This is a normal distribution standardized to a mean of zero and a standard deviation (referred to as a z score) of 1. Its main function is to allow reference to be made to the proportional areas under the curve (and hence to the probabilities of occurrence of different data values) in a way which is quite independent of any specific set of scores.

The key concept in understanding parameter estimation is the notion of the sampling distribution. This is the distribution which can be obtained for any statistic (which, remember, is a value, such as the mean, computed from a sample), if a population is repeatedly sampled, and the values of the statistic are plotted on a frequency distribution. It turns out that the sampling distribution of a statistic such as the mean possesses particularly useful properties which permit the bridging of the gap between a sample and its parent population. It thus becomes possible to generate an estimate of the population parameters on the basis of sample data alone.

Note, though, that the population mean provides only one example of a parameter which one might wish to estimate. Other statistics, such as the median and standard deviation, also possess their own sampling distributions, and these can be used in a similar way to estimate their population parameters. The important point to be made about sampling distributions in this context is that as long as sampling has been random, and the samples are sufficiently large, even samples taken from a grossly non-normal population will still produce a sampling distribution which is close to normal in form. We also know that the standard deviation of the sampling distribution (called the standard error) can be estimated directly by formula from the standard deviation of any random sample. So, by using the characteristics of the standard normal curve (or if you have to use an estimate of the population standard deviation, the appropriate t distribution), it becomes possible to reason about the range of values (or confidence interval) which a population mean might take, and, most usefully of all, to attach a level of probability to any chosen interval.

The more precise the estimate (i.e. the narrower the range of the confidence interval), the lower is the probability that the population parameter actually lies in the predicted range. Conversely, the wider the range, the more confident one can be that it actually includes the parameter of interest. This means that arriving at an estimate of a population parameter involves trying to strike a balance between these two situations. In general, the dilemma is resolved in favour of widening the range of the confidence interval, and thereby increasing the degree of certainty that the possible value of the parameter in question has been identified.

9 Using Statistical Tests

This chapter contains background information on a selection of tests, providing computation instructions and worked examples.

- It explains the important distinction between parametric and non-parametric tests.

- It reviews the process of selecting a test and gives guidance on choosing an appropriate one.

- It discusses the power and robustness characteristics of tests and suggests strategies for increasing these when planning research.

Introduction

The following chapter contains the information you require in order to select an appropriate test and apply it to your data. Although there are obviously differences among these tests, at the general level they all perform the same service. They enable you to determine whether, at some level of probability, your data are unlikely to have occurred by chance, and thus permit the decision to be made about whether or not to reject the null hypothesis.

First of all, you will recall from chapters 6 and 8 the important concepts of **parameter** and **statistic**. The former was defined as a value, such as a mean, computed from a **population**, and the latter as the corresponding value computed from a **sample**. It follows that the **test statistics** in this chapter are so called because they all work with data obtained from samples rather than populations.

However, rather confusingly, a distinction is also made between 'parametric' and 'non-parametric' tests, and you need to know why this is so if you are to be able to select the correct test for your data. Here is the difference.

Parametric tests

A parametric test is one, such as the t-test, which is based on certain assumptions about the properties of the population from which samples were taken, and about the sampling process itself. For example, the t-test assumes that the variable sampled to generate the data has a normal distribution in the population from which the samples were taken, which in turn at least implies the interval scale of measurement; it also assumes that the sampling from that population was a random process. The implication of this is that, in general, a parametric test will only produce a valid decision on a null hypothesis when all the assumptions on which it is based have been satisfied (although see also the discussion on the robustness of tests which follows on p. 389).

Non-parametric tests

Non-parametric tests are those, such as the Mann-Whitney test, which are based on fewer and more easily satisfied assumptions about the population and the sampling process. For this reason they are known as 'distribution-free' tests, since they are effectively 'free' of some assumptions about the characteristics of the population distribution. Non-parametric tests are particularly useful in psychology as they can be used when (as is often the case) the nature of the underlying distribution is unknown, or if it is known to be grossly non-normal in form, or when the scale of measurement or sampling procedure is not adequate for a parametric test.

As you will now see, this distinction between parametric and non-parametric tests is essential to making the decision about which test to use.

Selecting a test

The selection of a test needs to be approached with some care. There are a number of different possibilities, and clearly you will wish to make sure you select the right statistic for the kind of data your investigation is going to generate. If you don't choose correctly, you may not make full use of your data, or more seriously, you may draw unjustified conclusions.

It is a good idea to try to train yourself to make this decision a key part of the whole planning process, and to do it before you actually gather any data. Although it *is* possible to leave the decision about which test to use until after all the data have actually been collected, this is never very satisfactory. It is far better to design the investigation around a test rather than to try to do it the other way round.

Fortunately, selecting a test for your data is a straightforward process, *as long as you are in possession of certain key pieces of information.* The first thing to do is to check that you have answers to each of the following questions. Then consult the decision table to decide which procedure you need to use. Immediately after the table is a summary of what each of them is able to tell you. You can use it to check that you will obtain the information you need from the test you have selected.

Important questions to ask when selecting a test

1   What kind of decision do you want the test to help you with?

- Do you wish to investigate non-causal (correlational) relations, where you want to know whether there is significant **co-variation** between two sets of data?
- Do you want to know whether two or more means or medians are significantly different from each other?
- Or whether a distribution is significantly different from one predicted by the null hypothesis?

(Note: If you wish to obtain a correlation coefficient you need to consider the scale of measurement of the data before choosing a procedure using the table in box 9.1. Otherwise, continue to question 2 below.)

2   Do your data satisfy the theoretical assumptions of a parametric test?
In this book only the t-test falls squarely into this category, although the Pearson product-moment correlation coefficient requires measurements to have been made on at least an interval scale.

3   What design is the investigation?

- **A one-sample design?** (One group of participants who generate one set of data.)
- **A two or more samples independent subjects design?** (Two or more groups of participants who each generate one set of data.)
- **A two or more samples repeated measures design?** (One group of participants who generate two or more sets of data under different conditions.)

See chapter 5 for information on the difference between these designs.

Once you have answers to these questions you can use the information in box 9.1 to select the test you need. When you have a choice among options, as in the case of non-parametric procedures, use the summary of tests which follows to check that your choice is correct.

Box 9.1 A test decision table

	Design		
	1 sample	**2 or more samples**	
		Independent subjects	**Repeated measures**
Parametric tests		t-test for independent subjects	t-test for repeated measures
Non-parametric tests	Chi-squared test of goodness of fit	Mann-Whitney U-test Chi-squared test of association	Wilcoxon test Sign test
	Both sets of data measured on at least an interval scale	**Both sets of data measured on at least an ordinal scale**	
Correlation coefficients	Pearson's product-moment coefficient	Spearman's rank order coefficient	

A Summary of the Information provided by the Tests in this Book

Parametric tests

The t-test (for independent subjects or repeated measures designs)

This is a test of significant difference between two means. It tells you whether the difference between the means of two samples is sufficiently great to be unlikely to have occurred by chance alone. There are two versions, one for the independent subjects and a slightly different one for repeated measures designs.

Non-parametric tests

The Wilcoxon test

This is a test of significant difference between two sets of ordinal data obtained from a repeated measures design. It tells you whether the difference between the two medians is sufficiently great to be unlikely to have occurred by chance alone.

The Sign test

This test performs the same function as the Wilcoxon test, but should be used in preference to it when you have only weak ordinal data. (In this context 'weak' means that when you compare a subject's scores in condition 1 with the corresponding score in condition 2 you feel confident that you are able to state whether the change has been positive or negative, but you have little confidence that the magnitude of the change has much meaning.)

The Mann-Whitney test

This is a test of significant difference between two sets of ordinal data obtained from an independent subjects design. It tells you whether the difference between the two medians is sufficiently great to be unlikely to have occurred by chance alone.

The chi-squared (goodness of fit) test

This is a test to determine whether an observed distribution of frequencies (which has been obtained by counting the number of observations falling into several categories) is significantly different from that predicted by the null hypothesis. The scale of measurement need only be nominal. Use this test when the frequencies are contained in a 1 × n table.

The chi-squared test of association

This is a test to determine whether an observed distribution of frequencies (which has been obtained by counting the number of observations falling into several categories) is significantly different from that predicted by the null hypothesis. The scale of measurement need only be nominal. Use this test to determine whether there is a significant association between two variables, when the frequencies are contained in an m × n table. (The symbols m and n here refer to the number of rows (m) and columns (n) in a table or matrix. Thus, a 1 × n table is one consisting of only a single row of cells, but with any number of cells in the row. An m × n table is one which can have any number of both rows and columns (although some, such as the 2 × 2 table, are most common).)

Correlation coefficients

The Pearson product-moment correlation coefficient

This procedure provides a measure of the extent of co-variation between any two variables based on sets of interval or ratio scale data. The significance of correlation (i.e. the probability of any given correlation coefficient being equalled or exceeded by chance alone) can be determined if the variables are normally distributed.

The Spearman rank order correlation coefficient

This provides a measure of the extent of co-variation between any two variables based on sets of ordinal scale data. The significance of correlation (i.e. the probability of any given correlation coefficient being equalled or exceeded by chance alone) can be determined.

Power and Robustness of Tests

Power

The power of a test statistic is a measure of that test's ability to do the job it was designed to do when it is given appropriate data to work on.

More formally, the power of a test is defined as the probability that it will lead to the correct rejection of the null hypothesis (that is, to rejection when the null hypothesis is in fact false). This definition implies that the power of a test can be quantified with some precision, and, in fact, it is possible to calculate the power of a test for any given situation, though the procedure for doing so lies beyond the scope of this book.

There are two points to be made regarding the power of tests. The first is that parametric tests are always likely to be more powerful than non-parametric tests in any given situation. Parametric tests, as we have already seen, are based on a set of assumptions about the data which, while they limit the range of situations in which the test can be used, also mean that, as long as the assumptions are satisfied, the test will be more powerful than any non-parametric equivalent. The difference in power can, however, be quite small.

Secondly, because high power is a very desirable quality in a test, it is necessary to find ways of maximizing the power of a test. Basically, there are two ways of doing this:

1   Increase sample size. The most straightforward strategy for raising the power of a test is simply to increase the sample size by as much as possible without thereby making the experiment unwieldy or too expensive. As the sample size increases so the probability of a correct rejection of the null hypothesis increases.

2   Decrease the variability in the samples. You do this by removing as far as

possible sources of error variance from the sampling and measurement process; for example, by using a matched subjects design and ensuring that all research participants generate scores under identical conditions.

The test will also appear to be more powerful if you ask it to do less by increasing the significance level. As the significance level moves from (say) p = 0.01 to 0.05 and beyond, so the power of the test increases. However, this strategy may increase to an unacceptable degree the probability of making a type 1 error. Similarly, the power of a test will appear to increase if you use a directional (i.e. a one-tailed) hypothesis instead of a non-directional (two-tailed) one. However, you should really do so only if you are sure that the alternative possibility is of no interest to you.

Robustness

The robustness of a test refers to the extent to which any underlying assumptions about the population and sample can be disregarded without seriously compromising the conclusions based on the test. Not all tests are equally robust, but apart from knowing this fact, you don't really need to concern yourself with just how robust each of them is. All the procedures in this book describe tests which are relatively robust, meaning that they can each permit some degree of violation of their basic assumptions without seriously invalidating the test result. It is safe to assume that, in general, non-parametric tests are more tolerant of such violations than parametric tests.

However, that said, if you are a relative newcomer to using statistics, or, indeed, regard yourself as a non-statistician, you should regard the robustness of a test as an insurance policy rather than as a licence to ignore test requirements. Always play safe and try to ensure that, as far as possible, you meet fully the underlying assumptions of any test statistic which you use.

One final point. Because both parametric and non-parametric tests work on samples of data, there is, as was noted earlier, a relationship between the robustness of the test and the size of the sample which it is given to deal with. Essentially the robustness of a test (defined as its ability to provide a meaningful result despite some degree of violation of its basic assumptions) increases as the sample size increases. However you should also be aware of the fact that this increase can be very slow since power is proportional only to the square root of sample size. So, although large samples do indeed help protect against the consequences of disregarding the test assumptions, they are not the only, nor indeed the best, way to assure a valid result. You also need to consider the other aspects of the research design which were mentioned earlier.

The t-Test

The t-test is a powerful parametric procedure which compares the **means** of two sets of scores in order to determine whether the difference between them is significant at the chosen level of probability. If the result of the test indicates that the difference *is* significant, and as long as the assumptions in the under-lying statistical model have been met, then it can be concluded that there is a significant difference between the means of the two populations from which the samples were drawn.

There are two versions of the t-test. Both perform the same function, and are based on the same statistical model.

1   The **independent subjects** (or independent samples) version is used to work with data obtained from an independent subjects design. The numbers of subjects in the two samples can differ, although the difference should not be too great – a conservative rule of thumb would be that any difference should not amount to more than 10 per cent of the larger of the two samples.

2   The **repeated measures** (also sometimes called correlated samples) version is used when the data have been obtained from a repeated measures design.

The assumptions underlying the t-test

The independent subjects version of the test involves comparing two samples of data which are thought to have been drawn from populations with different means. The repeated measures version, however, involves two samples of data drawn from the same population and the comparison is between data drawn from the same source under different conditions – i.e. the test assesses the significance of within-subject differences.

Because this is a parametric test it is based on assumptions concerning the nature of the population(s) involved, the sampling procedure and the scale of measurement achieved in the data.

Assumption 1   The variable being measured is normally distributed in the population(s) from which the samples are drawn.

In practice, you have to be reasonably certain that the variable in question is likely to be approximately normally distributed – and the closer to normal the better – although in the nature of things, you are not able to say this with certainty. If a random or quasi-random procedure has been used to obtain the samples, then the mean and standard deviation of the samples can be used as estimates of the population parameters, and can thus be used, by means of a box and whisker graph, to assess the shape of the underlying population distribution.

Assumption 2   The population(s) have the same variance.

This can be checked by comparing the variances or standard deviations for the two samples – the smaller the difference, the better. A more precise check is given by the F-ratio test (not in this book), which permits the significance of the difference in variances to be determined.

Assumption 3   The data are obtained by a process of random sampling from the population(s), and each score is obtained independently of the others.

Assumption 4   The data represent measures on at least the interval scale.

Because the t-test is a robust procedure, some degree of latitude in meeting the first two of these assumptions is sometimes allowed. However, as already noted, unless you are a statistician, it is better to treat this latitude as an insurance policy, rather than as a licence to neglect the assumptions of the test. It is particularly important to take a conservative approach and to check as carefully as you can that the assumptions of the t-test are satisfied, since if you are producing coursework for an examining authority they will require you to use the precise criteria in deciding whether to use the test.

How the t-test works

The t-test enables a researcher to ask about the significance of the difference between the means of two sets of data. However, because in any situation where the data are obtained by sampling from a population some degree of difference will always be observed, the question to be asked is not simply whether the two means are different (they will be), but whether the difference is so great as to be unlikely to have occurred by chance. To tackle this question, the t-test considers two pieces of information:

1   The difference between the means of the samples, which is easily obtained from the raw data.
2   An estimate of the dispersion of the differences between sample means in the form of the **standard error of the difference between the means**. This has to be computed from the data.

You will remember from chapter 8 that if a sample is taken from a population, and the sample standard deviation computed, then this can also be used to provide an estimate of the standard deviation of all possible sample means. This statistic, called the standard error of the mean, is important because it enables any given sample mean to be located on the distribution of sample means. Given that the standard error of the difference *between* means can be computed in a similar way, it follows that it is also possible to locate any given difference between means on its sampling distribution.

Clearly, the larger the difference which exists between sample means, the more likely it will be that such difference will turn out to be statistically significant. But at the same time, the greater the value of the standard error of the difference, the less likely it will be that a difference will turn out to be significant.

The t-test, therefore, puts these two pieces of information – the difference between the means and the standard error of the difference – together to compute the ratio between them, which is signified by the symbol t. So that:

$$t = \frac{\text{difference in means}}{\text{standard error of the difference in means}}$$

The details of the statistical theory behind this need not concern us here. It is enough to say that the value for the statistic t which results from the computation reflects the magnitude of the difference between the means.

There is only one further piece of information necessary before any inference can be drawn about the meaning of t. This concerns the t-distribution.

The t-distribution

The statistic t has its own distribution, called the t-distribution. Actually, there is a whole family of t-distributions, each member of which is slightly different from the others. The precise shape of any one particular distribution is determined by the number of degrees of freedom in the data (in effect by the sample size), but each is approximately normal, and the larger the sample size, the closer the t-distribution approaches to the standard normal distribution.

The importance of the t-distribution is that once a value for t (which indicates the magnitude of the difference between the sample means) has been computed, and the degrees of freedom determined, then the t-distribution can be used to decide whether the difference between the means is so great as to be unlikely to have occurred by chance.

Once you have calculated a value for t from your data, consult table 9 in appendix 5, which provides the critical values for t. These critical values are the t values, for a range of degrees of freedom, which are so extreme as to have a probability of being exceeded of $p = 0.05$ (i.e. are likely to be exceeded by chance no more than 5 per cent of the time). To use the table you simply compare your computed value for t with the table value for the correct number of degrees of freedom. If the obtained value is more extreme than the table value, then it follows that the observed value for t (and hence the difference between the two sample means) must have a p-value of no more than $p = 0.05$.

Power, sample size and the t-test

The t-test is a fairly powerful and robust test, and can therefore safely be used with smallish samples. However, as the sample size falls, so does the robustness of the test, and it may be better not to use it if there are fewer than 10 scores for each mean. A non-parametric test should be used instead.

If, on the other hand, you have obtained samples consisting of more than 20 scores for each mean, this will almost certainly mean that the power and robustness of the test will reach an acceptable level. The greater the size of the samples above 20, the more the power of the test approaches the point at which it is certain to reject the null hypothesis, if that is appropriate. So, theoretically at least, bigger is better as far as samples are concerned. However, in practice big samples confer no significant advantage, since any increase in power has to be balanced against the possibility of increased sampling error due to fatigue or other experiment-related factors, especially if the data are collected over several days. This means that for most experiments, a moderate sample size (say around 20 to 25), coupled with careful attention to the other factors affecting the reliability of the data, is probably the best strategy to adopt.

The t-Test for Independent Subjects

Overview of the test

(Note: If you wish, you can skip this section, and move on directly to the computation instructions.)

This test assumes that the population variances for the two samples are the same. If you doubt whether this is the case, because the box-plots look *very* different, then use an F-test (from a more advanced text) to determine whether the difference is significant at the $p = 0.05$ level. If it is, the text should suggest a way of overcoming the difficulty.

The computation of the t-test is carried out in three stages:

Stage 1

Obtain an unbiased estimate of the variance of the population from which the samples were drawn, using the formula:

$$s^2 = \frac{\Sigma(X_1 - \overline{X}_1)^2 + \Sigma(X_2 - \overline{X}_2)^2}{n_1 + n_2 - 2}$$

Formula 9.1

where:

X_1 is any item of data in sample 1
X_2 is any item of data in sample 2
$\overline{X}_1$ is the mean of sample 1
$\overline{X}_2$ is the mean of sample 2
n_1 is the number of observations in sample 1
n_2 is the number of observations in sample 2

In words, this formula instructs you to:

• Sum the squared deviations of the data in each sample about its mean
• Add the two sums together
• Divide by the number of degrees of freedom.

Stage 2

Use the estimate of the population variance to estimate the standard error of the difference between the means:

$$s_{\bar{x}_1-\bar{x}_2} = \sqrt{\frac{s^2}{n_1} + \frac{s^2}{n_2}}$$

Formula 9.2

Stage 3

Divide the difference between the means by the standard error of the difference to find t:

$$t = \frac{\bar{X}_1 - \bar{X}_2}{s_{\bar{x}_1-\bar{x}_2}}$$

Formula 9.3

The t-test for independent subjects: computation instructions

Step 1   Set up the column headings for the computation as follows:

Column 1	Column 2	Column 3	Column 4	Column 5	Column 6
Sample 1 (X_1)	Sample 2 (X_2)	Sample 1 differences $(X_1 - \bar{X}_1)$	Sample 2 differences $(X_2 - \bar{X}_2)$	Sample 1 squared differences	Sample 2 squared differences

Step 2   Enter the sample 1 data in column 1 and the sample 2 data in column 2.

Stage 1

To find:

$$\Sigma(X_1 - \bar{X}_1)^2 + \Sigma(X_2 - \bar{X}_2)^2$$

Step 3   Sum column 1 and find the mean: repeat for column 2.

If you are to use a two-tailed alternate hypothesis go to step 4 now. If, on the other hand, you are to use a one-tailed hypothesis, inspect the means before proceeding. If the positive or negative difference between the means supports the alternate hypothesis because the difference between means is in the required direction, then continue with step 4. Otherwise stop the test here and report that there is no evidence in the data to justify the rejection of the null hypothesis.

Step 4   Subtract the mean of the data in column 1 from each item of data in column 1, and enter each difference in column 3. Repeat for column 2, placing each answer in column 4.

Step 5   Square each difference in column 3 and place the result in column 5. Repeat the process with the values in column 4, and place the results in column 6.

Step 6   Sum column 5 and place the result at the foot of the column. Repeat for column 6.

To find the number of degrees of freedom:

$$(n_1 - 1) + (n_2 - 1)$$

Step 7   Subtract 1 from the number of items of data in each sample, and add the two values together.

To find s^2:

Step 8   Add together the sums of columns 5 and 6 (step 6), and divide the result by the number of degrees of freedom (step 7), to find s^2.

Stage 2

To find:

$$\frac{s^2}{n_1} + \frac{s^2}{n_2}$$

Step 9   Divide the result of step 8 by the number of observations in sample 1. Repeat for sample 2, and add the two results together.

To find:

$$s_{\bar{x}_1 - \bar{x}_2}$$

Step 10   Take the square root of the result of step 9.

Stage 3

Step 11   Subtract the smaller of the means of the samples from the larger (step 3), and divide the result by the result of step 10. This gives a value for t.

Step 12   Consult table 9 in appendix 5 to determine the critical value for t for the appropriate number of degrees of freedom and significance level.

Step 13   Present the results. After completing the t-test report the following information:

- The means of both sets of scores
- The computed value for t
- The significance level employed
- The number of degrees of freedom

- The critical value of t for that number of degrees of freedom and that significance level
- Whether the test is being used as a one- or two-tailed test
- The region of rejection.

Step 14   Make a decision about hypotheses. If the computed value for t is equal to, or numerically greater than, the critical value in table 9 it lies in the region of rejection, indicating that the means of the two sets of scores *are* significantly different from each other. The probability of such difference when the null hypothesis is correct (the p-value) is no greater than the significance level selected. **If this is so, accept the experimental hypothesis and reject the null hypothesis.**

Alternatively, if the observed value for t is numerically *less* than the table value, then the probability of the observed difference when the null hypothesis is correct (the p-value) is greater than the significance level. **If this is so, do not reject the null hypothesis. There is insufficient evidence to support the experimental hypothesis.**

Step 15   Translate the result of the procedure back into the terms of the investigation. If the experimental hypothesis has been accepted *and* if the data have been collected under sufficiently controlled conditions, it may be possible to conclude that the effect of the experimental treatment has been to cause a significant change in the behaviour of the experimental group. If this conclusion is drawn, then that change can also be expected to occur whenever the experiment is repeated with a sufficiently large randomly selected group of subjects.

The t-test for independent subjects: a worked example

As part of an investigation into male–female differences in cognitive functioning, male and female subjects were asked individually to perform a simple visuo-spatial task, and their performance was measured by the time it took them (in seconds) to complete the task.

As this is an independent subjects design, with data obtained by random sampling representing measures on an interval scale, the t-test for independent subjects is appropriate.

· The null hypothesis states that there will be no significant difference between the means of the two conditions, while the experimental hypothesis is one-tailed and predicts that a significant difference will be found, with the mean time of female subjects significantly below that of the males. The significance level chosen is $p = 0.05$, and the region of rejection is one-tailed. The null hypothesis will be rejected if the means differ in the predicted direction and the p-value (the probability that the null hypothesis is nevertheless correct) is equal to or less than the significance level.

Data: Time (in seconds) to complete a visuo-spatial task

Steps 1 and 2		Step 4	Step 4	Step 5	Step 5
Column 1 Sample 1 Males	Column 2 Sample 2 Females	Column 3 $X_1 - \overline{X}_1$	Column 4 $X_2 - \overline{X}_2$	Column 5 $(X_1 - \overline{X}_1)^2$	Column 6 $(X_2 - \overline{X}_2)^2$
193	112	45.15	−4.91	2038.52	24.11
143	160	−4.85	43.09	23.52	1856.75
104	73	−43.85	−43.91	1922.82	1928.09
92	121	−55.85	4.09	3119.22	16.73
188	140	40.15	23.09	1612.02	533.15
141	113	−6.85	−3.91	46.92	15.29
120	98	−27.85	−18.91	775.62	357.59
117	127	−30.85	10.09	951.72	101.81
186	155	38.15	38.09	1455.42	1450.85
124	101	−23.85	−15.91	568.82	253.13
217	86	69.15	−30.91	4781.72	955.43
165		17.15		294.12	
132		−15.85		251.22	
Step 3 $\Sigma X_1 = 1922$ $\overline{X}_1 = 147.85$	**Step 3** $\Sigma X_2 = 1286$ $\overline{X}_2 = 116.91$			**Step 6** $\Sigma(X_1 - \overline{X}_1)^2$ $= 17841.66$	**Step 6** $\Sigma(X_2 - \overline{X}_2)^2$ $= 7492.93$

The sample mean for females (column 2) is below that of males (column 1) in line with the one-tailed hypothesis: therefore proceed.

Step 7	Step 8
$df = (13 - 1) + (11 - 1) = 22$	$s^2 = \dfrac{17841.66 + 7492.93}{22}$ $= 1151.57$

Steps 9 and 10	Step 11
$s_{\overline{X}_1 - \overline{X}_2} = \sqrt{\dfrac{1151.57}{13} + \dfrac{1151.57}{11}}$ $= \sqrt{88.58 + 104.69}$ $= 13.90$	$t = \dfrac{147.85 - 116.91}{13.90}$ $t = 2.22$

(Note: We are working to two decimal places, so it is probable that some rounding error will creep into these calculations. As we saw in chapter 6 it is necessary to carry a sufficient number of decimal places to permit the precision of the original measurements to be maintained.)

Step 12   Consult table 9 in appendix 5. This gives the one-tailed critical value for 22 degrees of freedom at the $p = 0.05$ significance level as $t = 1.717$.

Step 13   Present the results:

Means Male sample 1 Female sample 2	147.85 secs 116.91 secs
Degrees of freedom	$df = (13 - 1) + (11 - 1) = 22$
Computed value for t	$t = 2.22$
Significance level (one-tailed test)	$p = 0.05$
Critical value for t	$t = 1.717$
Region of rejection	Values of t which are equal to, or greater than, 1.717

Step 14   The value computed for t is 2.22. This value is greater than the one-tailed critical value of $t = 1.72$ (rounded to two decimal places) for the $p = 0.05$ significance level with 22 degrees of freedom and thus lies within the region of rejection chosen for the test. Consequently, the null hypothesis can be rejected and the experimental hypothesis accepted.

Step 15   The research question asked whether the performance of males on a visuo-spatial task would be significantly inferior to that of females. The result of the t-test indicates that a significant difference exists between the two samples, with the probability no greater than $p = 0.05$ (i.e. 5 chances in 100) of such a difference having occurred by chance when the null hypothesis is correct.

Since this indicates that the two sets of data were drawn from statistical populations with different means, it can be concluded that these data represent evidence for a difference between the sexes in terms of visuo-spatial ability, with women on average able to complete the task more rapidly than men.

The t-Test for Repeated Measures

Overview of the test

(Note: As with the t-test for independent subjects, you can ignore this overview and proceed directly to the computation instructions if you so wish.)

The computation is carried out in three stages.

Stage 1

Obtain an unbiased estimate of the variance of the difference between pairs of scores:

$$s_D^2 = \frac{\Sigma(D - \overline{D})^2}{N - 1}$$ **Formula 9.4**

where:

D is the difference between each pair of scores
$\overline{D}$ is the mean difference between the pairs of scores
N is the number of pairs of scores

Stage 2

Use the estimate of the population variance to find the variance of the mean difference between pairs of scores:

$$s_{\overline{D}}^2 = \frac{s_D^2}{N}$$ **Formula 9.5**

Stage 3

Divide the mean difference between pairs of scores in the sample by the standard error of the mean difference to find t:

$$t = \frac{\overline{D}}{s_{\overline{D}}}$$ **Formula 9.6**

The t-test for repeated measures: computation instructions

Step 1 Set up the column headings for the computation as follows:

Column 1	Column 2	Column 3	Column 4	Column 5
Sample 1 (X_1)	Sample 2 (X_2)	differences $X_1 - X_2$	$D - \overline{D}$	$(D - \overline{D})^2$

Step 2   Enter the sample 1 data in column 1 and the sample 2 data in column 2.

Stage 1

To find:

$$\Sigma(D - \bar{D})^2$$

Step 3   For each pair of scores, subtract the score in column 2 from its pair in column 1. Enter the difference in column 3.

Step 4   Sum the differences and find the mean difference by dividing by the number of pairs of scores. Enter the result at the foot of column 3.

If you are to use a two-tailed alternate hypothesis go to step 5 now. If, on the other hand, you are to use a one-tailed hypothesis inspect the mean difference before proceeding. Does its sign support the direction of the one-tailed alternate hypothesis? If not, stop the analysis here and report there is no evidence in the data to justify the rejection of the null hypothesis. Otherwise proceed with step 5.

Step 5   Subtract the mean difference (step 4) from each of the differences in column 3, and enter each result in column 4.

Step 6   Square each value in column 4 and enter the result in column 5.

Step 7   Sum the values in column 5 and enter the result at the foot of the column.

Step 8   Find the df $= (N - 1)$ number of degrees of freedom in the data, by subtracting 1 from the number of pairs of scores.

To find:

$$s_{\bar{D}}^2$$

Step 9   Divide the result of step 7 by the result of step 8.

Stage 2

To find:

$$\frac{s_{\bar{D}}^2}{N}$$

Step 10   Divide the result of step 9 by the number of pairs of scores.

Stage 3

To find t:

Step 11   Take the square root of the result of step 10.

Step 12   Divide the result of step 11 *into* the mean difference between the two sets of scores (found at step 4). This is t. If its value is negative neglect the sign.

Step 13   Consult table 9 in appendix 5 to determine the critical value for t for the appropriate number of degrees of freedom and significance level.

Step 14 Present the results. After completing the t-test report the following information:

- The means of both sets of scores
- The computed value for t
- The significance level employed
- The number of degrees of freedom
- The critical value of t for that number of degrees of freedom and that significance level
- Whether the test is being used as a one- or two-tailed test
- The region of rejection.

Step 15 Make a decision about hypotheses. If the computed value for t is equal to, or numerically greater than, the critical value in table 9, it lies in the region of rejection, indicating that the means of the two sets of scores *are* significantly different from each other. The probability of such difference when the null hypothesis is correct (the p-value) is no greater than the significance level selected. **If this is so, accept the experimental hypothesis and reject the null hypothesis.**

Alternatively, if the observed value for t is numerically *less* than the table value, then the probability of the observed difference when the null hypothesis is correct (the p-value) is greater than the significance level. **If this is so, do not reject the null hypothesis. There is insufficient evidence to accept the experimental hypothesis.**

Step 16 Translate the result of the procedure back into the terms of the investigation. If the experimental hypothesis has been accepted *and* if the data have been collected under sufficiently controlled conditions, it may be possible to conclude that the effect of the experimental treatment has been to cause a significant change in the behaviour of the experimental group. If this conclusion is drawn, then that change can also be expected to occur whenever the experiment is repeated with a sufficiently large randomly selected group of subjects.

The t-test of repeated measures: a worked example

An investigation into the effects of prior expectations on problem-solving ability was designed to enable the ten participants to act as their own controls. Half the participants were asked to solve a problem which they were told was 'easy' followed by one which they believed to be 'difficult'. The other five were first asked to solve the 'hard' problem followed by the 'easy' one. In fact, both problems were of the same moderate level of difficulty. The raw data from the experiment consisted of the time taken by each participant to solve each of the problems.

The one-tailed experimental hypothesis was that the mean of the solution times for the problems in the 'hard' condition would be significantly greater (i.e. longer) than the mean of the 'easy' condition, while the null hypothesis predicted no difference between the two means. The significance level chosen is p = 0.05 and the region of rejection is one-tailed. The null hypothesis will be rejected if the means differ in the predicted direction and the p-value (the probability that the null hypothesis is nevertheless correct) is equal to or less than the significance level.

Data: Solution times (in seconds) for 'hard' and 'easy' problems

Steps 1 and 2		Step 3	Step 5	Step 6
Column 1 Sample 1 'Hard'	Column 2 Sample 2 'Easy'	Column 3 $X_1 - X_2$	Column 4 $D - \bar{D}$	Column 5 $(D - \bar{D})^2$
131.0	64.2	66.8	14.44	208.51
109.1	80.4	28.7	−23.66	559.80
102.0	100.3	1.7	−50.66	2566.44
158.1	70.3	87.8	35.44	1255.99
138.4	102.7	35.7	−16.66	277.56
125.3	83.7	41.6	−10.76	115.78
180.4	55.7	124.7	72.34	5233.08
170.4	123.6	46.8	−5.56	30.91
163.7	89.1	74.6	22.24	494.62
121.2	106.0	15.2	−37.16	1380.87

		Step 4		Step 7
$\Sigma X_1 = 1399.6$ $\bar{X}_1 = 139.96$	$\Sigma X_2 = 87.60$ $\bar{X}_2 = 87.6$	$\Sigma(X_1 - X_2) = 523.6$ $\bar{D} = 52.36$		$\Sigma(D - \bar{D})^2$ $= 12123.56$

The sign of the mean difference (column 3) supports the one-tailed hypothesis; therefore proceed.

Step 8	Step 9
$df = (N - 1) = (10 - 1) = 9$	$s_{\bar{D}}^2 = \dfrac{12123.56}{9} = 1347.06$

Step 10	Step 11
$s_{\bar{D}}^2 = \dfrac{1347.06}{10}$ $= 134.71$	$\sqrt{134.71} = 11.61$

Step 12
$t = \dfrac{52.36}{11.61} = 4.51$

Step 13 Consult table 9 in appendix 5. This gives the one-tailed critical value for 9 degrees of freedom at the p = 0.05 significance level as t = 1.833.

Step 14 Present the results:

Means	Sample 1	139.96 secs
	Sample 2	87.60 secs
Degrees of freedom		df = (N − 1) = 9
Computed value for t		t = 4.51
Significance level (one-tailed test)		p = 0.05
Critical value for t		t = 1.833
Region of rejection		Values of t which are equal to, or greater than, 1.833

Step 15 The value computed for t is 4.51. This value is greater than the one-tailed critical value of t = 1.83 (rounded to two decimal places) for the p = 0.05 significance level with 9 degrees of freedom and thus lies within the region of rejection chosen for the test. Consequently, the null hypothesis can be rejected and the experimental hypothesis accepted.

Step 16 The research question asked whether there would be a difference observable in the subjects' problem-solving performance, depending on whether they believed the problems to be 'hard' or 'easy'. The result of the t-test indicates that a significant difference exists between the conditions in the experiment, and as predicted, when subjects are led to believe that a problem is hard they perform significantly less well than when they believe it to be easy.

This indicates that the two sets of data were drawn from statistical populations with different means. We may conclude that in general, peoples' beliefs about the relative difficulty of problems are likely to affect the ease with which they can be solved.

The Mann-Whitney U-Test for Independent Samples

The Mann-Whitney U-test provides a useful way of testing for the existence of a significant difference between the medians of two sets of data, enabling you to determine whether the data are likely to have come from the same statistical population.

When to use the Mann-Whitney U-test

You can use this test if all the following conditions are met:

1 **Data** The data consist of measures on *at least* an ordinal scale of measurement. (See chapter 6 for information to help you decide whether your data represent measures on the ordinal scale.)
2 **Design** The data are drawn from two independent samples (which need not be of equal size).
3 **Purpose** You intend to test for the existence of a significant difference between medians. If such a difference is found it may be concluded that the data came from two different populations.

How the Mann-Whitney test works

The Mann-Whitney U-test requires at least ordinal data, that is, data which capture the **relative ordering** of the scores, but which ignore the **exact size** of the intervals between them. It is this characteristic which provides the basis for the test.

The test works by first merging the two sets of data. A single rank ordering of the merged sets is then obtained, which gives the lowest rank to the lowest value. The reason for the ranking process is that it places each score in a relation to every other score in a way which is independent of the exact magnitude of the difference between their values.

Because high values in the rankings indicate higher scores in the data, it follows that if the rankings for each of the sets of data are summed individually, and the two sums compared, the set for which the sum is larger will contain the higher relative scores.

The Mann-Whitney test uses these rankings to generate a measure of the difference between the two sets of scores, called U, whose value is determined by the number of times that a score from one set of data precedes (i.e. has been given a lower ranking than) a score from the other set. Because either set of scores could be used as the reference set, these relationships are different for each set of scores, so there are actually two possible values for U, which are called U and U_1 (read U_1 as 'U complement').

As you will see from the instructions for computation below, you need to make sure that you have the *smaller* of the two values of U before you consult the table of critical values. The procedure for doing this is quite straightforward, and is given in the instructions for the computation in the next section.

The distribution of U for all possible sample sizes can be computed, so critical values of U for any given significance level are known. Those for the $p = 0.05$ and $p = 0.01$ significance levels are given in table 6 of appendix 5.

The Mann-Whitney U-test: computation instructions

(Note: This procedure only applies to situations where you have up to 20 items of data in either group of scores. If you have more, you will need to consult a more advanced text, such as Siegel & Castellan (1988).)

Step 1   Set up the column headings for the computation as follows:

Column 1	Column 2	Column 3	Column 4
Sample 1	Ranks of sample 1	Sample 2	Ranks of sample 2

Step 2   Enter the data from sample 1 in column 1, the data from sample 2 in column 3, and compute the two medians. If the samples are unequal in size take care to place the larger of the two sets of data in column 1.

Step 3   Inspect all the values in both columns 1 and 3 and carry out the ranking procedure on all the items of data. Place a 1 in the appropriate rankings column against the *lowest* value in *both* sets of data, a 2 against the next lowest, a 3 against the next lowest, and so on, until all the items of data have been given a ranking. (See chapter 6 if detailed instructions on how to rank data, including how to deal with tied rankings, are required.)

Check that the direction of the difference between the medians supports the alternate hypothesis if it is one-tailed. If it does not, end the computation here and report that there is no evidence in the data to justify rejecting the null hypothesis. Otherwise continue to step 4.

Step 4   When all scores have been ranked, sum the rankings in columns 2 and 4.

Step 5   Find a value for R_1 by one of the following methods. If you have sets of data of *unequal* size, sum the ranks of the *smaller* of the two sets from column 4.

If you have sets of data containing *equal* numbers of scores sum the ranks for *either* of the two sets of scores.

Finally, use R_1 to determine a value for U, by the formula:

$$U = n_1 n_2 + \frac{n_1(n_1 + 1)}{2} - R_1 \qquad\qquad \textbf{Formula 9.7}$$

where:

n_1 and n_2 are the number of scores in each sample
R_1 is the sum of the ranks of *one* of the sets of scores

(Alternatively, if you prefer, you can ignore the formula and, after computing the rankings, simply follow the instructions below.)

5.1   Sum the rankings in column 4
5.2   Multiply the number of items of data in column 1 by the number of items of data in column 3

5.3   Multiply n_1, the number of items in column 1, by $(n_1 + 1)$, and divide the result by 2

5.4   Add the result of 5.2 to the result of 5.3 and subtract the result of 5.1. The answer is a value for U.

Step 6   However arrived at, check that the value you have for U is the value you need (i.e. that it is the *smaller* of U and U_1.). To do this you calculate the value for U_1 using the following formula:

$$U_1 = n_1 n_2 - U \hspace{4cm} \textbf{Formula 9.8}$$

(Multiply the number of items of data in column 1 by the number of items of data in column 3, and subtract from the result the value for U already obtained.)

Step 7   Compare the values you have for U and U_1 and discard the larger of the two: you only need to use the smaller. Consult table 6 in appendix 5 to determine the critical value for U for the appropriate sample size.

Step 8   Present the results. After completing the computation of the Mann-Whitney test, report the following information:

- The medians of both sets of scores
- The computed values for U and U_1
- The significance level employed
- The critical value of U for that size of sample and significance level
- Whether the test is being used to test a one- or two-tailed hypothesis
- The region of rejection.

Step 9   If the computed value of U or U_1 (whichever is the smaller) is equal to or less than the critical value in table 6, it lies in the region of rejection, indicating that the medians of the two sets of scores are significantly different from each other. The probability of such difference occurring when the null hypothesis is correct (the p-value) is no greater than the significance level selected. **If this is so, accept the experimental hypothesis, and reject the null hypothesis.**

Alternatively if the computed value for U is greater than the critical value in the table, then the probability of the observed difference when the null hypothesis is correct (the p-value) is greater than the significance level, indicating that the two samples of data may have come from the same population. **If this is so, do not reject the null hypothesis. There is insufficient evidence to support the experimental hypothesis.**

Step 10   Translate the result of the procedure back into the terms of the investigation. If the experimental hypothesis has been accepted *and* if the data have been collected under sufficiently controlled conditions, it may be possible to conclude that the data are drawn from different statistical populations. If this conclusion is drawn, then the same difference can also be expected to be found whenever the same two populations are randomly sampled.

The Mann-Whitney U-test: a worked example

A psychologist working on an AIDS education project wanted to find out which was likely to be the most effective procedure for delivering information about HIV and AIDS to young adults.

The research involved showing an official government health education film to two groups of students from a large urban comprehensive school who had earlier been assigned at random to one of two conditions:

Condition 1 subjects saw the film, followed by a short, formal talk by a doctor.

Condition 2 subjects saw the film followed by an informal discussion session led by the same doctor.

After the film and talk or film and discussion, the students were asked to complete a questionnaire intended to measure 'AIDS awareness', and each completed questionnaire was marked out of a possible 30 marks.

The two-tailed experimental hypothesis was that a difference would be observed between the median questionnaire scores achieved in the two conditions, while the null hypothesis stated that no such difference would be found. The data represent measures only on an ordinal scale so the research uses the Mann-Whitney test and, since no prediction is made about the direction of difference, the two-tailed test is appropriate. The significance level chosen is $p = 0.05$, and the region of rejection is two-tailed. The null hypothesis will be rejected if the medians differ and the p-value (the probability that the null hypothesis is nevertheless correct) is equal to or less than the significance level.

Data: Scores on an 'AIDS awareness' questionnaire

	Column 1	Column 2	Column 3	Column 4
Step 1	Sample 1	Ranks of sample 1	Sample 2	Ranks of sample 2
Steps 2 and 3	17	8	15	5.5
	10	1	21	13.5
	24	17.5	23	16
	11	2.5	19	11
	13	4	27	20
	19	11	18	9
	21	13.5	19	11
	11	2.5	26	19
	16	7	22	15
	15	5.5	24	17.5
	median = 15.5		median = 21.5	
Step 4		Σranks = 72.5		Σranks = 137.5

Step 5

$$U = n_1 n_2 + \frac{n_1(n_1 + 1)}{2} - R_1 \qquad\qquad \text{Formula 9.7}$$

$$= 10 \times 10 + \frac{10(10 + 1)}{2} - 72.5$$

$$= 100 + 55 - 72.5$$
$$= 82.5$$

Step 6   Checking that this is indeed the value we need:

$$U_1 = n_1 n_2 - U \qquad\qquad \text{Formula 9.8}$$
$$= 10 \times 10 - 82.5$$
$$= 17.5$$

Step 7   As this gives a value for U_1 which is less than the value obtained for U, we know that 17.5 is the value we need. Table 6 gives U = 23 for a two-tailed test at the p = 0.05 significance level when both n_1 and n_2 = 10.

Step 8   Present the results:

Medians	Sample 1 Sample 2	15.5 21.5
Computed values for U		U = 82.5 U_1 = 17.5
Significance level (two-tailed test)		p = 0.05
Critical value for U		U = 23
Region of rejection		Values of U which are equal to, or less than, 23

Step 9   The value computed for U is 17.5. This value is less than the two-tailed critical value of U = 23 for the p = 0.05 significance level when n_1 = 10 and n_2 = 10 and thus lies within the region of rejection chosen for the test. Consequently, the null hypothesis can be rejected and the experimental hypothesis accepted.

Step 10   The psychologist concludes from the test that the two sets of data are drawn from populations with different medians, and thus the two methods of AIDS education do not appear to be equally effective. Inspection of the data indicates that an informal discussion is likely to be more effective than a formal talk when they are each used in conjunction with the same film.

The Wilcoxon Test for Matched Pairs: The Repeated Measures Design

The Wilcoxon test provides a means of testing for the existence of a significant difference between the medians of two related samples of data, permitting a decision to be made on whether the data are likely to have been drawn from the same, or different, populations.

When to use the Wilcoxon test

You can use this test if:

1 **Data**   The data represent measures on at least the ordinal scale of measurement. (See chapter 6 for information to help you decide whether your data reach the ordinal scale.)
2 **Design**   The data consist of two related sets of scores, such as those produced by one group of subjects in a repeated measures design.
3 **Purpose**   You wish to test for a significant difference between the medians of two sets of scores. If such a difference is found it may be concluded that the data came from two different populations.

How the Wilcoxon test works

The computation is a simple one, requiring only the following three operations:

1 Finding the magnitude (size) of the difference between the two scores generated by each subject.
2 Ranking the differences, with larger differences receiving higher rankings.
3 Giving each ranking a sign (+ve or −ve), to indicate the direction of difference.

It is these signed rankings which provide the means of determining whether the differences between the two sets of data are statistically significant. The reasoning behind this is as follows.

If chance or random factors alone are responsible for any differences between the two sets of scores then one would expect that the differences between scores (and hence their rankings) would be reasonably equally divided between positive and negative directions. That is, for about one-half of the pairs of scores, those in condition 1 would be greater than those in condition 2, and for the other half, the opposite would be the case. If the positive and negative ranks are then summed separately, one would expect to find that the two sums are approximately equal.

If, on the other hand, the two sets of scores are very different, due to the effect of the experimental treatment to which the subjects were exposed, then the rankings will not be equally divided between the two conditions, and therefore the signs of the direction of difference will also be unequally distributed between the two conditions.

So if, when the two rankings (+ve and −ve) are summed, they turn out to be unequal in size, the difference between the sums reflects the overall difference between the two sets of scores. However, you also have to remember that because the rankings were originally carried out on a single set of differences between two groups of scores, the two sums are related to each other: the larger the size of one, the smaller must be the size of the other. The test therefore uses the smaller of the summed rankings, which is designated T.

The exact distribution of T for all possible sample sizes can be worked out, and is approximately normal for situations where the number of pairs of scores is greater than about 8. However, the method given below is for use when the number of subjects contributing data is no greater than 25. If you have more than 25 subjects (i.e. more than 50 individual scores), then you should consult a more advanced statistics text, such as Siegel & Castellan (1988) for guidance. Critical values of T for N of up to 25 subjects can be found in table 7 in appendix 5.

The Wilcoxon test: computation instructions

Step 1   Set up the column headings for the computation as follows:

Column 1	Column 2	Column 3	Column 4
Sample 1	Sample 2	Differences	Signed rank of differences

Step 2   Enter one set of scores in column 1 and the other in column 2. It is vital that you ensure that the two scores on the *same* line come from the *same person*. (Before you begin, it may be helpful to inset an additional column to the left of column 1 to take an identifying number for each subject.) Compute the median of each set of scores.

If the alternate hypothesis is one-tailed, check that the direction of difference between the medians supports the hypothesis. If it does not, stop the computation and report that the data do not justify rejection of the null hypothesis. Otherwise continue on to step 3.

Step 3   Subtract the first score in column 2 from its corresponding score in column 1 and enter the difference, including the sign of the direction of difference, on the same line in column 3. Continue until all differences have been found.

Step 4   Ignoring the signs, rank the differences giving the lowest numerical difference the rank of 1, and the highest rank to the highest difference. (See the note below on the treatment of zero differences and tied rankings.)

Step 5 Transfer the sign of each of the differences from column 3 to the rankings in column 4.

Step 6 Sum the values of all the positive rankings, and note the result. Do the same for all the negative rankings.

Step 7 Take the smaller of the two sums of ranks – this is the computed value of T for those data. (NB If all the rankings have the same sign, then T = 0.) Consult table 7 in appendix 5 to determine the critical value for T for the appropriate N (the number of pairs of scores with non-zero difference).

Step 8 Present the results. After completing the computation of the Wilcoxon test report the following information:

- The medians of both sets of scores
- The effective sample size – the number of non-zero differences between scores
- The computed value for T
- The significance level employed
- The critical value of T for that size of sample and that significance level
- Whether the test is being used as a one- or two-tailed test
- The region of rejection.

Step 9 Make a decision about hypotheses. If the computed value of T is equal to or less than the critical value in table 7 it lies in the region of rejection, indicating that the medians of the two sets of scores are significantly different from each other. The probability of such difference when the null hypothesis is correct (the p-value) is no greater than the significance level selected. **If this is so, accept the experimental hypothesis, and reject the null hypothesis.**

   Alternatively if the computed value for T is greater than the critical value in the table, then the probability of the observed difference (the p-value) is greater than the significance level, indicating that the two samples of data came from the same population. **If this is so, do not reject the null hypothesis. There is insufficient evidence to support the experimental hypothesis.**

Step 10 Translate the result of the procedure back into the terms of the investigation. If the experimental hypothesis has been accepted *and* if the data have been collected under sufficiently controlled conditions, it may be possible to conclude that the data are drawn from different statistical populations. If this conclusion is drawn, then the same difference can also be expected to be found whenever the same two populations are randomly sampled.

A note on the treatment of ties in both scores and differences

1 Where tied scores result in a difference of zero, these are ignored and are not ranked, and the value of N is reduced accordingly.
2 Where tied differences exist, these are dealt with in the usual way. (See the section on ranking data in chapter 6.)

The Wilcoxon test: a worked example

A psychologist was investigating the question of whether wives' perceptions of their husbands changed significantly during the first three months of marriage. The couples married in a single locality during one month were randomly sampled and a cohort of 13 newly married women who had agreed to participate in the study was obtained. They were asked to complete a questionnaire designed to measure both positive and negative attitudes to their spouses. Three months later, the same individuals were contacted again, and asked to complete the same questionnaire.

Each participant's answers to the questionnaire on each occasion were expressed as a single score out of 20, so that the data consisted of two sets of 13 scores. Because these are ordinal data, obtained from a repeated measures design, the Wilcoxon test can be used in order to determine whether there is any significant change in attitudes over the three-month period being studied. The null hypothesis predicts no shift in attitudes over the three-month period, while the two-tailed experimental hypothesis is that a significant shift in attitudes will be found. The significance level chosen is $p = 0.05$ and the region of rejection is two-tailed. The null hypothesis will be rejected if the medians differ and the p-value (the probability that the null hypothesis is nevertheless correct) is equal to or less than the significance level.

Data: Scores on a marital attitudes questionnaire

Steps 1 and 2		Step 3	Steps 4 and 5
Column 1	Column 2	Column 3	Column 4
Sample 1 (2-week test)	Sample 2 (3-month test)	Differences	Signed rank of differences
12	14	−2	−4
14	16	−2	−4
15	12	+3	+8
10	12	−2	−4
13	17	−4	−10
10	18	−8	−12
15	18	−3	−8
9	6	+3	+8
14	16	−2	−4
10	10	0	0
11	17	−6	−11
10	11	−1	−1
14	16	−2	−4
median = 12	median = 16		

Step 6 Sum of positive rankings = 8 + 8 = 16
Sum of negative rankings = 4 + 4 + 4 + 10 + 12 + 8 + 4 + 11 + 1 + 4 = 62
There is one zero difference, so N = (13 − 1) = 12

Step 7 As T is the smaller of the two sums of rankings (in this case T = 16), discard the sum of the negative rankings above and consult table 7 in appendix 5. For N = 12, table 7 gives the value for a two-tailed test at the p = 0.05 significance level of T = 14.

Step 8 Present the results:

Medians	Sample 1	12
	Sample 2	16
Effective sample size		N = 12
Computed value for T		T = 16
Significance level (two-tailed test)		p = 0.05
Critical value for T		T = 14
Region of rejection		Values of T which are equal to, or less than, 14

Step 9 The value computed for T is 16. This value is greater than the two-tailed critical value of T = 14 for the p = 0.05 significance level when the effective sample size is 12, and thus lies *outside* the region of rejection chosen for the test. Consequently, the null hypothesis *cannot* be rejected.

Step 10 The psychologist therefore concludes that there is insufficient evidence to support the idea of a change in the attitudes of new wives to their husbands during the first three months of marriage. This is despite the fact that 10 out of the 13 wives registered *some* change in attitudes over the period in question. This suggests to her that it might be worth trying to improve the questionnaire so that it is better able to register changes in attitudes in order to see whether a significant difference can then be obtained from a new sample of informants.

The Sign Test

The Sign test is a non-parametric test which can be used to determine whether there is a significant difference between two sets of data when these have been obtained by means of a repeated measures design. If such a difference is found, it permits the conclusion to be drawn that the samples came from different statistical populations.

This test offers a useful alternative to the Wilcoxon test (which performs the same task), because it requires less information from the data. The difference between any two individual scores can be expressed in terms of two measures: the direction of difference (i.e. whether one is greater or less than the other), and the magnitude of the difference (i.e. by how much one is greater or less than the other). Whereas the Wilcoxon test requires that both the **direction** and **magnitude** of difference between pairs of scores can be established, the Sign test needs only the **direction** of the difference to be known.

This makes the Sign test particularly useful for analysing subjective data; for example, where participants are asked to make a judgement about the relative intensity of different smells under different conditions. Typically, participants are able to report different intensities of smells (i.e. they can say whether they are strong or faint), but cannot assign a precise magnitude to the difference. It would be inappropriate to use the Wilcoxon test on such data, but the Sign test allows the significance of any differences between two sets of data to be assessed.

When to use the Sign test

This test can be used if the following conditions are met.

1 **Data**   The data constitute measures on an ordinal scale, representing only the direction of difference between scores. If a reliable measure of the magnitude of the differences has been attained, use the Wilcoxon test instead.
2 **Design**   The data consist of two related sets of scores, such as those produced by one group of subjects under different experimental conditions.
3 **Purpose**   You wish to determine whether the difference between the two sets of scores is so great as to be unlikely, at the probability set by the significance level, to have occurred by chance alone.

How the Sign test works

Each participant in a related measures design generates two scores, one in each of the conditions in the investigation.

The Sign test simply ranks each of the scores in one condition in relation to its corresponding score in the other. This involves no more than asking whether each score in condition 1 is greater or smaller than its corresponding score in condition 2, and marking the direction of difference with a + or − sign.

The probability of the number of plus or minus signs can be determined. If chance alone is responsible for the data (perhaps because the participants are answering at random) one would expect similar numbers of plus and minus signs. However, if there is a difference between the conditions which led to the pairs of scores, as the role of chance decreases (or as the amount of guessing declines), so the ratio of plus to minus signs will change until the point is reached at which it becomes unlikely that the observed ratio could have occurred by chance.

Having determined S, the relative number of plus and minus signs from the data, the final step is to consult table 5 in appendix 5, which gives critical values for S at both the $p = 0.01$ and $p = 0.05$ significance levels for both one- and two-tailed tests. If the value obtained for S is equal to or less than the value in the table, then the probability that it could have occurred when the null hypothesis is correct is below the significance level, and the null hypothesis can be rejected and the experimental hypothesis accepted. Otherwise the null hypothesis should not be rejected.

The Sign test: computation instructions

Step 1   Set up the column headings for the computation as follows:

Column 1	Column 2	Column 3
Sample 1	Sample 2	Sign of difference

Step 2   Insert the data from sample 1 into column 1, and that from sample 2 into column 2. Ensure that scores from the same participant are placed on the same line.

Step 3   Inspect each of the pairs of data. If the score in column 1 is greater than its corresponding score in column 2 place a plus sign in column 3; if it is less put in a minus sign. If there is no difference enter a zero.

Step 4   Determine S, the number of times the less frequent sign occurs (ignore all zeros). Check that the balance of plus and minus signs supports the alternate hypothesis if it is one-tailed. If it is not supported, end the computation here and report that the data do not justify rejecting the null hypothesis. Otherwise continue with the computation.

Step 5   Determine N, the effective sample size, by adding the number of pluses and minuses together (again ignoring all zeros).

Step 6   Consult table 5 in appendix 5 to find the critical value for S for the effective sample size and required significance level.

Step 7   Present the results. After completing the computation of the Sign test, report the following information:

- The effective sample size
- The significance level chosen
- The number of the least frequent sign

- The critical value for S
- The region of rejection.

Step 8   Make a decision about hypotheses. If the value for S obtained at step 4 is equal to or less than the table value, it lies in the region of rejection, indicating that the two sets of scores are significantly different from each other. The probability of such difference occurring when the null hypothesis is correct (the p-value) is no greater than the significance level selected. **If this is so, accept the experimental hypothesis, and reject the null hypothesis.**

Alternatively if the computed value for S is greater than the critical value in the table, then the probability of the observed difference when the null hypothesis is correct (the p-value) is greater than the significance level. **If this is so, do not reject the null hypothesis. There is insufficient evidence to support the experimental hypothesis.**

Step 9   Translate the result of the procedure back into the terms of the investigation. If the experimental hypothesis has been accepted *and* if the data have been collected under sufficiently controlled conditions, it may be possible to conclude that the data are drawn from different statistical populations. If this conclusion is drawn, then the same difference can also be expected to be found whenever the same two populations are randomly sampled.

The Sign test: a worked example

A researcher into the perception of odour was interested in the question of whether people experience different smells more intensely when they are blindfolded than when they are able to see. Fifteen participants were asked to rate the strength of a standard odour on a 9-point scale under the two conditions – blindfolded and non-blindfolded.

In this case the Sign test is more appropriate than the Wilcoxon test because although the researcher was confident that the participants would be able to report accurately on the existence of any difference in the relative intensities of the odour under the two conditions, she was not confident that the magnitude of any such differences could be accurately captured. The one-tailed experimental hypothesis is that the ratings of the standard odour will be higher (odour experienced as stronger) when participants are blindfolded than when they are not. The null hypothesis is that no difference will be observed between the ratings in the two conditions. The significance level chosen is $p = 0.05$ and the region of rejection is one-tailed. The null hypothesis will be rejected if the ratings differ in the predicted direction, and the p-value (the probability that the null hypothesis is nevertheless correct) is equal to or less than the significance level.

Data: *Ratings of the subjective intensity of a standard odour*
under blindfolded and non-blindfolded conditions

Column 1	Column 2	Column 3
Sample 1 (non-blindfolded)	Sample 2 (blindfolded)	Sign of difference
4	6	minus
1	4	minus
3	7	minus
6	5	plus
1	6	minus
3	8	minus
7	7	0
4	8	minus
2	2	0
3	4	minus
4	8	minus
6	6	0
4	7	minus
4	6	minus
4	5	minus

Step 2 (Column 1, Column 2) **Step 3** (Column 3) **Step 1** (left of table)

Step 4 There are 11 minus signs and 1 plus sign. Therefore S = 1.
Step 5 The effective sample size, N = 15 − 3 = 12.
Step 6 Table 5 gives a one-tailed critical value at the p = 0.05 significance level of S = 2.
Step 7 Present the results:

Effective sample size	N = 12
Significance level (one-tailed test)	p = 0.05
Smaller number of signs	S = 1
Critical value for S	S = 2
Region of rejection	Values of S which are equal to, or less than, 2

Step 8   The value computed for S is 1. This value is less than the one-tailed critical value of S = 2 for the p = 0.05 significance level and an effective sample size of 12 and thus lies within the region of rejection chosen for the test. Consequently, the null hypothesis can be rejected and the experimental hypothesis accepted.

Step 9   The research question concerned the extent of whether exposure to a standard odour under either blindfolded or non-blindfolded conditions would affect the perceived strength of the odour. The result of the Sign test indicates that participants exposed to the standard odour in the blindfolded condition were significantly more likely to perceive it as strong than when it was perceived in the non-blindfolded condition, and hence that the two groups were drawn from different statistical populations.

The Chi-Squared Tests

The chi-squared tests, so called because their symbol is the Greek letter χ (chi, pronounced 'ky'), are non-parametric tests. There are two versions of this test, consisting of fundamentally the same procedure, requiring exactly the same kind of data to work on, but providing ways of dealing with data arising out of different research designs. These are:

1   The chi-squared test of association
2   The chi-squared (goodness of fit) test.

The chi-squared tests are particularly useful because they can be used to analyse frequency data when the scale of measurement is only nominal. For this reason also, they can provide a way of rescuing a poorly designed research project since it is sometimes possible to convert defective interval scale data, which cannot be analysed by using the t-tests, into frequencies which can then be dealt with by means of a chi-squared test.

When to use one of the chi-squared tests

You can use one of the chi-squared tests if:

1 **Data**   The data to be analysed consist of frequencies obtained by counting the number of times possible events or observations occur in each of several categories. Data must be organized into the cells of a data table or matrix, with each cell of the table containing only one specific category of data. (See also 'Organizing data for a chi-squared test' below.)

2 **Design**   The categories used in the test must be defined so that any individual observation qualifies for inclusion in one (and only one) of the categories. In sampling, each observation must be completely independent of every other observation. This means that, for instance, each individual research participant is allowed to contribute once to only one cell.

   There are also two rule-of-thumb stipulations to be made concerning the total size of the sample:

   1 If you intend to work with only two categories of data then the sample must contain a minimum of twenty scores.
   2 If you intend to work with more than two categories of data, then the sample size must be such that the expected frequency for each cell must be at least five observations.

3 **Purpose**   You wish to test either for a significant association between two variables, or to see whether an observed frequency distribution differs significantly from the distribution predicted by the null hypothesis. Note that the chi-squared test allows only two-tailed alternate hypotheses to be tested. This is because both of the purposes mentioned above require only a general prediction to be made about the data: consequently, one-tailed hypotheses are inappropriate.

The chi-squared test of association between two variables

The chi-squared test of association is used when the data consist of frequencies (counts), and when the question to be asked of the data is whether there is a significant association between two variables. For example, variable 1 might be different categories of research participant, say, males and females; and variable 2 might be some aspect of their behaviour which could be categorized in different ways. In such cases, the research is asking whether or not the differences between the research participants could be **associated** with differences in behaviour as defined in the categories. (See the worked example below.) The variables are said to be associated if, in the population of all such research participants, the proportion of males to females differs significantly from one category of behaviour to another.

   The alternate hypothesis for this test is that, in the population, the proportions do differ; that is, there is an association between the variables. Conversely, the null hypothesis is that there is no difference between the proportions, and so we infer there is no association between the variables in the population. In any sample, however, we shall invariably see some association due to random factors, and the chi-squared test is designed to establish whether the association in the sample is so great that it is unlikely to be due to chance alone. If it is too great we reject the null hypothesis and accept the alternate hypothesis.

Interpreting the result of the test of association

When a significant value for chi-squared is obtained from the test of association, the results need to be interpreted with care. If a significant association has been found, it does not mean that one can automatically conclude that one variable has *caused* the observed pattern of frequencies on the other. The association *may* be due to the existence of a causal link between the two variables, or it may not, and a decision on this depends on the design of the investigation. If one of the variables consists of different treatment groups to which subjects are allocated at random, then causality can validly be inferred. If, on the other hand, the variable which determines the division of subjects into different groups is some pre-existing characteristic of the subjects (such as their sex), then no causal inference can be made. In the latter case, no matter how strong an association is indicated in the data, all that can really be said is that the test indicates a significant degree of **association**, or **co-variation** between the two variables. (See chapter 5 for a fuller explanation of the basis on which causal inferences may be made.)

The chi-squared goodness of fit test

As we saw in chapter 6, when the process of making measurements of the values of a variable produces a range of different values for that variable, then the resulting set of values constitutes a distribution. A distribution is produced every time more than one measure is taken of the value of a variable. For example, taking a measure of the daily temperature at noon will produce, over time, a range of different values of the temperature variable. These different values of temperature constitute a distribution.

When the data consist of frequencies (counts) of the number of times certain categories of events are observed, it is useful to be able to ask whether the observed distribution of frequencies differs significantly from that which could be expected by chance alone.

As its name suggests, the chi-squared 'goodness of fit' test is intended to perform exactly that task. It enables a researcher to test the 'fit' of an observed distribution of frequencies against a particular hypothetical distribution. In this book we shall deal only with the hypothetical distribution which represents the situation where each category of the variable is equally likely to occur. In any case, the null hypothesis offers a prediction of no significant difference between the observed and expected distributions, while the alternate hypothesis predicts that a difference will occur.

The null hypothesis cannot be rejected if the result of the test has a p-value that exceeds the significance level, and this will occur when the 'fit' between 'observed' and 'expected' distributions is relatively close. On the other hand, if the fit between the distributions is sufficiently poor, the p-value falls below the significance level, and the alternate hypothesis should be accepted.

How the chi-squared tests work

Both chi-squared tests conduct a comparison between the data which has been obtained by means of observation or experiment, the 'observed' frequencies and a set of 'expected' frequencies. The result of the procedure is a statistic called chi-squared. If the difference between observed and expected frequencies is small, then the value for chi-squared will also be small, and vice versa. The smaller the value of the chi-squared statistic, then, of course, the greater is the probability that the difference between observed and expected frequencies could have been observed by chance alone when the null hypothesis is correct. The values of chi-squared form a set of distributions – collectively called the chi-squared distribution. As in the case of the t-test, values of chi-squared for any desired significance level can be extracted from these distributions, and these form the tables of critical values from which the significance of any observed value of chi-squared can be ascertained.

The chi-squared distribution

Like the t-distribution, the chi-squared distribution is not one but a whole family of distributions, with the shape of each individual member of the family determined by the number of degrees of freedom in the data.

As with the t-test, you don't need to concern yourself with the whole set of chi-squared distributions, nor even with any one of them in its entirety. All you need to know in any particular situation is whether the value for chi-squared which you have obtained is so large as to lie in the extreme upper end of its distribution.

Table 8 in appendix 5 gives the critical values of chi-squared at the $p = 0.05$ and $p = 0.01$ significance levels for a range of degrees of freedom. Having obtained a value for chi-squared by computation from data, the next step is to compare the computed value with the table value for the appropriate number of degrees of freedom. If the computed value is greater than that in the table, then you can conclude that the probability of the observed frequencies in the data having occurred when the null hypothesis is correct is no greater than the significance level selected. This means, in turn, that you can accept the experimental hypothesis and reject the null hypothesis.

Organizing data for a chi-squared test

The data to be analysed have to be organized into the cells of a data table, or matrix, with each cell of the matrix containing one specific category of data. In theory, a data table intended for use with a chi-squared test can be almost any size. However, the more cells you have in the matrix, above about 8, the harder it becomes to interpret the results of the test. The 2×2 form (2 cells deep by 2 cells long) and the $1 \times n$ form (1 cell deep by at least 2 cells long) are probably the sizes you are most likely to want to use. If you find yourself wanting to use the chi-squared test on more complex data forms, it will probably be worth asking yourself whether you can't simplify it in some way. Merging some of the categories is one possibility, or, alternatively, you could try subdividing the matrix and treating some sections of it individually using the chi-squared test.

Degrees of freedom in the chi-squared test

You will recall that the number of degrees of freedom in a set of data can be defined as a measure of the extent to which the values in the data are free to vary under a constraint. In the chi-squared test, the data consist of frequencies (counts), which are distributed among a fixed number of categories represented by the cells in a matrix. The extent to which the frequency values can vary is thus determined by the *number* of categories (cells) among which the frequencies are distributed.

For example, imagine a total frequency of 100 (i.e. 100 observations) divided between the cells in a two-cell matrix. In this case there is only one degree of freedom in the data, because the frequency value is totally free to vary in only one of the cells. As soon as any frequency value is placed in one of the cells, then the value in the other is determined, because the total frequency was fixed in advance (this is the constraint mentioned in the earlier definition). If you put a frequency value of 45 in cell 1 then the value in cell 2 *must* be 55 for the total of the frequencies to add up to 100. Increasing the size of the matrix, say to 3×1 cells, increases the number of degrees of freedom (in this case to 2), because this time the values in two of the cells can vary before the value in the third is determined, and so on. The simple rule is that for any matrix containing $1 \times n$ cells the number of degrees of freedom will be one less than the number of cells in the table.

Tables which have more than one cell in each column (such as the 2×2 table) seem more complex, but are in reality just as easy to figure out. The principle is the same, and the rule for these larger matrices is that the number of degrees of freedom is calculated by the number of cells in any row minus one times the number of cells in any column minus one ($N_{row} - 1$) times ($N_{column} - 1$). So a 2×2 table has just 1 degree of freedom, while a 4×3 table has $(4 - 1) \times (3 - 1) = 6$ degrees of freedom.

The Chi-Squared Test of Association

The chi-squared test of association: computation instructions

Step 1 Draw up the table of frequencies. In order to be able to use the chi-squared in the test of association version, you have to be able to organize the data into a table which is at least two cells deep and two cells long. Enter O, the observed frequencies, including any zero frequencies, in each of the cells of the table. All cells must be filled.

Step 2 Calculate the marginal totals for each row and column by adding the cell frequencies across and down. Calculate the grand total by summing either the row or the column totals together. This gives you N, the total number of observations made in the investigation.

Step 3 Set up the headings for five columns across the page, as follows:

Column 1	Column 2	Column 3	Column 4	Column 5
Observed (O)	Expected (E)	$O - E$	$(O - E)^2$	$\dfrac{(O - E)^2}{E}$

Step 4 Enter O, the observed frequencies from the data table (step 1) into column 1. (Don't worry that the cells in the table are arranged vertically and horizontally, while the column gives you only a vertical arrangement. Simply start at the top left-most cell of the data table, and enter the frequencies cell by cell under the heading. (See the worked example which follows if you are unsure how to proceed.)

Step 5 Calculate E, the expected frequency for each cell in the table, using the following procedure. For each cell, take the totals of the row and column in which it is located, multiply them, and divide by N, the grand total found at step 2. Enter the result in column 2.

Step 6 Subtract each of the column 2 values from its corresponding column 1 value to obtain $(O - E)$. Enter the results in column 3. Don't worry if you have negative values to enter as they will be taken care of at the next step. (NB If (but only if) you have data organized in 2 × 2 data table, you need to apply a correction factor before entering the result of this step in column 3. To do this, simply subtract 1/2 from each of the results of $(O - E)$.)

Step 7 Square each of the column 3 values to obtain $(O - E)^2$ and enter the result in column 4. (Notice that this removes any minus signs.)

Step 8 Divide each value in column 4 by its corresponding value in column 2 to obtain

$$\frac{(O - E)^2}{E}$$

Enter the result in column 5.

Step 9   Sum the values in column 5. This gives you a value for chi-squared

$$\chi^2 = \sum \frac{(O - E)^2}{E}$$

Step 10   Determine the number of degrees of freedom for the frequencies in the data table, using the formula (no. of rows − 1) by (no. of columns − 1).

Step 11   Consult table 8 in appendix 5. This gives you the critical values of chi-squared at the $p = 0.05$ and $p = 0.01$ significance levels for a range of degrees of freedom.

Step 12   Present the results. After completing the computation of the chi-squared test report the following information:

- The computed value for chi-squared
- The number of degrees of freedom
- The significance level employed
- The critical value for chi-squared
- The region of rejection.

Step 13   Make a decision about hypotheses by comparing the computed value of chi-squared to the critical value in table 8 of appendix 5. If the computed value of chi-squared is equal to or greater than the critical value in the table, it lies in the region of rejection, indicating that there is a significant difference between the observed and expected frequencies. The probability of such difference occurring when the null hypothesis is correct (the p-value) is no greater than the significance level selected. **If this is so, accept the experimental hypothesis, and reject the null hypothesis.**

Conversely, if the computed value of chi-squared is less than the critical value in the table, then the probability of obtaining that difference between the observed and expected frequencies (the p-value) is greater than the significance level. **If this is so, do not reject the null hypothesis. There is insufficient evidence to accept the experimental hypothesis.**

Step 14   Translate the result of the procedure back into the terms of the investigation. If the experimental hypothesis has been accepted *and* if the data have been collected under sufficiently controlled conditions, it may be possible to conclude that there is a significant association between the variables in question. If this conclusion is drawn, then the same association can also be expected to be found whenever the same population is randomly sampled.

The chi-squared test of association: a worked example

A group of 30 children aged 7 and 8 years were studied in order to assess the influence of parenting on play. A questionnaire was devised to assess child rearing styles, and the children were divided into three groups according to their parents' responses to the questionnaire.

The play behaviour of each child was subsequently observed, and the number of incidents of co-operative and competitive play occurring in a 30-minute period were counted. Behaviour which did not fall within the definitions of these two categories was ignored.

As the investigation is examining the possibility of an association between two nominal variables, with data in frequency form, the chi-squared test is appropriate. The null hypothesis to be tested in this case is that there is no association between child rearing styles and behaviour, while the experimental hypothesis is that there is such an association. The significance level chosen is p = 0.05. The null hypothesis will be rejected if there is evidence of an association between the variables and the p-value (the probability that the null hypothesis is nevertheless correct) is equal to or less than the significance level.

Data: Frequency of different play behaviours by child rearing style

Steps 1 and 2

Play behaviour	Child rearing styles			
	Permissive	Balanced	Authoritarian	Total
Co-operative	7	21	4	32
Competitive	15	9	28	52
Totals	22	30	32	N = 84

	Step 4	Step 5	Step 6	Step 7	Step 8
Step 3	Column 1	Column 2	Column 3	Column 4	Column 5
	Observed frequencies (O)	Expected frequencies (E)	$O - E$	$(O - E)^2$	$\dfrac{(O - E)^2}{E}$
	7	8.3	−1.3	1.69	0.2
	21	11.4	9.6	92.16	8.08
	4	12.1	−8.1	65.61	5.42
	15	13.6	1.4	1.96	0.14
	9	18.5	−9.5	90.25	4.87
	28	19.8	8.2	67.24	3.39

Step 9   Sum of column 5 (χ^2) = 22.1

Step 10

$$df = (\text{rows minus } 1) \times (\text{columns minus } 1)$$
$$= (3 - 1)\ (2 - 1)$$
$$= 2$$

Step 11   From table 8 the critical value at the p = 0.05 significance level for 2 degrees of freedom is $\chi^2 = 5.99$.

Step 12   Present the results:

Computed value for χ^2	$\chi^2 = 22.1$
Degrees of freedom	df = 2
Significance level	p = 0.05
Critical value for χ^2	$\chi^2 = 5.99$
Region of rejection	Values of χ^2 which are equal to, or greater than, 5.99

Step 13   The value computed for chi-squared is 22.1, while the critical value in table 8 of appendix 5 at the p = 0.05 significance level for 2 degrees of freedom is 5.99.

As the computed value exceeds the table value, it lies within the region of rejection chosen for the test and indicates that the difference between the observed and expected frequencies is so great that the p-value, when the null hypothesis is correct, is equal to or less than p = 0.05. The experimental hypothesis can therefore be accepted, and the null hypothesis rejected.

Step 14   The research concerned the question of whether there was an association between the kind of child rearing styles adopted by parents and the play styles of their offspring. On the evidence of these data, it can be concluded that there is such an association. Inspection of the observed frequencies shows that children whose parents adopt a balanced style of child rearing are more likely to play co-operatively, while those whose parents follow the authoritarian or permissive styles are more likely to play competitively. The same pattern of association can also be expected to be found whenever the same population is randomly sampled.

The Chi-Squared (Goodness of Fit) Test

The chi-squared (goodness of fit) test: computation instructions

Step 1   Draw up the table of frequencies. In order to be able to use the chi-squared in the goodness of fit version, you have to be able to organize the data into a table which is one cell deep and at least two cells long. Enter O, the observed frequencies, including any zero frequencies, in each of the cells of the table. No cells must be empty.

Step 2 Calculate the row total by adding the cell frequencies across. This should equal the total number of observations made in the investigation.

Step 3 Set up the headings for five columns across the page, as follows:

Column 1	Column 2	Column 3	Column 4	Column 5
Observed (O)	Expected (E)	$O - E$	$(O - E)^2$	$\dfrac{(O - E)^2}{E}$

Step 4 Enter O, the observed frequencies from the data table (step 1) into column 1. (Don't worry that the cells in the table are arranged vertically and horizontally, while the column gives you only a vertical arrangement. Simply start at the top left-most cell of the data table, and enter the frequencies cell by cell under the heading. See the worked example which follows if you are unsure how to proceed.)

Step 5 Calculate E, the expected frequencies. If, as is likely to be the case, it is hypothesized that these are determined by chance or random factors, then the value for E for each cell in the table is found by:

$$E = \frac{\text{total frequency}}{\text{number of cells}}$$

Enter the values for E in column 2.

Step 6 Subtract each of the column 2 values from its corresponding column 1 value to obtain $(O - E)$. Enter the result in column 3. Don't worry if you have negative values to enter as they will be taken care of at the next step.

Step 7 Square each of the column 3 values to obtain $(O - E)^2$ and enter the result in column 4. (Notice that this removes any minus signs.)

Step 8 Divide each value in column 4 by its corresponding value in column 2 to obtain

$$\frac{(O - E)^2}{E}$$

Enter the result in column 5.

Step 9 Sum the values in column 5. This gives you a value for chi-squared:

$$\chi^2 = \sum \frac{(O - E)^2}{E}$$

Step 10 Determine the number of degrees of freedom for the data, using the formula $(n - 1)$, no. of cells in the table minus 1.

Step 11 Consult table 8 in appendix 5. This gives you the critical values of chi-squared for a range of degrees of freedom at the $p = 0.05$ and $p = 0.01$ significance levels.

Step 12 Present the results. After completing the computation of the chi-squared test report the following information:

- The computed value for chi-squared
- The number of degrees of freedom
- The significance level employed
- The critical value for chi-squared
- The region of rejection.

Step 13 Make a decision about hypotheses by comparing the computed value of chi-squared to the critical value in the table. If the computed value of chi-squared is equal to or greater than the critical value in the table, it lies in the region of rejection, indicating that there is a significant difference between the observed and expected frequencies. The probability of such difference occurring when the null hypothesis is correct (the p-value) is no greater than the significance level selected. **If this is so, accept the experimental hypothesis, and reject the null hypothesis.**

Conversely, if the computed value of chi-squared is less than the critical value in the table, then the probability of obtaining that difference between the observed and expected frequencies (the p-value) is greater than the significance level. **If this is so, do not reject the null hypothesis. There is insufficient evidence to accept the experimental hypothesis.**

Step 14 Translate the result of the procedure back into the terms of the investigation. If the experimental hypothesis has been accepted *and* if the data have been collected under sufficiently controlled conditions, it may be possible to conclude that there is a significant difference between the two distributions. If this conclusion is drawn, then the same difference can also be expected to be found whenever the same population is randomly sampled.

The chi-squared (goodness of fit) test: a worked example

Research into the interaction between experimenters and their subjects suggests that research personnel benefit from a version of the 'halo effect' which leads research subjects to see them as highly competent simply because they are engaged in research. Some data from an investigation into this phenomenon takes the form of ratings by 50 research participants of a researcher's competence using the following five categories:

- Very competent
- Competent
- No opinion

- Incompetent
- Very incompetent.

Each participant was allowed to make only one judgement about the re-searcher, and all participants responded. As the number of responses in each category can be easily determined, the chi-squared test of goodness of fit is an appropriate choice to analyse the data.

The null hypothesis predicts that the distribution of choices among the five categories will not differ significantly from that expected by chance, while the experimental hypothesis predicts that it will. The significance level chosen is $p = 0.05$. The null hypothesis will be rejected if there is evidence of a difference between the observed and expected distributions and the p-value (the probability that the null hypothesis is nevertheless correct) is equal to or less than the significance level.

Data: Frequency of judgements in each of five categories made by 50 research participants

Steps 1 and 2

Very competent	Competent	No opinion	Incompetent	Very incompetent	Row total
9	23	6	9	3	50

	Step 4	Step 5	Step 6	Step 7	Step 8
Step 3	Column 1	Column 2	Column 3	Column 4	Column 5
	Observed frequencies (O)	Expected frequencies (E)	$O - E$	$(O - E)^2$	$\dfrac{(O - E)^2}{E}$
	9	10	−1	1	0.1
	23	10	13	169	16.9
	6	10	−4	16	1.6
	9	10	−1	1	0.1
	3	10	−7	49	4.9

Step 9   Sum of column 5 $(\chi^2) = 23.6$

Step 10

$$df = (n - 1) = (5 - 1) = 4$$

Step 11   From table 8, the critical value of chi-squared at the $p = 0.05$ significance level for 4 degrees of freedom is $\chi^2 = 9.49$.

Step 12   Present the results:

Computed value for χ^2	$\chi^2 = 23.6$
Degrees of freedom	df = 4
Significance level	p = 0.05
Critical value for χ^2	$\chi^2 = 9.49$
Region of rejection	Values of χ^2 which are equal to, or greater than, 9.49

Step 13   The value computed for chi-squared is 23.6, while the critical value in table 8 at the $p = 0.05$ significance level for 4 degrees of freedom is 9.49.

As the computed value exceeds the table value, it lies within the region of rejection chosen for the test and indicates that the difference between the observed and expected frequencies is so great that the p-value when the null hypothesis is correct is $p = 0.05$, or less. The experimental hypothesis can therefore be accepted and the null hypothesis rejected.

Step 14   The research question asked whether there would be a significantly non-chance distribution of choices among the five categories of experimenter competence. The result of the chi-squared test indicates that the distribution of such choices is significantly different from what would be expected by chance alone. Inspection of the data reveals a strong tendency for the subjects to rate the researcher as 'competent' while tending to avoid the 'very incompetent' rating. The frequencies for the ratings of 'very competent', 'no opinion' and 'incompetent' were close to those to be expected by chance.

A similar distribution of frequencies can be expected to be found whenever the same population is randomly sampled.

The Spearman Rank Order Correlation Coefficient

The Spearman rank order coefficient should always be used in preference to the Pearson procedure if either of the sets of data to be correlated consists of measures on an ordinal scale of measurement. (If you need a reminder about the ordinal scale of measurement see chapter 6.)

A different correlation procedure is needed for ordinal data because data of this type preserve only the *general* relationships of magnitude between different values in the data (that is, that one item of data is greater or less than another). The *exact* magnitude, or size, of the differences between items is not preserved because although ordinal data can say that one observation or score is greater or smaller than another, it cannot provide an exact measure of the difference. Unlike the Pearson procedure, which works with the exact differences of magnitude between data, the Spearman coefficient is designed to work with data of this type. The procedure simply requires that the data to be correlated are ranked, and then the differences between the individual rankings of each of the pairs of data items are used in order to assess the degree of co-variation between the two sets. If you look at the procedure for calculating the Spearman correlation coefficient you will be able to see this happening quite clearly.

The Spearman correlation coefficient also permits hypotheses about the co-variation between variables to be tested. The null hypothesis is always that the coefficient of correlation of the two variables in the population is zero, while the alternate hypothesis states that it is non-zero. Table 3 in appendix 5 gives critical values of Spearman's rank order coefficient for a range of sample sizes.

The Spearman rank order correlation coefficient: computation instructions

Step 1 Check that both of the sets of data to be correlated consist of measures on at least an ordinal scale.

Step 2 Write the column headings across the page as follows. Sample 1 and sample 2 denote the two sets of data to be correlated:

Column 1	Column 2	Column 3	Column 4	Column 5	Column 6
Sample 1	Sample 1 ranks	Sample 2	Sample 2 ranks	Difference in ranks of sample 1 and sample 2	Squared differences

Step 3 Enter the set of data you call sample 1 in column 1 and sample 2 in column 3. Ensure that both items in a pair are placed on the same line.

Step 4 Compute the rankings for sample 1, giving rank 1 to the lowest value, and so on. Enter them in column 2.

Step 5 Repeat step 4 for sample 2, entering the rankings in column 4.

Step 6 Subtract the value of each rank in column 2 from its corresponding one in column 4, ensuring that you always work with values on the same line. Place the result in column 5.

Step 7 Square each of the differences between rankings in column 5 and enter the result in column 6.

Step 8   Sum the squared differences in column 6 and enter the result at the foot of the column.

Step 9   Insert the result of step 8 in the following formula. (r_s is usually used as the symbol for the Spearman coefficient):

$$r_s = 1 - \frac{6\Sigma d^2}{(n^3 - n)} \qquad \text{Formula 9.9}$$

where:

n   is the number of pairs of scores
Σd^2 is the result of step 8 above
6   is a constant

To obtain a value for r_s using this formula:

*   Multiply the result of step 8 (Σd^2) by 6
*   Divide the result by $n^3 - n$
*   Subtract that result from 1 to get r_s.

(Note that the correlation coefficient has an inbuilt checking device! If your value for r_s is *outside* the range of −1 to +1 then you can be certain you must have made an error somewhere in the computation.)

If the alternate hypothesis is one-tailed you should also check that the sign of the correlation coefficient lies in the required direction. If it doesn't, the data do not justify rejection of the null hypothesis.

Step 10   Determine n_p, the number of pairs of scores, and consult table 3 of appendix 5. This gives the critical values of r_s for the $p = 0.05$ and $p = 0.01$ significance levels.

Step 11   Present the results. After completing the computation of the Spearman coefficient report the following information:

*   The computed value for Spearman's coefficient
*   The number of pairs of scores
*   The significance level employed
*   Whether it is a one-tailed or two-tailed test
*   The critical value
*   The region of rejection.

Step 12   Make a decision about hypotheses. If the computed value of r_s is of greater magnitude than the value in table 3 for the appropriate number of pairs of scores, then it lies within the region of rejection, indicating that it is significantly different from zero. The probability of such difference occurring by chance when the null hypothesis is correct (the p-value) is no greater than the significance level selected. **If this is so, accept the alternate hypothesis and reject the null hypothesis.**

Conversely, if the computed value for r_s is less than the value in the table, then the probability of the observed difference (the p-value) is greater than the significance level. **If this is so, do not reject the null hypothesis. There is insufficient evidence to accept the alternate hypothesis.**

Step 13   Translate the result of the procedure back into the terms of the investigation. If the alternate hypothesis has been accepted *and* if the variables are appropriately related (see chapter 6), it may be possible to conclude that there is a significant association between them. If this conclusion is drawn, then the same association can also be expected to be found whenever the same populations are randomly sampled.

The Spearman rank order correlation coefficient: a worked example

A psychologist working as a designer of psychometric tests wished to evaluate the validity of a newly constructed test of emotional stability. In order to do this she decided to compare the scores obtained by a sample of 12 subjects on the new test with the scores obtained by the same people on an established test. The null hypothesis is that the coefficient of correlation of the two variables in the population is zero, while the one-tailed alternate hypothesis states that it is non-zero and positive. The significance level chosen is $p = 0.05$ and the region of rejection is one-tailed. The null hypothesis will be rejected if the observed correlation differs from zero in the predicted direction and the p-value (the probability that the null hypothesis is nevertheless correct) is equal to or less than the significance level.

Data: *Scores on two tests of emotional stability*

Sample 1	Sample 2
Scores on established test/50	Scores on new test/20
17	20
48	13
44	17
19	11
30	20
36	16
41	19
40	12
42	10
22	14
24	16
47	15

Steps 1 to 8

Column 1 Sample 1 (X)	Column 2 Sample 1 ranks	Column 3 Sample 2 (Y)	Column 4 Sample 2 ranks	Column 5 Difference in ranks	Column 6 Squared differences
17	1	20	11.5	10.5	110.25
48	12	13	4	−8	64
44	10	17	9	−1	1
19	2	11	2	0	0
30	5	20	11.5	6.5	42.25
36	6	16	7.5	1.5	2.25
41	8	19	10	2	4
40	7	12	3	−4	16
42	9	10	1	−8	64
22	3	14	5	2	4
24	4	16	7.5	3.5	12.25
47	11	15	6	−5	25
					$\Sigma d^2 = 345$

Step 9

$$r_s = 1 - \frac{6\Sigma d^2}{(n^3 - n)}$$ **Formula 9.9**

$$= 1 - \frac{6(345)}{12^3 - 12}$$

$$= 1 - \frac{2070}{1716}$$

$$= 1 - 1.21$$

$$= -0.21$$

(Note that we have obtained a negative coefficient when the alternate hypothesis has specified that a positive correlation will be obtained. Therefore we may not reject the null hypothesis. However, we will continue by checking the table of critical values and presenting the results.)

Step 10   The number of pairs of scores (n_p) is 12, and the one-tailed critical value of r_s for the $p = 0.05$ significance level is therefore $r_s = 0.503$.

Step 11   Present the results:

Computed value for r_s	$r_s = -0.21$
No. of pairs of scores	$n_p = 12$
Significance level (one-tailed)	$p = 0.05$
Critical value for r_s	$r_s = 0.503$
Region of rejection	Values of r_s whose magnitude is greater than 0.503

Step 12   The Spearman rank order correlation procedure yields a correlation coefficient of −0.21 from these data. As this lies in the opposite direction from that predicted by the one-tailed alternate hypothesis, the null hypothesis must be accepted. Moreover, table 3 in appendix 5 gives $r_s = 0.503$ as the one-tailed critical value when $n_p = 12$ at the $p = 0.05$ significance level. Since the observed value of r_s (ignoring the sign) is only 0.21, the null hypothesis must again be accepted.

Step 13   The original research question asked whether the scores on the two tests would co-vary in a positive direction. However, research has shown only a weak negative relationship between the variables with a correlation coefficient which was too small to reach significance. The psychologist concludes that the new test of emotional stability may be measuring a different set of variables compared to the older test, and that therefore it cannot be used as an alternative to it.

The Pearson Product-Moment Correlation Coefficient

The Pearson product-moment correlation can be used to work with data which reach at least the interval scale of measurement. If your data represent measures on only the ordinal scale you should use the Spearman rank order coefficient described in the previous section. As always, the data to be correlated should consist of two sets of scores, each of which should contain exactly the same number of items. More information on the concept of correlation can be found in chapter 6.

Like the Spearman correlation coefficient, Pearson's also permits hypotheses about the co-variation between variables to be tested. Again, the null hypothesis is always that the coefficient of correlation of the two variables in the population is zero, while the alternate hypothesis states that it is non-zero. Table 4 in appendix 5 gives critical values of the Pearson product-moment coefficient for a range of sample sizes.

The formula for the Pearson correlation (symbol r) appears rather complicated at first, but is easy to understand if you take it slowly and break it down into its constituent parts. In the formula, X and Y identify the two sets of data to be correlated, n_p is the no. of pairs of scores, and Σ is simply the instruction to sum the values indicated.

$$r = \frac{n_p \Sigma XY - \Sigma X \Sigma Y}{\sqrt{\left[n_p \Sigma X^2 - (\Sigma X)^2\right]\left[n_p \Sigma Y^2 - (\Sigma Y)^2\right]}}$$

Formula 9.10

The Pearson product-moment correlation coefficient: computation instructions

Step 1   Place the following column headings in line across the page:

Column 1	Column 2	Column 3	Column 4	Column 5
Sample 1 (X)	X^2	Sample 2 (Y)	Y^2	$X \times Y$

Step 2   Insert one set of data (X) in column 1, and the other (Y) in column 3, ensuring that scores from the same pair are placed on the same line (row). Sum the data in each column and place the total at the foot of the column.

Step 3   Square each X item of data in column 1, and write the answer in column 2. Repeat the procedure with the Y data in column 3, placing the answer this time in column 4. Sum the values in column 2 and then do the same for column 4.

The main computation

Step 4   To find ΣXY: multiply each item of data in column 1 with its corresponding item in column 3, and place the answers in column 5. Sum column 5.

Step 5   Find the value of n_p by counting the number of *pairs* of scores.

Step 6   To find $n_p \Sigma XY$: Multiply the total of column 5 by n_p.

Step 7   To find $\Sigma X \Sigma Y$: Multiply together the totals of columns 1 and 3.

To find $[n_p \Sigma x^2 - (\Sigma X)^2]$:

Step 8   Multiply the total of column 2 by n_p.

Step 9   Square the total of column 1.

Step 10   Subtract the result of step 9 from the result of step 8.

To find $[n_p \Sigma Y^2 - (\Sigma Y)^2]$:

Step 11   Multiply the total of column 4 by n_p.

Step 12   Square the total of column 3.

Step 13   Subtract the result of step 12 from the result of step 11.

To complete the calculation of r from the formula above:

Step 14   Multiply together the results of steps 10 and 13.

Step 15   Take the square root of the result of step 14.

Step 16   Subtract the result of step 7 from that of step 6 (this can produce a negative value).

Step 17   Divide the result of step 16 by the result of step 15 to obtain the correlation coefficient r. The sign of the answer (+ or −) is the same as the sign of the result of step 16. (Note that the correlation co-efficient has an inbuilt checking device! If your value for r is *outside* the range of −1 to +1 then you can be certain you must have made an error somewhere in the computation.)

   If the alternate hypothesis is one-tailed you should also check that the sign of the correlation coefficient lies in the required direction. If it doesn't, the data do not justify rejection of the null hypothesis.

Step 18   Use the formula $n_p - 2$ to find the number of degrees of freedom for the data and consult table 4 in appendix 5. This gives critical values of r for the $p = 0.05$ and $p = 0.01$ significance levels.

Step 19   Present the results. After completing the computation of the Pearson coefficient report the following information:

- The computed value for the Pearson coefficient
- The number of degrees of freedom
- The significance level employed
- Whether it is a one-tailed or two-tailed test
- The critical value
- The region of rejection.

Step 20   Make a decision about hypotheses. If the computed value of r is of greater magnitude than the value in table 4 for the appropriate number of degrees of freedom, then it lies within the region of rejection, indicating that it is significantly different from zero. The probability of such difference occurring by chance when the null hypothesis is correct (the p-value) is no greater than the significance level selected. **If this is so, accept the alternate hypothesis and reject the null hypothesis.**

   Conversely, if the computed value for r is less than the value in the table, then the probability of the observed difference (the p-value) is greater than the significance level. **If this is so, do not reject the null hypothesis. There is insufficient evidence to accept the alternate hypothesis.**

Step 21   Translate the result of the procedure back into the terms of the investigation. If the alternate hypothesis has been accepted *and* if the variables are appropriately related (see chapter 6), it may be possible to conclude that there is a significant association between them. If this conclusion is drawn, then the same association can also be expected to be found whenever the same populations are randomly sampled.

The Pearson product-moment correlation coefficient: a worked example

A psychologist, studying problem solving, decided to investigate the question of how the ability to solve pencil and paper problems in a test situation co-varied with the ability to solve problems in real life. Two sets of problems were put together. One set consisted of logical problems, or syllogisms, which the subjects were required to solve by deciding whether the statements contained in them were 'true' or 'false'. The other set consisted of 'real-life' problem scenarios, where, for example, the subjects were asked to describe what they would do if they were unexpectedly stranded in a foreign country with no money. There was no expectation that the scores would co-vary in a particular direction.

One half of the ten subjects each first attempted to solve the logic problems, and then tackled the 'real-life' problems, while the other half attempted the 'real-life' problems first. The data consisted of the total time in minutes which each subject took to answer the problems in each set, and as they represent interval scale measures of a continuous variable, the Pearson product-moment correlation can be applied.

The null hypothesis is that the coefficient of correlation of the two variables in the population is zero, while the two-tailed alternate hypothesis states that it is non-zero. The significance level chosen is $p = 0.05$ and the region of rejection is two-tailed. The null hypothesis will be rejected if the observed correlation differs from zero in either direction and the p-value (the probability that the null hypothesis is nevertheless correct) is equal to or less than the significance level.

Data: Scores on two tests of problem solving

Subject	Time taken in minutes to complete the logic problems (X)	Time taken in minutes to complete the 'real-life' problems (Y)
1	16	12
2	16	17
3	12	8
4	19	12
5	7	17
6	14	8
7	24	12
8	3	24
9	21	7
10	13	4
	$\Sigma X = 145$	$\Sigma Y = 121$

Steps 1 to 4

Column 1	Column 2	Column 3	Column 4	Column 5
X	X^2	Y	Y^2	$X \times Y$
16	256	12	144	192
16	256	17	289	272
12	144	8	64	96
19	361	12	144	228
7	49	17	289	119
14	196	8	64	112
24	576	12	144	288
3	9	24	576	72
21	441	7	49	147
13	169	4	16	52
$\Sigma X = 145$	$\Sigma X^2 = 2457$	$\Sigma Y = 121$	$\Sigma Y^2 = 1779$	$\Sigma XY = 1578$

Step 5   Count the number of pairs of scores:

$n_p = 10$

Step 6   Multiply the total of column 5 by n_p:

$n_p \Sigma XY = 10 \times 1578$
$= 15780$

Step 7   Multiply together the totals of columns 1 and 3:

$\Sigma X \Sigma Y = 145 \times 121$
$= 17545$

Step 8   Multiply the total of column 2 by n_p:

$n_p \Sigma X^2 = 2457 \times 10$
$= 24570$

Step 9   Square the total of column 1:

$(\Sigma X)^2 = 145 \times 145$
$= 21025$

Step 10   Subtract the result of step 9 from the result of step 8:

$[n_p \Sigma X^2 - (\Sigma X)^2]$
$= 24570 - 21025$
$= 3545$

Step 11   Multiply the total of column 4 by n_p:

$n_p \Sigma Y^2 = 1779 \times 10$
$= 17790$

Step 12 Square the total of column 3:

$$(\Sigma Y)^2 = 121 \times 121$$
$$= 14641$$

Step 13 Subtract the value of step 12 from the result of step 11:

$$[n_p \Sigma Y^2 - (\Sigma Y)^2]$$
$$= 17790 - 14641$$
$$= 3149$$

Step 14 Multiply together the results of steps 10 and 13:

$$3545 \times 3149$$
$$= 11163205$$

Step 15 Take the square root of the result of step 14:

$$\sqrt{11163205}$$
$$= 3341.1383$$

Step 16 Subtract the result of step 7 from that of step 6:

$$15780 - 17545$$
$$= -1765$$

Step 17 Divide the result of step 16 by the result of step 15 to obtain the correlation co-efficient r.

$$r = -1765 \div 3341.14$$
$$= -0.528$$

Step 18 The degrees of freedom $= n_p - 2 = 8$. Consulting table 4 in appendix 5 gives a two-tailed critical value for 8 degrees of freedom of $r = 0.632$ at the $p = 0.05$ significance level.

Step 19 Present the results:

Computed value for r	$r = -0.528$
Degrees of freedom	$df = 8$
Significance level (two-tailed)	$p = 0.05$
Critical value for r	$r = 0.632$
Region of rejection	Values of r whose magnitude is greater than 0.632

Step 20 Since the observed value of r is -0.528 the null hypothesis (of nil difference between the observed coefficient and zero) cannot be rejected at the 5 per cent level.

Step 21   Translating the result of the test back into the terms of the investigation, there is evidence of a negative relation between the variables, although the magnitude of the coefficient fails to reach significance. Inspection of the data reveals that more subjects completed the 'real-life' problems faster than the logic problems, which suggests that a more careful investigation using a larger sample might find a significant correlation. However, there is not enough evidence here to make any such claim for a wider population, and further research is required.

Appendix 1: Ethical Standards in Psychological Research

The ethical standard for psychological research in the UK, to which all workers in psychology at whatever level, are expected to adhere, is published by The British Psychological Society (British Psychological Society, 1993). The following represents a summary of the key points of that standard, which covers all matters likely to be of concern to a beginning researcher.

1 The right of informed consent

Research participants are entitled to be fully informed about the reason, aims and purpose of the investigation, to be told exactly what will be involved, and what will happen to the data they generate. You don't have to go into exhaustive detail on any of these points, but you are required to satisfy yourself that the reason for the experiment, and the nature of the contribution to be made by each individual has been clearly understood.

It is important that a participant's agreement to participate in research be sought only *after* they have been informed, and understood, the nature of the research. Any form of deception about any aspect of research should always be regarded as something to be avoided if it is at all possible, since it undermines the trust between researcher and participant. If you feel some form of deception is essential to your research you should always consult with a more experienced researcher before proceeding. If you decide to continue with the deception you must satisfy yourself that participants will not be annoyed or upset in any way when you reveal that it has taken place, and you must take particular care over the debriefing (see below).

2 The right to withdraw at any time

All participants in psychological research have an absolute right to withdraw from the research at any time without giving a reason, taking with them any data that they have contributed to the investigation up to that point, if they wish to do so. They must be explicitly informed of this right before the research commences, and reminded of it, if at any time during the research session you believe that they are experiencing any physical or psychological discomfort or distress.

3   Debriefing

All participants should be offered the opportunity of a debriefing after data have been collected. Sometimes this will be unnecessary, particularly if full information about the research has already been provided, but on occasions participants will welcome the opportunity to find out more about the research to which they have contributed. Whatever the nature of the research, it is essential at least to check that a participant is not leaving the situation with negative feelings of any kind.

If the research design has involved deception of any kind, no matter how mild, the debriefing must be conducted with particular care. You must explain fully the reasons for the deception and satisfy yourself, as far as is possible, that no adverse effects have been experienced. If you believe that a participant has taken the deception badly, you must, if they wish to do so, arrange for them to discuss their feelings with someone who possesses the appropriate skills, such as trained counsellor, and do anything else you can to put things right.

4   Confidentiality

All data obtained in the course of a research project should be treated as confidential, and therefore should not be released to another person, or published unless the identity of the source has been disguised. This means that numbers rather than names should always be used to identify individuals on all working documents such as data sheets, as well as in the final research report. If you need to store names and addresses (perhaps in order that you can follow up an inquiry) you should keep these in a secure place separately from the data.

The data in an inquiry belongs to the participant who provided it, and they therefore have the right to withdraw their data from your investigation, or to ask you to destroy it, if they so wish. You can minimize the likelihood of this happening by ensuring that every participant is fully informed about what will happen to data once it has been contributed.

5   Protection from harm

Research must not be carried out if it appears possible that it will threaten the physical or psychological well-being, or human dignity of a participant in any way. Note that this standard not only prohibits the obvious ways of causing harm to others (electric shocks spring to mind), but it also excludes from the research situation all the less obvious ways in which harm can occur, such as by making someone look absurd before other people.

6   Children

An investigator has a special responsibility to consider carefully any research involving children. Consent to the research, if possible in writing, must be given by the child's parent, or someone, such as a headteacher who is *in loco parentis*. If the research is to take place in a school, the consent of the Head must always be obtained. The informed consent of the child herself should also be sought, though clearly any explanations of the research must be tailored to the child's age and capacity to understand.

In doing research with child participants, the researcher must be particularly aware of the way in which any failure to complete a task can adversely affect a child, even when care is taken not to communicate criticism or negative assessment in any way. Where the research involves such a task, at which failure is possible, care must always be taken to debrief the child fully, and advice should be sought if there are any concerns.

7   Responsibility to seek advice

Whenever any doubt or uncertainty exists about the appropriateness, or possible consequences of a particular procedure, it is the responsibility of the researcher to seek the advice of someone more experienced.

8   Not to claim knowledge or expertise you don't possess

Any researcher in psychology may be regarded as an expert on psychological matters by non-psychologists. If a research participant solicits advice or asks for an opinion, the safest response is to offer to help them find someone who is qualified to answer their question. It is always unethical to claim psychological knowledge or expertise that you don't possess.

9   Research into animal behaviour

In general, laboratory studies of animals should not be undertaken outside university departments where adequate facilities and levels of supervision will exist. However, where good facilities for keeping animals exist in schools and colleges a researcher, in consultation, may feel that animal research is justified and possible, and the following guidelines are given by the British Psychological Society (British Psychological Society, 1985) to assist this decision. Note that some examination boards may not allow the submission of reports of animal research.

- A researcher who is considering research using animals should consult first with a more experienced researcher, preferably one with expertise in research using non-human species.
- The research should not proceed at all unless it can be shown that genuine knowledge is to be gained. Replication studies should not be attempted.
- There is a responsibility to ensure that the animals are adequately housed and cared for in a way which ensures as far as possible a reasonable quality of life. Particular consideration should be given to the question of what is likely to happen to the animal(s) after the research is completed.
- Animals should not be subjected to procedures which distress them in any way. All experimental research using animals which may cause distress is strictly regulated by the Home Office, and must not be carried out except in research centres specially licensed for the purpose.
- If observing behaviour in the wild, disturbance to individuals and to habitat should be minimized, especially during the breeding season.

Appendix 2: Presenting the Results of an Investigation

Communicating the results of research by writing up and publishing a research report is a vital part of the process of 'doing science'. Publication, in whatever form, places the information obtained from an investigation in the public domain, so that it can be scrutinized by other researchers who can then attempt the important task of replication. As we have already seen (chapter 1) this is a key process in science since it is only through repeated replication by different investigators that a phenomenon can be established as stable and 'real' and not an artefact of a particular situation. Unreplicated results are best regarded as curiosities – phenomena which are possibly significant and important, but which cannot be evaluated accurately until it has been shown that they can be made to occur at will.

It follows that the accurate communication of scientific information in a research report is a key skill, needed by everyone who does research, at whatever level of expertise, because unless the results of research are written up fully, the task of trying to replicate them cannot even begin.

Writing the research report

The task of writing up the results of research is greatly helped by the fact that there is a conventional structure, consisting of a fixed set of sections, for the reporting of experimental research. (This can, to some extent be customized to meet the specific of other, non-experimental, research methods, and suggestions about the ways in which this can be achieved are made below).

The conventional headings for an report of experimental research are as follows:

1 Title
2 Abstract
3 Introduction

These headings are helpful to both the writer and reader because they provide a clear and logical framework for the report, and thereby reduce the possibility that anything of importance may be omitted. They also act as an index to the report and permit the reader to know exactly where to find each of the several different categories of information which it contains.

The research report: a section by section analysis

1 Title

Because the title is the first thing the reader encounters it needs to be put together with care. The basic principle to be followed is that it should be as informative as possible about the research (in order to help the reader find out what the report is about as quickly as possible) without on the other hand falling into the trap of being too long-winded. Witty, or tricksy titles are always best avoided, as are those which simply pose a bald question without providing any clues as to the answer which will be offered.

Within these limits, a glance through the references section of a text book will show that any one of several different title formats may be adopted. The most straightforward approach if you are reporting an experiment and are also relatively new to the disciplines involved in writing-up is to use the title to draw the reader's attention to the IV and DV. It is relatively straightforward to get these into the title, and if you add a mention of any special characteristics of the participants, or the nature of the research task you will have a more than adequate title for your work.

As an example, consider,

> The effect of physical appearance on the judgement of guilt, interpersonal attraction and severity of recommended punishment in a simulated jury task.
> (Efran, M. G. 1974. *Journal of Experimental Research in Personality, 8*, 45–54.)

which mentions the IV (physical appearance), the three DVs (judgement of guilt, interpersonal attraction, and severity of recommended punishment) and the task environment in which these variables were being measured (a simulated jury).

2 Abstract

The purpose of this section of a report is to provide a concise summary of the whole contents which can be used to obtain an overview of the whole work. Because it is a summary, it is virtually impossible to write the abstract properly until the other sections of the report have been written at least in draft form.

The abstract permits a reader to identify key pieces of information, such as the results of the investigation, without having to read every single word. The information in the abstract should be placed in the same order as it appears in the main body of the report, and should summarize the introduction, method, results, discussion and conclusion sections, each within the space of a sentence or two. The whole section should be as concise as possible, and should take about 200 words.

3   Introduction

The introduction is the section of the report in which the background to the investigation is explained, in order to place the reported research within an appropriate context.

As a guide, the appropriate length for an introduction will probably lie between 500 and 1000 words, although very concise introductions of a couple of hundred words are to be found in published research. Generally you should aim to achieve the shortest and most concise expression which is consistent with a full and clear explanation of the ideas.

In terms of the organization of ideas, it is often said that the introduction to a report should have a funnel-like structure – that is, it should 'start broad and end narrow'. It should begin by reviewing the ideas which provide the most general context for the research, and then become progressively more detailed and specific until those which provide the immediate basis for the investigation are reached.

An alternative way of visualizing the structure of the introduction is to see the proposed piece of research as lying at the centre of a set of concentric circles. The outermost circle contains the most general context of the ideas of the research, with the ideas becoming progressively more specific and more closely related to the proposed research as the centre is approached.

In more detail, the introduction should include the following categories of information:

There should be a **general statement** of the problem to be addressed, and the general area of ideas or questions which are to be investigated should be clearly identified. For example, an investigation into some aspect of memory has to be connected to a general problem or some aspect of understanding memory, so it is necessary to refer in general terms to previous approaches to the same problem and to describe, again in general terms the results of those researches.

There should also be a **review the relevant previous research** beginning with that which has the least direct connection with the present research. The key word here is undoubtedly the word 'relevant'. It is all too easy to fall into the trap of attempting an essay length review of the literature on a particular topic. This is not what needs to be done. What is needed, instead, is a selective, and concise description, focusing on method and results of those pieces of research which relate directly to the work in hand. It is neither necessary nor likely that this will involve the discussion of more than three or four pieces of research. The main criteria to be applied in selecting research for inclusion are:

It has attempted to answer the same or similar question

Or

It has produced research findings (perhaps in relation to a somewhat different question) which nevertheless throw some light on the problem with which you

are concerned. It may, for example, suggest a new way of looking at the problem, or a different method, or identify new variables which need to be controlled.

In reporting the results of previous research, the general rule is that the closer the relationship to the proposed research, the greater the detail that needs to be given.

There should be a **clear identification of the main issues which arise** out of earlier work. For example, the previous research might suggest two completely different ways of looking at a problem, which your research aims to resolve. In that case you need to explain the point at issue, and the nature of the connection between the previous research and the research you intend to carry out, and you would need to explain quite clearly how your research might permit such a decision to be made about which is correct.

Finally, all the foregoing points are gathered together into **one final statement** which defines the aim of the investigation. You should say what specific point of information you hope the research will reveal, and make a statement of the null and experimental (alternate) hypotheses which you will be testing.

4 Method

The purpose of the method section is to permit any other competent person to undertake an exact replication of the research. It therefore needs to contain a concise and accurate description of the mechanics of the investigation – how, exactly, the research was done, at a level of detail which will be sufficient to enable another person to repeat the whole process exactly.

If this sounds a formidable proposition, it isn't really. In fact, in some ways the method section is the most straightforward section to write since it consists simply of straight description. Any difficulty which may be experienced comes from having to achieve the high level of detail and precision in the description needed to permit replication by another investigator. The best rule here is to assume that *nothing* will be obvious to a reader and to describe absolutely everything which could conceivably influence the results, including, possibly, any mundane or everyday aspects of the situation.

This requirement means that it is difficult to give any guidance on the appropriate length of the method section. It simply has to be as long as it needs to be in order to perform its function, though you should aim always to express your thoughts as precisely and economically as possible in order to keep the word count as low as possible.

Design   This section should be used to describe the basic design of the research, for example, if you are reporting an experiment say whether an independent or repeated samples design has been used. The reason for the selection of that particular method should be briefly explained.

Conditions   The conditions sub-section of the report is primarily for reporting the way in which groups of participants are organized in the investigation. The number of groups of participants, and the nature of any different treatments (the different levels of the IV in an experiment or quasi experiment) should be fully described.

Subjects   The minimum requirement is that this section should specify the total number of research participants, and the number of members of each sex, and age group together with a description of the sampling method employed and, if appropriate, a description of the sampling frame. Beyond this minimum, the kind of information to be provided will be dictated by the nature of the research project. Any information which is relevant to the selection or treatment of the participants must be provided, for example, the handedness of participants should be reported after an experiment on eye–hand co-ordination.

Apparatus   List here the apparatus and equipment used in the research, including where appropriate, details of the manufacturer, model number, type, dimensions, method of construction, or any other information which would be needed to enable another researcher to obtain or construct an identical apparatus. Paper-based apparatus, such as mazes, word lists, or drawings should be both described, and clear examples provided.

There is no need to include everyday articles such as pens, paper chairs and tables, unless they have been specially prepared for the research.

Procedure   The procedure section should contain a precise description of the research procedure in the order in which it took place, from the moment that the first partici- pant enters the environment or situation in which the research is to be conducted. It should cover everything of relevance to the research which occurs between the re- searcher and the subjects during the course of the investigation. It should therefore include description of such things as the instructions given to participants, the proce- dures carried out by the researcher, the recording of participants' responses.

Where the members of a group of participants are all treated identically, the descrip- tion naturally needs only to be given once, though it is essential to record any differ- ences in instructions or treatment given to different groups of participants.

5   Results

The results section of the report should provide the reader with four closely related items of information. These are:

- A summary of the raw quantitative data
- The name of the test statistic which has been used (if appropriate) and the reason(s) for the choice
- The numerical result of the test statistic
- The decision on hypotheses on the basis of the result of the test statistic.

Each of these should be clearly indicated in the text of the report. See the worked example of the appropriate test statistic for an example of how the third of these points should be approached.

Presentation of data   Most investigations which generate quantitative data produce more than can conveniently be accommodated within the results section of a report. It is distracting to the reader to find five or ten, or more, pages of raw data sandwiched between the procedure and discussion sections. The tidiest approach is to give only a summary of the raw data, using descriptive statistics together with some form of graphical representation, in the results section, so that the reader can easily extract the general trends. If it is essential that the mass of raw data is presented with the research report, it can then be given in the first appendix where it will be accessible, but out of the way. If, however, there is no need to provide it within the report, then it should be stored somewhere safe in case you ever need to refer to it again, and destroyed after an appropriate interval has passed. *On no account should raw data be destroyed as soon as the summary has been made.* (See chapter 6 for more information on drawing graphs and basic data presentation.)

Treatment of results   Secondly, the results section should make it plain which infer- ential test statistic (if any) has been applied to the raw data, and why that statistic was selected. The following example, which obviously needs to be suitably amended to meet specific cases shows the approach:

> **The data were analysed using the t-test for independent samples since they represent measures on at least an interval scale, and were obtained by random sampling from two populations of approximately equal variance.**

Numerical results of the test statistic and decisions on hypotheses   Finally, the results section should communicate the numerical result of the test statistic, and the decision on hypotheses which follows from that result. See the worked examples of test statistics for guidance on the layout of this information.

6   Discussion

The purpose of the discussion section of the report is to provide a place for the researcher to review the specific results of the research, as expressed by the decision on hypotheses, and put them into the general context of related knowledge and research. Structurally, the discussion needs to be organized in the opposite way to the introduction. That is, instead of progressing from the most general point to the most specific, it needs to move from the highly specific (the actual decision on hypotheses), to consider more and more general issues raised by the research: 'starting narrow and ending broad'.

In general, the introduction and discussion can be seen as mirror images of each other, although as you will see below, there are obviously some issues which need to be mentioned in the discussion which are not touched in the introduction.

If necessary the discussion section can be a little longer than the introduction, and should come out at somewhere between 750 and 1500 words, though some may be even shorter. Longer discussions – and particularly those which get too close to or exceed the 2000 word mark – are in grave danger of becoming full-blown essays in their own right, and probably stand in need of a little judicious surgery.

The specific points which should be addressed in the discussion section are as follows:

1   Begin with a brief restatement of the results of the research and the decision which was taken on the hypotheses. Say whether they were as predicted, or otherwise.
2   The main body of the discussion should consist of a series of paragraphs in which you systematically relate the findings to each of the pieces of research cited in the introduction, beginning with that which is most clearly relevant. The questions to be addressed here are whether the present results confirm the results of other researchers or not. Do your results require explanation, and if so can any explanation be suggested?
3   If the research returns a result which was not predicted, you should review the technical effectiveness of your implementation of the method. What, if any flaws might there be in the way your chosen research method was applied? For example, were all relevant extraneous variables controlled as tightly as they might have been in an experiment? Could this have affected the outcome?
4   Consider extensions of the present research. One important criterion which identifies good research is not whether it succeeds in answering some particular question, but how many further questions it succeeds in provoking. The more successful the research, the more new questions are revealed. Every piece of research, including even those which are exact replications of previous work, should suggest a further problem or issue which needs to be worked on. It may be that the answer

offered by the present research is incomplete, and needs to be continued; or that it was addressed to what now can be seen to be the wrong questions; or that it was technically flawed, and needs to be done again more carefully; or that it was successful research which suggests a new approach to a question, or a whole range of new questions. Whichever it was, the most effective way in which to end the discussion section is to consider briefly any ways in which the research stimulates new ideas or approaches to the problem.

7   Conclusion

The conclusion section should contain a concise statement of the main conclusion which you draw from your results, together with a sentence or two in which the main implications of the findings are identified. The emphasis here should be on brevity. If the reader requires more detailed information it should be available in the discussion section.

8   References

The purpose of the references section is to provide all the publication details of the research mentioned in the introduction and discussion sections of the report so that the reader will be able to locate the original source. It should consist of a complete listing, in alphabetic order of all the pieces of research which have been cited using one of the recognized formats. The American Psychological Association (APA) format is probably the most consistently used in psychology, and information on this is provided below in appendix 3.

9   Appendices

Appendices should be used to present any information which, while it belongs with the report, does not fit easily or neatly into any of the report's other sections. The raw data has already been mentioned as one such type of information, and examples of materials used, or the calculations for the test statistic might be others.

Reporting qualitative data

As we have already noted at various points, the reporting and analysis of qualitative data presents certain problems, which may make it difficult to see how the information can be most effectively presented. The standard report format, which was developed for the reporting of quantitative experimental data, may not seem appropriate, and published works containing qualitative data, such as Freud's case studies, may either be too long, too literary or simply too idiosyncratic in their approach, to be of use as models.

The aim in what follows is to suggest how the standard report format can be adapted at various points to allow the effective reporting of purely qualitative data such as might be obtained from an interview or a piece of participant-observation work.

The advantage in taking this approach rather than simply devising your own format is that it is most likely to be acceptable to examiners if the work is to be done for assessment purposes. The GCE examination boards, organize their coursework marking schemes around the structure of the standard report, and unless the broad outlines of the standard form are followed, for example, by making sure you provide an abstract, you will lose some proportion of the marks available. In effect you will penalize yourself for taking a non-standard approach.

To avoid this possibility, then, these are ways in which the standard report can be customized. (I assume you have already read, and are familiar with the main comments on analysing and reporting quantitative data which precede this section.)

1 & 2   Title and Abstract

There is no need to treat either of these sections any differently to accommodate qualitative data. Simply do as indicated earlier.

3   Introduction

For the most part the introduction can also be treated in the same way. The exceptions to this will be the dropping of the null and experimental hypotheses, which are clearly inappropriate, in favour of a more general statement of the aims of the investigation. This can incorporate a general prediction about the expected results of the research if you wish to make one.

4   Method

The method section will still, of course, be required in the report, but will need surgery. The design and conditions sub-sections are redundant, and can be dropped. They will need, though to be replaced with a general statement or description of the method of research which was used, and how it was applied in the specific circumstances of your research. For example, if you have interviewed someone for a case study, you will need to use this section to describe why you have selected the interview method of data collection, whether the structured or unstructured approach to interviewing was chosen. Details of how the schedule of interview questions was developed, and the schedule itself would be placed in a retained apparatus section. If there is nothing that qualifies as 'apparatus' in your research (as in a participant-observational project), you can leave the apparatus section out as well.

Subjects   The subjects section will need to stay, but must also be tailored to the requirements of the research. It should be used to provide all the information about the informant(s) that you judge is needed to illuminate the research project. If you have conducted an interview on a single informant, for example, you may wish to present a brief pen-portrait of your informant, or a description of the salient characteristics of the group of individuals studied by participant research.
Procedure   The procedure section is also required in any report of qualitative research, and needs to contain essentially the same information as would be provided for an experiment. You need to put in as much information as is necessary to permit the reader to build up a picture of how you went about the research. For example, if you are reporting an interview, explain how the schedule of questions was constructed for an interview, how the interview was planned, and for what reasons, how contact was made with an appropriate informant, the number of times you met, and what in general was discussed, what arrangements were made for debriefing, how the debriefing was carried out, and so on. In short, provide information about everything that you actually did in connection with your research.

5 Results

This section must also be retained in the report, although for the reporting of qualitative research its character is required to be quite radically altered. In particular it may become quite lengthy, especially if you decide to support your remarks by quoting directly from an informant.

What information should be provided?

A **statement** should be given of the findings or general results of the research, which says whether or not, or how far, the aims of the study were achieved. Note, this is not conclusions that you draw about the data, but merely a summary of the data themselves. For example, if you have been making a participant study of peer relationships among adolescent girls, you will probably have set out with the aim of finding out more about what factors appear to influence peer relationships, and what functions such relationships seem to perform for young girls. This is the place in the report at which you state whatever you have found out about these aspects of peer relationships, buttressing it with some of your evidence.

6 Discussion

The discussion section remains essentially the same as for the standard report. The main task here is to assess the data you have obtained and to connect those results to whichever theory you see as relevant to the research. Include a review of the good, and any less good features of the project and consider what further research may be needed.

7 & 8 Conclusion and References

It may not be possible to draw a very firm conclusion on the basis of the data, but if any kind of conclusion should be possible, then this is the place to put it. The references section, of course remains as for the standard report.

9 Appendices

Use the appendix to the main report to place interview transcripts, examples of field notes, or any similar material which you wish to present with the report, but also want to keep out of the main body.

Appendix 3: Making Reference to Other Research

The method most used by psychologists to refer to books and articles in scholarly papers and research reports is the one devised by the American Psychological Association. However, the APA rules are extremely detailed and an acceptable approximation of them would be to use the name–date format described below. Although there are a number of other ways of putting references into your work, this is the nearest thing there is to a standard method in psychology, so that if you learn to use this one it is unlikely that you will ever need to learn another, at least for your psychological work.

All references to other work consist of two parts:

The citation is a reference to another piece of work which is placed in the body of the report.

The references list is a list containing the full bibliographical information for each of the citations.

The citation

The APA method is to use the name–date format, consisting of the author's surname followed in parentheses by the year of publication thus, for example:

Single author Tulving (1974)
Two authors Tulving & Pearlstone (1966)
More than two authors Give only the first author's name and use 'et al.' (which means 'and others') to stand for the rest:

   Hewstone, et al. (1988)

The references list

The references list consists of a list of all the works you have cited in the body of your report, giving the information needed to enable a reader to obtain a copy of the original.

The list should be organized in strict alphabetical order by first author's surname. Single authored items should be placed before those which have been jointly authored, and these in turn come before any works with multiple authors. If you have a number of works authored by the same person, they should be placed in date order.

To see examples of this system in action you can look in the references list of almost any textbook, as long as you check that it does use the APA format (to tell this compare some of the items with the examples below). If you find you need to refer to type of document which is not mentioned here, you could look in a library for one of the many guides to academic writing, such as Hubbuch (1981), which will almost certainly provide the help you seek.

The basic information which is required in the references list is:

- Author(s) surname and initial(s)
- Year of publication
- Title
- Place of publication (either a town or city or a scholarly journal)
- Publisher's name (or volume number and page references of a journal article).

Examples of items from a references list using the APA standard

Note particularly that the punctuation, capitalization and underlining, are all part of the APA standard, and should be followed exactly.

For a book with a single author:

Graham, H. (1986). *The human face of psychology*. Milton Keynes: Open University Press.

For a book with multiple authors:

Hewstone, M., Stroebe, W., Codol, J-P. & Stephenson, G. M. (1988). *Introduction to social psychology*. Oxford: Basil Blackwell.

For a book which had been edited:

Blakemore, C. & Greenfield, S. (Eds). (1987). *Mindwaves*. Oxford: Basil Blackwell.

For a chapter from an edited collection:

Fiedler, F. E. (1968). Personality and situational determinants of leadership effectiveness. In D. Cartwright and A. Zander (Eds), *Group dynamics*. New York: Harper & Row.

For a paper published in a scholarly journal:

Stratton, G. M. (1896). Some preliminary experiments on vision. *Psychological Review, 3*, 611–17.

Appendix 4: Statistical Notation

One of the things which many people find difficult and and also somewhat intimidating about statistics are the symbols. They appear to dominate the pages of every statistics text, and they can sometimes look like a deliberate attempt by statisticians to make their discipline as hard as possible for the beginner to grasp.

The symbols come from two sources. Some of them are familiar members of the Roman alphabet such as n and x. Others, the more formidable looking ones, come from the Greek alphabet. These are the ones that can be hard to remember, and feel difficult to use. However, it is worth reminding yourself that this is only because they are unfamiliar. The average English speaker, even on holiday in Greece, is unlikely to try to use the Greek alphabet. This means that every new worker with statistics has to undergo a process of familiarization during which the symbols, and especially the Greek ones, will feel difficult to use. Be assured that this feeling will pass as you become more practised at using them.

It is good practice to use the proper statistical notation, including all the Greek letters, in your work. You will find, once you get used to using them, that the symbols actually make working with data easier rather than harder. And of course, you will be much less likely to make mistakes in your work if you use the recognized notation rather than one that you may have made up for yourself.

Don't feel you need to master all the symbols immediately.

The following is a list of the more important symbols used in this book. Refer to it whenever you feel you need to refresh your memory.

Statistical Symbols

From the Greek alphabet

Symbol	Name	
Symbol	*Name*	
Σ	sigma upper case	Directs you to sum (add up) a set of values
σ	sigma lower case	The symbol for the standard deviation of a population
$\sigma_{\overline{X}}$	sigma ex-bar	The standard error of the mean
μ	mu (mew)	The symbol for the mean of a population
ρ	rho (row)	The symbol for Spearman's rank order correlation coefficient (alternative to r_s)
χ^2	chi ('ky') squared	The symbol for the chi-squared non-parametric test statistic

From the Roman alphabet

Symbol	Description
D	The difference between two scores
d	The difference between a score and the mean of the set of scores
N	Number of independent cases in a statistical test
n	Number of independent cases in a single sample
p (lower case)	Symbol for the probability of a given event
r	Symbol for the Pearson product-moment correlation coefficient
r_s	Symbol for the Spearman rank order correlation coefficient (alternative to ρ)
S	Symbol for the Sign test statistic
s (lower case)	Symbol for the standard deviation of a sample
T	Symbol for the Wilcoxon test statistic
t	Symbol for the t-test statistic
U	Symbol for the Mann-Whitney statistic
$\overline{X}$ ('ex-bar') upper case	The mean of a sample
X upper case	The variable being measured: a score in a sample
Var (X)	The variance of a set of scores

Appendix 5: Statistical Tables

The table of random numbers

The table of random numbers (overleaf), consists of a large number of integers generated by means of a computer procedure which virtually guarantees that as every integer is selected it is entirely independent of those which have preceded it. This means that even in very large sets of such numbers there will be no patterns or regularities which could lead to bias or error when the integers are used.

You may wonder why it is necessary to use a table of random numbers at all, instead of just generating a 'random' list of numbers for yourself whenever you need them. The reason is that this is one activity for which the human mind is rather poorly designed, and although it is certainly very easy to generate lists of different numbers, you would almost certainly find sooner or later (probably sooner) repetitions of various kinds beginning to appear in your list. For some purposes, of course this won't matter at all, but if you wish to operate within the strict definition of randomness given on p. 100 of chapter 3 you must use the table.

The integers in the table are generated independently, and therefore, although they are placed in groups of four on the page, this is purely to make the table easier to use, and has no other significance. You can obtain one, two three, four or indeed five digit random numbers with equal ease simply by reading off the required number of digits.

You can begin to read off numbers from any point on the table, and can proceed in any direction that takes your fancy. Taking a starting point somewhere in the middle and then continuing up the column will give just as random a set of numbers as starting at the top left-hand corner and reading from left to right.

Using the table:

1 To select a **random sample** give every individual in the sample a different number from the table, place them in number order and take individuals from the top of the ordered list until the required sample is obtained.

   If the individuals have already been numbered for some reason (as in the example in chapter 3), choose a starting point on the table and look for numbers within that range. As you find them, each individual denoted by the number is taken up into the sample until the desired sample size has been achieved.

2 To conduct **random assignment to independent groups** (i.e. in an independent subjects design), first give each individual to be assigned a different number from the table and place them in number order. Then divide the ordered list into the same number of sections as there are groups to be created. In a simple experiment there will be two groups, and so the subjects in the top half of the ordered list will become one condition in the experiment and the remainder the other condition.

3 To conduct **random assignment to groups in a matched subjects design** first pair the subjects on the desired variable, and then give each individual a different number from the table. Within each pair, assign the individual with the lower number to one condition and the one with the higher to the other.

Table 1 Random numbers

2889	6587	0813	5063	0423	2547	5791	1352	6224	1994	9167	4857
1030	2943	6542	7866	2855	8047	4610	9008	5598	7810	7049	9205
1207	9574	6260	5351	5732	2227	1272	7227	7744	6732	2313	6795
0776	3001	8554	9692	7266	8665	6460	5659	7536	7546	4433	6371
5450	0644	7510	9146	9686	1983	5247	5365	0051	9351	3080	0519
2956	2327	1903	0533	1808	5151	7857	2617	3487	9623	9589	9993
3979	1128	9415	5204	4313	3700	7968	9626	6070	3983	6656	6203
5586	5777	5533	6202	0585	4025	2473	5293	7050	4821	4774	6317
2727	5126	3596	2900	4584	9090	6577	6399	2569	0209	0403	3578
1979	9507	2102	8448	5197	2855	5309	4886	2830	0235	7130	3206
4793	7421	8633	4990	2169	7489	8340	6980	9796	4759	9756	3324
8736	1718	1690	4675	2728	5213	7320	9605	6893	4169	9607	9750
8179	5942	3713	8183	9242	8504	3110	8907	7621	4024	7436	4240
3304	4624	3563	0231	6134	5943	3696	9150	2778	3706	0616	2598
1778	8036	8526	4177	6337	7163	9494	3303	4544	6688	9781	2603
8939	4667	2117	9810	3933	1561	6300	2592	8941	5891	6365	9959
9784	9014	7961	5556	1688	8760	3215	9967	4313	4300	9726	1691
2132	4160	2266	7217	3185	3369	0768	4920	4329	7171	0051	7262
0389	2632	3527	9918	2578	1203	0970	5093	1935	5619	2815	0041
9227	7340	3837	1105	7516	9881	9937	2992	2032	3967	5638	3092
3045	5194	6904	0084	1436	3795	6639	0109	2168	4095	7939	2752
8911	0081	0628	4812	0805	7526	0335	6305	7713	1381	2067	5873
1328	5801	0506	4224	0760	6029	9993	7293	7804	3625	7601	5403
8160	8451	5712	6846	5589	6009	7187	8970	8110	9591	8379	6820
6605	6298	0785	0779	2669	6167	8572	3741	8579	7648	2361	5887
0805	6297	1629	1852	1616	2356	6295	8097	6332	2534	0336	4884
6037	6531	1363	2108	1601	9258	2148	7974	7372	0864	8091	3807
2866	6159	9738	3534	1989	8405	3447	4788	0931	5488	9796	8601
6946	1395	6596	3211	7833	8251	9998	4439	1275	1060	3680	6639
9497	4236	3116	5981	9913	3705	0812	6039	2361	7384	8918	2602
0437	9596	1869	0630	4574	0003	0569	9947	2652	4806	3000	1803
3028	5559	6610	7144	0511	8413	6901	8891	2879	5071	4214	9655
9859	9601	3688	7790	4559	1466	1287	2259	4527	0851	8564	2385
4164	7208	5944	6798	3665	5640	2567	8782	8427	1730	3748	6949
0258	9802	5058	1195	3906	3563	4448	9749	4365	4553	4107	1483
4674	1176	6663	6008	9054	3365	8441	9454	0657	4828	0183	8409
1121	9173	9728	4474	0622	3095	6972	0712	1558	8493	1831	8345
5452	6229	9153	5854	6605	4719	6392	7564	2790	4352	1826	3296
8350	5845	2757	1496	3964	8573	8796	7623	8071	8641	0345	6263
4088	3569	3410	9432	2252	0474	6963	2183	4127	0608	0992	2622
5928	2738	5822	1479	2432	1238	4233	5690	9257	5468	9720	5433
2674	0330	7422	1913	4830	2801	9249	5861	5227	0302	9265	6899
0553	1526	7004	6922	6407	0473	2574	8278	3522	2188	8352	5778
6298	6170	4822	6850	6455	7542	7032	0960	5870	6143	9782	8276
3133	8513	4138	1016	4761	4377	8327	1970	4134	7877	6025	3861
3409	4904	4166	0976	2050	7340	9524	7795	9573	2047	4280	6103
0101	1188	3803	1016	8224	3958	2012	3982	7702	1888	3311	4915
1621	1438	2854	0818	0704	9217	6336	7533	1411	1178	9730	5362
3832	2930	6959	6850	3331	4715	6488	7527	0451	4161	9686	6293
6671	0459	2165	4739	9089	8677	4686	8688	8650	0913	2491	5480
6778	6638	6450	0736	5650	4594	2548	2848	3051	6073	7303	8768
4737	1084	4833	5083	5359	7764	5990	5892	6250	1893	9945	8906

Taken from Table XXXIII of Fisher, R. A. and Yates, F. (1953). *Statistical Tables for Biological, Agricultural and Medical Research*, Published by Longman Group UK Ltd., 1974 (6th edition).

Table 2   Areas under the normal distribution curve from the 0 to z

This table gives the area beneath the curve between the mean and any point on the x axis denoted by a z score.

To read the table, first determine the values of z required up to the first decimal place in the leftmost column, then read across to find the area in the column indicated by the second decimal position. Thus, the area under the curve between the mean and a z score of 1.37 is 0.4147.

The table can also be read in reverse to find the z score marking off any given area above or below the mean, by reading from the body of the table out to the margins.

z	00	01	02	03	04	05	06	07	08	09
0.0	.0000	.0040	.0080	.0120	.0160	.0199	.0239	.0279	.0319	.0359
0.1	.0398	.0438	.0478	.0517	.0557	.0596	.0636	.0675	.0714	.0754
0.2	.0793	.0832	.0871	.0910	.0948	.0987	.1026	.1064	.1103	.1141
0.3	.1179	.1217	.1255	.1293	.1331	.1368	.1406	.1443	.1480	.1517
0.4	.1554	.1591	.1628	.1664	.1700	.1737	.1772	.1808	.1844	.1879
0.5	.1915	.1950	.1985	.2019	.2054	.2088	.2123	.2157	.2190	.2224
0.6	.2258	.2291	.2324	.2357	.2389	.2422	.2454	.2486	.2518	.2549
0.7	.2587	.2612	.2642	.2673	.2704	.2734	.2764	.2794	.2823	.2852
0.8	.2882	.2910	.2939	.2967	.2996	.3023	.3051	.3079	.3106	.3133
0.9	.3159	.3186	.3212	.3238	.3264	.3289	.3315	.3340	.3365	.3389
1.0	.3414	.3438	.3461	.3485	.3508	.3531	.3554	.3577	.3599	.3621
1.1	.3643	.3665	.3686	.3708	.3729	.3749	.3770	.3790	.3810	.3830
1.2	.3849	.3859	.3888	.3907	.3925	.3944	.3962	.3980	.3997	.4015
1.3	.4032	.4049	.4066	.4082	.4099	.4115	.4131	.4147	.4162	.4177
1.4	.4192	.4207	.4222	.4236	.4251	.4265	.4279	.4292	.4306	.4319
1.5	.4332	.4345	.4358	.4370	.4382	.4394	.4406	.4418	.4430	.4441
1.6	.4452	.4463	.4474	.4485	.4495	.4505	.4515	.4525	.4535	.4545
1.7	.4554	.4564	.4573	.4582	.4591	.4599	.4608	.4616	.4625	.4633
1.8	.4641	.4649	.4656	.4664	.4671	.4678	.4686	.4693	.4700	.4706
1.9	.4713	.4719	.4726	.4732	.4738	.4744	.4750	.4756	.4762	.4769
2.0	.4772	.4778	.4783	.4788	.4793	.4798	.4803	.4808	.4812	.4817
2.1	.4821	.4826	.4830	.4834	.4838	.4842	.4846	.4850	.4854	.4857
2.2	.4861	.4865	.4868	.4871	.4875	.4878	.4881	.4884	.4887	.4890
2.3	.4893	.4896	.4898	.4901	.4904	.4906	.4909	.4911	.4913	.4916
2.4	.4918	.4920	.4922	.4925	.4927	.4929	.4931	.4932	.4934	.4936
2.5	.4938	.4940	.4941	.4943	.4945	.4946	.4948	.4949	.4951	.4952
2.6	.4953	.4955	.4956	.4957	.4959	.4960	.4961	.4962	.4963	.4964
2.7	.4965	.4966	.4967	.4968	.4969	.4970	.4971	.4972	.4973	.4974
2.8	.4975	.4975	.4976	.4976	.4977	.4978	.4979	.4980	.4980	.4981
2.9	.4981	.4982	.4983	.4983	.4984	.4984	.4985	.4985	.4986	.4986
3.0	.4987	.4987	.4987	.4988	.4988	.4988	.4989	.4989	.4989	.4990
3.1	.4990	.4990	.4991	.4991	.4991	.4992	.4992	.4992	.4992	.4993
3.2	.4993	.4993	.4993	.4994	.4994	.4994	.4994	.4994	.4995	.4995
3.3	.4995	.4995	.4995	.4996	.4996	.4996	.4996	.4996	.4996	.4997
3.4	.4997	.4997	.4997	.4997	.4997	.4997	.4997	.4997	.4997	.4998
3.5	.4998	.4998	.4998	.4998	.4998	.4998	.4998	.4998	.4998	.4998
3.6	.4998	.4999	.4999	.4999	.4999	.4999	.4999	.4999	.4999	.4999
3.7	.4999	.4999	.4999	.4999	.4999	.4999	.4999	.4999	.4999	.4999
3.8	.4999	.4999	.4999	.4999	.4999	.4999	.4999	.5000	.5000	.5000

See chapter 7 pp. 334–9, for a discussion of the normal distribution curve.

Table 3 Critical values for the Spearman rank order correlation coefficient at the p = 0.01 and p = 0.05 significance levels

No. of pairs of scores	one-tailed test		two-tailed test	
	p = 0.01	p = 0.05	p = 0.01	p = 0.05
5	1.000	.900	–	1.000
6	.943	.829	1.000	.886
7	.893	.714	.929	.786
8	.833	.643	.881	.738
9	.783	.600	.833	.700
10	.745	.564	.794	.648
11	.709	.536	.755	.618
12	.671	.503	.727	.587
13	.648	.484	.703	.560
14	.622	.464	.675	.538
15	.604	.443	.654	.521
16	.582	.429	.635	.503
17	.566	.414	.615	.485
18	.550	.401	.600	.472
19	.535	.391	.584	.460
20	.520	.380	.570	.447
25	.466	.337	.511	.398
30	.425	.306	.467	.362

Taken from Table 1 of Zar, J.H. (1972). Significance testing of the Spearman rank correlation coefficient. *Journal of the American Statistical Association, 67*, 578–80. Reprinted with permission. Copyright 1972 by the American Statistical Association. All rights reserved.

Table 4 Critical values for the Pearson product-moment correlation coefficient at p = 0.01 and p = 0.05 significance levels

Degrees of freedom	one-tailed test		two-tailed test	
	p = 0.01	*p = 0.05*	*p = 0.01*	*p = 0.05*
5	.833	.669	.875	.755
6	.789	.622	.834	.707
7	.750	.582	.798	.666
8	.716	.549	.765	.632
9	.685	.521	.735	.602
10	.658	.497	.708	.576
11	.640	.476	.684	.553
12	.612	.458	.661	.532
13	.592	.441	.641	.514
14	.574	.426	.623	.497
15	.558	.412	.606	.482
16	.543	.400	.590	.468
17	.529	.389	.575	.456
18	.516	.378	.561	.444
19	.503	.369	.549	.433
20	.492	.360	.537	.423
25	.445	.323	.487	.381
30	.409	.296	.449	.349

Taken from Table VII of Fisher, R.A. & Yates, F. (1953). *Statistical Tables For Biological, Agricultural and Medical Research*, Published by Longman Group UK Ltd., 1974 (6th edition).

Table 5   One- and two-tailed critical values of S for the Sign test at the
$p = 0.01$ and $p = 0.05$ significance levels

N	one-tailed test		two-tailed test	
	$p = 0.01$	$p = 0.05$	$p = 0.01$	$p = 0.05$
5	–	0	–	–
6	–	0	–	0
7	0	0	–	0
8	0	1	0	0
9	0	1	0	1
10	0	1	0	1
11	1	2	0	1
12	1	2	1	2
13	1	3	1	2
14	2	3	1	2
15	2	3	2	3
16	2	4	2	3
17	3	4	2	4
18	3	5	3	4
19	4	5	3	4
20	4	5	3	5
25	6	7	5	7
30	8	10	7	9

Taken from Table 12.1 of Owen, Donald B. (1972). *Handbook of Statistical Tables*, © 1962 by
Addison-Wesley Publishing Company Inc. Reprinted by permission.

Table 6 One- and two-tailed critical values of U for the Mann-Whitney test at the p = 0.01 and p = 0.05 significance levels

To use this table:
Find the appropriate value for n2, the number of scores in the larger of the two samples (if there is one), followed by n1, the number of scores in the other sample. Then read off the critical value for the chosen significance level and decision type. Where there is no entry in the table, it means that no critical value can be computed, and you will need either to use a different significance level or decision type or collect more data.

n2	n1	one-tailed test $p = 0.01$	one-tailed test $p = 0.05$	two-tailed test $p = 0.01$	two-tailed test $p = 0.05$
5	2	–	0	–	–
	3	–	1	–	0
	4	0	2	–	1
	5	1	4	0	2
6	2	–	0	–	–
	3	–	2	–	1
	4	1	3	0	2
	5	2	5	1	3
	6	3	7	2	5
7	2	–	0	–	–
	3	0	2	–	1
	4	1	4	0	3
	5	3	6	1	5
	6	4	8	3	6
	7	6	11	4	8
8	2	–	1	–	0
	3	0	3	–	2
	4	2	5	1	4
	5	4	8	2	6
	6	6	10	4	8
	7	7	13	6	10
	8	9	15	7	13
9	1	–	–	–	–
	2	–	1	–	0
	3	1	4	0	2
	4	3	6	1	4
	5	5	9	3	7
	6	7	12	5	10
	7	9	15	7	12
	8	11	18	9	15
	9	14	21	11	17

Table 6 (cont.)

n2	n1	one-tailed test		two-tailed test	
		$p = 0.01$	$p = 0.05$	$p = 0.01$	$p = 0.05$
10	1	–	–	–	–
	2	–	1	–	0
	3	1	4	0	3
	4	3	7	2	5
	5	6	11	4	8
	6	8	14	6	11
	7	11	17	9	14
	8	13	20	11	17
	9	16	24	13	20
	10	19	27	16	23
11	1	–	–	–	–
	2	–	1	–	0
	3	1	5	0	3
	4	4	8	2	6
	5	7	12	5	9
	6	9	16	7	13
	7	12	19	10	16
	8	15	23	13	19
	9	18	27	16	23
	10	22	31	18	26
	11	25	34	21	30
12	1	–	–	–	–
	2	–	2	–	1
	3	2	5	1	4
	4	5	9	3	7
	5	8	13	6	11
	6	11	17	9	14
	7	14	21	12	18
	8	17	26	15	22
	9	21	30	18	26
	10	24	34	21	29
	11	28	38	24	33
	12	31	42	27	37
13	1	–	–	–	–
	2	0	2	–	1
	3	2	6	1	4
	4	5	10	3	8
	5	9	15	7	12
	6	12	19	10	16
	7	16	24	13	20
	8	20	28	17	24
	9	23	33	20	28

Table 6 (cont.)

n2	n1	one-tailed test		two-tailed test	
		p = 0.01	p = 0.05	p = 0.01	p = 0.05
	10	27	37	24	33
	11	31	42	27	37
	12	35	47	31	41
	13	39	51	34	45
14	1	–	–	–	–
	2	0	3	–	1
	3	2	7	1	5
	4	6	11	4	9
	5	10	16	7	13
	6	13	21	11	17
	7	17	26	15	22
	8	22	31	18	26
	9	26	36	22	31
	10	30	41	26	36
	11	34	46	30	40
	12	38	51	34	45
	13	43	56	38	50
	14	47	61	42	55
15	1	–	–	–	–
	2	0	3	–	1
	3	3	7	2	5
	4	7	12	5	10
	5	11	18	8	14
	6	15	23	12	19
	7	19	28	16	24
	8	24	33	20	29
	9	28	39	24	34
	10	33	44	29	39
	11	37	50	33	44
	12	42	55	37	49
	13	47	61	42	54
	14	51	66	46	59
	15	56	72	51	64
16	1	–	–	–	–
	2	0	3	–	1
	3	3	8	2	6
	4	7	14	5	11
	5	12	19	9	15
	6	16	25	13	21
	7	21	30	18	26
	8	26	36	22	31
	9	31	42	27	37

Table 6 (*cont.*)

n2	n1	one-tailed test		two-tailed test	
		p = 0.01	p = 0.05	p = 0.01	p = 0.05
	10	36	48	31	42
	11	41	54	36	47
	12	46	60	41	53
	13	51	65	45	59
	14	56	71	50	64
	15	61	77	55	70
	16	66	83	60	75
17	1	–	–	–	–
	2	0	3	–	2
	3	4	9	2	6
	4	8	15	6	11
	5	13	20	10	17
	6	18	26	15	22
	7	23	33	19	28
	8	28	39	24	34
	9	33	45	29	39
	10	38	51	34	45
	11	44	57	39	51
	12	49	64	44	57
	13	55	70	49	63
	14	60	77	54	69
	15	66	83	60	75
	16	71	89	65	81
	17	77	96	70	87
18	1	–	–	–	–
	2	0	4	–	2
	3	4	9	2	7
	4	9	16	6	12
	5	14	22	11	18
	6	19	28	16	24
	7	24	35	21	30
	8	30	41	26	36
	9	36	48	31	42
	10	41	55	37	48
	11	47	61	42	55
	12	53	68	47	61
	13	59	75	53	67
	14	65	82	58	74
	15	70	88	64	80
	16	76	95	70	86
	17	82	102	75	93
	18	88	109	81	99

Table 6 (cont.)

		one-tailed test		two-tailed test	
n2	n1	p = 0.01	p = 0.05	p = 0.01	p = 0.05
19	1	–	0	–	–
	2	1	4	0	2
	3	4	10	3	7
	4	9	17	7	13
	5	15	23	12	19
	6	20	30	17	25
	7	26	37	22	32
	8	32	44	28	38
	9	38	51	33	45
	10	44	58	39	52
	11	50	65	45	58
	12	56	72	51	65
	13	63	80	57	72
	14	69	87	63	78
	15	75	94	69	85
	16	82	101	74	92
	17	88	109	81	99
	18	94	116	87	106
	19	101	123	93	113
20	1	–	0	–	–
	2	1	4	0	2
	3	5	11	3	8
	4	10	18	8	14
	5	16	25	13	20
	6	22	32	18	27
	7	28	39	24	34
	8	34	47	30	41
	9	40	54	36	48
	10	47	62	42	55
	11	53	69	48	62
	12	60	77	54	69
	13	67	84	60	76
	14	73	92	67	83
	15	80	100	73	90
	16	87	107	79	98
	17	93	115	86	105
	18	100	123	92	112
	19	107	130	99	119
	20	114	138	105	127

Taken from Table 11.4 of Owen, Donald B. (1962). *Handbook of Statistical Tables*, © 1962 by Addison-Wesley Publishing Company Inc. Reprinted by permission.

Table 7 One- and two-tailed critical values of T for the Wilcoxon test at the p = 0.01 and p = 0.05 significance levels

N	one-tailed test		two-tailed test	
	p = 0.01	*p = 0.05*	*p = 0.01*	*p = 0.05*
5	–	1	–	–
6	–	2	–	1
7	0	4	–	2
8	2	6	0	4
9	3	8	2	6
10	5	11	3	8
11	7	14	5	11
12	10	17	7	14
13	13	21	10	17
14	16	26	13	21
15	20	30	16	25
16	24	36	19	30
17	28	41	23	35
18	33	47	28	40
19	38	54	32	46
20	43	60	37	52
25	77	101	68	90

Table 8 Critical values of chi-squared at the p = 0.01 and p = 0.05
significance levels

	critical values of χ^2	
df	p = 0.01	p = 0.05
1	6.635	3.841
2	9.210	5.991
3	11.345	7.815
4	13.277	9.488
5	15.086	11.070
6	16.812	12.592
7	18.475	14.067
8	20.090	15.507
9	21.666	16.919
10	23.209	18.307
11	24.725	19.675
12	26.217	21.026
13	27.688	22.362
14	29.141	23.685
15	30.578	24.996
16	32.000	26.296
17	33.409	27.587
18	34.805	28.869
19	36.191	30.144
20	37.566	31.410
21	38.932	32.671
22	40.289	33.924
23	41.638	35.172
24	42.980	36.415
25	44.314	37.652
26	45.642	38.885
27	46.963	40.133
28	48.278	41.337
29	49.588	42.557
30	50.892	43.773

Taken from Table IV of Fisher, R. A. and Yates, F. (1953). *Statistical Tables For Biological,
Agricultural and Medical Research*, Published by Longman Group UK Ltd., 1974 (6th edition).

Table 9   One- and two-tailed critical values of t for the t-test at the p = 0.01 and p = 0.05 significance levels

df	one-tailed test		two-tailed test	
	p = 0.01	*p = 0.05*	*p = 0.01*	*p = 0.05*
1	31.821	6.314	63.657	12.706
2	6.965	2.920	9.925	4.303
3	4.541	2.353	5.841	3.182
4	3.747	2.132	4.604	2.776
5	3.365	2.015	4.032	2.571
6	3.143	1.943	3.707	2.447
7	2.998	1.895	3.499	2.365
8	2.896	1.860	3.355	2.306
9	2.821	1.833	3.250	2.262
10	2.764	1.812	3.169	2.228
11	2.718	1.796	3.106	2.201
12	2.681	1.782	3.055	2.179
13	2.650	1.771	3.012	2.160
14	2.624	1.761	2.977	2.145
15	2.602	1.753	2.947	2.131
16	2.583	1.746	2.921	2.120
17	2.567	1.740	2.898	2.110
18	2.552	1.734	2.878	2.101
19	2.539	1.729	2.861	2.093
20	2.528	1.725	2.845	2.086
21	2.518	1.721	2.831	2.080
22	2.508	1.717	2.819	2.074
23	2.500	1.714	2.807	2.069
24	2.492	1.711	2.797	2.064
25	2.485	1.708	2.787	2.060
26	2.479	1.706	2.779	2.056
27	2.473	1.703	2.771	2.052
28	2.467	1.701	2.763	2.048
29	2.462	1.699	2.756	2.045
30	2.457	1.697	2.750	2.042
40	2.423	1.684	2.704	2.021
60	2.390	1.671	2.660	2.000
120	2.358	1.658	2.617	1.980
∞	2.326	1.645	2.576	1.960

Taken from Table III of Fisher, R. A. and Yates, F. (1953). *Statistical Tables for Biological, Agricultural and Medical Research*, Published by Longman Group UK Ltd., 1974 (6th edition).

References

Argyris, C. (1968). Some unintended consequences of rigorous research. *Psychological Bulletin, 70,* 185–7.

Asch, S. (1956). Studies of independence and conformity: A minority of one against a unanimous majority. *Psychological Monographs, 70,* No. 416.

Baddeley, A. (1983). *Your memory: A user's guide.* Harmondsworth, Middlesex: Penguin Books.

Bales, R. F. (1950a). A set of categories for the analysis of small group interaction. *American Sociological Review, 15,* 257–68.

Bales, R. F. (1950b). *Interaction process analysis: A method for the study of small groups.* Reading, Massachusetts: Addison-Wesley.

Berko, J. & Brown, R. (1960). Psycholinguistic research methods. In P. H. Mussen, (Ed.), *Handbook of research methods in child development,* (pp. 517–57). New York: Wiley.

Bower, G. H., Clark, M., Lesgold, A., & Winzenz, P. (1969). Hierarchical retrieval schemes in recall of categorised word lists. *Journal of Verbal Learning and Verbal Behaviour, 8,* 323–43.

Bowlby, J. (1969). *Attachment and loss. Vol. 1: Attachment.* Harmondsworth, Middlesex: Penguin Books.

British Psychological Society. (1985). Guidelines for the use of animals in research. *The Psychologist, 3,* (6), 269–72.

British Psychological Society. (1993). Ethical principles for conducting research with human participants. *The Psychologist, 6,* (1), 33–5.

Bromley, D. B. (1977). *Personality descriptions in ordinary language.* New York: Wiley.

Burgess, R. G. (1984). *In the field: An introduction to field research.* London: Allen & Unwin.

Child, I. L. (1973). *Humanistic psychology and the research tradition: Their several virtues.* New York: Wiley.

Cialdini, R. D., Reno, R. R. & Kallgren, C. A. (1990). A focus theory of normative conduct: Recycling the concept of norms to reduce littering in public places. *Journal of Personality and Social Psychology, 58,* 1015–26.

Cooper, L. A. & Shepard, R. N. (1984). Turning something over in the mind. *Scientific American, 251,* (6), 106–14.

Dement, W. & Kleitman, N. (1957). The relation of eye movements during sleep to dream activity: An objective method for the study of dreaming. *Journal of Experimental Psychology, 53,* 339–46.

Duck, S. (1988). *Relating to others.* Milton Keynes: Open University Press.

Dukes, W. F. (1965). N = 1. *Psychological Bulletin, 64,* 74–9.

Ebbinghaus, H. (1913). *Memory.* New York: Teacher's College Press. (Original published 1885).

Eysenck, H. J. & Eysenck, S. B. G. (1975). *Manual of the Eysenck personality questionnaire.* London: Hodder & Stoughton.

Festinger, L. (1957). *A theory of cognitive dissonance.* New York: Harper & Row.

Festinger, L., Riecken, H. W. & Schachter, S. (1956). *When prophecy fails.* Minneapolis, Minnesota: University of Minnesota Press.

Freud, S. (1986). *The essentials of psychoanalysis.* Harmondsworth, Middlesex: Penguin Books.

Freud, S. & Breuer, J. (1974). *Studies on hysteria.* Harmondsworth, Middlesex: Penguin Books. (Original published 1894).

Gardner, R. A. & Gardner, B. T. (1969). Teaching sign language to a chimpanzee. *Science, 165,* 664–72.

Godden, D. R. & Baddeley, A. D. (1975). Context-dependent memory in two natural environments: On land and under water. *British Journal of Psychology, 66,* 325–31.

Gregory, R. L. & Wallace, J. G. (1963). Recovery from early blindness: A case study. *Experimental Psychology Society Monographs.* No. 2. Cambridge: Heffer.

Gregory, R. L. (1974). *Concepts and mechanisms of perception.* London: Duckworth.

Gregory, R. L. (1972). *Eye and Brain.* (2nd edn). London: Weidenfeld & Nicolson. World University Library Series.

Gross, R. D. (1992). *Psychology: The science of mind and behaviour.* (2nd edn). London: Hodder & Stoughton.

Haney, C., Banks, C. & Zimbardo, P. (1988). A study of prisoners and guards in a simulated prison. In E. Aronson, (Ed.), *Readings about the social animal,* (pp. 52–67) (5th edn). New York: Freeman.

Held, R. & Hein, A. (1963). Movement-produced stimulation in the development of visually guided behaviour. *Journal of Comparitive and Physiological Psychology, 56,* 872–6.

Hubbuch, S. M. (1981). *Writing research papers across the curriculum.* New York: Holt, Rinehart & Winston.

Hull, C. L. (1943). *Principles of behaviour.* New York: Appleton, Century, Crofts.

Huxley, T. H. (1910). *Lectures and lay sermons.* New York: E. P. Dutton.

Jenni, D. A. & Jenni, M. A. (1976). Carrying behaviour in humans: Analysis of sex differences. *Science, 194,* 859–60.

Kelly, G. A. (1955). *The psychology of personal constructs.* New York: W. W. Norton.

Kline, P. (1989). Objective tests of Freud's theories. In A. M. Colman and J. G. Beaumont, (Eds), *Psychology Survey No. 7.* Leicester: British Psychological Society.

Latane, B. and Darley, J. M. (1968). Group inhibitions of bystander intervention in emergencies. *Journal of Personality and Social Psychology, 10,* 215–21.

Likert, R. (1932). A technique for the measurement of attitudes. *Archives of Psychology, 140,* 44–53.

Lofland, J. (1971). *Analysing social settings: A guide to qualitative observation.* Belmont, California: C. A. Wadsworth.

Lofland, J. (1976). *Doing social life: The qualitative study of human interaction in natural settings*. New York: Wiley.

Luria, A. R. (1968). *The mind of a mnemonist*. New York: Basic Books Inc.

Maple, T. & Zucker, G. L. (1978). Ethological studies of play behaviour in captive great apes. In E. O. Smith, (Ed.), *Social play in primates*, (pp. 113–42). New York: Academic Press.

Milgram, S. (1963). A behavioural study of obedience. *Journal of Abnormal and Social Psychology, 67*, 391–8.

Minitab Inc. (1991). *MINITAB reference manual*.

Murstein, B. I. (1972). Physical attractiveness and marital choice. *Journal of Personality and Social Psychology, 22*, 8–12.

Oatley, K. (1984). Depression: Crisis without alternatives. *New Scientist, 103*, 29–31.

Orne, M. T. (1962). On the social psychology of the psychological experiment. *American Psychologist, 17*, 776–83.

Orne, M. T. (1969). Demand characteristics and the concept of quasi controls. In R. Rosenthal & R. L. Rosnow (Eds), *Artifact in behavioural research*, (pp. 143–79). New York: Academic Press.

Osgood, C. E., Suci, G. J. & Tannenbaum, P. H. (1957). *The measurement of meaning*. Urbana, Illinois: University of Illinois Press.

Patrick, J. (1973). *A Glasgow gang observed*. London: Eyre Methuen.

Peterson, L. R. & Peterson, M. J. (1959). Short-term retention of individual verbal items. *Journal of Experimental Psychology, 58*, 193–8.

Popper, K. R. (1963). *Conjectures and refutations*. London: Routledge & Kegan Paul.

Reason, P. & Rowan, J. (Eds). (1981). *Human inquiry: A sourcebook of new paradigm research*. Chichester, Sussex: Wiley.

Rees, W. D. (1971). The hallucinations of widowhood. *British Medical Journal, 4*, 37–41.

Rosenberg, M. (1969). The conditions and consequences of evaluation apprehension. In R. Rosenthal & R. L. Rosnow (Eds), *Artifact in behavioural research*, (pp. 279–349). New York: Academic Press.

Rosenhan, D. L. (1973). On being sane in insane places. *Science, 179*, 250–8.

Rosenthal, R. (1966). *Experimenter effects in behavioural research*. New York: Appleton, Century, Crofts.

Rosenthal, R. & Rosnow, R. L. (1975). *The volunteer subject*. New York: John Wiley & Co.

Rosenthal, R. & Jacobson, L. F. (1968). Teacher expectations for the disadvantaged. *Scientific American, 218*, 19–23.

Rubin, Z. & Mitchell, C. (1976). Couples research as couples counselling: Some unintended effects of studying close relationships. *American Psychologist, 31*, 17–25.

Rutter, M. (1976). *Maternal deprivation re-assessed*. (2nd edn). Harmondsworth, Middlesex: Penguin Books.

Schachter, S. & Singer, S. (1962). Cognitive, social and physiological determinants of emotional state. *Psychological Review, 69*, 379–99.

Scheerer, M. (1963). Problem-solving. *Scientific American, 208*, 118–28.

Shepard, R. N. & Metzler, J. (1971). Mental rotation of three-dimensional objects. *Science, 171*, 701–3.

Shotter, J. (1975). *Images of man in psychological research*. London: Methuen & Co.

Siegel, S. & Castellan, N. J. (1988). *Non-parametric statistics for the behavioural sciences*. New York: McGraw-Hill.

Tulving, E. (1974). Cue-dependent forgetting. *American Scientist, 62*, 74–82.

Walster, E., Aronson, E., Abrahams, D. & Rottman, L. (1966). Importance of physical attractiveness in dating behaviour. *Journal of Personality and Social Psychology*, 4, 508–16.

Watson, J. B. (1913). Psychology as the behaviourist views it. *Psychological Review*, 20, 158–77.

Watson, J. B. & Rayner, R. (1920). Conditioned emotional reactions. *Journal of Experimental Psychology*, 3, 1–14.

Watson, P. (1978). *War on the mind*. London: Hutchinson.

Weisberg, R. W. & Alba, J. W. (1981). An examination of the alleged role of 'fixation' in the solution of several insight problems. *Journal of Experimental Psychology (General)*, 110, 169–92.

Index